AP* COMPARATIVE GOVERNMENT AND POLITICS: A STUDY GUIDE

THIRD EDITION

by Ethel Wood

WoodYard Publications, Reading, Pennsylvania

AP Comparative Government and Politics: A Study Guide, Third Edition

Published by
WoodYard Publications
PO Box 3856
Reading, PA 19606 U.S.A.
Ph. 610-207-1366
Fax 610-372-8401
apcomparative@comcast.net

http://apcomparative.home.comcast.net/

ISBN 978-0-9743481-3-1

TABLE OF CONTENTS

A Note from the Author

Why Comparative Government and Politics?

I have taught social studies classes for many years, mostly at Princeton High School in Princeton, New Jersey. Like most social studies teachers, my experience includes classes in United States history and government. I have also published review books, textbooks, readers, and web materials that have required me to do extensive research in various types of American studies. Needless to say, I believe that an education in these areas is incredibly important for high school students, and every secondary curriculum should include them. So why is comparative government and politics so important?

The 21st century has taught us that we cannot ignore the world around us. Happenings around the globe now directly impact our lives, and social studies teachers and students around the country face the challenge of interpreting complex, puzzling events. The AP comparative course focuses on government and politics in other countries and provides a theoretical framework to compare political systems around the world. It is my hope that this book will help students to grasp something of the political complexities of our global environment, and gain some understanding of both commonalities and differences among modern political systems. In today's world, we cannot afford not to know.

Ethel Wood
Reading, Pennsylvania
October 2007

Other Books by Ethel Wood

American Government: A Complete Coursebook

AP Human Geography: A Study Guide

The Immigrants: An Historical Reader

Introduction to Sociology

Multiple Choice and Free-Response Questions in Preparation for the AP United States Government and Politics Examination

Multiple Choice and Free-Response Questions in Preparation for the AP World History Examination

Teacher's Guide - AP Comparative Government and Politics

The Best Test Preparation for the Graduate Record Examination in Political Science

The Presidency: An Historical Reader

PREFACE: THE COMPARATIVE EXAMINATION

The AP Comparative Government and Politics Examination includes some significant revisions beginning in May 2006. The description below reflects those changes and gives you an overview of what to expect on the exam.

The examination administered by the College Board in May lasts for two hours and 25 minutes and consists of the following parts:

- 55 multiple-choice questions (45 minutes allowed; 50% of AP grade)

- a 100-minute free response section consisting of 8 questions (50% of AP grade)

The multiple-choice questions cover all the topics listed below, and test knowledge of comparative theory, methods, and government and politics in Britain, Russia, China, Mexico, Iran, and Nigeria. In scoring the exam, the College Board penalizes you for incorrect answers (1/4 of a point each), so it is generally better to leave answers blank to questions you have no idea how to answer. However, if you can eliminate at least two of the choices, it is generally better to take an educated guess.

The free-response questions are of three types:

- Definition and description (25% of free-response grade) – Students provide brief definitions or descriptions of five concepts or terms, briefly explaining their significance. Students may have to provide an example of the definition or description in one or more of the core countries.

- Conceptual analysis (one question; 25% of free-response grade) – Students must use major concepts from comparative politics, explain important relationships, or discuss the causes and implications of politics and policy.

- Country context (two questions; 50% of free-response grade; each question 25%) – These questions focus on specific countries, and require students to use core concepts to analyze one country or compare two countries.

The recommended total time for definition and description terms is 30 minutes; for the conceptual analysis question 30 minutes; and for each of the country context questions 20 minutes. However, there are no time divisions among the free-response questions. Instead, a total of 100 minutes is allotted to answer all of them.

Generally, multiple-choice questions are distributed fairly evenly among the six countries. In addition, many questions are not country-specific, but instead test knowledge of the major concepts. According to the College Board, the topics of the multiple choice questions are distributed as follows:

Introduction (methods, purpose of comparisons)..........................5%

Sovereignty, Authority, and Power 20%

Political Institutions...35%

Citizens, Society, and State..15%

Political and Economic Change...15%

Public Policy...10%

This newly revised 3rd Edition of *AP Comparative Government and Politics: A Study Guide* is designed to help you prepare for the exam by giving you a sound footing in comparative concepts as well as country-specific information about the six core countries. The book is divided into three parts:

- **Part One** - Introduction to Comparative Government and Politics: A Conceptual Approach

- **Part Two** - Country Cases: Advanced Democracies (Great Britain), Communist and Post Communist Regimes (Russia and China), and Less Developed and Newly Developing Countries (Mexico, Iran, and Nigeria)

- **Part Three** - Practice Examinations: Two complete sample exams, each with 55 multiple-choice questions and 9 free-response questions

Your best preparation for the exam is to know your stuff. The questions do require reading and writing skills, but the surer you are of the material, the more likely you are to answer the questions correctly. This book provides the concepts and information, as well as plenty of practice questions that will prepare you for the exam. The most important things are that you learn something about comparative government and politics, and that you learn to love it, too!

Ethel Wood

PART ONE:
INTRODUCTION TO COMPARATIVE GOVERNMENT AND POLITICS: A CONCEPTUAL APPROACH

Comparative government and politics provides an introduction to the wide, diverse world of governments and political practices that currently exist in modern times. Although the course focuses on specific countries, it also emphasizes an understanding of conceptual tools and methods that form a framework for comparing almost any governments that exist today. Additionally, it requires students to go beyond individual political systems to consider international forces that affect all people in the world, often in very different ways. Six countries form the core of the course: Great Britain, Russia, China, Mexico, Iran, and Nigeria. The countries are chosen to reflect regional variations, but more importantly, to illustrate how concepts operate both similarly and differently in different types of political systems: "advanced" democracies, communist and post communist countries, and newly industrialized and less developed nations. This book includes review materials for all six countries.

Goals for the course include:

- Gaining an understanding of major comparative political concepts, themes, and trends
- Knowing important facts about government and politics in Great Britain, Russia, China, Mexico, Iran, and Nigeria
- Identifying patterns of political processes and behavior and analyzing their political and economic consequences
- Comparing and contrasting political institutions and processes across countries
- Analyzing and interpreting basic data for comparison of political systems

WHAT IS COMPARATIVE GOVERNMENT AND POLITICS?

Most people understand that the term **government** is a reference to the leadership and institutions that make policy decisions for the country. However, what exactly is **politics?** Politics is basically all about power. Who has the power to make the decisions? How did they get the power? What challenges do leaders face from others – both inside and outside the country's borders – in keeping the power? So, as we look at different countries, we are not only concerned about the ins and outs of how the government works. We will also look at how power is gained, managed, challenged, and maintained.

College-level courses in comparative government and politics vary, but they all cover topics that enable meaningful comparisons across countries. These topics are introduced in the pages that follow, and will be addressed with each of the countries covered separately.

The topics are:

- The Comparative Method
- Sovereignty, Authority, and Power
- Political and Economic Change

- Citizens, Society, and the State
- Political Institutions
- Public Policy

TOPIC ONE: THE COMPARATIVE METHOD

Political scientists sometimes argue about exactly what and how countries should be studied and compared. One approach is to emphasize **empirical data** based on factual statements and statistics, and another is to focus on **normative** issues that require value judgments. For example, the first approach might compare statistics that reflect economic development of a group of countries, including information about Gross National Product, per capita income, and amounts of imports and exports. The second approach might not reject those statistics, but would focus instead on whether or not the statistics bode well or ill for the countries. Empiricists might claim that it is not the role of political scientists to make such judgments, and their critics would reply that such an approach leads to meaningless data collection. Both approaches give us different but equally important tools for analyzing and comparing political systems.

As for research in any social science, comparative government and politics relies on the scientific method to objectively and logically evaluate data. After reviewing earlier research, the researchers formulate a **hypothesis**, a speculative statement about the relationship between two or more factors known as **variables.** Variables are measurable traits or characteristics that change under different conditions. For example, poverty levels in a country may change over time. One question that a comparative researcher might ask is, "Why are poverty rates higher in one country than in others?" The research is then led in the direction of discovering **causation**, or the idea that one variable causes or influences another. An **independent variable** is one that influences the **dependent variable** because its action depends on the influence of the independent variable. So, a credible hypothesis might be that poverty level (a dependent variable) might be caused by low levels of formal education (an independent variable). A **correlation** exists when a change in one variable coincides with a change in the other. Correlations are an indication that causality *may* be present; they do not necessarily indicate causation. Comparative researchers seek to identify the causal link between variables by collecting and analyzing data.

How do we go about comparing countries? The model most frequently used until the early 1990s was the **three-world approach,** largely based on cold war politics. The three worlds were 1) the United States and its allies; 2) the Soviet Union and its allies; and 3) "**third world**" nations that did not fit into the first two categories and were all economically underdeveloped and deprived. Even though the Soviet Union collapsed in 1991, this approach is still taken today by many comparative textbooks. Comparisons are based on democracy vs. authoritarianism and communism vs. capitalism. Even though this method is still valid, newer types of comparisons are reflected in these trends:

- **The impact of informal politics** – Governments have formal positions and structures that may be seen on an organizational chart. For example, Great Britain is led by a prime minister and has a House of Lords and a House of Commons. In comparison, the United States has a President, a Senate, and a House of Representatives. You may directly compare the responsibilities and typical activities of each position or structure in Britain to its counterpart in the United States. However, you can gain a deeper understanding of both political systems if you connect **civil society** – the way that citizens organize and define themselves and their interests – to the ways that the formal government operates. **Informal politics** takes into consideration not only the ways that politicians operate outside their formal powers, but also the impact that beliefs, values, and actions of ordinary citizens have on policymaking.

- **The importance of political change** – One reason that the three-world approach has become more problematic in recent years is that the nature of world politics has changed. After 1991, the world was no longer dominated by two superpowers, and that fact has had consequences that have reverberated in many areas that no one could have predicted. However, what better opportunity to compare the impact of change on different countries!

- **The integration of political and economic systems** – Even though we may theoretically separate government and politics from the economy, the two are often almost inextricably intertwined. For example, communism and capitalism are theoretically economic systems, but how do you truly separate them from government and politics? Attitudes and behavior of citizens are affected in many ways by economic inefficiency, economic inequality, and economic decision-making. They then may turn to the government for solutions to economic problems, and if the government does not respond, citizens may revolt, or take other actions that demand attention from the political elite.

Keeping these trends in mind, in this book we will study countries in three different groups that are in some ways similar in their political and economic institutions and practices. These groups are:

- **"Advanced" democracies** – These countries having well established democratic governments and a high level of economic development. Of the six core countries, Great Britain represents this group.

- **Communist and post-communist countries** – These countries have sought to create a system that limits individual freedoms in order to divide wealth more equally. Communism flourished during the 20th century, but lost ground to democratic regimes by the beginning of the 21st century. Russia (as a post-communist country) and China (currently a communist country) represent this group in our study of comparative government and politics.

- **Less developed and newly industrializing (or developing) countries** – We will divide the countries traditionally referred to as the "Third World" into two groups, still very diverse within the categories. The newly industrializing countries are experiencing rapid economic growth, and also have shown a tendency toward democratization and political and social stability. Mexico and Iran represent this group, although, as you will see, Iran has many characteristics that make it difficult to categorize in this scheme. Less developed countries lack significant economic development, and they also tend to have authoritarian governments. Nigeria represents this group, although it has shown some signs of democratization in very recent years.

Important concepts that enable meaningful comparisons among countries are introduced in this chapter, and will be addressed in each of the individual countries separately. However, it is important to remember that the main point of comparative government and politics is to use the categories to compare among countries. For example, never take the approach of "Here's Britain," "Here's Russia," without noting what similarities and differences exist between the two countries.

TOPIC TWO: SOVEREIGNTY, AUTHORITY, AND POWER

We commonly speak about individuals who are powerful, but in today's world power is territorially organized into **states**, or countries, that control what happens within their borders. What exactly is a state? German scholar Max Weber defined state as the organization that maintains a monopoly of violence over a territory. In other words, the state defines who can and cannot use weapons and force, and it sets the rules as to how violence is used. States often sponsor armies, navies, and/or air forces that legitimately use power and sometimes violence, but individual citizens are very restricted in their use of force. States also include **institutions**, stable, long lasting organizations that help to turn political ideas into policy. Common examples of institutions are bureaucracies, legislatures, judicial systems, and political parties. These institutions make states themselves long lasting, and often help them to endure even when leaders change. By their very nature, states exercise **sovereignty,** the ability to carry out actions or policies within their borders independently from interference either from the inside or the outside.

A state that is unable to exercise sovereignty lacks autonomy, and because it is not independent, it may be exploited by leaders and/or organizations that see the state as a resource to use for their own ends. Frequently, the result is a high level of corruption. The problem is particularly prevalent in newly industrializing and less-developed countries, largely because their governments lack autonomy. For example, military rulers in Nigeria stole vast amounts of money from the state during the 1990s, making it one of the most corrupt countries in the world. Today Nigeria's tremendous revenues from oil have largely evaporated before they reach ordinary citizens, providing evidence that corruption is still a major issue in Nigeria today.

STATES, NATIONS, AND REGIMES

States do much more than keep order in society. Many have important institutions that promote general welfare – such as health, safe transportation, and effective communication systems - and economic stability. The concept of state is closely related to a **nation,** a group of people that is bound together by a common political identity. **Nationalism** is the sense of belonging and identity that distinguishes one nation from another. Nationalism is often translated as patriotism, or the resulting pride and loyalty that individuals feel toward their nations. For more than 200 years now, national borders ideally have been drawn along the lines of group identity. For example, people in one area think of themselves as "French," and people in another area think of themselves as "English." Even though individual differences exist within nations, the nation provides the overriding identity for most of its citizens. However, the concept has always been problematic – as when "Armenians" live inside the borders of a country called "Azerbaijan." Especially now that globalization and fragmentation provide counter trends, the nature of nationalism and its impact on policymaking are clearly changing.

The rules that a state sets and follows in exerting its power are referred to collectively as a **regime.** Regimes endure beyond individual governments and leaders. We refer to a regime when a country's institutions and practices carry over across time, even though leaders and particular issues change. Regimes may be compared by using these categories: democracies and authoritarian systems.

DEMOCRACIES

This type of regime bases its authority on the will of the people. Democracies may be **indirect,** with elected officials representing the people, or they may be **direct**, when individuals have immediate say over many decisions that the government makes. Most democracies are indirect, mainly because large populations make it almost impossible for individuals to have a great deal of direct influence on how they are governed. Democratic governments typically have three major branches: executives, legislatures, and constitutional courts. Some democracies are **parliamentary systems** – where citizens vote for legislative representatives, which in turn select the leaders of the executive branch. Others are **presidential systems** – where citizens vote for legislative representatives as well as for executive branch leaders, and the two branches function with separation of powers. Democratic governments vary in the degree to which they regulate/control the economy, but businesses, corporations, and/or companies generally operate somewhat independently from the government.

- **Parliamentary systems** – In this type of democracy, the principle of **parliamentary sovereignty** governs the decision-making process. Theoretically, the legislature makes the laws, controls finances, appoints and dismisses the prime minister and the cabinet, and debates public issues. In reality, however, strong party discipline within the legislature has developed over time, so that the cabinet initiates legislation and makes policy. The majority party in the legislature almost always votes for the bills proposed by its leadership (the prime minister and cabinet members). Even though the opposition party or parties are given time and opportunity to criticize, the legislature eventually supports decisions made by the executive branch. Because the prime minister and cabinet are also the leaders of the majority party in the legislature, no separation of powers exists between the executive and legislative branches. Instead, the two branches are fused together. Also typical of the parliamentary system is a separation in the executive branch between a **head of state** (a role that symbolizes the power and nature of the regime) and a **head of government** (a role that deals with the everyday tasks of running the government). For example, in Great Britain, the queen is the head of state who seldom formulates and executes policy, and the prime minister is the head of government who directs the country's decision-making process in his or her position as leader of the majority party in parliament.

- **Presidential systems** – In this type of democracy, the roles of head of state and head of government are given to one person – the president. This central figure is directly elected by the people and serves as the chief executive within a system of **checks and balances** between the legislative and executive (and sometimes judicial) branches. The **separation of powers** between branches ensures that power is shared and that one branch does not come to dominate the others. As a result, power is diffused and the policymaking process is sometimes slowed down because one branch may question decisions that another branch makes. In order for presidential systems to truly diffuse power, each branch must have an independent base of authority recognized and respected by politicians and the public. The United States is a presidential system, as are Nigeria and Mexico. As we will see, the question of whether or not truly independent bases of authority exist for the branches of government is important to consider in evaluating the nature of democracy in Mexico and Nigeria.

Some countries combine elements of the presidential and parliamentary systems, as is illustrated in Russia's 1993 Constitution. Although Russia is a questionable democracy, the Constitution clearly provides for a **semi-presidential system** where a prime minister coexists with a president who is directly elected by the people and who holds a significant degree of power. In Russia today, the president has a disproportionate amount of power, but in other semi-presidential systems – such as France and India – the power balance between the two executives is quite different.

AUTHORITARIAN REGIMES

In this type of regime, decisions are made by political **elites** – those that hold political power – without much input from citizens. These regimes may be ruled by a single dictator, an hereditary monarch, a small group of aristocrats, or a single political party. The economy is generally tightly controlled by the political elite. Some authoritarian regimes are based on **communism**, a theory developed in the 19th century by Karl Marx and altered in the early 20th century by Vladimir Lenin. In these regimes, the communist party controls everything from the government to the economy to social life. Others practice **state corporatism** – an arrangement in which government officials interact with people/groups outside the government before they set policy. These outside contacts are generally business and labor leaders, or they may be heads of huge **patron-client systems** that provide reciprocal favors and services to their supporters.

Common characteristics of authoritarian regimes include:

- A small group of elites exercising power over the state
- Citizens with little or no input into selection of leaders and government decisions
- No constitutional responsibility of leaders to the public
- Restriction of civil rights and civil liberties

A common misconception about authoritarian regimes is that they are not legitimate governments. If the people accept the authority of the leaders, and other countries recognize the regime's right to rule, authoritarian regimes may be said to be legitimate.

Totalitarianism

Many people think of authoritarianism and **totalitarianism** as the same thing, but the term "totalitarian" has many more negative connotations, and is almost always used to describe a particularly repressive, often detested, regime. For example, during the Cold War era, westerners often referred to the Soviet Union as a "totalitarian regime." However, authoritarian systems are not necessarily totalitarian in nature. Unlike totalitarian regimes, authoritarian governments do not necessarily seek to control and transform all aspects of the political and economic systems of the society. Totalitarian regimes generally have a strong ideological goal (like communism) that many authoritarian systems lack, and authoritarian governments do not necessarily use violence as a technique for destroying any obstacles to their governance.

Military Regimes

One form of nondemocratic rule is **military rule**, especially prevalent today in Latin America, Africa, and parts of Asia. In states where legitimacy and stability are in question, and especially when violence is threatened, the military may intervene directly in politics as the organization that can solve the problems. Military rule usually begins with a **coup d'etat**, a forced takeover of the government. The coup may or may not have widespread support among the people. Once they take control, military leaders often restrict civil rights and liberties, and, in the name of order, keep political parties from forming and elections from taking place. Military rule usually lacks a specific ideology, and the leaders often have no charismatic or traditional source of authority, so they join forces with the state bureaucracy to form an authoritarian regime. Military rule may precede democracy, as occurred in South Korea and Taiwan during the 1990s, or it may create more instability as one coup d'etat follows another, reinforcing a weak, vulnerable state.

CORPORATISM IN AUTHORITARIAN AND DEMOCRATIC SYSTEMS

Modern **corporatism** is a method through which business, labor, and/or other interest groups bargain with the state over economic policy. In its earliest forms corporatism emerged as a way that authoritarian regimes tried to control the public by creating or recognizing organizations to represent the interests of the public. This practice, known as **state corporatism,** makes the government appear to be less authoritarian, but in reality the practice eliminates any input from groups not sanctioned or created by the state. Only a handful of groups have the right to speak for the public, effectively silencing the majority of citizens in political affairs. Often non-sanctioned groups are banned altogether. For example, in Mexico's one-party system that existed for most of the 20th century, the oil wells and refineries were placed under the control of state-run PEMEX, and many private oil businesses were kicked out of the country. Corporatism gives the public a limited influence in the policymaking process, but the interest groups are funded and managed by the state. Most people would rather have a state-sanctioned organization than none at all, so many participate willingly with the hope that the state will meet their needs.

A less structured means of **co-optation**, or the means a regime uses to get support from citizens, is **patron-clientelism**, a system in which the state provides specific benefits or favors to a single person or small group in return for public support. Unlike corporatism, clientelism relies on individual patronage rather than organizations that serve a large group of people. We will see examples of clientelism in China, Russia, Mexico, and Nigeria.

More recently corporatist practices have emerged in democratic regimes as well. In democracies corporatism usually comes into play as the state considers economic policy planning and regulation. In some cases, such as in the Scandinavian countries, many major social and economic policies are crafted through negotiations between the representatives of interests and the government agencies. In democracies that have nationalized industries, the directors are state officials who are advised by councils elected by the major interest groups involved. In democracies that do not nationalize industries, many regulatory decisions are made through direct cooperation between government agencies and interests.

A basic principle of democracy is **pluralism,** a situation in which power is split among many groups that compete for the chance to influence the government's decision-making. This competition is an important way that citizens may express their needs to the government, and in a democracy, the government will react to citizens' input. **Democratic (or neo) corporatism** is different from pluralism in two ways:

> 1) In democratic pluralism, the formation of interest groups is spontaneous; in democratic corporatism, interest representation is institutionalized through recognition by the state. New groups can only form if the state allows it.

2) In democratic pluralism, the dialogue between interest groups and the state is voluntary, and groups remain autonomous; in democratic corporatism organizations develop institutionalized and legally binding links with the state agencies, so that the groups become semi-public agencies, acting on behalf of the state. As a result, groups and individuals lose their freedoms.

Just how much corporatism a democracy will allow before it becomes an authoritarian state is a question of much debate. For example, in the United States, the National Recovery Act of 1934 was judged by the Supreme Court to be unconstitutional, largely because it gave the government too much say in private industries' hiring and production decisions. In more recent years, U.S. government agencies have been criticized for hiring people from private interest groups to fill regulatory positions, allegedly destroying the ability of the government to guard the public interest and giving special interests control of policy. In the 1970s labor unions in Great Britain were often accused of strong-arming public officials, including the prime minister, into passing labor-friendly policies into law. In all of these cases, the entangling of government and private interests has been criticized for undermining the principle of diffusion of power basic to a democracy.

LEGITIMACY

Who has political power? Who has the authority to rule? Different countries answer these questions in different ways, but they all answer them in one way or another. Countries that have no clear answers often suffer from lack of political **legitimacy** – or the right to rule, as determined by their own citizens.

Legitimacy may be secured in a number of ways, using sources such as social compacts, constitutions, and ideologies. According to political philosopher Max Weber, legitimacy may be categorized into three basic forms of authority:

- **Traditional authority** rests upon the belief that tradition should determine who should rule and how. For example, if a particular family has had power for hundreds of years, the current ruling members of that family are legitimate rulers because it has always been so. Traditional authority often involves important myths and legends, such as the idea that an ancestor was actually born a god or performed some fantastic feat like pulling a sword out of a stone. Rituals and ceremonies all help to reinforce traditional legitimacy. Most monarchies are based on traditional legitimacy, and their authority is symbolized through crowns, thrones, scepters, and/or robes of a particular color or design.

- **Charismatic authority** is based on the dynamic personality of an individual leader or a small group. Charisma is an almost indefinable set of qualities that make people want to follow a leader, sometimes to the point that they are willing to give their lives for him or her. For example, Napoleon Bonaparte was a charismatic leader that rose in France during a time when the traditional legitimacy of the monarchy had been challenged. By force of personality and military talent, Napoleon seized control of France and very nearly conquered most of Europe. However, Napoleon also represents the vulnerability of charismatic authority. Once he was defeated, his legitimacy dissolved, and the nation was thrown back into chaos. Charismatic legitimacy is notoriously short-lived because it usually does not survive its founder.

- **Rational-legal authority** is based neither on tradition nor on the force of a single personality, but rather on a system of well-established laws and procedures. This type of authority, then, is highly institutionalized, or anchored by strong institutions (such as legislatures, executives, and/or judiciaries) that carry over across generations of individual leaders. People obey leaders because they believe in the rules that brought them to office, and because they accept the concept of a continuous state that binds them together as a nation. Rational-legal legitimacy is often based on the acceptance of the rule of law that supersedes the actions and statements of individual rulers. The rule may take two forms: 1) **common law** based on tradition, past practices, and legal precedents set by the courts through interpretations of statutes, legal legislation, and past rulings; 2) **code law** based on a comprehensive system of written rules (codes) of law divided into commercial, civil, and criminal codes. Common law is English in origin and is found in the United States and other countries with a strong English influence. Code law is predominant in Europe and countries influenced by the French, German, or Spanish systems. Countries in the comparative government course that have code law systems are China, Mexico, and Russia.

Most modern states today are based on rational-legal authority, although that does not mean that traditional and charismatic authority are not still important. Instead, they tend to exist within the rules of rational-legal legitimacy. For example, charismatic leaders such as Martin Luther King still may capture the imagination of the public and have a tremendous impact on political, social, and economic developments. Likewise, modern democracies, such as Britain and Norway, still maintain the traditional legitimacy of monarchies to add stability and credibility to their political systems.

Many factors contribute to legitimacy in the modern state. In a democracy, the legitimacy of leaders is based on fair, competitive elections and open political participation by citizens. As a result, if the electoral process is compromised, the legitimacy of leadership is likely to be questioned as well. For example, the controversial counting of votes in Florida in the U.S. presidential election of 2000 was a crisis for the country largely because the basic fairness of the electoral process (an important source of legitimacy) was questioned. Factors that encourage legitimacy in both democratic and authoritarian regimes are:

- **Economic well-being** – Citizens tend to credit their government with economic prosperity, and they often blame government for economic hardships, so political legitimacy is reinforced by economic well being.

- **Historical tradition/longevity** – If a government has been in place for a long time, citizens and other countries are more likely to view it as legitimate.

- **Charismatic leadership** – As Max Weber says, charismatic authority is a powerful factor in establishing legitimacy, whether the country is democratic or totalitarian.

- **Nationalism/shared political culture** – If citizens identify strongly with their nation, not just the state, they are usually more accepting of the legitimacy of the government.

- **Satisfaction with the government's performance/responsiveness** – Chances are that the government is a legitimate one if citizens receive benefits from the government, if the government wins wars, and/or if citizens are protected from violence and crime.

POLITICAL CULTURE AND POLITICAL IDEOLOGIES

Historical evolution of political traditions shapes a country's concept of who has the authority to rule and its definition of legitimate political power. This evolution may be gradual or forced, long or relatively brief, and the relative importance of tradition varies from country to country. **Political culture** refers to the collection of political beliefs, values, practices, and institutions that the government is based on. For example, if a society values individualism, the government will generally reflect this value in the way that it is structured and in the way that it operates. If the government does not reflect basic political values of a people, it will have difficulty remaining viable.

Political culture may be analyzed in terms of **social capital**, or the amount of reciprocity and trust that exists among citizens, and between citizens and the state. Societies with low amounts of social capital may be more inclined toward authoritarian and anti-individual governments, and societies with more social capital may be inclined toward democracy. Some argue that Islam and/or Confucianism are incompatible with democracy because they emphasize subservience and respect for differing statuses in life. Social capital, then, is not valued. Critics of social capital theory say that it relies too heavily on stereotypes, and that it ignores the fact that democracy has flourished in traditional societies, such as India, South Africa, and Turkey.

TYPES OF POLITICAL CULTURE

The number and depth of disagreements among citizens within a society form the basis for dividing political cultures into two types: consensual and conflictual.

- **Consensual political culture** – Although citizens may disagree on some political processes and policies, they tend generally to agree on how decisions are made, what issues should be addressed, and how problems should be solved. For example, citizens agree that elections should be held to select leaders, and they accept the election winners as their leaders. Once the leaders take charge, the problems they address are considered by most people to be appropriate for government to handle. By and large, a **consensual political culture** accepts both the legitimacy of the regime and solutions to major problems.

- **Conflictual political culture** – Citizens in a **conflictual political culture** are sharply divided, often on both the legitimacy of the regime and solutions to major problems. For example, if citizens disagree on something as basic as capitalism vs. communism, conflict almost certainly will be difficult to avoid. Or if religious differences are so pronounced that followers of one religion do not accept an elected leader from another religion, these differences strike at the heart of legitimacy, and threaten to topple the regime. When a country is deeply divided in political beliefs and values over a long period of time, political subcultures may develop, and the divisions become so imbedded that the government finds it difficult to rule effectively.

No matter how we categorize political cultures, they are constantly changing, so that over time, conflictual political cultures may become consensual, and vice versa. However, political values and beliefs tend to endure, and no political system may be analyzed accurately without taking into consideration the political culture that has shaped it. So when the Russian president dictates a major change of policy, the Chinese government enforces economic development of rural lands, the British prime minister endures another round of derision, or Mexican citizens take a liking to a leftist leader, you may be sure that political culture is a force behind the stories in the news.

POLITICAL IDEOLOGIES

Political culture also shapes political ideologies that a nation's citizens hold. **Political ideologies** are sets of political values held by individuals regarding the basic goals of government and politics. Examples of political ideologies are:

- **Liberalism** places emphasis on individual political and economic freedom. Do not confuse liberalism as an ideology with its stereotype within the U.S. political system. As a broad ideology, liberalism is part of the political culture of many modern democracies, including the United States. Liberals seek to maximize freedom for all people, including free speech, freedom of religion, and freedom of association. Liberals also believe that citizens have the right to disagree with state decisions and act to change the decisions of their leaders. For example, in recent years many U.S. citizens have openly expressed their disagreements with the George W. Bush administration concerning the war in Iraq and homeland security issues. The U.S. political culture supports the belief that government leaders should allow and even listen to such criticisms. Public opinion generally has some political impact in liberal democracies, such as the U.S. and Britain.

- **Communism**, in contrast to liberalism, generally values equality over freedom. Whereas liberal democracies value the ideal of equal opportunity, they usually tolerate a great deal of inequality, especially within the economy. Communism rejects the idea that personal freedom will ensure prosperity for the majority. Instead, it holds that an inevitable result of the competition for scarce resources is that a small group will eventually come to control both the government and the economy. For communists, liberal democracies are created by the rich to protect the rights and property of the rich. To eliminate the inequalities and exploitation, communists advocate the takeover of all resources by the state that in turn will insure that true economic equality exists for the community as a whole. As a result, private ownership of property is abolished. Individual liberties must give way to the needs of society as a whole, creating what communists believe to be a true democracy.

- **Socialism** shares the value of equality with communism but is also influenced by the liberal value of freedom. Unlike communists, socialists accept and promote private ownership and free market principles. However, in contrast to liberals, socialists believe that the state has a strong role to play in regulating the economy and providing benefits to the public in order to ensure some measure of equality. Socialism is a much stronger ideology in Europe than it is in the United States, although both socialism and liberalism have shaped these areas of the world.

- **Fascism** is often confused with communism because they both devalue the idea of individual freedom. However, the similarity between the two ideologies ends there. Fascism also rejects the value of equality, and accepts the idea that people and groups exist in degrees of inferiority and superiority. Fascists believe that the state has the right and the responsibility to mold the society and economy and to eliminate obstacles (including people) that might weaken them. The powerful authoritarian state is the engine that makes superiority possible. The classic example is of course Nazi Germany. No strictly fascist regimes currently exist, but fascism still is an influential ideology in many parts of the world.

- **Religions** have always been an important source of group identity and continue to be in the modern world. Many advanced democracies, such as the United States, have established principles of separation of church and state, but even in those countries, religion often serves as the basis for interest groups and voluntary associations within the civil society. Even though some European countries, such as Great Britain, have an official state religion, their societies are largely secularized, so that religious leaders are usually not the same people as political leaders. In our six countries we will see religion playing very different roles in all of them – from China, whose government has recently squelched the Falon Gong religious movement, to Iran, that bases its entire political system on Shia Islam.

TOPIC THREE: POLITICAL AND ECONOMIC CHANGE

Comparativists are interested not only in the causes and forms of change, but also in the various impacts that it has on the policymaking process. Profound political and economic changes have characterized the 20th and early 21st centuries, and al of the six core countries of the AP Comparative Government and Politics course illustrate this overall trend toward change. More often than not, political and economic changes occur together and influence one another. If one occurs without the other, tensions are created that have serious consequences. For example, rapid economic changes in China have strongly pressured the government to institute political changes. So far, the authoritarian government has resisted those changes, a situation that leaves us with the question of whether or not authoritarian governments can effectively guide market economies.

TYPES OF CHANGE

Change occurs in many ways, but it may be categorized into three types:

- **Reform** is a type of change that does not advocate the overthrow of basic institutions. Instead, reformers want to change some of the methods that political and economic leaders use to reach goals that the society generally accepts. For example, reformers may want to change business practices in order to preserve real competition in a capitalist country, or they may want the government to become more proactive in preserving the natural environment. In neither case do the reformers advocate the overthrow of basic economic or political institutions.

- **Revolution,** in contrast to reform, implies change at a more basic level, and involves either a major revision or an overthrow of existing institutions. A revolution usually impacts more than one area of life. For example, the Industrial Revolution first altered the economies of Europe from feudalism to capitalism, but eventually changed their political systems, transportation, communication, literature, and social classes. Likewise, the French and American Revolutions were directed at the political systems, but they significantly changed the economies and societal practices of both countries, and spread their influence throughout the globe.

- **Coup d'etats** generally represent the most limited of the three types of change. Literally "blows to the state," they replace the leadership of a country with new leaders. Typically coups occur in countries where government institutions are weak and leaders have taken control by force. The leaders are challenged by others who use force to depose them. Often coups are carried out by the military, but the new leaders are always vulnerable to being overthrown by yet another coup.

ATTITUDES TOWARD CHANGE

The types of change that take place are usually strongly influenced by the attitudes of those that promote them. Attitudes toward change include:

- **Radicalism** is a belief that rapid, dramatic changes need to be made in the existing society, often including the political system. Radicals usually think that the current system cannot be saved and must be overturned and replaced with something better. For example, radicalism prevailed in Russia in 1917 when the old tsarist regime was replaced by the communist U.S.S.R. Radicals are often the leaders of revolutions.

- **Liberalism** supports reform and gradual change rather than revolution. Do not confuse a liberal attitude toward change with liberalism as a political ideology. The two may or may not accompany one another. Liberals generally do not believe that the political and/or economic systems are broken, but they do believe that they need to be repaired or improved. They may support the notion that eventual transformation needs to take place, but they almost always believe that gradual change is best.

- **Conservatism** is much less supportive of change in general than are radicalism and liberalism. Conservatives tend to see change as disruptive, and they emphasize the fact that it sometimes brings unforeseen outcomes. They consider the state and the regime to be very important sources of law and order that might be threatened by making significant changes in the way that they operate. Legitimacy itself might be undermined, as well as the basic values and beliefs of the society.

- **Reactionary beliefs** go further to protect against change than do conservative beliefs. Reactionaries are similar to conservatives in that they oppose both revolution and reform, but they differ in that reactionaries also find the status quo unacceptable. Instead, they want to turn back the clock to an earlier era, and reinstate political, social, and economic institutions that once existed. Reactionaries have one thing in common with radicals: both groups are more willing to use violence to reach their goals than are liberals or conservatives.

THREE TRENDS

In comparing political systems, it is important to take notice of overall patterns of development that affect everyone in the contemporary world. Two of these trends – democratization and the move toward market economies – indicate growing **commonalities** among nations, and the third represents **fragmentation** – the revival of ethnic or cultural politics.

1) **Democratization**

Even though democracy takes many different forms, more and more nations are turning toward some form of popular government. One broad, essential requirement for democracy is the existence of **competitive elections** that are regular, free, and fair. In other words, the election offers a real possibility that the incumbent government may be defeated. By this standard, a number of modern states that call themselves "democracies" fall into a gray area that is neither clearly democratic nor clearly undemocratic. Examples are Russia, Nigeria, and Indonesia. In contrast, **liberal democracies** display other democratic characteristics beyond having competitive elections:

- **Civil liberties**, such as freedom of belief, speech, and assembly
- **Rule of law** that provides for equal treatment of citizens and due process
- **Neutrality of the judiciary** and other checks on the abuse of power
- **Open civil society** that allows citizens to lead private lives and mass media to operate independently from government
- **Civilian control of the military** that restricts the likelihood of the military seizing control of the government

Countries that have regular, free, and fair competitive elections, but are missing these other qualities (civil liberties, rule of law, neutrality of the judiciary, open civil society, and civilian control of the military) are referred to as **illiberal democracies.**

According to political scientist Samuel Huntington, the modern world is now in a **"third wave" of democratization** that began during the 1970s. The "first wave" developed gradually over time since the revolutions of the late 18th century; the "second wave" occurred after the Allied victory in World War II, and continued until the early 1960s. This second wave was characterized by de-colonization around the globe. The third wave is characterized by the defeat of dictatorial or totalitarian rulers from South America to Eastern Europe to some parts of Africa. The recent political turnover in Mexico may be interpreted as part of this "third wave" of democratization.

Why has democratization occurred? According to Huntington, some factors are:

- The **loss of legitimacy** by both right and left wing authoritarian regimes
- The **expansion of an urban middle class** in developing countries
- A new emphasis on **"human rights"** by the United States and the European Union
- The **"snowball" effect**, when one country in a region becomes democratic, it influences others to do so. An example is Poland's influence on other nations of Eastern Europe during the 1980s.

One of the greatest obstacles to democratization is poverty because it blocks citizen participation in government. Huntington gauges democratic stability by this standard: democracy may be declared when a country has had at least two successive peaceful turnovers of power. An authoritarian regime may transition to a democracy as a result of a "trigger event," such as an economic crisis or a military defeat. Political discontent is generally fueled if the crisis is preceded by a period of relative improvement in the standard of living, a condition called the **"revolution of rising expectations."** The changes demanded may not necessarily be democratic. Democratization begins when these conditions are accompanied by a willingness on the part of the ruling elite to accept power-sharing arrangements, as well as a readiness on the part of the people to participate in the process and lend it their active support.

2) Movement Toward Market Economies

A second trend of the 20th and early 21st centuries is a movement toward market economies. Political scientists disagree about the relationship between democratization and marketization. Does one cause the other, or is the relationship between the two spurious? Many countries have experienced both, but two of the country cases for the comparative government course offer contradictory evidence. Mexico has moved steadily toward a market economy since the 1980s, and democratization appears to have followed, starting in the late 1980s. On the other hand, China has been moving toward capitalism since the late 1970s without any sign of democratization.

Many political economists today declare that the economic competition between capitalism and socialism that dominated the 20th century is now a part of the past. The old **command economies**, with socialist principles of centralized planning and state ownership are fading from existence, except in combination with market economies. The issue now is what type of **market economy** will be most successful: one that allows for significant control from the central government - a "**mixed economy**" - or one that does not – a pure market economy. For example, modern Germany has a "social market economy" that is team-oriented and emphasizes cooperation between management and organized labor. In contrast, the United States economy tends to be more individualistic and anti-government control.

Two factors that have promoted the movement toward market economies are:

- **Belief that government is too big** – Command economies require an active, centralized government that gets heavily involved in economic issues. Anti-big government movements began in the 1980s in the United States and many Western European nations, where economies had experienced serious problems of inefficiency and stagnation. Margaret Thatcher in Britain and Ronald Reagan in the United States rode to power on waves of public support for reducing the scale of government.

- **Lack of success of command economies** – The collapse of the Soviet Union is the best example of a failed command economy that reverberated around the world. This failure was accompanied by changes among the Eastern European satellite states from command to market economies. Meanwhile, another big command economy – China – had been slowly infusing capitalism into its system since its near collapse in the 1970s. Today China is a "socialist market economy" that is fueled by its ever growing doses of capitalism.

Marketization is the term that describes the state's re-creation of a market in which property, labor, goods, and services can all function in a competitive environment to determine their value. **Privatization** is the transfer of state-owned property to private ownership.

COMMAND ECONOMY	MIXED ECONOMY	MARKET ECONOMY
Right to own property is greatly restricted. All industry is owned by the government. Competition and profit are prohibited.	Elements of command and market economies present.	Right to own property is accepted/guaranteed. Most industry is owned by private individuals. Competition and profit are not controlled by the government.

All economies fall somewhere on the continuum between command and market systems, as illustrated by the graph above. For example, the United States is mostly a market economy, but competition and profit are regulated by the government, so it has some characteristics of a mixed economy. On the other end of the continuum is the former Soviet Union, where the government controlled the economy and allowed virtually no private ownership. Countries may move along the continuum over time. A good example is China, which has moved steadily away from a command economy toward a market economy since 1979.

3) Revival of Ethnic or Cultural Politics

Until recently, few political scientists predicted that **fragmentation** - divisions based on ethnic or cultural identity - would become increasingly important in world politics. A few years ago **nationalism** – identities based on nationhood - seemed to be declining in favor of increasing globalization. However, nationality questions almost certainly did in Mikhail Gorbachev's attempts to resuscitate the Soviet Union, and national identities remain strong in most parts of the world. Perhaps most dramatically, the **politicization of religion** has dominated world politics of the early 21st century. Most Westerners have been caught off guard by this turn of events, especially in the United States, where separation of church and state has been a basic political principle since the founding of the country. In the Middle East, political terrorism are carried out in the name of Islam, and some frame modern international interactions in terms of tensions that occur between Islamic and Christian states.

Samuel Huntington has argued that our most important and dangerous future conflicts will be based on clashes of civilizations, not on socioeconomic or even ideological differences. He divides the world into several different cultural areas that may already be poised to threaten world peace: the West, the Orthodox world (Russia), Islamic countries, Latin American, Africa, the Hindu world, the Confucian world, the Buddhist world, and Japan. Some political scientists criticize Huntington by saying that he distorts cultural divisions and that he underestimates the importance of cultural conflicts within nations. In either case – a world divided into cultural regions or a world organized into multicultural nations – the revival of ethnic or cultural politics tends to emphasize differences among nations rather than commonalities.

TOPIC FOUR: CITIZENS, SOCIETY AND THE STATE

Government and politics are only part of the many facets of a complex society. Religion, ethnic groups, race, social and economic classes – all of these interact with the political system and have a tremendous impact on policymaking. These divisions – theoretically out of the realm of politics – are called **social cleavages**.

- **Bases of social cleavages** – What mix of social classes, ethnic and racial groups, religions, languages does a country have? How deep are these cleavages, and to what degree do they separate people from one another (form **social boundaries)?** Which of these cleavages appear to have the most significant impact on the political system?

- **Cleavages and political institutions** – How are the cleavages expressed in the political system? For example, is political party membership based on cleavages? Do political elites usually come from one group or another? Do these cleavages block some groups from fully participating in government?

COMPARING CITIZEN/STATE RELATIONSHIPS

Governments connect to their citizens in a variety of ways, but we may successfully compare government-citizen relationships by categorizing, and in turn noting differences and similarities among categories. For example, citizens within democracies generally relate to their governments differently than do citizens that are governed by authoritarian rulers. Or, different countries may be compared by using the categories below:

- **Attitudes and beliefs of citizens** – Do citizens trust their government? Do they believe that the government cares about what they think? Do citizens feel that government affects their lives in significant ways?

- **Political socialization** – How do citizens learn about politics in their country? Does electronic and print media shape their learning? Does the government put forth effort to politically educate their citizens? If so, how much of their effort might you call "propaganda"? How do children learn about politics?

- **Types of political participation** – In authoritarian governments, most citizens contact government through **subject activities** that involve obedience. Such activities are obeying laws, following military orders, and paying taxes. In democracies, citizens may play a more active part in the political process. The most common type of participation is voting, but citizens may also work for political candidates, attend political meetings or rallies, contribute money to campaigns, and join political clubs or parties.

BASES OF SOCIAL CLEAVAGES

Social Class - Even though class awareness has declined in industrial and post-industrial societies, it is still an important base of cleavages. For example, traditionally in Great Britain, middle class voters have supported the Conservative Party and working class voters have supported the Labour Party. These differences have declined significantly in recent elections. In less developed countries class tensions may appear between landless peasants and property owners. In India, vestiges of the old caste system (now illegal) have slowed India's movement toward a democratic political system.

Ethnic Cleavages - In the early 20th century, ethnic cleavages are clearly the most divisive and explosive social cleavages in countries at all levels of development. Ethnic clashes are the cause of several full-scale civil wars in the former Yugoslavia, some of the former USSR republics and African countries such as Liberia, Rwanda, and Angola. Ethnic cleavages are based on different cultural identities, including religion and language, and are important considerations in evaluating the political systems of all six country cases in the AP Comparative course.

Religious Cleavages - Religious differences are often closely intertwined with ethnicity. For example, the conflict in Northern Ireland has a strong religious dimension, with the Irish nationalists being ardent Catholics and the loyalists strong Protestants. However, religious differences can also exist among people of similar ethnic backgrounds. For example, some have argued that a basic cleavage exists in the United States between fundamentalist and non-fundamentalist Christians.

Regional Cleavages - In many modern states, differing political values and attitudes characterize people living in different geographic regions. These populations compete for government resources such as money, jobs, and development projects. Regional differences are often linked to varying degrees of economic development. For example, regional conflicts in Nigeria based largely on economic inequalities resulted in the secession of Biafra and a tragic civil war.

Coinciding and Cross-cutting Cleavages - When every dispute aligns the same groups against each other, **coinciding cleavages** exist, and they are likely to be explosive. **Cross-cutting cleavages** divide society into many potential groups that may conflict on one issue but cooperate on another, and they tend to keep social conflict to more moderate levels.

- **Voting behavior** – Do citizens in the country have regular elections? If so, are the elections truly competitive? If not, what is the purpose of the elections? What citizens are eligible to vote, and how many actually vote? Do politicians pay attention to elections, and do elections affect policy-making?

- **Factors that influence political beliefs and behaviors** - Consider the important cleavages in the country. Do they make a difference in citizens' political beliefs and behaviors? For example, do the lower classes vote for one political party or the other? Are women's beliefs and behaviors different from those of the men? Are younger people as likely to vote as older people are? Do people in rural areas participate in government?

SOCIAL MOVEMENTS

Social movements refer to organized collective activities that aim to bring about or resist fundamental change in an existing group or society. Social movements try to influence political leaders to make policy decisions that support their goals. Members of social movements often step outside traditional channels for bringing about social change, and they usually take stands on issues that push others in mainstream society to reconsider their positions. For example, early leaders in the women's suffrage movement in Great Britain and the United States were considered to be radicals, but their goals were eventually recognized and accomplished. The modern civil rights movement in the United States consisted of collective action that influenced state, local, and national governments to support racial equality. The African National Congress (ANC), a political organization that sought to overthrow the state-supported system of apartheid in South Africa, eventually pushed the government to lift the decades-old ban and release ANC leader Nelson Mandela from prison. The success of social movements varies from case to case, but even if they fail, they often influence political opinion.

CIVIL SOCIETY

Civil society refers to organizations outside the government that help people define and advance their own interests. Civil society is usually strong in liberal democracies where individual freedoms are valued and protected. The organizations that compose it may represent class, religious, or ethnic interests, or they may cross them, creating strong personal bonds that exist outside of government controls. Political scientists are interested in civil society as it helps to define the people's relationship to and role in politics and community affairs. Groups in civil society may be inherently apolitical, but they serve as a cornerstone of liberty by allowing people to articulate and promote what is important to them. In many ways, civil society checks the power of the state and helps to prevent the **tyranny of the majority**, or the tendency in democracies to allow majority rule to neglect the rights and liberties of minorities. Advocacy groups, social networks, and the media all may exist within the civil society, and if they are strong enough, they may place considerable pressure on the state to bring about reform.

By the early 21st century, a global civil society has emerged, with human rights and environmental groups providing international pressures that have a significant effect on government-citizen relations. Some argue that a global **cosmopolitanism** – or a universal political order that draws its identity and values from everywhere – is emerging. This global civil society can take shape in **nongovernmental organizations (NGOs)** or more informally through people that find common interests with people who live in other corners of the globe. Nongovernmental organizations are national and international groups, independent of any state, that pursue policy objectives and foster public participation. Examples are Doctors without Borders and Amnesty International. Societal globalization, then, may change the definition of who is "us" and who is "them," and reshape a world that formerly defined reality in nationalistic terms.

By their very nature, authoritarian states do not encourage civil society, and they often feel that their power is threatened by it. Civil society does not necessarily disappear under authoritarian rule, as is illustrated by the survival of the Russian Orthodox Church and social reform movements in Eastern Europe during decades of communist rule. Generally, civil society is weak in less-developed and newly

COMPARATIVE VOTER TURNOUT
SELECTED PRESIDENTIAL ELECTIONS 2006-7

Country	Date of Election	Voter Turnout
Nigeria	April 21, 2007	57.5%*
Uganda	February 23, 2006	69.19%
Yemen	September 20, 2006	65.16%
Colombia	May 28, 2006	45.05%
Haiti	February 7, 2006	59.26%
France	April 27, 2007	83.77%
Portugal	January 22, 2006	61.53%

*Figure is estimate, not official.

Voter turnouts may be compared across countries, as shown in the chart of recent presidential elections above. The chart does not explain why some voter rates are lower than others, but a little research will yield some hypotheses. For example, the French election was of very high interest because an incumbent was not running, so the voter turnout was much higher than it had been in previous recent presidential elections. Nigeria's election results are less reliable than many, partly because of widespread fraud.

industrializing countries. Individuals tend to be divided by ethnic, religious, economic, or social boundaries, and do not identify with groups beyond their immediate surroundings that might help them articulate their interests to the government. One step in the development of civil society is civic education, in which communities learn their democratic rights and how to use those rights to give meaningful input to political institutions. One positive sign in less developed countries is the growing involvement of women in NGOs that deal with a variety of health, gender, environmental, and poverty issues.

TOPIC FIVE: POLITICAL INSTITUTIONS

An important part of studying comparative government and politics is developing an understanding of **political institutions,** structures of a political system that carry out the work of governing. Some governments have much more elaborate structures than others, but they often have similarities across cultures. However, just because you see the same type of institution in two different countries, don't assume that they serve the same functions for the political system. For example, a legislature in one country may have a great deal more power than a comparable structure in another country. Only by studying the way that the structures operate and the functions they fill will you be able to compare them accurately. Common structures that exist in most countries are legislatures, executives, judicial systems, bureaucracies, and armies.

LEVELS OF GOVERNMENT

Every state has multiple levels of authority, though the geographic distribution of power varies widely. A **unitary system** is one that concentrates all policymaking powers in one central geographic place; a **confederal system** spreads the power among many sub-units (such as states), and has a weak central government. A **federal system** divides the power between the central government and the sub-units. All political systems fall on a continuum from the most concentrated amount of power to the least. Unitary governments may be placed on the left side, according to the degree of concentration; confederal governments are placed to the right; and federal governments fall in between. Most countries have unitary systems, including all six of the core countries, although Britain is moving toward more federalism and the Nigerian state is generally too weak to effectively concentrate its power in one place.

Unitary Systems	Federal Systems	Confederal Systems

SUPRANATIONAL ORGANIZATIONS AND GLOBALIZATION

All political systems exist within an environment that is affected by other governments, but more and more they are affected by **supranational organizations** that go beyond national boundaries. Some have more international and/or regional contacts than others, but most countries in the world today must cope with influences from the outside and interactions with others. These organizations reflect a trend toward integration, a process that encourages states to pool their sovereignty in order to gain political, economic, and social clout. Integration binds states together with common policies and shared rules. In the 20th century, many national governments established relationships with regional organizations – such as NATO, the European Union, NAFTA, and OPEC – and with international organizations, such as the United Nations.

These **supranational organizations** reflect the phenomenon of **globalization** - an integration of social, environmental, economic, and cultural activities of nations that has resulted from increasing international contacts. Globalization has changed the nature of comparative politics, largely because it breaks down the distinction between international relations and domestic politics, making many aspects of domestic politics subject to global forces. Likewise, it also internationalizes domestic issues and events. Because globalization deepens and widens international connections, local events, even small ones, can have ripple effects throughout the world. Perhaps most apparent is the effect of technology and its ability to ignore national boundaries. The Internet allows news from every corner of the globe to rapidly spread to other areas, so that what happens in one place affects others around the world. On the other hand, many political scientists point out a counter trend – **fragmentation** – a tendency for people to base their loyalty on ethnicity, language, religion, or cultural identity. Although globalization and fragmentation appear to be opposite concepts, they both transcend political boundaries between individual countries.

MODERN CHALLENGES TO THE NATION-STATE CONFIGURATION

Nation states have always had their challenges, both internal and external, but today new supranational forces are at work that have led some to believe that the nation-state political configuration itself may be changing. Is it possible that large regional organizations, such as the European Union, will replace the smaller state units as basic organizational models? Or will international organizations, such as the United Nations, come to have true governing power over the nation-states? If so, then the very nature of sovereignty may be changing, especially if nation-states of the future have to abide by the rules of **supranational organizations** for all major decisions and rules.

Centripetal vs. Centrifugal Forces

A recurring set of forces affects all nation-states: **centripetal forces** that unify them, and **centrifugal forces** that tend to fragment them.

- **Centripetal forces** bind together the people of a state, giving it strength. One of the most powerful centripetal forces is **nationalism**, or identities based on nationhood. It encourages allegiance to a single country, and it promotes loyalty and commitment. Such emotions encourage people to obey the law and accept the country's overall ideologies. States promote nationalism in a number of ways, including the use of symbols, such as flags, rituals, and holidays that remind citizens of what the country stands for. Even when a society is highly heterogeneous, symbols are powerful tools for creating national unity. Institutions, such as schools, the armed forces, and religion, may also serve as centripetal forces. Schools are expected to instill the society's beliefs, values, and behaviors in the young, teach the nation's language, and encourage students to identify with the nation. Fast and efficient transportation and communications systems also tend to unify nations. National broadcasting companies usually take the point of view of the nation, even if they broadcast internationally. Transportation systems make it easier for people to travel to other parts of the country, and give the government the ability to reach all of its citizens.

- **Centrifugal forces** oppose centripetal forces. They destabilize the government and encourage the country to fall apart. A country that is not well-organized or governed stands to lose the loyalty of its citizens, and weak institutions can fail to provide the cohesive support that the government needs. Strong institutions may also challenge the government for the loyalty of the people. For example, when the U.S.S.R. was created in 1917, its leaders grounded the new country in the ideology of communism. To strengthen the state, they forbid the practice of the traditional religion, Russian Orthodoxy. Although church membership dropped dramatically, the religious institution never disappeared, and when the U.S.S.R. dissolved, the church reappeared and is regaining its strength today. The church was a centrifugal force in creating and maintaining loyalty to the communist state. Nationalism, too, can be a destabilizing force, especially if different ethnic groups within the country have more loyalty to their ethnicity than to the state and its government. These loyalties can lead to **separatist movements** in which nationalities within a country may demand independence. Such movements served as centrifugal forces for the Soviet Union as various nationalities - such as Lithuanians, Ukrainians, Latvians, Georgians, and Armenians - challenged the government for their independence. Other examples are the Basques of Northern Spain, who have different customs (including language) from others in the country, and the Tamils in Sri Lanka, who have waged years of guerrilla warfare to defend what they see as majority threats to their culture, rights, and property.

Characteristics that encourage separatist movements are a peripheral location and social and economic inequality. One reaction states have had to centrifugal force is **devolution,** or the tendency to decentralize decision-making to regional governments. Britain has devolved power to the Scottish and Welsh parliaments in an effort to keep peace with Scotland and Wales. As a result, Britain's unitary government has taken some significant strides toward federalism, ahtough London is still the geographic center of decision-mkaing in the country.

Devolution: Ethnic, Economic, and Spatial Forces

Devolution of government powers to sub-governments is usually a reaction to centrifugal forces – those that divide and destabilize. Devolutionary forces can emerge in all kinds of states, old and you, mature and newly created. We may divide these forces into three basic types:

- **Ethnic forces** – An **ethnic group** shares a well-developed sense of belonging to the same culture. That identity is based on a unique mixture of language, religion, and customs. If a state contains strong ethnic groups with identities that differ from those of the majority, it can threaten the territorial integrity of the state itself. **Ethnonationalism,** the tendency for an ethnic group to see itself as a distinct nation with a right to autonomy or independence, is a fundamental centrifugal force promoting devolution. The threat is usually stronger if the group is clustered in particular spaces within the nation-state. For example, most French Canadians live in the province of Quebec, creating a large base for an independence movement. If ethnically French people were scattered evenly over the country, their sense of identity would be diluted, and the devolutionary force would most likely be weaker. Devolutionary forces in Britain – centered in Wales, Scotland, and Northern Ireland – have not been strong enough to destabilize the country, although violence in Northern Ireland has certainly destabilized the region. Ethnic forces broke up the nation-state of Yugoslavia during the 1990s, devolving it into separate states of Slovenia, Croatia, Bosnia, Macedonia, and Serbia-Montenegro.

- **Economic forces** - Economic inequalities may also destabilize a nation-state, particularly if the inequalities are regional. For example, Italy is split between north and south by the "Ancona Line", an invisible line extending from Rome to the Adriatic coast at Ancona. The north is far more prosperous than the south, with the north clearly part of the European core area, and the south a part of the periphery. The north is industrialized, and the south is rural. These economic differences inspired the formation of the Northern League, which advocated an independent state called Padania that would shed the north of the "economic drag" they considered the south to be. The movement failed, but it did encourage the Italian government to devolve power to regional governments, moving it toward a more federal system. A similar economic force is at work in Catalonia in northern Spain, with Catalonians only about 17% of Spain's population, but accountable for 40% of all Spanish industrial exports.

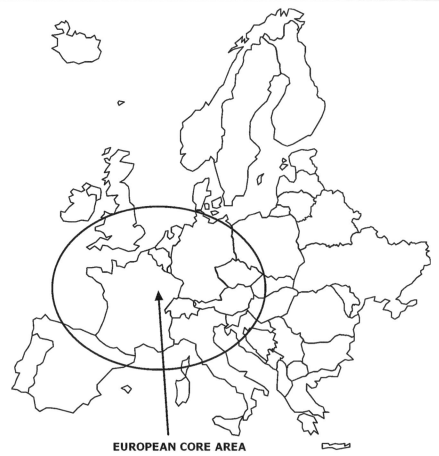

EUROPEAN CORE AREA

Economic Devolutionary Forces in Italy and Spain. Geographically, southern Italy and most of Spain lie outside the European core, creating economic devolutionary forces within the two nation-states. In Spain, the Catalonians in the north are connected to the core, but the bulk of Spain is not. In Italy the core extends its reach over the northern half of the country, creating cetrifugal tensions between north and south.

- **Spatial forces** – Spatially, devolutionary events most often occur on the margins of the state. Distance, remoteness, and peripheral location promote devolution, especially if water, desert, or mountains separate the areas from the center of power, and neighbor nations that may support separatist objectives. For example, the United States claims Puerto Rico as a territory, and has offered it recognition as a state. However, Puerto Ricans have consistently voted down the offer of statehood, and a small but vocal pro-independence movement has advocated complete separation from the U.S. The movement is encouraged by spatial forces – Puerto Rico is an island in the Caribbean, close to other islands that have their independence.

EXECUTIVES

The executive office carries out the laws and policies of a state. In many countries the executive is split into two distinct roles: **the head of state** and **the head of government.** The head of state is a role that symbolizes and represents the people, both nationally and internationally, and may or may not have any real policymaking power. The head of government deals with the everyday tasks of running the state, and usually directs the activities of other members of the executive branch. The distinction is clearly seen in a country such as Britain, where formerly powerful monarchs reigned over their subjects, but left others (such as prime ministers) in charge of actually running the country. Today Britain still has a monarch that is head of state, but the real power rests with the prime minister, who is head of government. Likewise, the Japanese emperor still symbolically represents the nation, but the prime minister runs the government. In the United States, both roles are combined into one position – the president. However, in other countries, such as Italy and Germany, the president is the head of state with weak powers, and the prime minister is the head of government. In still others, such as Russia and France, the president is head of state with strong powers, and the prime minister is the head of government with subordinate powers.

FUNCTIONS OF THE CHIEF EXECUTIVE

Usually the chief executive is the most important person in the policymaking process, initiating new policies and playing an important role in their adoption. In presidential systems, the president usually has the power to veto legislation, while the executive in a parliamentary system usually does not have that authority. The political executive also oversees policy implementation and can hold other officials in the executive branch accountable for their performance. The central decisions in a foreign policy crisis are generally made by the chief executive.

THE CABINET

In parliamentary systems, the cabinet is the most important collective decision-making body. Its ministers head all the major departments into which the executive branch is divided, and the cabinet is led by the prime minister, or "first among equals." The ministers are also leaders of the majority party in parliament, or if the country has a multi-party system with no clear majority party, a **cabinet coalition** will form, where several parties join forces and are represented in different cabinet posts. In presidential systems, the president chooses the cabinet members from almost any area of political life, and his appointments may have to be approved by the legislature, as with the U.S. Senate. Because the cabinet members are not necessarily party leaders, nor are they usually members of the legislature, they often have more independence from the president than ministers do from the prime minister. However, the president usually has the power to remove them from office, so they can't stray too far from the president's wishes.

BUREAUCRACIES

Bureaucracies consist of agencies that generally implement government policy. They usually are a part of the executive branch of government, and their size has generally increased over the course of the 20th and early 21st centuries. This is partly due to government efforts to improve the health, security, and welfare of their populations.

German political philosopher Max Weber created the classic conception of bureaucracy as a well-organized, complex machine that is a "rational" way for a modern society to organize its business. He did not see them as necessary evils, but as the best organizational response to a changing society.

According to Weber, a bureaucracy has several basic characteristics:

- **Hierarchical authority structure** - A chain of command that is hierarchical; the top bureaucrat has ultimate control, and authority flows from the top down

- **Task specialization** - A clear division of labor in which every individual has a specialized job
- **Extensive rules** - Clearly written, well-established formal rules that all people in the organization follow
- **Clear goals** - A clearly defined set of goals that all people in the organization strive toward
- **The merit principle** - Merit-based hiring and promotion; no granting of jobs to friends or family unless they are the best qualified
- **Impersonality** - Job performance that is judged by productivity, or how much work the individual gets done

Bureaucracies have acquired great significance in most contemporary societies and often represent an important source of stability for states.

BUREAUCRACIES IN DEMOCRACIES

Max Weber developed the above characteristics of bureaucracies with European democracies in mind. He was less than enthusiastic about their growing importance largely because of the alienation that he believed they created among workers. A modern issue has to do with the **discretionary power** given to bureaucrats – the power to make small decisions in implementing legislative and executive decisions. These small decisions arguably add up to significant policymaking influence. Yet democratic beliefs require decisions to be made by elected officials, not by appointed bureaucrats. The bureaucracy is often an important source of stability in a democracy, since the elected officials may be swept out of office and replaced by new people with little political experience. The bureaucrats stay on through the changes in elected leadership positions, and as a result, they provide continuity in the policymaking process.

BUREAUCRACIES IN AUTHORITARIAN REGIMES

Bureaucracies in authoritarian regimes differ from those in democracies in that the head of government exercises almost complete control over their activities. For example, Joseph Stalin placed his own personal supporters (members of the communist party) in control of bureaucratic agencies, such as the secret police and the network of political commissars who served as watchdogs over the military. These bureaucracies not only managed the economy but directly controlled vast resources, including human labor. For example, the number of prisoners in labor camps under secret police administration increased dramatically under Stalin's rule. Executive power over the bureaucracy was questioned in the 19th century in the United States, when presidents had a great deal of control over who got government jobs under the **patronage system**, in which political supporters received jobs in return for their assistance in getting the president elected. However, this system was reformed after President James Garfield was assassinated by a disgruntled supporter, and was replaced by a merit-based system meant to curtail the president's patronage powers. As a result, bureaucratic appointments came to abide by more democratic, less authoritarian rules.

Other examples of bureaucratic-authoritarian regimes developed in Brazil, Argentina, Chile, and Uruguay during the 1960s and 1970s. In these Latin American countries a military regime formed a ruling coalition that included military officers and civilian bureaucrats, or **technocrats.** The coalition seized control of the government and determined which other groups were allowed to participate. The authoritarian leaders were seen as modernizers seeking to improve their countries' economic power in the world economy. They controlled the state partly in the name of efficiency – democratic input into the government was seen as an obstacle in the modernization process, and so the governments in these countries have often been oppressive.

COMMON CHARACTERISTICS OF BUREAUCRACIES

All bureaucracies, whether they are democratic or authoritarian, tend to have many features in common:

- **Non-elected positions** – Bureaucrats are appointed, usually salaried, and are not elected by the public.
- **Impersonal, efficient structures** – Bureaucracies tend to be impersonal because they are goal-oriented and have little concern for personal feelings. Bureaucracies are meant to be efficient in accomplishing their goals.
- **Formal qualifications for jobs** – Although authoritarian leaders may appoint whoever they want to government positions, they must at least factor in formal qualifications (education, experience) in making their appointments. Otherwise, the bureaucracy cannot fulfill its goals of efficiency and competent administration. Most democracies have institutionalized formal qualifications as prerequisites for appointments to the bureaucracy.
- **Hierarchical organization** – Most bureaucracies are hierarchical, top-down organizations in which higher officials give orders to lower officials. Everyone in the hierarchy has a boss, except for the person at the very top.
- **Red tape/inefficiency** – Despite their common goal of efficiency, large bureaucracies seem to stumble under their own weight. Once the bureaucracy reaches a certain size and complexity, the orderly flow of business appears to break down, so that one hand doesn't appear to know what the other is doing.

LEGISLATURES

The legislature is the branch of government charged with making laws. Their formal approval is usually required for major public policies, although in authoritarian states, legislatures are generally dominated by the chief executive. Today more than 80 percent of the countries belonging to the United Nations have legislatures, suggesting that a legitimate government today must formally include a representative popular component.

BICAMERALISM

Legislatures may be **bicameral**, with two houses, or **unicameral**, or only one. The most usual form is bicameral, and may be traced back to Britain's House of Lords and House of Commons. Despite the fact that one house is referred to as "upper" and the other as "lower," the upper house does not necessarily have more power than the lower house. In the United States, it is debatable which house is more powerful than the other, and in Britain, Russia, and France, the upper house has very little power.

Why do most countries have a bicameral legislature? If the country practices federalism, where power is shared between a central and subunit governments, bicameralism allows for one house (usually the upper chamber) to represent regional governments and local interests. Seats in the other chamber are usually determined by population, and so the body (usually the lower house) serves as a direct democratic link to the voters. Bicameralism may also counterbalance disproportionate power in the hands of any region. For example, in the United States, populous states such as California, New York, and Texas have large numbers of representatives in the lower house, so the voices of citizens in those states are stronger than those in more sparsely populated states. However, that large state advantage is counterbalanced in the Senate, where all states are equally represented by two senators each. Even in a unitary state where all power is centralized in one place, bicameralism may serve to disperse power by requiring both houses to approve legislation. Some scholars view the upper house as a "cooling off" mechanism to slow down impulsive actions of the "hotheaded" lower house that is directly elected by the people.

Memberships in the legislature may be determined in different ways, with many houses being elected directly by voters. However, others are selected by government officials, or their membership may be determined by political parties. The six core countries offer a variety of contrasting methods for determining legislative memberships.

FUNCTIONS OF LEGISLATURES

Assembly members formulate, debate, and vote on political policies. They often control the country's budget, in terms of both fund-raising and spending. Some assemblies may appoint important officials in the executive and judicial branches, and some (such as the British House of Lords) may serve as courts of appeal. They may also play a major role in **elite recruitment**, or identifying future leaders of the government, and they may hold hearings regarding behaviors of public officials.

Regarding policymaking, legislatures in different countries hold varying degrees of power. For example, the U.S. Congress plays a very active role in the formulation and enactment of legislation. In contrast, the National People's Congress of the People's Republic of China is primarily a rubberstamp organization for policies made by the leadership of the Chinese Communist Party.

JUDICIARIES

The judiciary's roles in the political system vary considerably from one country to another. All states have some form of legal structure, and the role of the judiciary is rarely limited to routinely adjudicating civil and criminal cases. Courts in authoritarian systems generally have little or no independence, and their decisions are controlled by the chief executive. Court systems that decide the guilt or innocence of lawbreakers go back to the days of medieval England, but **constitutional courts** that serve to defend democratic principles of a country against infringement by both private citizens and the government are a much more recent phenomenon. The constitutional court is the highest judicial body that rules on the constitutionality of laws and other government actions.

In some states the judiciary is relatively independent of the political authorities in the executive and legislative branches. It may even have the authority to impose restrictions on what these political leaders do. **Judicial review**, the mechanism that allows courts to review laws and executive actions for their constitutionality, was well established in the United States during the 19th century, but it has developed over the past decades in other democracies. The growth of judicial power over the past century has been spurred in part by the desire to protect human rights. Some have criticized the acceptance of the constitutional court in liberal democracies today, saying that the judges are not directly elected, so they do not represent the direct will of the people. Despite these developments, the judiciary is still a relatively weak branch in most of the six core countries of the Comparative Government and Politics course, but it takes a variety of forms in each of them.

LINKAGE INSTITUTIONS

In many countries we may identify groups that connect the government to its citizens, such as political parties, interest groups, and print and electronic media. Appropriately, these groups are called **linkage institutions.** Their size and development depends partly on the size of the population, and partly on the scope of government activity. The larger the population, and the more complex the government's policymaking activities, the more likely the country is to have well developed linkage institutions.

PARTIES

Political parties perform many functions in democracies. First, they help bring different people and ideas together to establish the means by which the majority can rule. Second, they provide labels for candidates that help citizens decide how to vote. Third, they hold politicians accountable to the electorate and other political elites. Most democracies have multi-party systems, with the two-party system in the United States being a more unusual arrangement. Communist states have one-party systems that dominate the governments, but non-communist countries have also had one-party systems. An example is Mexico during most of the 20th century as it was dominated by PRI.

The **two-party system** is a rarity, occurring in only about 15 countries in the world today. The United States has had two major political parties – the Republicans and the Democrats – throughout most of its history. Although minor parties do exist, most believe those two parties have the only reasonable chance to win national elections. The most important single reason for the existence of a two-party system is the plurality electoral system. Most European countries today have **multiparty systems.** They usually arise in countries with strong parliamentary systems, particularly those that use a proportional representation method for elections.

ELECTORAL SYSTEMS AND ELECTIONS

Electoral systems are the rules that decide how votes are cast, counted, and translated into seats in a legislature. All democracies divide their populations by electoral boundaries, but they use many different arrangements. The United States, India, and the Great Britain use a system called **first-past-the-post**, in which they divide their constituencies into **single-member districts** in which candidates compete for a single representative's seat. It is also called the **plurality system,** or the **winner-take-all system,** because the winner does not need a majority to win, but simply needs to get more votes than anyone else. In contrast, many countries use **proportional representation** that creates **multi-member districts** in which more than one legislative seat is contested in each district. Under proportional representation, voters cast their ballots for a party rather than for a candidate, and the percentage of votes a party receives determines how many seats the party will gain in the legislature. South Africa and Italy use a system based solely on proportional representation, and many countries, including Germany,

Mexico, and Russia, used a **mixed system** that combines first-past-the-post and proportional representation. For example, in Mexico, 300 of the 500 members of the Chamber of Deputies (the lower house) are elected through the winner-take-all system from single member districts, and 200 members are selected by proportional representation.

Plurality systems encourage large, broad based parties because no matter how many people run in a district, the person with the largest number of votes wins. This encourages parties to become larger, spreading their "umbrellas" to embrace more voters. Parties without big groups of voters supporting them have little hope of winning, and often even have a hard time getting their candidates listed on the ballot. In contrast, the proportional representation electoral system encourages multiple parties because they have a good chance of getting their representatives elected. This system allows minor parties to form coalitions to create a majority vote so that legislation can be passed.

Democracies also vary in the types of elections that they hold. A basic distinction between a presidential and parliamentary system is that the president is directly elected by the people to the position, and the prime minister is elected as a member of the legislature. The prime minister becomes head of government because (s)he is the leader of the majority party or coalition.

In general, these types of elections are found in democracies:

- **Election of public officials** – The number of elected officials varies widely, with thousands of officials elected in the United States, and far fewer in most other democracies. However, even in a unitary state, many local and regional officials are directly elected. Legislators are often directly elected, both on the regional and national levels. Now citizens of many European countries also elect representatives to the European Union's Parliament. Lower houses are more likely to be directly elected than upper houses, with a variety of techniques used for the latter.
- **Referendum** – Besides elections to choose public officials, many countries also have the option of allowing public votes on particular policy issues. A national ballot, called by the government on a policy issue is called a **referendum**, which allows the public to make direct decisions about policy itself. Referenda exist only on the state and local level in the United States and Canada, but many other countries have used them nationally. The French and Russian presidents have the power to call referenda, and they have sometimes had important political consequences. For example, when a referendum proposed by French President Charles DeGaulle failed, he resigned his office in reaction to the snub by the voters. In Russia, the Constitution of 1993 was presented as a referendum for approval by the voters. In Britain, devolution of powers to the Scottish and Welsh parliaments was put before the voters in those regions in the form of referenda, and national referenda have been proposed on adoption of the Euro and the European Constitution. A variation of a referendum is a **plebiscite**, or a ballot to consult public opinion in a nonbinding way.
- **Initiative** – Whereas a referendum is called by the government, an **initiative** is a vote on a policy that is initiated by the people. Although less common than the referendum, the initiative must propose an issue for a nation-wide vote and its organizers must collect a certain number of supporting signatures from the public. The government is then obliged to schedule a vote.

ELECTORAL SYSTEMS

PLURALITY SYSTEM	PROPORTIONAL REPRESENTATION	MIXED SYSTEM
Individual candidates run in single-member districts.	Voting is arranged in multimember districts.	Voting is arranged in combination of multi-member and single-member districts.
Voters cast votes for individual candidates.	Voters cast votes for parties.	Voters cast votes for individuals and parties.
Candidates with more votes than other candidates wins the seat.	Seats are divided among parties on the basis of percentage of overall vote.	Some seats are filled by winners in plurality races; others are filled by party.
One result is a two (or few) party system.	Proportional representation generally results in a multi-party systeym.	A mixed system results in an in-between number of parties.

INTEREST GROUPS

Interest groups are organizations of like-minded people whose goal is to influence and shape public policy. In liberal democracies, interest groups that are independent from the government are usually an important force in the maintenance of a strong civil society. Groups may be based on almost any type of common interest – occupations, labor, business interests, agriculture, community action, or advocacy for a cause. Groups may be formally organized on a national level, or they may work almost exclusively on the local level. Interest groups often have nonpolitical goals, too. For example, a business group might organize to promote the growth of its products by directly advertising them to the public. Most interest groups have a political side, too, that focuses on influencing the decisions that governments make.

The Strength of Interest Groups

An important factor in assessing how important interest groups are in setting public policy is to determine the degree of autonomy they have from the government. To exercise influence on public policy, groups need to be able to independently decide what their goals are and what methods they will use to achieve them.

In authoritarian states, groups have almost no independence. For example, in China, only government-endorsed groups may exist. Groups in communist China have often been agents to extend the party's influence beyond its own membership to shape the views of its citizens. The government cracks down on unrecognized groups, such as the religious organization, Falon Gong, so that they are either forced underground or out of existence. Frank Wilson refers to interest groups in this type of system **"transmission belts"** that convey to their members the views of the party elite.

At the other extreme are the interest groups in many Western industrial democracies. These groups guard their independence by selecting their own leaders and raising their own funds. These autonomous groups compete with each other and with government for influence over state policies in a pattern called **interest group pluralism.** Working from outside the formal governmental structures, rival groups use a variety of tactics to pressure government to make policies that favor their interests. A major criticism of interest group pluralism is that it increases inefficiency in policymaking, often slowing down or thwarting the work of political leaders.

In between these two extreme patterns is **corporatism**, where fewer groups compete than under pluralism, with usually one for each interest sector, such as labor, agriculture, and management. The group's monopoly over its sector is officially approved by the state and sometimes protected by the state. There are two forms of corporatism: **state corporatism**, where the state determines which groups are brought in; and **societal corporatism (or neocorporatism)**, where interest groups take the lead and dominate the state.

POLITICAL ELITES AND RECRUITMENT

All countries have **political elites,** or leaders that have a disproportionate share of policymaking power. In democracies, these people are selected by competitive elections, but they still may be readily identified as political elites. Every country must establish a method of **elite recruitment**, or ways to identify and select people for future leadership positions. Also, countries must be concerned about leadership **succession**, or the process that determines the procedure for replacing leaders when they resign, die, or are no longer effective.

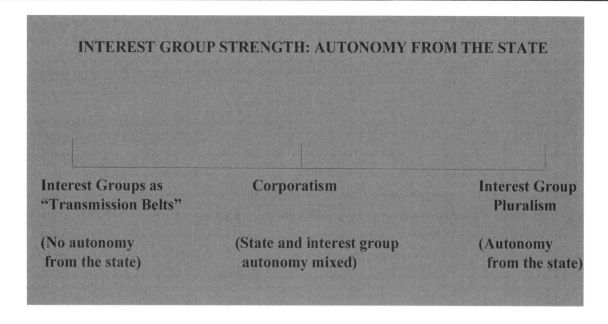

INTEREST GROUP STRENGTH: AUTONOMY FROM THE STATE

Interest Groups as "Transmission Belts"	Corporatism	Interest Group Pluralism
(No autonomy from the state)	(State and interest group autonomy mixed)	(Autonomy from the state)

TOPIC SIX: PUBLIC POLICY

All political systems set policy, whether by legislative vote, executive decision, judicial rulings, or a combination of the three. In many countries interest groups and political parties also play large roles in policymaking. Policy is generally directed toward addressing issues and solving problems. Many issues are similar in all countries, such as the needs to improve or stabilize the economy or to provide for a common defense against internal and external threats. However, governments differ in the approaches they take to various issues, as well as the importance they place on solving particular problems.

Common policy issues include:

- **Economic performance** – Governments are often concerned with the economic health/or problems within their borders. Most also participate in international trade, so their economies are deeply affected by their international imports and exports. The six core countries provide a variety of approaches that states may take, as well as an assortment of consequences of both good and poor economic performances. Economic performance may be measured in any number of ways including 1) **Gross Domestic Product (GDP)** – all the goods and services produced by a country's economy in a given year, excluding income citizens and groups earn outside the country; 2) **Gross National Product (GNP)** – like GDP, but also includes income citizens earned outside the country; 3) **GNP (or GDP) per capita** – divides the GNP by the population of the country; 4) **Purchasing Power Parity (PPP)** – a figure like GDP, except that it takes into consideration what people can buy using their income in the local economy.

- **Social welfare** – Citizens' social welfare needs include health, employment, family assistance, and education. States provide different levels of support in each area, and they display many different attitudes toward government responsibility for social welfare. Some measures of social welfare are literacy rates, distribution of income, life expectancy, and education levels. Two commonly used measures of social welfare are: 1) **The Gini Index**, a mathematical formula that measures the amount of economic inequality in a society; and 2) the **Human Development Index (HDI)** that measures the well-being of a country's people by factoring in adult literacy, life expectancy, and educational enrollment, as well as GDP.

THE GINI INDEX FOR SELECTED COUNTRIES 2006*

Country	Gini
Norway	.26
Canada	.33
United Kingdom	.36
New Zealand	.36
Russia	.40
United States	.41
Iran	.43
Nigeria	.44
China	.45
Mexico	.50

*A low Gini coefficient indicates more equal income or wealth distribution, while a high Gini coefficent indicates unequal income or wealth distribution. "0" corresponds to perfect equality (everyone has the same income), and "1" corresponds to complete inequality (one person has all the income; everyone else has zero income).

Source: UN Human Development Report, 2006 http://hdr.undp.org/hdr2006/statistics/indicators/147.html

- **Civil liberties, rights, and freedoms** – The constitutions of many liberal democracies guarantee civil liberties and rights, and most communist, post-communist, developing, and less developed countries pay lip service to them. **Freedom House**, an organization that studies democracy around the world, ranks countries on a 1 to 7 freedom scale, with countries given a 1 being the most free and those given a 7 being the least free. A number of post communist countries have made significant strides in this area in recent years, but many others remain highly authoritarian.

- **Environment** – Many modern democratic states take a big interest in protecting the environment. European countries in particular have had a surge of interest expressed through the formation of "green" parties that focus on the environment.

IMPORTANT TERMS AND CONCEPTS

advanced democracies
authoritarian regime
authority (traditional, charismatic, rational-legal)
bicameral, unicameral legislatures
bureaucratic authoritarian regimes
bureaucracy
cabinet coalition
causation
checks and balances
civil society
coinciding/crosscutting cleavages
command economies
common law/code law
communism
competitive elections
confederal system
conflictual political culture
consensual political culture
conservatism
constitutional courts
co-optation
corporatism
correlation
cosmopolitanism
coup d'etat
democratic corporatism
direct democracy
electoral systems
elites
empirical data
fascism
federal system
first past the post (plurality, winner-take-all)
fragmentation
Freedom House ratings
globalization
government
head of government
head of state
hypothesis
illiberal democracies
independent variable/dependent variable
indications of democratization
indirect democracy

informal politics
initiative
institutions, institutionalized
integration
interest group pluralism
judicial review
legitimacy
liberal democracies
liberalism as a political ideology
liberalism as an approach to economic and political change
linkage institutions
market economies
marketization
military rule
mixed economies
mixed electoral system
multi-member districts, single-member districts
multi-party system
nation
nationalism
normative questions
parliamentary system
patronage
patron-client system
plebiscite
pluralism
political culture
political elites
political frameworks
political ideologies
political socialization
politicization of religion
presidential system
privatization
proportional representation
radicalism
reactionary beliefs
recruitment of elites
referendum
reform
regime
revolution
revolution of rising expectations
rule of law
Samuel Huntington's "clash of civilizations"
semi-presidential system
separation of powers

social boundaries
social capital
social cleavages
social movements
socialism
societal (neo) corporatism
sovereignty
state corporatism
state
subject activities
succession
technocrats
"third wave" of democratization
third world
three-word approach
totalitarianism
"transmission belt"
two-party system
tyranny of the majority
unitary systems

MULTIPLE CHOICE QUESTIONS
INTRODUCTION TO COMPARATIVE GOVERNMENT
AND POLITICS: A CONCEPTUAL APPROACH

1. Suppose that a comparative government research project begins with a hypothesis that a high level of corruption within the Nigerian government has caused poverty rates to increase and foreign investments in the Nigerian economy to decrease. The independent variable in the hypothesis is

   a) the chief executive of Nigeria
   b) increasing poverty rates
   c) decreasing foreign investments
   d) high level of corruption in the government
   e) the global investment environment

2. Which of the following is NOT an example of informal politics?
   a) the Russian president consulting with the chief executive officer of a private oil company in Russia
   b) the prime minister of Great Britain granting an interview to the British Broadcasting Corporation
   c) the president of the United States signing a bill into law
   d) a citizen of Mexico joining a non-government sponsored labor union
   e) an Iranian student joining a protest at her university regarding the firing of a professor

3. If a state's boundaries do not closely follow the outline of a group bonded by a common political identity, the state is not consistent with

   a) its sovereignty
   b) its core area
   c) devolutionary forces
   d) its size
   e) the nation

4. Which of the following is the BEST description of the geographic distribution of power within states today?

   a) Most states are federal systems.
   b) Most states are confederal systems.
   c) Most states are unitary systems.
   d) States with federal systems are about equal in number to states with unitary systems.
   e) States with confederal systems are about equal in number to states with unitary systems.

5. Which of the following is MOST likely to serve as a centripetal force within a state?

    a) a tendency for the government to keep its power focused in a central geographical location
    b) strong institutions that challenge the government
    c) numerous separatist movements
    d) minority ethnic groups that live in the periphery
    e) overall strong sense of nationalism

6. Which of the following is the BEST definition of a regime?

    a) a group of people bound together by a common political identity
    b) the rules that a state sets and follows in exerting its power
    c) the organization that maintains a monopoly of violence over a territory
    d) stable, long lasting organizations that help to turn political ideas into policy
    e) the ability of a state to carry out actions or policies within their borders independently from outside or inside interference

7. A parliamentary system is usually characterized by

    a) a chief executive that is elected directly by the people
    b) separation of powers among the branches of government
    c) a prime minister that coexists with a president
    d) fusion between the executive and legislative branches
    e) a president with a disproportionate amount of power

8. Which of the following types of political systems is MOST likely to have a strong ideological goal?

    a) totalitarianism
    b) corporatism
    c) authoritarianism
    d) a military regime
    e) a patron-client system

9. A political system in which the state provides specific benefits or favors to a single person or small group in return for public support is called

    a) pluralism
    b) democratic corporatism
    c) patron-clientelism
    d) traditionalism
    e) totalitarianism

10. Common law differs from code law in that it is based more on

    a) written laws
    b) tradition and past practices
    c) the wishes of the chief executive
    d) the wishes of the legislature
    e) judicial review

11. The argument that Islam and/or Confucianism are incompatible with democracy is usually based on a devaluation in the political culture of

    a) human rights
    b) nationalism
    c) social capital
    d) law codes
    e) charismatic leadership

12. Which of the following political blocs would be MOST likely to advocate the elimination of inequality by the state taking over all resources to insure that true economic equality exists for the community as a whole?

    a) liberalism
    b) socialism
    c) communism
    d) fascism
    e) Islamists

13. Which of the following changes is MOST likely to impact more than one area of life?

    a) social reform
    b) political reform
    c) a military coup d'etat
    d) a revolution
    e) an economic depression

14. Which of the following democratic characteristics is an illiberal democracy MOST likely to display?

    a) rule of law
    b) regular, competitive elections
    c) an open civil society
    d) neutrality of the judiciary
    e) guarantee of some civil liberties and rights

15. Which of the following are generally willing to use violence to reach their goals?

    I. radicals
    II. liberals
    III. conservatives
    IV. reactionaries

    a) I only
    b) I and II only
    c) II and III only
    d) I and IV only
    e) II and IV only

16. Under which of the following circumstances is a revolution MOST likely to occur?

    a) a country whose citizens experience an economic crisis after a period of relative improvement in the standard of living
    b) an authoritarian regime that politically represses and economically limits its citizens
    c) a democracy whose citizens have limited literacy skills and access to health care
    d) a corporatist state that refuses to allow any input from groups other than those that the state endorses
    e) a military regime in which military officers frequently quarrel with one another

17. The anti-big government movements that began in the U.S. and western Europe in the 1980s promoted the 20th century trend toward

    a) nationalization of industry
    b) fascism
    c) market economies
    d) fragmentation
    e) democratization

18. Cleavages that split a society into the same groups against each other, no matter what the issue, are referred to as

    a) neocorporatist
    b) coinciding
    c) mobilizing
    d) crosscutting
    e) destabilizing

19. The most common type of political participation in most countries is

    a) voting in local elections
    b) protesting
    c) supporting candidates for office
    d) contacting government representatives concerning problems
    e) voting in national elections

20. Civil society is usually strongest in

    a) liberal democracies
    b) illiberal democracies
    c) authoritarian states
    d) less developed countries
    e) Latin American countries

21. Which of the following organizations MOST directly reflects a recent global trend toward integration?

    a) National Association for the Advancement of Colored People (NAACP)
    b) European Union
    c) National Organization of Women (NOW)
    d) United Arabs Emirate
    e) USA Today

22. Which of the following countries clearly combines the roles of head of state and head of government into one political position?

    a) Great Britain
    b) France
    c) Japan
    d) The United States
    e) Germany

23. A cabinet coalition is MOST likely to form in a country with a

    a) presidential system
    b) strong bureaucracy
    c) one-party system
    d) multi-party system
    e) head of state separated from the head of government

24. Bureaucrats that have a great deal of policymaking power in a bureaucratic-authoritarian regime are known as

    a) patrons
    b) technocrats
    c) politicos
    d) elites
    e) corporatists

(Questions 25 and 26 are based on the following map):

EUROPEAN CORE AREA

25. The European Core Area on the map above designates

    a) the heart of European economic activity
    b) countries that belong to the European Union vs. those that don't
    c) the cultural identity of being European
    d) the area of most intense ethnic strife in Europe
    e) people with an Anglo-Saxon identity

26. A country that has experienced centrifugal forces within its borders because of its position in regard to the European Core Area is

    a) France
    b) Switzerland
    c) Ireland
    d) Germany
    e) Italy

27. Which of the following is NOT a common reason why most countries have bicameral legislatures?

    a) to slow down impulsive legislation
    b) to disperse power
    c) to make the legislative process more efficient
    d) to represent regional governments in one house
    e) to counterbalance disproportionate power of one region

28. Which of the following is a likely outcome when a country has a plurality electoral system?

    a) a two (or few) party system
    b) low voter turnouts
    c) a parliamentary system
    d) separation of powers
    e) corporatism

29. In 1993 the Russian Constitution was presented for approval by the voters in the form of a(n)

    a) referendum
    b) approval vote for the president
    c) initiative
    d) plebiscite
    e) primary election

30. Interest groups are MOST likely to have influence in the policymaking process in the presence of

    a) "transmission belts"
    b) neocorporatism
    c) state corporatism
    d) fragmentation
    e) interest group pluralism

UNIT ONE CONCEPTUAL ANALYSIS QUESTION

(a) Define devolution.

(b) Discuss two reasons why a political leader of a unitary state might choose to support a policy for devolution. Include in your discussion a definition of a unitary state.

(c) Describe two implications of devolution for the policymaking process.

PART TWO: COUNTRY CASES

ADVANCED DEMOCRACIES

During the era of the Cold War, most political science scholars categorized countries of the world according to the "Three Worlds" approach. The First World included the United States and its allies; the Second World centered on the U.S.S.R. and its allies; and the Third World included all countries that could not be assigned to either camp. Today, with the Cold War over and the world encompassed with forces of globalization and fragmentation, we will use these three categories to more effectively compare political systems: advanced democracies, communist and post communist countries, and developing/less developed countries. In this section of the book, we will consider advanced democracies.

What do we mean by the term, "advanced democracies"? Generally, we are referring to two dimensions: political type and level of economic development.

POLITICAL DIMENSIONS

Politically, advanced democracies exemplify many facets of democracy, not just the characteristic of holding regular and fair elections. Other qualities of advanced democracies are:

- **Civil liberties**, such as freedom of belief, speech, and assembly

- **Rule of law** that provides for equal treatment of citizens and due process

- **Neutrality of the judiciary** and other checks on the abuse of power

- **Open civil society** that allows citizens to lead private lives and mass media to operate independently from government

- **Civilian control of the military** that restricts the likelihood of the military seizing control of the government

Advanced democracies generally have a high degree of legitimacy, partly because their systems have been in place for a long time. Another source of legitimacy is a large amount of **social capital** (see page 16), or reciprocity and trust that exists among citizens, and between citizens and the state. All advanced democracies guarantee participation, competition, and liberty, but they differ in the methods that they use. For example, some have proportional representation electoral systems; others use the plurality system; and still others combine the two systems. Participation rates vary considerably, too. The use of referenda and initiatives differ greatly across these countries; most advanced democracies use them, although the United States, Japan, Canada, and Germany, allow for such votes only at the local level. In most of the countries, it is the responsibility of the state to ensure that all eligible voters are automatically registered to vote. However, in the United States and France, the responsibility to register is on the individual. In several Scandinavian countries, citizenship is not required for voting; anyone who is a permanent resident may vote. In Australia, Argentina, Uruguay, and Belgium, voting is mandatory.

POLITICAL SYSTEMS IN ADVANCED DEMOCRACIES

PARLIAMENTARY	SEMI-PRESIDENTIAL	PRESIDENTIAL
Australia	Austria	The United States
Belgium	Finland	
Canada	France	
Denmark	Portugal	
Germany		
Israel		
Italy		
Japan		
Netherlands		
New Zealand		
Norway		
Spain		
Sweden		
Great Britain		

Parliamentary, Semi-Presidential and Presidential Systems. As the chart demonstrates, most advanced democracies have a parliamentary system. Although the United States is the only advanced democracy with a presidential system, other countries – such as Mexico and Nigeria – use it.

ECONOMIC DIMENSIONS

In thinking about the values that form the political culture of advanced democracies, they may be described as reflecting **post-modernism. Modernism** is a set of values that comes along with industrialization. Values of modernism include secularism (an emphasis on non-religious aspects of life), an emphasis on reasoning (rationalism), materialism (valuing concrete objects and possessions), technology, bureaucracy, and an emphasis on freedom rather than collective equality. In other words, industrialization encouraged making money and gaining economic success. Advanced democracies, such as Britain and the United States, experienced this transformation in the 19th century. Others were later, but all advanced democracies have also experienced post-modernism, a set of values that emphasizes quality of life over concern with material gain. Some examples of post-modern values are the preservation of the environment and the promotion of health care and education. These values accompany the economic changes of **post-industrialism**, in which the majority of people are employed in the **service sector**, including such industries as technology, health care, business and legal services, finance, and education. These contrast to the most common type of job created earlier by industrialization, the **industry sector,** which employs people to create tangible goods, such as cars, clothing, or machinery. The **agricultural sector** of post-modern societies is very small since mechanized farming (first developed during the industrial era) means that only a few farmers can produce enough food to feed all the workers in the industry and service sectors.

The sector percentages for some advanced democracies look something like this:

ECONOMIC SECTORS IN ADVANCED DEMOCRACIES

	Services	Industry	Agriculture
United States	78.6%	20.4%	.9%
Canada	68.5%	29.2%	2.3%
Japan	73.1%	25.3%	1.6%
United Kingdom	73.4%	25.6%	1%
France	77.2%	20.6%	2.2%
Germany	70%	29.1%	.9%

Source: *CIA Factbook*, 2006 estimate

We may also refer to advanced democracies as liberal democracies, although the latter term refers more directly to the political rather than the economic dimension. Many advanced democracies, but not all, established a democratic political system many years ago, and now operate under a stable government that has long followed democratic traditions.

Many countries in Europe are among the most stable democracies in the modern world. Although their political systems operate in very different ways, they share common characteristics that help students begin to effectively compare across countries, and allow them to see both similarities and differences. The citizens of each country are diverse, and they actively participate in political affairs. In the AP Comparative Government and Politics course, Britain represents this group. Britain has a well-organized and competitive party system and interest groups, as well as a representative form of government.

SUPRANATIONAL ORGANIZATIONS: THE EUROPEAN UNION AND NAFTA

One of the most important developments of the past few decades in Europe has been the slow but steady march toward integration of countries within the continent. After World War II the most obvious need was to rebuild the infrastructures of countries devastated by the conflict. As the Cold War set in, the "Iron Curtain" separated western and eastern Europe based on economic and political differences, with countries in the east dominated by communism. Still, the urge to integrate, first economically and eventually politically, continued throughout the century. By the early 21st century, the European Union had emerged as a strong supranational organization that encouraged cooperation among nations and promised to redefine the meaning of national sovereignty.

The North American Free Trade Agreement (NAFTA) is a supranational organization that binds the United States, Canada, and Mexico. Created in 1995 mainly as a free trade area, NAFTA has much narrower integration goals than the EU. Unlike the EU, no common currency has been adopted for North American countries, and no parliament or court systems have been set up.

In the pages that follow, the political system of Britain will be discussed, and students should note that the outline of concepts in Chapter One is followed throughout. The second part of this section is a brief review of the development and current status of the European Union, a major force that shapes policy-making in Britain and all other European countries.

IMPORTANT TERMS AND CONCEPTS

modernism
postmodernism
postindustrialism
sectors of the economy (agriculture, industry, service)

GOVERNMENT AND POLITICS IN BRITAIN

GREAT BRITAIN OR LITTLE ENGLAND?

Britain clearly has had one of the most influential and powerful political systems in world history. It was the first country in Europe to develop a limited monarchy, achieved gradually so as to maintain stability. Modern democratic institutions and industrialization have their roots in English soil, and English influence spread all over the world during the 18th and 19th centuries throughout a far-flung empire. At the beginning of the 20th century, Britain was undoubtedly the most powerful country in the world. Truly the name "Great Britain" is illustrated by many accomplishments.

Yet many British subjects refer to their homeland affectionately as "Little England." Perhaps there is something of the "David and Goliath" appeal - the little island that conquered the world! At any rate, the two names aptly define Britain's dilemma at the dawn of the 21st century. As a precursor in the development of modern democracy, industrialization, and imperialism, it is now a model in the art of growing old gracefully. Britain has lost much of the empire and has slipped out of the front rank of the economies of Western Europe, and yet the country is still a major player in world politics.

The world watches as Britain helps define the meaning of progress. Perhaps it is not unilateral - onward ever, backward never. Instead, Britain is adjusting to its new reality as one European country among many, and yet the nation's influence remains strong. Many believe that regeneration is in the making - politically, economically, and socially.

SOVEREIGNTY, AUTHORITY, AND POWER

Great Britain has the oldest democratic tradition of any country in the world, and as a result, has many sources of authority and power that provide stability and legitimacy. This section is divided into three parts:

- Social Compacts and Constitutionalism
- Historical Evolution of National Political Traditions
- Political Culture

SOCIAL COMPACTS AND CONSTITUTIONALISM

The legitimacy of the government has developed gradually, so that today tradition is a primary source of stability. Like so many other advanced democracies in Europe, **traditional authority** for many years was based on the belief that an hereditary ruling family had the right to rule. Although the tradition includes a monarchy, the limitation of the king's power began early, until the power of Parliament gradually eclipsed that of the king by the end of the 17th century. Today most British citizens accept democracy as a basic component of their government. With the notable exception of Protestant/Catholic conflicts in Northern Ireland, most British citizens accept a church/state relationship in which the church does not challenge the authority of the government.

Ironically, the country that influenced the development of so many other modern democracies has never had a written constitution as such. Instead, the "constitution" has evolved over time, with important documents, common law, legal codes, and customs combining to form what is often called the **"Constitution of the Crown."**

RATIONAL-LEGAL AUTHORITY IN BRITAIN

Like most other advanced democracies, Britain's political system is based on **rational-legal authority** - a system of well-established laws and procedures. Despite Britain's beginnings centuries ago in the traditional legitimacy of an hereditary monarch, the country has gradually developed its "Constitution of the Crown" through many important documents and legal principles, including these:

• **Magna Carta** – In 1215 King John signed this document, agreeing to consult nobles before he made important political decisions, especially those regarding taxes. Magna Carta, then, forms the basis of limited government that places restrictions on the power of monarchs.

• **The Bill of Rights** – This document bears little resemblance to the American Bill of Rights, because it lists rights retained by Parliament, not by individual citizens. William and Mary signed this document in 1688, giving important policymaking power to Parliament, including the power of the purse.

• **Common Law** - This legal system is based on local customs and precedent rather than formal legal codes. It is English in origin and is found in Great Britain, the United States, and other countries with a strong English influence. Common law allows the decisions that public officials and courts make to set precedents for later actions and decisions, eventually forming a comprehensive set of principles for governance.

HISTORICAL EVOLUTION OF NATIONAL POLITICAL TRADITIONS

The British political system is influenced by many traditions from the country's long history. Britain's political culture has developed for the most part gradually and consensually, although not totally without conflict. However, many current political conflicts result from unresolved issues from the dramatic changes brought by the Industrial Revolution in the late 18th and 19th centuries. The evolution of British political traditions may be analyzed in these historical categories:

• **The shaping of the monarchy** - The British monarchy has been in place for many centuries and has survived many transformations. Britain established a limited monarchy as early as the 13th century when nobles forced King John to sign the Magna Carta. During the English Civil War of the 1640s, the monarch, Charles I, was beheaded, but the monarchy was brought back later in the 17th century with powers seriously restricted by Parliament. Today, the monarchy has no decision-making power but plays an important ceremonial role in British society.

- **The ascendancy of Parliament** – The English Civil War was a conflict between the supporters of the king, Charles I, and those of Parliament (the Roundheads). Parliament won, the king was executed, and the Roundhead leader, Oliver Cromwell, took over the country. However, the "Protectorate" that followed was short-lived, and the monarchy was restored when Parliament brought Charles II, the beheaded king's son, to the throne. Succeeding kings did not always respect the power of Parliament, so the balance of power was decided by the Glorious Revolution of 1688. This bloodless revolution established the constitutional monarchy when William and Mary agreed to written restrictions on their power by signing the Bill of Rights. Parliament and its ministers continued to gain strength as the monarchy lost it through succeeding kings. The power of the king's prime minister was firmly established in the 18th century by Robert Walpole, minister to Kings George I and George II.

- **Challenges of the industrial revolution** - During the 18th century, two very important economic influences - colonial mercantilism and the industrial revolution - established England as a major economic power. The results radically changed traditional English society and its economic basis in the feudal relationship between lord and peasant. The brisk trade with colonies all over the world and the manufacture of goods created unprecedented wealth held by a new class of merchants and businessmen. Lives of peasants were transformed as they left rural areas, moved to cities, and went to work in factories. New merchants, businessmen, and workers all demanded that the political system respond by including them in decision-making. The 19th century reforms reflect their successes.

- **Britain in the 20th and early 21st centuries** – At the dawn of the 20th century, Britain was the greatest imperialist nation in the world. By the early 21st century, its power had been diminished by two world wars, serious economic problems of the 1970s, and the rising power of the United States. After World War II, Britain developed a strong welfare state, which was curtailed during the 1980s by a wave of "**Thatcherism**," a conservative, capitalist backlash led by Prime Minister Margaret Thatcher. In more recent years, Labour Prime Minister Tony Blair charted a course toward what he called "A Third Way." Modern Britain, then, is adjusting to a new level of world power, and is trying to find the right balance between the benefits of the welfare state and the trend toward greater reliance on a market economy.

POLITICAL CULTURE

"This fortress built by Nature for herself,
Against infection and the hand of war,
This happy breed of men, this little world,
This precious stone set in the silver sea,
Which serves it in the office of a wall,
Or as a moat defensive to a house,
Against the envy of less happier lands;
This blessed plot, this earth, this realm, this England."

Richard II
William Shakespeare

This famous quote from Shakespeare tells us a great deal about the political culture of Great Britain. It reflects a large amount of **nationalism**, or pride in being English. It also reflects **insularity,** or the feeling of separation from the continent of Europe. In modern times, insularity has caused Britain to have a cautious attitude toward participation in the European Union. When most of the EU members accepted the euro as a common currency in January 2002, Britain refused, and instead kept the English pound. However, despite Shakespeare's joy in this "fortress" state, his country has been far from isolated and has spread its influence around the world.

England's geographic features have shaped her political culture through the years. Important features include:

- **An island** – Britain is far enough away from mainland Europe for protection as long as a good navy is maintained. Yet the island is close enough to the mainland to allow interaction.

- **Small size** - As a result, resources are limited. This geographical fact shaped her efforts to colonize other lands and become an imperial power.

- **A short supply of fertile soil, short growing season** - Britain's ability to feed its population is limited as a result.

- **Temperate climate, but cold, chilly, and rainy** – Britain's population density is one of the highest in the world, but it is considerably lower in northern areas.

- **No major geographical barriers** – No mountains, deserts, or raging rivers hamper transportation/ communication within the country.

Other characteristics of the political culture include:

- *Noblesse oblige* **and social class** - Although the influence of social class on political attitudes is not as strong as it has been in the past, a very important tradition in British politics is *noblesse oblige,* the duty of the upper classes to take responsibility for the welfare of the lower classes. The custom dates to feudal times when lords protected their serfs and their land in return for labor. Today, *noblesse oblige* is reflected in the general willingness of the British to accept a welfare state, including the National Health Service. During the 1980s, Margaret Thatcher's government brought this willingness into question by cutting social services significantly. However, most of these services have been restored in recent years. A major concern is cost, but the NHS is an accepted part of government.

- **Multi-nationalism** – Although Britain has a relatively large amount of **cultural homogeneity,** its boundaries include England, Scotland, Wales, and Northern Ireland, all of which have been different nations in the past, but are united under one government today. Although English is a common language, it is spoken with different dialects, and religious differences between Catholics and Protestants in Northern Ireland remain a major source of conflict today. These national identities are still strong, and they greatly impact the way that the political system functions.

The legitimacy of the British government is evidenced by the willingness of the English people to obey the law. Britain's police force is smaller than that of most other advanced democracies, and crimes tend to be based on individual violence, and not on strikes against the state, such as assassinations. Until relatively recently, the only notable exception was Northern Ireland, where many crimes have been carried out with the political objective of overturning an elected government. In more recent years Britain has experienced terrorist acts as part of the larger wave of terrorism that has swept over many advanced democracies in the post-9/11 world.

POLITICAL AND ECONOMIC CHANGE

Political change in Britain has always been characterized by its gradual nature. **Gradualism** in turn established strong **traditions.** This process helps to explain the transition in policymaking power from the king to Parliament. That transition may be traced to the days shortly after William the Conqueror defeated Harold II at the Battle of Hastings in 1066. In order to ensure his claims to English lands, William (a Norman) gathered support from the nobility by promising to consult them before he taxed them. This arrangement led to a gradual acceptance of a "House of Lords," and as commercialism created towns and a new middle class, eventually the establishment of a "House of Commons." Both were created through evolution, not revolution. Of course, there are important "marker events" that demonstrate the growing power of Parliament – the signing of the Magna Carta, the English Civil War, and the Glorious Revolution – but the process was gradual and set strong traditions as it developed.

Despite the overall pattern of gradualism, Britain's political system has had to adjust to internal economic changes, as well as international crises. Some sources of change have been the Industrial Revolution, imperialistic aspirations, the two world wars of the 20th century, and the economic crisis of the 1970s. These events have had significant consequences as Britain's political system initiated a gradual agenda of reform to meet the challenges.

ADJUSTING TO THE INDUSTRIAL REVOLUTION

The Industrial Revolution that began in England during the late 18th century created two new social classes that were not accommodated under the parliamentary system: the middle class and laborers. At first, Parliament resisted including them, thinking that it might lead to disaster, perhaps even a revolution like the one that France had in 1789. However, the tradition of gradualism guided their decision to incorporate the new elements into the political system. The decision is a reflection of *noblesse oblige.* Starting in 1832, the franchise gradually broadened:

EXTENSION OF VOTING RIGHTS

- **Great Reform Act of 1832** - About 300,000 more men gained the right to vote, and the House of Commons gained more power in relation to the House of Lords.

- **Reform Act of 1867**- The electorate reached 3,000,000, as many working class people were allowed the right to vote.

- **Representation of the People Act of 1884 -** The electorate was further expanded so that the majority of the voters are working class.

- **Women's suffrage**- All women over the age of 28 and all men over 21 were granted the right to vote in 1918. By1928, all women over the age of 21 were allowed to vote.

The gradual inclusion of the people in the political process meant that Marxism did not take root as it did in many other European countries.

19TH CENTURY WORK AND WELFARE REFORMS

During the 19th century, labor unions formed to protect workers' rights on the job. By the end of the 19th century, some basic provisions were made for social services. For example, in 1870, mandatory elementary education was put into law. From 1906 until 1914, laws were enacted providing for old age pensions.

POLITICAL EFFECTS OF THE EXTENSION OF RIGHTS TO THE "COMMON MAN"

The balance of power between the House of Commons and the House of Lords changed slowly but surely, as the new commercial elites became Members of Parliament. By 1911, the House of Lords was left with only one significant power - to delay legislation. The House of Commons was clearly the dominant legislative house by the early 20th century. By then political party membership generally fell along class lines. The **Labour Party** was created in 1906 to represent the rights of the newly enfranchised working man, and the **Conservative Party** drew most of its members from middle class merchants and businessmen.

With the enfranchisement of the working class, a demand for welfare measures put pressure on the political system to change. Reform measures were passed by Parliament, including legislation for public education, housing, jobs, and medical care. With these demands came a new party - Labour. By the end of World War I, Labour had pushed the Liberals into third place where they have remained ever since. Labour was never Marxist, but it combined militant trade unionism with intellectual social democracy to create a pragmatic, gradualist ideology that sought to level class differences in Britain. The **Trade Union Council** emerged as a coalition of trade unions that has been a major force in British politics since. The British labor movement has always been tough, and its members resentful of being treated like inferiors. That militancy carries through to today, only to be softened in very recent years by party leaders Neil Kinnock, John Smith, and Tony Blair.

EFFECTS OF WORLD WAR II – COLLECTIVE CONSENSUS

Under the leadership of Winston Churchill Britain united behind the World War II effort. Churchill emphasized the importance of putting class conflicts aside for the duration of the war. Although he gained the Prime Minister's post as leader of the Conservative party, he headed an all-party **coalition government** with ministers from both major parties. The primary objective was to win the war. After the war was over, the spirit of **collective consensus** continued until well into the 1960s, with both Labour and Conservative parties supporting the development of a modern welfare system. Before the war was over, both parties accepted the **Beveridge Report,** which provided for a social insurance program that made all citizens eligible for health, unemployment, pension, and other benefits. One goal of the Beveridge Report was to guarantee a subsistence income to every British citizen. In 1948, the **National Health Service** was created under the leadership of the Labour Party. Even when Conservatives regained control in 1950, the reforms were not repealed. Although the electorate was divided largely by social class, with 70% of working class voting Labour and even larger percentages of middle class voting Conservative, both parties shared a broad consensus on the necessity of the welfare state. As a result, the foundations were laid for a **mixed economy**, with the government directing the economy and nationalizing major industries without giving up basic principles of capitalism, such as private ownership of property.

CHALLENGES TO THE COLLECTIVE CONSENSUS SINCE 1970

During the late 20th and early 21st centuries, Britain has experienced considerable economic and political turmoil. The era began with a serious decline in the economy, followed by a growing divide between the Labour and Conservative parties. Labour took a sharp turn to the left, endorsing a socialist economy and serving as a mouthpiece for labor union demands. The Conservatives answered with a sharp turn to the right, advocating denationalization of industries and support for a pure market economy. During the 1990s, both parties moderated their stances, and the economy showed some signs of recovery.

ECONOMIC CRISIS OF THE 1970s

The collective consensus began to break apart with social and economic problems in the late 1960s. Britain's economic problems included declining industrial production and a decline in international influence, both exaggerated by the loss of colonies and the shrinking of the old empire. The impact of **OPEC** (Organization for Petroleum Exporting Countries) was devastating. The quadrupling of oil prices and the oil embargo by oil producing countries caused recession, high unemployment rates, a drop in the GNP, and inflation. The economic problems led labor unions to demand higher wages, and crippling strikes, such as the coal strike of 1972-73, plagued the nation. The Labour Party lost membership, and many voters turned to the Liberals, the Conservatives, or the various nationalist parties. Many middle class voters reacted against Labour, and the Conservatives selected Margaret Thatcher as their leader. Her very conservative stance on political issues was appealing enough to sweep the conservatives to power in 1979.

THATCHERISM

Margaret Thatcher blamed the weakened economy on the socialist policies set in place by the government after World War II. Her policies were further influenced by a distinct movement left by the Labour Party that gave a great deal of power to labor unions. In response, she privatized business and industry, cut back on social welfare programs, strengthened national defense, got tough with the labor unions, and returned to market force controls on the economy. She was the controversial prime minister for eleven years. Her supporters believed her to be the capable and firm **"Iron Lady"**, but her critics felt that her policies made economic problems worse and that her strong personality further divided the country. Thatcher resigned office in 1990 when other Conservative Party leaders challenged her leadership.

TONY BLAIR'S THIRD WAY

After the jolts of the economic crisis of the 1970s and Margaret Thatcher's firm redirection of the political system to the right, moderation again became characteristic of political change in Britain. Thatcher's hand-picked successor, **John Major**, at first followed her policies, but later moderating them by abolishing Thatcher's poll tax, reconciling with the European Union, and slowing social cutbacks and privatization. The Conservative Party retained the majority in the 1993 parliamentary elections, but only by a very slim margin. Then, in 1997, Labour's gradual return in the center was rewarded with the election of **Tony Blair**, who promised to create a "New Labour" Party and rule in a **"third way"** – a centrist alternative to the old Labour Party on the left and the Conservative Party on the right. Tony

Blair's popularity slipped sharply after he supported the United States in the Iraq War. By sending troops and publicly committing his support to U.S. President George Bush, he not only alienated other European leaders, but much of the British public as well. In 2007 Blair stepped down from his post to be replaced by long-time cabinet member **Gordon Brown**.

CITIZENS, SOCIETY, AND THE STATE

In many ways, Britain is a homogeneous culture. English is spoken by virtually all British citizens, and only about 5% of Britain's 60 million people are ethnic minorities. For much of British history, the major **social cleavages** that shape the way the political system worked were based on multi-national identities, social class distinctions, and the Protestant/Catholic split in Northern Ireland. In recent years a major cleavage has developed based on race and ethnicity, with tensions regarding Muslim minorities increasing, as evidenced in race riots in May 2001 in the northern town of Oldham, and similar disturbances in Burnley, Leeds, and Bradford a few weeks later. In more recent years, terrorist activities have deepened the divisions, a situation that many advanced democracies of Europe and North America have faced.

MULTI-NATIONAL IDENTITIES

The "United Kingdom" evolved from four different nations: England, Wales, Scotland, and part of Ireland. England consists of the southern 2/3 of the island, and until the 16th century, did not rule any of the other lands. By the 18th century, England ruled the entire island, and became known as "Great Britain." In the early 20th century, Northern Ireland was added, creating the "United Kingdom." These old kingdoms still have strong national identities that greatly impact the British political system.

- **England -** The largest region of Great Britain is England, which also contains the majority of the population. Throughout most of the history of the British Isles, the English have dominated the other nationalities, and they still have a disproportionate share of political power. Today the challenge is to integrate the nationalities into the country as a whole, but at the same time allow them to keep their old identities.

- **Wales** – West of England, Wales became subject to the English king in the 16th century, and has remained so till the present. Modern Welsh pride is reflected in their flag – the **Plaid Cymru** – and in the fact that the language is still alive and currently being taught in some Welsh schools. Even though Wales accepted English authority long ago, some resentment remains, as well as feelings of being exploited by their richer neighbors.

- **Scotland** – For many years the Scots resisted British rule, and existed as a separate country until the early 1600s. Ironically, Scotland was not joined to England through conquest, but through intermarriage of the royalty. When Queen Elizabeth I died without an heir in 1603, the English throne went to her nephew James I, who also happened to be king of Scotland. A century later both countries agreed to a single Parliament in London. However, Scots still have a strong national identity, and tend to think of themselves as being very different from the English. The Scots too have their own national flag, and the Scottish Parliament has recently been revived.

- **Northern Ireland** – England and Ireland have a long history of arguing about religion. After Oliver Cromwell won the English Civil War in the mid 17th century, he tried to impose Protestantism on staunchly Catholic Ireland to no avail. English claims to Irish lands were settled shortly after World War I ended, when Ireland was granted **home rule**, with the exception of its northeast corner, where Protestants outnumbered Catholics by about 60% to 40%. Home rule came largely because of pressure from the **Irish Republican Army (the IRA)**, who used guerilla warfare tactics to convince the British to allow Irish independence. Finally, in 1949, the bulk of Ireland became a totally independent country, and Northern Ireland has remained under British rule, but not without a great deal of conflict between Protestants and Catholics.

SOCIAL CLASS DISTINCTIONS

Distinctions between rich and poor have always been important in Britain, with the most important divide today being between working and middle class people. The two classes are not easily separated by income, but psychologically and subjectively, the gulf between them is still wide. German sociologist Ralf Dahrendorf explains the difference in terms of **solidarity**, particularly among the working class. The sense is that keeping the old job and living in the old neighborhood – the sense of family and friends – is more important than individual success.

British social classes have traditionally been reinforced by the education system. **"Public schools"** were originally intended to train boys for "public life" in the military, civil service, or politics. They are expensive, and they have educated young people to continue after their parents as members of the ruling elite. A large number of Britain's elite have gone to "public" boarding schools such as Eton, Harrow, Rugby, St. Paul's, and Winchester. Middle classes commonly attend private grammar schools, where students wear uniforms but do not live in. Only 65 percent of British seventeen-year-olds are still in school, the lowest level of any industrialized democracy.

The most important portal to the elite classes is through Oxford and Cambridge Universities, or **Oxbridge**. Nearly half of all Conservative Members of Parliament went to Oxbridge, as have about one quarter of all Labour MPs. Percentages in cabinet positions are even higher, and prime ministers almost always graduate from one or the other school. Since World War II, more scholarships have been available to Oxbridge, so that working and middle class youths may attend the elite schools. Also, the number of other universities has grown, so that higher education is more widespread than before. Still, university attendance in Britain is generally lower than in other industrialized democracies.

ETHNIC MINORITIES

According to the 2001 census, only about 7.1% of the British population is of non-European origin, with most coming from countries that were formerly British colonies. However, the minority ethnic population grew by 53 percent between 1991 and 2001, from 3 million in 1991 to 4.6 million in 2001. The main groups are:

- **Indian** – 23% of all non-European population
- **Pakistani** – 16%
- **Afro-Caribbean** – 12.2%
- **Black African** – 10.5%

Because of tight immigration restrictions in the past, most ethnic minorities are young, with about half of the population under the age of 25. The percentages of minorities has grown despite the restrictions that were placed on further immigration during the Thatcher administration of the 1980s. Immigration restrictions are currently under debate, but the Labour government has allowed the restrictions to remain in place.

The British have often been accused of adjusting poorly to their new ethnic population. Reports abound of unequal treatment by the police and physical and verbal harassment by citizens. The May 2001 race riots in several cities increased tensions, and new fears of strife have been stoked by post 9/11 world politics. Today there is some evidence that whites are leaving London to settle in surrounding suburban areas, resulting in a higher percentage of minority population living in London. Despite this segregation, the mixed race population appears to be increasing, with the census of 2001 offering for the first time in British history a category for mixed race people.

Terrorist attacks, successful and attempted, have occurred in Britain over the past few years, with a major attack in 2005, schemes foiled by the government in the summer of 2006, and car-bombings in 2007. Other advanced democracies have suffered attacks and plots as well. Of course, the United States was attacked on September 11th, 2001, and the Madrid bombings in 2004 were Europe's most lethal terrorist outrage. In Canada 17 people were arrested in June 2007 on suspicion of scheming to blow up buildings there. However, Britain's risk for home-grown terrorist attacks may be greater than many other countries. Several problems for Britain are:

- **Distinct minority/majority cleavages** - Muslims have an identity of being a minority distinct from a well-established majority, such as the English in Britain, the French in France, and the Germans in Germany. In contrast, many people in the United States are immigrants, and the "majority" ethnicity of white Americans has already become a minority in many U.S. cities. With so many different ethnic and racial identities, the majority identity in the United States is not as clearcut as it is in most European countries.

- **Social class differences of Muslims** – In the United States, many Muslims tend to be relatively well-off, while many British Muslims are disaffected and unemployed. Many British Muslims are the children of illiterate workers slipped in as cheap industrial labor, and their childhood experiences have not endeared them to British culture.

- **Pakistani Muslims** – Many Muslims in the rest of Europe came from Turkey and Africa, while the largest group of British Muslims comes from Pakistan. Since Osama bin Laden and his companions are believed to be under the protection of Pakistanis, some scholars think that the links of British Muslims to al-Qaeda (bin Laden's group) are stronger than they are in other European countries.

- **Opposition to the Iraqi War** – The fact that many British citizens are very hostile toward the war may be helping to radicalize young Muslims, who appear to believe that the British government is supporting the U.S. in a war against Islam.

- **Lack of integration of minorities** – Polls suggest that alienation of minorities in Britain may be higher than it is in other countries because the national culture has not absorbed the groups into mainstream culture. This problem is apparent in France as well, where girls may not wear headscarves at school. In Britain they may attend classes in full *hijab*, but minorities still tend to feel as if they are treated as second-class citizens.

POLITICAL BELIEFS AND VALUES

In the early 1960s political scientists Gabriel Almond and Sidney Verba wrote that the "**civic culture**" (political culture) in Britain was characterized by trust, deference to authority and competence, pragmatism, and harmony. The economic crisis of the 1970s and the continuing conflicts regarding Northern

Ireland have challenged this view of citizenship in Britain, but the overall characteristics seem to still be in place today.

British citizens reflect what Almond and Verba saw as good qualities for democratic participation: high percentages of people that vote in elections, acceptance of authority, tolerance for different points of view, and acceptance of the rules of the game. However, social and economic changes during the 1970s altered these characteristics so that today British citizens are less supportive of the collective consensus and more inclined to values associated with a free market economy. Many observers believe that the "**politics of protest**" – or the tendency to disagree openly and sometimes violently with the government – have become increasingly acceptable.

Some manifestations of changing political beliefs and values include:

- **Decreasing support for labor unions** – British labor unions have strong roots in the Industrial Revolution, and class solidarity supports union membership. However, when unions staged crippling strikes during the 1970s, public opinion turned against them, as people began to view unions as "bullies" to both the government and the general population. Margaret Thatcher's tough stance against the unions intensified strife between unions and the Conservative government. Since then, the Labour Party has moved toward the center to diversify its appeal to non-union voters.

- **Increased violence regarding Northern Ireland** – The issues surrounding British claims to Northern Ireland intensified during the early 1970s after British troops killed thirteen Catholics in a "bloody Sunday" incident in January 1972. The IRA and Protestant paramilitaries stepped up their campaigns of violence. Although in recent years the groups have consented to negotiate with the government, the threat of violent eruptions remains strong today.

- **Thatcherism** – The Conservative Party controlled British government from 1979 until 1997. Although later modified by Prime Minister John Major, Margaret Thatcher's "revolution" toward a free market economy certainly affected political attitudes. She rejected collectivism and its emphasis on the redistribution of resources from rich to poor and government responsibility for full employment. Thatcherism fostered entrepreneurial values of individualism and competition over the solidarity of social classes and the tradition of *noblesse oblige.*

- **New Labour** - Despite these radical changes of the 1970s and 80s, Britain has not deserted its traditional political culture. **Tony Blair** led a Labour Party that loosened its ties to labor unions, and a new "Good Friday" Agreement on Northern Ireland was reached in 1998. Thatcherism has been incorporated into political attitudes, but in the early 21st century, both parties are more inclined to a middle path, or "**third way.**"

- **Protests over the Iraq War** – Not only have ordinary citizens vocally protested Britain's involvement in the Iraq War, many political leaders have openly criticized it as well. In a political system where party loyalty is valued above all, many Labour MPs (Members of Parliament) have withdrawn their support for Blair's policy in Iraq. Their resistance to the party leadership extended to the cabinet, with several party leaders resigning their posts, despite the strong tradition of collective consensus. The ill will spread into domestic affairs as well, so that Blair had little choice but to resign in June 2007.

VOTING BEHAVIOR

Like most other Europeans, British citizens have relatively high percentages of qualified voters who go to the polls. Although there was a notable decline in the elections of 2001 and 2005, more than 70% of eligible citizens normally vote in parliamentary elections. Today voters have less party loyalty than they once did, but voting behavior is still clearly tied to social class and region.

- **Social class -** Until World War II, voting in Britain largely followed class lines. The working class supported the Labour Party, and the middle class voted Conservative. However, today the lines of distinction are blurred, partly because the society and the parties themselves have changed.   For example, some middle class people who grew up in working class homes still vote the way their parents did. On the other hand, many in the working classes have been attracted to the Conservative platform to cut taxes, and to keep immigrants out. In recent years, both parties have come back to the center from the extreme views of the 1970s and 1980s, as reflected in Labour leader Tony Blair's program to provide a "**third way**," or a centrist alternative. However, statisics from the Labour victories of 1997, 2001 and 2005 show that the party is strongest among people who feel disadvantaged: the Scots, the Welsh, and the poor.

- **Regional factors –** The Labour Party usually does well in urban and industrial areas and in Scotland and Wales. The industrial cities of the north – around Liverpool, Manchester, and Newcastle, and in Yorkshire – almost always support the Labour candidates, as do people that vote in central London. The areas where Conservatives usually win are mostly in England, especially in rural and suburban areas. These voting patterns are tied to social class, but they also reflect urban vs. rural values.

POLITICAL INSTITUTIONS

Strong political traditions and institutions that have been in place for hundreds of years guide Britain's stable democratic regime. The monarch still rules as head of state, but the prime minister and his/her cabinet form the policymaking center. The system is **parliamentary,** which means that the prime minister and cabinet ministers are actually members of the legislature. In this section, we will explore the parts of the British political system and the ways that they interact to make policy.

LINKAGE INSTITUTIONS

Linkage institutions play a very important role in British government and politics. Political parties, interest groups, and print and electronic media have long connected the government to British citizens. The British government's policymaking activities are complex, and its linkage institutions are well developed.

POLITICAL PARTIES

Britain's political parties began to form in the 18th century, and their organization and functions have shaped the development of many other party systems (including the United States) through the years. At first they were simply **caucuses**, or meetings of people from the same area or of like mind. Only in the 19th century did a two-party system emerge with roots in the electorate. The labels "**Whig**" and "**Tory**" first appeared under Charles II, with the Tories supporting the king and the Whigs opposing. Both were derisive names: Whigs were Scottish bandits, Tories Irish bandits. The Whigs eventually became the

Liberal Party and the Tories (still a nickname today) the Conservatives. The Labour Party emerged in the early 20th century in response to new voter demands created by the Industrial Revolution.

Today the two major political parties are **Labour** and **Conservative,** but several other significant parties are represented in Parliament. Historically, Britain has had strong third parties that significantly affect election results. For example, in the 1980s, the **Liberal Democratic Alliance Party**, garnered as much as 26% of the popular vote, but because of Britain's single-member plurality election system (one member per district who only has to get more votes than anyone else, not a majority), never claimed more than 62 seats in the House of Commons. The House of Commons is dominated by the two largest parties, but three or four way elections for MPs are usual.

The Labour Party

The largest party on the left is the Labour Party. It has controlled the British government since 1997 when their leader, Tony Blair became Prime Minister. The party began in 1906 as an alliance of trade unions and socialist groups that were strengthened by the expansion of rights for the working class during the 19th century. Traditionally, labor unions have provided most party funds, although Blair loosened the union ties and sought to broaden the base of party membership.

The early history of the party was defined partially by the controversial **"Clause 4"** that called for nationalization of the "commanding heights" of British industry. The growing moderation of the party was reflected by the removal of the clause from the Labour Party Constitution in the early 1990s. The shift in policies toward the center became apparent shortly after Neil Kinnock became the party leader in the early 1980s, and has continued under leaders John Smith (1993-1994), Tony Blair (1994-2007), and Gordon Brown (2007-present).

Labour's 1992 loss in an election that they were widely predicted to win almost certainly was a turning point in its development. Its failure to capture the majority led to the resignation of Neil Kinnock as party leader, and the appointment of John Smith, a moderate Scotsman who the party hoped would solidify support from Scottish nationalist groups. Smith died suddenly in 1994, and was replaced by Tony Blair, a young leader that did not come from union ranks. Instead, he was an Oxford educated barrister-turned-politician who hoped to bring more intellectuals and middle class people into the party. Labour won the elections of 1997, 2001, and 2005, and has tried to redefine itself as a moderate party with support from many different types of voters. Even though the party won the 2005 election, its margin of victory was much smaller than before, contributing to the resignation of Blair as party leader in 2007.

The Conservative Party

The Conservative Party was the dominant party in Britain between World War II and 1997, holding the majority in Parliament for all but sixteen years during that period. The Conservative Party is the main party on the right, but it prospered partly because it traditionally has been a pragmatic, rather than an ideological party. Although the party supported a market controlled economy, privatization, and fewer social welfare programs during the 1980s under the leadership of Margaret Thatcher, the Conservatives moved back toward the center under Prime Minister John Major (1990-1997).

The party is characterized by *noblesse oblige*, and its power is centered in London. The organization of the party is usually viewed as elitist, with the MPs choosing the party leadership. No formal rules for choosing the leader existed until recently, but now the leadership must submit to annual leadership elections. This new process proved to be problematic for Margaret Thatcher in 1990, when she was challenged strongly in the election and virtually forced to resign. The senior party members formed the cabinet and were chosen by the party leader.

Since Labour seized control of the government in 1997, the Conservative Party has been weakened by deep divisions between two groups:

- **The traditional wing (one-nation Tories)** values *noblesse oblige* and wants the country ruled by an elite that takes everybody's interests into account before making decisions. This wing generally supports Britain's membership in the European Union.

- **The Thatcherite wing** of strict conservatives wants to roll back government and move to a full free market. The members of this wing are often referred to as **Euroskeptics** because they see the EU's move toward European integration as a threat to British sovereignty.

The current party leader is **David Cameron**, who won the position in December 2005. Cameron's youth and debating ability, as well as Tony Blair's vulnerability as Labour leader, revived the Conservative Party's hope of recapturing the majority. During 2006 and early 2007 the party established a lead in opinion polls, but with Blair's resignation and the rise of **Gordon Brown** to the prime minister's post, Labour regained its lead in major polls during the summer of 2007.

The Liberal Democrats

Two parties – the Liberals and the Social Democrats - formed an alliance in the 1983 and 1987 elections, and formally merged in 1989, establishing the **Liberal Democrats.** Their goal was to establish a strong party in the middle as a compromise to the politics of the two major parties: Thatcher's extremely conservative leadership and Labour's leftist views and strategies. The party won an impressive 26% of the votes in 1983, but because of the single member district **plurality voting system** (see pages 35-37) in Britain, they only won 23 seats (3.5%). They campaigned for **proportional representation**, which would have given them an equal percentage of the MP seats, and for a **Bill of Rights** modeled after the first ten amendments of the U.S. Constitution.

The party's strength declined in the early 1990s as both the Conservative and Labour Parties moved to the center of political opinion, and in the 1992 election the party picked up only about 17% of the total votes cast. The party held on, though, partly due to the popularity of its leader, **Paddy Ashdown**, and to some strong stands on the environment, health, and education. Ashdown retired in 1999, and was replaced by a Scottish MP, **Charles Kennedy**, and the Liberal Democrats picked up seven seats in the 2001 election. The party also benefited from public disillusionment with the Blair government's support for the war in Iraq, picking up 11 more MPs in the election of 2005. However, the party still remains tremendously underrepresented in Parliament, considering their relative popularity at the polls. After the 2005 elections, the Liberal Democrats had 62 MPs (out of 646), even though they won more than 22% of the vote.

Other Parties

Britain has many smaller parties including nationalist groups for Wales, Scotland, and Northern Ireland. **Plaid Cymru** in Wales and the **Scottish National Party** in Scotland both won seats in the House of Commons during the 1970s, and they have managed to virtually shut the Conservative Party out in the elections in their regions in 1997, 2001 and 2005. However, Labour is strong in the two regions, and the two parties combined won only nine seats in the House of Commons in 2005. The parties' fortunes were strengthened after Labour's return to power in 1997, when the Blair leadership created regional assemblies for Scotland and Wales. The Plaid Cymru currently has 12 of 60 seats in the Welsh Assembly, and the Scottish National Party has 27 of 129 seats in the Scottish Assembly.

Northern Ireland has always been dominated by regional parties, including **Sinn Fein** (the political arm of the IRA) and the **Democratic Unionist Party**, led by Protestant clergymen. Together they captured nine parliamentary seats in 2005.

ELECTIONS

The only national officials that British voters select are Members of Parliament. The prime minister is not elected as prime minister but as an MP from a single electoral district, averaging about 65,000 registered voters. Elections must be held every five years, but the prime minister may call them earlier. Officially, elections occur after the Crown dissolves Parliament, but that always happens because the prime minister requests it. The power to call elections is very important, because the prime minister – as head of the majority party – always calls them when (s)he thinks that the majority party has the best chance of winning.

The Plurality Electoral System

Like the United States, British parliamentary elections are "**winner-take-all**," with no runoff elections. Within this single-member plurality system, each party selects a candidate to run for each district post, although minor parties don't always run candidates in all districts. The person that wins the most votes gets the position, even if (s)he does not receive the majority of votes in the district. The British nickname this system "**first-past-the-post**" (like a race horse). Since MPs do not have to live in the districts that they represent, each party decides who runs in each district. So party leaders run from safe districts – or districts that the party almost always wins. Political neophytes are selected to run in districts that a party knows it will lose. They are usually happy to just make a good showing by receiving more votes than the party usually gets.

The "winner-take-all" system often exaggerates the size of the victory of the largest party and reduces the influence of minor parties. This system is the main reason that the Liberal Democrats have not been able to get a good representation in Parliament. Regional parties tend to fare better. For example, The Scottish National Party generally has a good chance of picking up some districts in Scotland. However, Parliament still remains a two-party show, even though many other parties may get a sizeable number of votes. For example, in the election of 2005, the Labour party received 35.3% of the vote (not a majority), but they received 356 out of 646 seats (a majority).

Elections for Regional Governments

Some signs of change in the electoral system have emerged in very recent years. For example, in the **Good Friday Agreement** of April 1998, Britain agreed to give Northern Ireland a regional government, in which all parties would be represented on a proportional basis. In other words, the religion-based parties would each have a percentage of representatives that matches the percentage of the total vote each received. In later agreements with Scotland and Wales, their regional parliaments also are based on **proportional representation**. Other changes have occurred on the local level, with the mayor of London now elected directly for the first time ever.

U.S. vs. British Elections*

United States	Britain
Parties are less powerful.	Party determines who runs where.
Members must live in districts.	Members usually don't live in their districts.
Party leaders run in their respective districts.	Party leaders run in "safe districts."
Individual votes for four officials on the national level.	Individual votes for only one official on the national level.
Between 30 and 50 percent of the eligible voters actually vote (more in 2004).	About 70 percent of the eligible voters actually vote (less in 2001 and 2005).
Elections are by first-past-the-post, single-member districts; virtually no minor parties get representation.	Elections are by first-past-the-post, single-member districts; minor parties get some representation, but less than if they had proportional representation (regional elections in Ireland, Scotland and Wales use proportional representation).

*Note: The Comparative AP Exam does not require knowledge of U.S. government, but this chart is intended to help students understand British elections.

Campaign Financing

British campaigns for public office are much shorter and less expensive than those in the United States. However, in 2006 both major political parties were under police investigation for campaign financing. The two areas of investigation were the use of peerages (seats in the House of Lords) and the disclosure of non-commercial loans. In the first, parties were investigated for breaking a parliamentary act of 1925 that prohibited the offering of peerages in return for money. Secondly, parties were suspected of breaking a law passed in 2000, which requires parties to disclose the benefits they derive from personal loans.

In question were secret loans from wealthy well-wishers. The investigation increased the pressure on Tony Blair to step down as Labour leader.

INTEREST GROUPS

Like most other advanced democracies, Britain has well-established interest groups that demonstrate **interest group pluralism** (p. 36) with relatively autonomous groups competing with one another for influence in policymaking. However, patterns may also be seen of **neo-corporatism**, in which interest groups take the lead and sometimes dominate the state. Perhaps the greatest influence of British interest groups comes through **quangos** (quasi-autonomous nongovernmental organizations), or policy advisory boards appointment by the government. Using a neo-corporatist model, quangos, together with government officials, develop public policy. Although they weakened while Margaret Thatcher was prime minister, there are still over 5,000 such organizations working in different policy areas. Some simply advise on policy while others deliver public services.

Not surprisingly, the most influential interest groups have been those linked to class and industrial interests. Between 1945 and the 1970s, business interests and trade union organization fiercely competed for influence over the policymaking process. The powerful **Trades Union Congress (TUC),** that represents a coalition of unions, had a great deal of clout because the government often consulted them on important decisions. While no comparable single group represents business interests, they too had an open door to inner government circles. For example, in 1976, Chancellor of the Exchequer Denis Healy negotiated with TUC and **the Confederation of Business Industries** – CBI - to limit TUC's wage demands in exchange for 3% reduction in income tax rates. All of this changed when Margaret Thatcher took control in 1979. Thatcher wanted to reduce the power of interest groups in general, but she slammed the door shut on TUC. As labor unions lost public support, they also lost political sway, and the Labour Party loosened ties to unions and began to broaden its voter base. Since Thatcher left in 1990, interest groups have regained power, but Blair's "third way" partnered not only with unions, but with businesses as well.

THE ROLE OF THE MEDIA

Not surprisingly, British newspapers reflect social class divisions. They are sharply divided between quality news and comments that appeal to the middle and upper class, and mass circulation tabloids that carry sensational news. Radio and television came to life during the collective consensus era, so originally they were monopolized by the **British Broadcasting Corporation (BBC)**. The BBC sought to educate citizens, and it was usually respectful of government officials. Commercial television was introduced in the 1950s, and now there are five stations that compete, as well as cable. A variety of radio stations also exist. Despite the competition from private companies, the government strictly regulates the BBC and the commercial stations. For example, no advertisements may be sold to politicians, parties, or political causes.

The BBC had a significant clash with the Blair government in 2003 over support for the war in Iraq. BBC reporter Andrew Gilligan wrote that a government statement that Iraqi forces could deploy weapons of mass destruction within 45 minutes was based on false intelligence that officials knew was unreliable. The conflict grew into a crisis when weapons inspector Michael Kelly (the alleged source of the "false intelligence") committed suicide. Tony Blair appointed appeals judge Lord Hutton to investigate the death, and the judge ended the crisis when he exonerated the Blair government in early 2004 and criticized BBC for its reporting. The report prompted the chairman of BBC board of governors to resign, an action that signaled an almost unprecedented embarrassment for the network.

THE INSTITUTIONS OF NATIONAL GOVERNMENT

Like most other countries of the world today, the British government has three branches of government and a bureaucracy. Furthermore, the legislature is divided into two houses, a bicameral model that the British invented, and now widely copied. However, their system is **parliamentary**, and the interactions among the branches are very different from those in a **presidential system,** such as the United States. In a parliamentary system, the executive branch is fused with the legislative branch because the prime minister and his cabinet are actually the leaders of parliament. As a result, separation of powers – a major principle of American government – does not exist. Also, the judicial branch lacks the power of judicial review, so they have no role in interpreting the "Constitution of the Crown."

Britain is a **unitary state** with political authority centralized in London. Decisions made by the central government – both laws passed by Parliament and regulations prepared by the bureaucrats in Whitehall - are binding on all public agencies.

COMPARATIVE EXECUTIVES*

PRIME MINISTER OF BRITAIN	PRESIDENT OF THE U.S.
Serves only as long as he/she remains leader of the majority party	Elected every four years by an electoral college based on popular election
Elected as a member of parliament (MP)	Elected as President
Has an excellent chance of getting his/her programs past Parliament	Has an excellent chance of ending up in gridlock with Congress
Cabinet members not always MPs and leaders of the majority party	Cabinet member usually not from Congress (although they may)
Cabinet members not experts in policy areas; rely on bureaucracy to provide expertise	Expertise in policy areas one criteria for appointment to cabinet; members head vast bureaucracies

*Note: The Comparative AP Exam does not require knowledge of U.S. government, but this chart is intended to help students understand the British executiv

---

THE CABINET AND THE PRIME MINISTER

The cabinet consists of the prime minister and ministers, with each handling a major bureaucracy of the government. Unlike the U.S. cabinet, the British cabinet members are party leaders from Parliament chosen by the prime minister. The **collective cabinet** is the center of policy-making in the British political system, and the prime minister has the responsibility of shaping their decisions into policy. The cabinet does not vote, but all members publicly support the prime minister's decisions. In other words, as the leaders of the majority party elected by the people, they take "**collective responsibility**" for making policy for the country. The unity of the cabinet is extremely important for the stability of the government. The prime minister is the "**first among equals**", but he/she stands at the apex of the **unitary government**. Despite many recent changes, political authority in Britain is still centralized in the London-based government. The prime minister is not directly elected by the people, but is a Member of Parliament and the leader of the majority party. Currently, the Labour Party is in power, and has been since 1997.

The prime minister

- speaks legitimately for all Members of Parliament
- chooses cabinet ministers and important subordinate posts
- makes decisions in the cabinet, with the agreement of the ministers
- campaigns for and represents the party in parliamentary elections

PARLIAMENT

Although British government consists of three branches, little separation of powers exists between the cabinet and parliament. Like most other parliamentary systems, the executive and legislative branches are fused, largely because the leaders of the majority party in parliament are also the cabinet members.

The House of Commons

Even though Britain has multiple political parties, the House of Commons is based on the assumption that one party will get the majority number of seats, and another will serve as the "opposition." So, one way to look at it is that Britain has a multi-party system at the polls, but a two-party system in the House of Commons. Whichever party wins a plurality at the polls becomes the majority party, and the second party becomes the "**loyal opposition.**"

Set-up of the House of Commons

The House of Commons is set up with long benches facing one another with a table in between that is by tradition two-sword-lengths wide. The prime minister – who is elected as an MP like all the rest – sits on the front bench of the majority side in the middle. He or she becomes prime minister because all the members of the majority party have made that selection. The majority party may vote to change their leader, and the prime minister will change as a result. Right across from the prime minister sits the leader of the "opposition" party, who sit on benches facing the majority party. Between them is the table. Cabinet members sit on the front rows on the majority side, and the "**shadow cabinet**" faces them on the opposition side. On the back benches sit less influential MPs – the "**backbenchers**" – and MPs from other political parties sit on the opposition side, but at the end, far away from the table.

Debate

The "**government**", then, consists of the MPs on the first rows of the majority party side, and they are the most important policymakers as long as they hold power. Debate in the House is usually quite spirited, especially once a week during **Question Time**. During the hour the prime minister and his cabinet must defend themselves against attack from the opposition, and sometimes from members of their own party. The **speaker of the house** presides over the debates. Unlike the speaker in the U.S. House of Representatives, the speaker is supposed to be objective and often is not a member of the majority party. The speaker's job is to allow all to speak, but not to let things get out of hand. (S)he often has to gavel MPs down that get too rowdy.

One reason that debate can be so intense is that the floor of Parliament is the place where MPs can gain attention from others, possibly casting themselves as future leaders. Also, the opposition is seen as the **"check"** on the majority party, since checks and balances between branches do not exist.

Party Discipline

Because the majority party in essence is the government, party discipline is very important. If party members do not support their leadership, the government may fall into crisis because it lacks legitimacy. Above all, the majority party wants to avoid losing a **"vote of confidence,"** a vote on a key issue. If the issue is not supported, the cabinet by tradition must resign immediately, and elections for new MPs must be held as soon as possible. This drastic measure is usually avoided by settling policy differences within the majority party membership. If a party loses a vote of confidence, all MPs lose their jobs, so there is plenty of motivation to vote the party line. A recent vote of confidence occurred in early 2005, when the Labour government's Higher Education Bill squeaked by with an approval vote of 316 to 311. The bill proposed raising university fees, a measure criticized by not only the opposition, but also by some outspoken Labour MPs. The vote narrowly allowed Blair's government to continue to control Commons. The policymaking power of the House is very limited since many government decisions are ratified by the Cabinet and never go to Parliament.

Since the 1970s, backbenchers have been less deferential to the party leadership than in the past. A backbench rebellion against John Major's EU policy weakened the prime minister significantly. Tony Blair faced a major rebellion of Labour backbenchers on key votes in February and March 2003 regarding the use of force in Iraq. Many have been outspoken in their opposition to government policy regarding the adoption of the euro, so it looks likely that the trend will continue.

Parliament has some substantial powers because its members

- debate and refine potential legislation

- are the only ones who may become party leaders and ultimately may head the government.

- scrutinize the administration of laws

- keep communication lines open between voters and ministers

House of Lords

Britain is no exception to the rule in its bicameral legislative structure. However, many of the benefits of bicameralism (including the dispersing of power between two houses) do not operate because the House of Lords has so little power. House of Lords is the only hereditary parliamentary house in existence today, and although historically it was the original parliament, today it has minimal influence. The House of Commons established supremacy during the 17th century, and Lords gradually declined in authority. Since the turn of the 20th century, the only remaining powers are to delay legislation, and to debate technicalities of proposed bills. Lords may add amendments to legislation, but the House of Commons may delete their changes by a simple majority vote. The chamber also includes five **law lords** who serve as Britain's highest court of appeals, but they cannot rule acts of Parliament unconstitutional. Until 1999 about one-half of the members of Lords were **hereditary peers**, who hold seats that have been passed down through family ties over the centuries. The remaining were **life peers**, people appointed to nonhereditary positions as a result of distinguished service to Britain.

In 1999 the Labour government took seats away from most of the hereditary peers, so that today only 92 hereditary seats remain, while 567 seats are life peers. In late 2001, the government announced plans for a new upper house with about 550 mostly appointed members, but with no hereditary posts. In March 2007 the House of Commons voted, in principle, in favor of replacing the Lords with an elected chamber, (either 100% elected or 80% elected, 20% appointed.). However, the House of Lords, feeling threatened by the idea of dismantlement, rejected this proposal and voted for an entirely appointed House of Lords. Despite these changes and proposals, the fact remains that the House of Lords has very little policymaking power in the British government.

One criticism of the British parliamentary system is that the lack of separation between the prime minister and the legislature is a dangerous concentration of power, since both are controlled by the same party. Supporters of the parliamentary system praise its efficiency, since it does not experience the crippling "gridlock" found between Congress and the President in the United States.

THE BUREAUCRACY

Britain has hundreds of thousands of civil servants who administer laws and deliver public services. Most civil servants do clerical work and other routine work of a large bureaucracy. However, a few hundred higher civil servants directly advise ministers and oversee work of the departments. They coordinate the policies that cabinet members set with their actual implementation by the bureaucracy.

The British bureaucracy is a stable and powerful force in the political system. Top level bureaucrats almost always make a career of government service, and most are experts in their area. Because the ministers are party leaders chosen by the prime minister, they understand a great deal about British politics, but they generally are not experts in particular policy areas. In contrast, the top bureaucrats usually stay with their particular departments, and the ministers rely on their expertise. As a result, the top civil servants often have a great deal of input into policymaking, including **discretionary power** to make many decisions in implementing legislative and executive decisions. The minister has a powerful position on the cabinet, but he/she relies heavily on the advice of the bureaucrats. Bureaucrats almost never run for public office and are usually not active in party politics. Therefore, as cabinets come and go, the bureaucrats stay and fulfill an important role in government.

THE JUDICIARY

English ideas about justice have shaped those of many other modern democracies. For example, the concept of trial by jury goes back to the time of Henry II in the 13th century. Britain has had a judicial branch for centuries, but ironically, the modern judiciary has much more limited powers than those in the United States, France, and Germany. In Britain, the principle of **parliamentary sovereignty** (parliament's decisions are final) has limited the development of judicial review (the courts' ability to determine actions, laws and other court decisions unconstitutional). British courts can only determine whether government decisions violate the common law or previous acts of Parliament. Even then, the courts tend to rule narrowly because they defer to the authority of Parliament. By tradition, the courts may not impose their rulings on Parliament, the prime minister, or the cabinet.

The British legal system based on **common law** contrasts to the stricter **code law** (see p. 15) practiced in the rest of Europe. Code law is much less focused on precedent and interpretation than common law. British courts, like those in most other advanced democracies, do make distinctions between original and appellate jurisdiction. District Courts hear cases that may be appealed to the High Courts, which may in turn be appealed to the highest court in the land - the **law lords**. They are actually members of the House of Lords who are designated as the highest judicial authority in Great Britain to settle disputes from lower courts. The law lords do not have the power of judicial review, so their authority is limited.

By and large, judges have the reputation of being independent, impartial, and neutral. Few have been MPs, and almost none are active in party politics. Judges are appointed on "good behavior," but they are expected to retire when they reach the age of 75. Most judges are educated at public schools and at Oxford and Cambridge, and their positions are prestigious.

Despite the limited policymaking power of the judiciary, Britain's membership in the European Union has given judges a new responsibility that promises to become even more important in the future. Since Britain is now bound by EU treaties and laws, it is the judges' responsibility to interpret them and determine whether or not EU laws conflict with parliamentary statutes. Since the British tend to be skeptical about their EU membership, the way that possible conflicts between supranational and national laws are settled by British judges may impact the policymaking process considerably.

PUBLIC POLICY AND CURRENT ISSUES

The election of 2005 secured an historic third term for Tony Blair and the Labour Party. However, Blair's support of the war in Iraq was very controversial among British voters, and probably cost Labour a good many votes. Labour MPs slipped from 403 to 356, a loss of 47 members. The biggest beneficiary was the Liberal Democratic Party that picked up 11 MPs for a total of 62. Conservatives picked up 33, but their total numbers rose to 198, still far behind Labour's lead. For now, Labour still has a solid majority, and the government gained enough votes to continue the course they have followed since 1997. Many issues confront the British political system today, but some of the most important are:

- The evolving relationship between government and the economy

- British relationships with the European Union

- Blair's balancing act between the U.S. and the EU

- Direction of post-Blair policy

- Terrorism

- Devolution and constitutional reform

THE EVOLVING RELATIONSHIP BETWEEN GOVERNMENT AND THE ECONOMY

The historical basis for Britain's political economy is **liberalism**, the philosophy that emphasizes political and economic freedoms for the individual and the market. Yet liberalism in Great Britain has been reshaped over the years, particularly in recent decades.

Since the end of World War II, the British government has redefined its relationship with the economy several times. Until the 1970s, the **collective consensus** philosophy was based on social democratic values that support a great deal of government control of the economy, including the nationalization of many major industries. The approach taken was **Keynesianism** (after British economist John Maynard Keynes), in which the government took action to secure full employment, expand social services, maintain a steady rate of growth, and keep prices stable. Then, Margaret Thatcher reversed this trend by emphasizing **neo-liberalism,** a revival of the old political and economic philosophy of liberalism that had guided Britain in earlier years. Thatcher's policies moved toward a free market economy and denationalization of industries. Since then, the government has tried to establish a middle way, but the correct balance between state control and the free market is a matter of great dispute.

During the Blair years (1997-2007) the prime minister teamed with Gordon Brown, the chancellor of the exchequer (treasury), to craft the direction of the political economy. By 2001 the Blair-Brown team had succeeded in bringing Britain's **"misery index"** (inflation plus unemployment) down to a new low. While holding income tax rates steady, the government still managed to fund a variety of welfare programs, including those intended to improve living standards and job opportunities for the poor. This balancing act is illustrated by the current debate over what to do with the National Health Service (NHS). Some support it, saying that the British population is much healthier than it used to be, and that the British working class has especially benefited. Others criticize the service for its increasing expense to the government and for its long wait lists for medical treatment. Private medical care is becoming more common, but many Britons want to keep the NHS, especially if it can be reformed.

BRITISH RELATIONSHIPS WITH THE EUROPEAN UNION

British insularity has always meant that the country tends to keep its allies at arm's length. The British government did not enter the Common Market (a precursor to the European Union) when it was established in 1957. When Britain finally decided to enter in the early 1960s, its membership was vetoed twice by French President Charles DeGaulle. Finally, in 1978, Britain joined the Common Market, but the Thatcher government was opposed to rapid integration of European markets. She was adamantly opposed to the adoption of the euro in place of the pound. Under Prime Minister John Major, Britain signed the Maastricht Treaty that created the European Union, and under Labour's Tony Blair, the government was still more favorable. When the Labour government first took power, it openly advocated adoption of the euro and further integration with the EU. However, once in power, Labour backed away from its initial commitment, although during the 2005 campaign Blair promised future **referenda** on the new EU constitution and the euro. The referenda did not take place during the remainder of Blair's time in office, and the Conservative Party is openly split over EU matters. Polls indicate that the majority of the British public still wants to hold on to the British pound, so it appears as if Britain will continue to play its age-old cat and mouse game with the European continent.

DIRECTION OF POST-BLAIR POLICY

As Tony Blair stepped down from office in June 2007, most British citizens were relieved to end the last years of controversy over his policies, particularly his highly unpopular support for the Iraq War. However, it is too soon to judge his accomplishments, which supporters say are considerable. For example, his admirers point out that the British economy has stabilized, globalization has made London one of the most dynamic cities in the world, schools and hospitals have improved, devolution is well underway, and British citizens are paying more attention to climate change and worldwide poverty. The future will reveal how much of this is true, especially in terms of the direction that the new prime minister, Gordon Brown, takes as he heads the Labour government.

Gordon Brown has been a Labour leader for many years, rising at the same time that Tony Blair climbed the ranks of party power. He was first elected to Parliament in 1983, and became shadow chancellor of the exchequer (treasury) in the years before Labour's victory in 1997. During Blair's years in office, Brown served as the chancellor, largely crafting overall economic strategy, and apparently gaining a great deal of power in other policy areas as well, including foreign aid and management of health and education. Once Blair's unpopularity made it apparent that he would have to step down, it became clear that Gordon Brown was the heir-apparent. Brown's personality is more low-key than Blair's, and how that might affect Britain's place in international politics is a source of much speculation. Critics had accused Tony Blair of being George Bush's "poodle" in his Iraq policy, and the new prime minister's visit to George Bush at Camp David in the summer of 2007 did not reveal much about how the relationship between the U.S. president and the British prime minister might or might not change in the future.

TERRORISM

Tony Blair aptly described changes in the nature of terrorism in Britain in an essay published in *The Economist* at the end of his tenure:

> "Over ten years I have watched this [terrorism] grow. (If you had told me a decade ago that I would be tackling terrorism, I would have readily understood, but thought you meant Irish Republican terrorism.)"

The meaning of terrorism certainly changed after four British Muslim suicide bombers attacked the London transit system in July 2005, killing 52 people. Two other major terrorist plots were uncovered in 2006, and in 2007 several car bombs exploded – one parked outside a London nightclub, one near Trafalgar Square in London, and one in the Glasgow airport. Within four days of the car bombs, the main players had been arrested. The government is now earmarking extra money for security, a mosque watchdog is in operation, and the M15 (British security service) is keeping track of many suspected terrorists.

In his first press conference as prime minister, Gordon Brown reacted to the 2007 attacks by affirming his government's commitment to nonviolence, and expressed his distaste for the "extreme message of those who practice violence and would maim and murder citizens on British soil." Shortly afterward, the government began a pilot curriculum to be taught in some Muslim religious classes that emphasizes nonviolence among British Muslims. The program has been criticized as singling out young Muslims for civics lessons, and the British government is still struggling with how to isolate the extremist Muslim minority from the moderate majority.

THE BALANCING ACT BETWEEN THE U.S. AND THE EU

When Tony Blair became prime minister of the United Kingdom in 1997, he took on a very ambitious agenda. Domestically, he wanted to sustain economic prosperity and increase social equality, as well as reinforce traditional British national identity and political institutions. Internationally, he sought to develop a new relationship with Europe in which the United Kingdom would play a central and self-confident role, and yet maintain a special relationship with the United States that had been in place since World War II.

Blair's efforts seemed to succeed until the Iraq crisis drove Washington in the opposite direction from Paris and Berlin. France and Germany were outspoken in their criticism of the U.S. invasion of Iraq and of Britain's support for the war under Blair's watch. The crisis challenged the cornerstone of Tony Blair's vision that the United Kingdom could act as a bridge across the Atlantic. It damaged Britain's relationship with France and raised questions about the wisdom of its special relationship with the United States. It caused dissent within the Labour leadership, and seriously undermined Blair's popular support, a situation that resulted in the party losing many seats in the House of Commons in the election of 2005, and eventually led to Blair's resignation in 2007.

DEVOLUTION AND CONSTITUTIONAL REFORM

The British government is still a **unitary** one, with the most authority emanating from London. However, continuing desire by the Scottish and the Welsh for their independence and the problems with Northern Ireland have led to the development and implementation of the policy of **devolution**. Even before Margaret Thatcher delayed the process when she took office in 1979, the Labour party supported **devolution**, or the turning over of some political powers to regional governments. However, a 1977 referendum to create Scottish and Welsh assemblies failed. In 1999, though, referenda in both regions passed, and each now has its own regional assembly, which has powers in taxation, education, and economic planning. In the 1998 Good Friday Agreement, a parliament was set up for Northern Ireland as well, although London shut down its activities after violence broke out in 2002. The Northern Ireland Assembly remained suspended for almost five years, not reopening until May 2007. Just how much these new parliaments will affect London's authority is yet to be seen. Devolution has also included the creation of the office of mayor and a general assembly for London, giving the city more independence from the central government over its affairs.

Some critics have argued that devolution should be only one step toward modernizing the political system. Other reforms under consideration include a written Bill of Rights for individual citizens, a written constitution, freedom of information, and a new electoral system. Whatever reforms are made, Britain still retains a strong attachment to its many traditions, and the government's long lists of accomplishments are not all in the past. As the nation redefines both external and internal political relationships, Britain still serves as a role model for the development of democratic traditions in the modern world.

IMPORTANT TERMS AND CONCEPTS

backbenchers
Beveridge Report
Blair, Tony
British Broadcasting Corporation

Brown, Gordon
Cameron, David
caucuses
"civic culture"
Clause 4
coalition government
collective consensus
collective responsibility
Confederation of Business Industries
Conservative Party
"Constitution of the Crown"
cultural heterogeneity
Democratic Unionist Party
devolution
the English Bill of Rights
Euroskeptics
"first-past-the-post" voting system
the Glorious Revolution
the "government"
gradualism
hereditary peers
home rule
insularity
Irish Republican Army
"Iron Lady"
Kennedy, Charles
Keynesianism
Labour Party
law lords
Liberal Democratic Alliance
liberalism
life peers
limited government
"loyal opposition"
Magna Carta
"misery index"
mixed economy
multi-nationalism
neo-corporatism
neo-liberalism
noblesse oblige
OPEC
Oxbridge
parliamentary system
Plaid Cymru
plurality voting system
politics of protest

proportional representation
quangos
Question Time
rational-legal legitimacy
referendum
safe districts
Scottish National Party
"shadow cabinet"
Sinn Fein
solidarity
Speaker of the House
Thatcherism
The Third Way
Tories
Trades Union Congress
traditional leadership
unitary government
vote of confidence
Whigs

MULTIPLE-CHOICE QUESTIONS
GOVERNMENT AND POLITICS IN BRITAIN

1. All of the following are examples of rational-legal authority in Britain EXCEPT:

    a) the Magna Carta
    b) the Bill of Rights
    c) common law
    d) hereditary monarchy
    e) the "Constitution of the Crown"

2. Which of the following countries have legal and justice systems based on common law?

    I. Great Britain
    II. The United States
    III. France
    IV. Germany

    a) I only
    b) I and II only
    c) II, III, and IV only
    d) III and IV only
    e) I, II, III, and IV

3. In the early 21st century, which of the following social cleavages appears to be getting stronger in Britain?

    a) social class
    b) multi-nationalism
    c) ethnicity
    d) age groups
    e) political ideologies

4. Controversy in Britain over the European Union has most frequently centered on

    a) elections of representatives to the European Parliament
    b) competition with France over who heads the Council of Ministers
    c) cooperation with other countries regarding anti-terrorism
    d) competitive educational opportunities on the continent
    e) the adoption of the euro as the national currency

5. Despite Britain's numerous political parties, one political party has always been able to claim a majority in Parliament. The BEST single reason is that

   a) parliamentary majorities are usually based on coalitions
   b) the plurality electoral system is used
   c) very few people actually vote for parties other than Conservative or Labour
   d) regional parties are forbidden by law from controlling Parliament
   e) Britain has a conflictual political culture

6. Neo-liberalism is most closely associated with British policymaking under

   a) Winston Churchill
   b) Clement Attlee
   c) Gordon Brown
   d) Tony Blair
   e) Margaret Thatcher

7. Which of the following characteristics of Britain's political culture may be linked most directly to its cautious attitude toward the European Union?

   a) insularity
   b) noblesse oblige
   c) traditionalism
   d) nulti-nationalism
   e) gradualism

8. Which of the following BEST describes the nature of political and economic change over the long course of Britain's history?

   a) frequent coup d'etats
   b) economic revolution
   c) political revolution
   d) gradual reform
   e) periods of reform followed by periods of revolution

9. Which of the following is the best description of Britain's political party system since its inception in the 17th century?

   a) Britain has always had a multi-party system characterized by coalitions among parties.
   b) Britain has always been a two-party system: Conservative and Labour parties.
   c) Britain has always been dominated by two parties, but Labour replaced the Liberals as a main party in the early 20th century.
   d) British political parties were very weak until the 20th century, when Conservatives, Labour, and Liberals all gained access to the policymaking process.
   e) Political parties were strong until the mid-20th century, when their power began to decline.

10. What do Neil Kinnock, John Smith, Tony Blair, and Gordon Brown all have in common?

    a) They have all been British prime ministers.
    b) They have all been leaders of the Conservative Party.
    c) They have all been leaders of the Liberal Democratic Party.
    d) They have all been chancellors of the exchequer.
    e) They have all been leaders of the Labour Party.

11. The post-World War II cabinet laid the foundations for a

    a) free market economy
    b) socialist economy
    c) command economy
    d) mixed economy
    e) decentralized economy

12. Tony Blair's "third way" was an attempt to balance the socialist policies of the Labour Party during the 1970s with

    a) collective consensus
    b) Margaret Thatcher's free-market policies
    c) Winston Churchill's internationalism
    d) Bill Clinton's new direction for the Democratic Party in the United States
    e) the demands made by the Democratic Liberal Party for more personal liberties

13. Tony Blair's support for devolution was primarily stimulated by Britain's problems with

    a) multi-national identities
    b) increasing numbers of immigrants from India and Pakistan
    c) urban vs. rural areas
    d) emigration of educated citizens to the United States
    e) social class differences

14. In modern times political elites in Britain have most often been recruited from

    a) the military
    b) business and industry
    c) the middle class
    d) Oxbridge
    e) aristocratic families

15. Which of the following is an accurate description of British Muslims?

   a) They form roughly 20% of Britain's population.
   b) Most of them emigrated from Africa.
   c) Most of them are well educated.
   d) Most of them are involved with terrorist activities.
   e) Most are not well integrated into British society.

16. The "Good Friday" agreement addressed the issue of

   a) protest over the Iraq War
   b) the adoption of the euro
   c) religious conflict in Northern Ireland
   d) sovereignty powers of the Scottish Parliament
   e) government control of the media

17. The political party that gets most of its support from rural and suburban areas of England is

   a) Labour
   b) Plaid Cymru
   c) Liberal Democratic
   d) Conservative
   e) Democratic Unionist

18. The British political party most disadvantaged by the plurality voting system is

   a) Labour
   b) Scottish Nationalist
   c) Conservative
   d) Sinn Fein
   e) Liberal Democratic

19. Which of the following is characteristic of British elections?

   a) Party leaders run in "safe districts."
   b) MP candidates must live in their districts.
   c) Individuals vote for four officials on the national level.
   d) Virtually no minor parties win MP seats.
   e) Elections for the House of Commons are held at different times than elections for the House of Lords.

20. Quangos best represent which pattern of interest group involvement in policymaking?

    a) interest group pluralism
    b) solidarity
    c) state corporatism
    d) neo-corporatism
    e) liberalism

21. Which of the following is NOT an accurate description of the relationship between the British government and the British Broadcasting Corporation?

    a) The government strictly regulates the BBC and private media companies.
    b) The BBC has competition from private media outlets.
    c) The BBC seldom criticizes the government's officials.
    d) The government prohibits the BBC from selling advertisements to politicians, parties, and political causes.
    e) The government allows the BBC to broadcast internationally.

22. Which of the following is an accurate description of the British political system?

    a) It is a unitary state with political authority centralized in London.
    b) It is a federal state with a central government that shares power with sub-units of government.
    c) Although officials are directly elected, the fusion between the executive and legislative branches makes it an authoritarian state.
    d) It has a confederal government that suits the multi-national country very well.
    e) It is a corporatist state that allows interest group input but chooses which groups have access to the government.

23. Collective responsibility is a concept that applies most clearly to the British

    a) House of Commons
    b) House of Lords
    c) cabinet
    d) bureaucracy
    e) judiciary

24. All of the following are accurate statements about the British executive EXCEPT:

    a) the prime minister serves only as long as (s)he remains leader of the majority party
    b) the prime minister is elected as a member of parliament
    c) cabinet members are always MPs and leaders of the majority party
    d) the cabinet members rely on bureaucrats to provide expertise in specific policymaking areas
    e) the prime minister has an excellent chance of ending up in gridlock with parliament

25. The shadow cabinet is formed by the

   a) majority party in Parliament
   b) House of Lords
   c) bureaucracy
   d) judiciary
   e) loyal opposition

26. If a vote of confidence is lost in the House of Commons, by tradition, what happens next?

   a) The opposition party takes over.
   b) The prime minister and cabinet resign.
   c) The House votes for a new leadership team.
   d) The prime minister chooses a new cabinet.
   e) The vote goes to the House of Lords.

27. Britain's highest court of appeals consists of

   a) the law lords
   b) specially elected judges
   c) judges selected by the queen
   d) cabinet members
   e) judges appointed by the prime minister and confirmed by the House of Lords

28. The most important shapers of the British political economy during the Blair years were Tony Blair and

   a) Gordon Brown
   b) Jack Straw
   c) John Major
   d) David Cameron
   e) John Maynard Keynes

29. Referenda on British policy issues have actually been held for

   a) the European Constitution
   b) the adoption of the euro as a currency
   c) regional assemblies
   d) the National Health Service
   e) support for the Iraq War

30. The nature of the issue of terrorism in Britain has changed over the past few years from a focus on

   a) international terrorism to violence in Northern Ireland
   b) violence in Northern Ireland to international terrorism
   c) solutions crafted by the government in London to solutions collectively considered through the European Union
   d) control of British citizens to control of immigration into the country
   e) individual acts of terror to actions sponsored by organized groups

GREAT BRITAIN – COUNTRY BASED FREE-RESPONSE QUESTION

The two major political parties in Great Britain are the Labour Party and the Conservative Party.

(a) Contrast the political positions that each party currently holds on TWO of the following issues:

- integration with the European Union

- devolution

- the welfare state

(b) For each of the two issues that you chose in (a), describe a change in policy that one of the parties has made since 1991.

THE EUROPEAN UNION

As we have seen, one major trend in Britain is **devolution**, or the process of decentralizing the unitary state to share policymaking power with regional governments. Yet all the countries of Europe, including Britain, are deeply affected by a countertrend – **integration.** Integration is a process that encourages states to pool their sovereignty in order to gain political, economic, and social clout. Integration binds states together with common policies and shared rules. The **supranational organization** that integrates the states of Europe is called the European Union.

Europe's history is one of diverse national identities. Its wars have encompassed the continent as first its kingdoms, and then its countries, fought over religion, power, land, and trade. Perhaps most dramatically, its conflicts erupted in two devastating world wars during the 20th century. Shortly after World War II ended, European leaders decided on a new direction – cooperation among nations – that led to the creation of the European Union, a supranational organization that has not supplanted nationalism, but has altered its members' policymaking practices substantially.

A BRIEF HISTORY

The organization began in an effort to revitalize a war-torn Europe after World War II ended. The most immediate need was to repair the nations' broken economies, so the initial goals were almost completely economic in intent. In 1949 the Council of Europe was formed, which had little power, but did provide an opportunity for national leaders to meet. The following year a supranational authority was formed to coordinate the coal and steel industries, both damaged heavily in the war. Later evolutions of the new organization included:

- **The EEC** (European Economic Community) - The Treaty of Rome established the EEC - informally named the "**Common Market**" - in 1957. Its most important provisions called for the elimination of all tariffs between European nations and the creation of new ones that applied to all.

- **The EC** (European Community) – Established in 1965, the EC expanded the organization's functions beyond economics. One major concern other than tariffs and customs was a unified approach to the peaceful use of atomic energy. However, the development of the EC was limited by disagreements as to how much power it should be given, with many nations concerned that their national sovereignty would be weakened. The urge toward integration was given a boost by the collapse of Soviet dominance in Eastern Europe in the late 1980s. With new democracies emerging, their transitions from communism to capitalism demanded guidance from a supranational regional power.

- **The EU** (European Union) – The 1991 Maastricht Treaty created the modern organization, and gave it authority in new areas, including monetary policy, foreign affairs, national security, transportation, the environment, justice, and tourism. The treaty established the **three pillars,** or spheres of authority:

  1) Trade and other economic matters, including economic and monetary union into a single currency, and the creation of the European Central Bank

2) Justice and home affairs, including policy governing asylum, border crossing, immigration, and judicial cooperation on crime and terrorism

3) Common foreign and security policy, including joint positions and actions, and common defense policy

MEMBERSHIP

Ongoing expansion is a major characteristic of the European Union, with a total membership of 27 countries as of 2007. The European Union began with six members in 1957: Belgium, France, Germany, Italy, Luxembourg, and the Netherlands. Denmark, Great Britain, and Ireland joined in the early 1970s; Greece in 1981; Portugal and Spain in 1986; and Austria, Finland, and Sweden in 1995. Ten countries joined on May 2, 2004: Cyprus (Greek part), the Czech Republic, Estonia, Hungary, Latvia, Lithuania, Malta, Poland, Slovakia and Slovenia. Bulgaria and Romania joined on January 1, 2007.

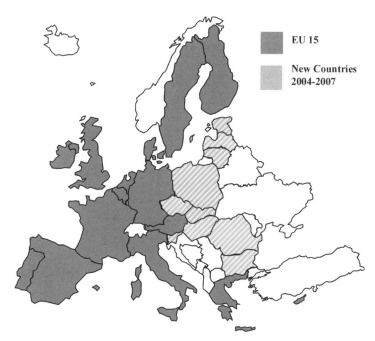

EU 15

New Countries
2004-2007

The Expansion of the EU. A major challenge for the EU is the integration of many new members since 2004.

Several countries are currently under consideration as candidates for membership, including Croatia, Macedonia, and Turkey. Turkey is controversial for many reasons, including its relatively low Gross Domestic Product per capita of less than 7,000 euro, or 1/3 of the EU average. Turkey has been questioned because of its history of authoritarian governments, and its candidacy brings up a question of eligibility, since most of the country is technically not in Europe, but in Asia. A deeper issue is the largely Muslim population of Turkey. If the EU is mainly an economic organization, then it shouldn't matter that all Turkey's religious leanings are quite different from those of current members, whose populations are overwhelmingly Christian. However, if the EU fulfills its other pillars (justice and home affairs, and common foreign and security policy), some fear that religious differences could hinder the integration process.

Even though the political and economic muscle of so many countries united is considerable, this rapid integration presents many difficult issues for the EU. First, organizational issues abound. Structures that work for six countries do not necessarily operate smoothly for 27. Second, the expansion brings in many former communist countries whose economies were relatively weak by the end of the 20th century. Older member states worry that immigrants from the east will flood their labor markets and strain their economies. EU supporters believe that these problems will be overshadowed by the benefits of common markets, currencies, political policies, and defense.

In order to be accepted for membership, candidate nations must provide evidence to meet three important criteria:

- a stable and functioning democratic regime
- a market-oriented economy
- willingness to accept all EU laws and regulations

The rapid growth of the EU has brought about what some have called **enlargement fatigue.** Polls show a decline in support for enlargement among EU voters, and many believe that the French and Dutch rejections of the European Constitution (see p. 93) partly reflected dissatisfaction over the 2004 enlargement. Also, many EU governments have lost their enthusiasm for further growth, particularly France, Germany, and Austria. The economic benefits of the recent expansions are still unknown, and the questions surrounding Turkey have cooled some support. Of course, there is a limited amount of growth potential remaining because only a few countries of the continent are non-members, including Norway, Switzerland, Yugoslavia, Bosnia, Belarus, Moldova, and the Ukraine.

ORGANIZATION

The European Union is composed of four major bodies: The Commission, the Council of Ministers, the European Court of Justice, and the European Parliament.

- **The Commission** – This body currently has twenty-seven members, one from each member state of the EU, supported by a bureaucracy of several thousand European civil servants. Each Commissioner takes responsibility for a particular area of policy, as well as a department called a Directorate General. The Commission is headed by a president, currently Jose Manuel Durao Barroso of Portugal. Although their home governments nominate them, commissioners swear an oath of allegiance to the EU and are not supposed to take directions from their national governments. The Commission's main responsibility is to initiate and implement new programs, and it forms a permanent executive that supervises the work of the EU, much in the way that a national cabinet operates.

- **The Council of Ministers** - Whereas the Commission acts cooperatively as the director of EU activities, the Council demonstrates the continuing power of the states. The Council consists of foreign ministers, finance ministers, the president of France, and all the prime ministers of the other members. They hold frequent meetings – some for only one type of minister – and the heads of state meet every six months as the **European Council**. The council is central to the EU's legislative process. The president of the council rotates every six months, so each country now fills the chair once every 13 ½ years. The Commission may initiate legislation, but its proposals don't become law until they have been passed by the Council. Each country is assigned a number of votes in proportion to its share of population.

- **The European Parliament** – Contrary to the implications of its name, the European Parliament does not have a great deal of legislative power. However, since 1979 its members (MEPs) have been directly elected by the people of their respective countries, so they do have some independence from their national governments. Parliament may propose amendments to legislation, and they may reject proposals from the Council outright. However, the Council may override their rejection by a unanimous vote. EU citizens vote directly for representatives to the parliament every five years. Apportionment of representatives is not strictly based on population, and smaller member states have disproportionately greater representation than larger ones. The meetings of the parliament are held in Strasbourg, although committees meet in Brussels.

- **The European Court of Justice** – The ECJ is the supreme court of the European Union, and it has the power of **judicial review**. The Court meets in Luxembourg, where it interprets European law, and its decisions may limit national sovereignty. As such, it is more powerful than most national judicial systems of its member states. The Court has a broad jurisdiction, and hears cases that rule on disagreements among the Commissioners, the Council of Ministers, and the members of parliament. It also may settle disputes among member nations, private companies, and individuals. The ECJ consists of 27 judges, with each one nominated by a different member state. Cases are decided by a simple majority.

POLICYMAKING POWER

Although the European Union has made only rudimentary policy in many areas – such as defense and social policy – it clearly sets strong policies in other areas that previously had been controlled by the individual countries. Three areas of active policymaking are:

- **Creating and maintaining a single internal market** - The EU has removed most of the old tariffs and other barriers to trade among its members. For example, trucking goods across national borders is much easier today than it was before the EU was created. Also, most professional licenses, such as those for doctors and beauticians, are accepted in all member states. The exception is that lawyers' licenses are only good in the country that issues them. So policy differences still exist among the nations, but the single market has greatly affected both European governments and their citizens. More options are available to shoppers and consumers now that goods are freely transported across national borders.

- **Union of monetary policy** – The EU has made remarkable strides in its ability to set European **monetary policy,** or the control of the money supply. Today the euro has replaced most of the old national currencies, which are well on their way to being phased out. Also, the power to set basic interest rates and other fiscal policies is being passed from national banks and governments to the **European Monetary Union** and its new central bank. Today, in 12 of the member countries, the euro is accepted as a common currency both in banking and for everyday business transactions. Two exceptions to the rule are Britain and Sweden, which as of 2007 still refuse to give up their national currencies in favor of the euro.

- **Common agricultural policy** – Implementation of policy in this area has generally been less successful than others, but the EU has put in place significant new agricultural programs, with almost half of the organization's budget going to this policy. One goal has been to modernize inefficient farms so that they might compete in the common market. In order to meet this goal, the EU established **farm subsidies**, guarantees of selling goods at high prices. The subsidies have proved very expensive and have yet to improve farm efficiency in any measurable way. Recent reforms of the system have transferred subsidies away from price supports for specific crops and toward direct payments to farmers. A growing chunk of the money goes to rural-development projects, not farming as such.

By the late 1990s, the European Union began to lay the groundwork for future policies in these areas:

- **Common defense** – European integration began with economic policy, so EU defense policy is much less well developed than those for trade and common currency. However, the 1993 Maastrict Treaty made foreign and defense policy one of the three "pillars" of the EU, so some defense policies have been put in place. In 1999 the European Council placed **crisis management** tasks at the core of the development of common security and defense of EU members. Crises were defined as humanitarian, rescue, and peacemaking tasks. The Council set as a goal that the EU should be able to deploy up to 60,000 troops within sixty days that could be sustained for at least one year. The agreement left troop commitment and deployment up to the member states, and, as a result, did not create a European army.

- **Justice and Home Affairs** – The 1997 **Treaty of Amsterdam** set major policy initiatives for judicial affairs. The aim was to establish within a few years the **free movement** of European Union citizens and non-EU nationals throughout the Union. Free movement has involved setting policy regarding visas, asylum, and immigration. Additionally, the Treaty of Amsterdam helped to define cooperation among national police forces and judicial authorities in combating crime. Although member nations may support a EU structure in areas of justice, freedom, and security, they are not compelled to participate. In these areas, Britain, Ireland, and Denmark restrict their participation to only a few select provisions.

- **Terrorism** – The EU has become very concerned about terrorism since the September 11, 2001 attacks on the World Trade Towers and the Pentagon in the United States. More recent bombings have rocked transportation systems in Spain (2004) and Britain (2005), reminding Europeans that terrorists have almost certainly taken advantage of the increasing ease of travel across country borders created by integration of nations. Beginning in April 2004, United States and European Union officials have held a series of policy dialogues on border and transportation security that have focused on better addressing common security concerns and identifying areas where U.S.-EU cooperation and coordination might be enhanced.

THE EUROPEAN CONSTITUTION

On October 29, 2004, European heads of government signed a treaty establishing a **European Constitution.** The intention of the Constitution is to replace the overlapping set of treaties that govern member states' interactions, and to streamline decision-making as the organization has grown to its current 27 states. The Constitution is now in the process of ratification by member states, and was scheduled to go into effect on November 1, 2006. However, in mid-2005, French and Dutch voters rejected the treaty in separate referenda, prompting other countries, including Britain, to postpone their ratification procedures.

The negative reactions in France and the Netherlands to the European Constitution reflect a growing resistance to integration, especially as the European Union membership continues to grow so rapidly. Many fear that the power shift from national to supranational institutions will result in a **democratic deficit**, or the loss of direct control of political decisions by the people. The European Parliament is the only directly elected body, and it is the weakest of the major EU bodies.

The post-World War II visionaries that first conceived of a European Union saw not only an economically united Europe, but one with close political cooperation as well. So far, the European Union has shown little movement toward political integration, although the Maastricht Treaty of 1991 did include it within their "three pillars", or spheres of authority. More cooperation in foreign and national security policy is still on the EU's agenda, but economic integration remains the focus today.

ECONOMIC ISSUES

By mid-2007 EU economies, especially the areas where the euro is the common currency, were underperforming the American economy, causing some to question the success of the economic integration of Europe. GDP per capita is almost 30% lower than in the United States, and the gap appears to be widening. Unemployment in Europe has been persistently higher than across the Atlantic, and Europeans have also been slower to take up information technology, limiting their potential for innovation and research. Neo-liberalists advocate more flexible labor markets and a cut-back in welfare benefits. European labor unions have won good salaries and benefits for workers over the years, and are not about to hand their victories back to the free market without resistance. At stake is the familiar issue of the right balance between the welfare state and free enterprise in the **mixed economies** (p. 21) of most European countries. One bright spot is a huge improvement in recent months in German competitiveness, brought about partly through limiting the growth of salaries and reducing the benefits of German workers. The economic effects of the expansions of membership in 2004 and 2007 are still not clear.

Does the European Union represent the trend toward globalization in the world? Or is it a better example of fragmentation? Perhaps the EU is forging the way toward global connections, particularly in terms of trade and economic cooperation. On the other hand, it may be forming a bloc that invites other parts of the world to create blocs of their own, setting the stage for fragmentation and conflict among cultural areas. Only time will tell.

IMPORTANT TERMS AND CONCEPTS

The Commission
Common Market
The Council of Ministers
crisis management
democratic deficit
EC
EEC

enlargement fatigue
European Constitution
European Council
European Court of Justice
European Parliament
European Monetary Union
EU
farm subsidies
free movement
integration
judicial review
Maastrict Treaty
MEPs
mixed economy
monetary policy
requirements for EU membership
supranational organization
"three pillars"
Treaty of Amsterdam

MULTIPLE CHOICE QUESTIONS
THE EUROPEAN UNION

1. An opposite concept to devolution is

   a) succession
   b) fragmentation
   c) sovereignty
   d) integration
   e) globalization

2. The European Union must operate within the long established political culture of Europe, best described as

   a) culturally homogeneous
   b) broadly consensual
   c) diverse, often contentious national identities
   d) diverse, yet cooperative national identities
   e) chaotic, with weak national identities

3. The main motivation for the formation of a supranational organization in post-World War II Europe was to

   a) improve communication among national governments
   b) provide for a common defense
   c) regulate immigration and emigration
   d) improve the economies of European countries
   e) create judicial cooperation

4. All of the following are problems for the EU caused by rapid expansion EXCEPT:

   a) organizational and operational strain
   b) inflation caused by rapidly growing national economies
   c) relatively weak economies of new nations
   d) large numbers of immigrants from the east moving west
   e) integration of non-communist and formerly communist countries

5. All of the following are arguments against Turkey joining the EU EXCEPT:

   a) Turkey has not followed the correct procedures for obtaining membership
   b) the main religion in Turkey is Islam; the main religion in EU countries is Christianity
   c) Turkey has a low Gross Domestic Product per capita
   d) Turkey is not geographically a part of Europe
   e) Turkey has a tradition of authoritarian governments

6. The body of the EU that BEST demonstrates the continuing power of the nation-states is the

   a) Commission
   b) Council of Ministers
   c) European Parliament
   d) European Court of Justice
   e) European Monetary Union

7. Which of the following is an accurate description of the European Parliament?

   a) Its members are directly elected by the people of their respective countries.
   b) The Parliament has the ultimate power to pass laws.
   c) Apportionment of representatives is strictly based on population.
   d) Members of the European Parliament (MEPs) have no real independence from their national governments.
   e) The European Parliament meets in Strasbourg.

8. In which of the following economic areas has EU policy been the LEAST successful?

   a) removing tariffs and other barriers to trade
   b) increasing options for shoppers and consumers in Europe
   c) controlling the money supply
   d) replacing most national currencies with the euro
   e) common agricultural policy

9. All of the following are goals of the EU as defined by treaties or other international agreements EXCEPT:

   a) to develop and enforce crisis management tasks
   b) to establish a central European bank
   c) to form a regional government
   d) to define cooperation among national police forces
   e) to improve agricultural efficiency

10. The European Parliament is the only directly elected body of the EU, and it is the weakest one. This fact may be used to argue that the EU

    a) has not successfully formed a common market
    b) can never replace national governments
    c) will have problems integrating its newest members
    d) does not have true separation of powers
    e) has a democratic deficit

COMMUNIST AND POST-COMMUNIST COUNTRIES

Over the course of the past century, the advanced industrialized democracies (represented by Britain in this book) have become the wealthiest and most powerful countries in the world. However, these countries have been widely criticized for the degree of economic inequality that they allow among their citizens, as well as the big divide in wealth and power between them and the other countries of the world. Have advanced democracies encouraged and valued freedom at the expense of equality to such a degree that we may see them as basically unjust societies? Communist countries answer this question with a resounding "Yes!" and base their governments on the belief that equality is undervalued in capitalist countries such as Britain, France, and the United States.

During the 20th century two large countries declared themselves to be communist nations – the Soviet Union and the People's Republic of China. Together they were home to one and a half billion people, and the economic and political influence of communism was indisputable. Today the Soviet Union has collapsed, leaving in its wake dozens of fledgling democracies, all struggling for their survival. Among major nations, only China remains under communist rule, although Cuba and North Korea are well-known communist regimes as well.

Communism has taken many forms since its birth in the mid-nineteenth century. The variations are so vast that they often appear to have little in common, although all claim to have roots in Marxism.

MARXISM

The father of communism is generally acknowledged to be Karl Marx, who first wrote about his interpretation of history and vision for the future in ***The Communist Manifesto*** in 1848. He saw capitalism – or the free market – as an economic system that exploited workers and increased the gap between the rich and the poor. He believed that conditions in capitalist countries would eventually become so bad that workers would join together in a revolution of the **proletariat** (workers), and overcome the **bourgeoisie**, or owners of factories and other means of production. Marx envisioned a new world after the revolution, one in which social class would disappear because ownership of private property would be banned. According to Marx, communism encourages equality and cooperation, and without property to encourage greed and strife, governments would be unnecessary, and they would wither away.

MARXISM-LENINISM

Russia was the first country to base a political system on Marx's theory. Their **"revolution of the proletariat"** occurred in 1917, but did not follow the steps outlined by Karl Marx. Marx believed that the revolution would first take place in industrialized, capitalist countries. Early 20th century Russia had only begun to industrialize in the late 19th century, and was far behind countries like Britain, Germany, and the United States. However, revolutionary Vladimir Lenin believed that the dictatorial tsar should be overthrown, and that Russian peasants should be released from oppression. Lenin changed the nature of communism by asserting the importance of the **vanguard of the revolution** – a group of revolutionary leaders who could provoke the revolution in non-capitalist Russia. The government he established in 1917 was based on **democratic centralism,** or rule by a few for the good of the many. He proceeded to direct industrialization and agricultural development from a centralized government, and capitalistic ventures were severely restricted in the Soviet Union.

The system that Lenin set up has been incredibly influential because all communist countries that followed based their systems on the Soviet model. Political power rests with the communist party, a relatively small "vanguard" organization that by its very nature allows no competing ideologies to challenge it. The legitimacy of the state rests squarely on the party as the embodiment of communist ideology. Ironically, this feature of communist systems transforms Marxism, with all of its idealistic beliefs in equality for the common citizen, into authoritarianism. Communist states are often associated with the use of force, but they also rely on **co-optation,** or allocation of power throughout various political, social, and economic institutions. Recruitment of elites takes place through *nomenklatura*, the process of filling influential jobs in the state, society, or the economy with people approved and chosen by the communist party. The *nomenklatura* includes not only political jobs, but almost all top positions in other areas as well, such as university presidents, newspaper editors, and military officers. Party approval translates as party membership, so the easiest way for an individual to get ahead is to join the party.

Despite the authoritarian nature of communist states, it is also true that the system does allow for a certain amount of **social mobility**, or the ability for individuals to change their social status over the course of their lifetimes.

MAOISM

China's version of communism began shortly after Lenin's revolution in Russia, but China's government was not controlled by communists until 1949. Almost from the beginning, China's communist leader was Mao Zedong, whose interpretation of Marxism was very different from that of the Soviet leaders. **Maoism** shares Marx's vision of equality and cooperation, but Mao believed very strongly in preserving China's peasant-based society. Although the government sometimes emphasized industrialization during Mao's long rule, Mao was more interested in promoting a revolutionary fervor that strengthened agriculturally-based communities. After Mao's death in 1976, Deng Xiaoping instituted **market-based socialism**, which today allows for a significant infusion of capitalism into the system.

COMMUNIST POLITICAL ECONOMY

Communist ideology led to political economies characterized by **central planning**, in which the ownership of private property and the market mechanism were replaced with the allocation of resources by the state bureaucracy. According to the basic tenets of Marxism, neither principle - ownership of private property nor the market economy – is capable of equitably distributing wealth. Countries with communist political economies have experienced these two problems:

1. **Logistical difficulties** – Planning an entire economy is an extremely difficult task. The larger the economy, the more difficult. In a market economy supply and demand interact spontaneously, so the active management of an economy in communist countries takes more work and energy.

2. **Lack of worker incentives** – Capitalist countries often repeat this criticism of communist political economies. Workers have no fear of losing their jobs, and factories don't worry about going out of business, so there are few incentives for producing good quality products. In the absence of competition and incentives, innovation and efficiency disappear, and as a result, communist economies generally fall behind market economies.

In the case of the USSR, these problems were insurmountable, ending in the dissolution of the Soviet Republics.

GENDER RELATIONS IN COMMUNIST REGIMES

Marxists often see traditional gender relations – with women in subservient roles to men – as resulting from the underlying inequality encouraged by capitalist societies. Men exploit women through the family structure in much the same way that the bourgeoisie exploit the proletariat in the workplace. Communism envisions complete economic, social, and political equality between men and women. As we will see in Russia and China, this ideal was not followed in reality in any of the communist countries. However, it almost certainly increased opportunities for women, so that until the late 20th century, women in communist countries were more likely to work outside the home than women in capitalist countries.

In the pages that follow, we will examine in more detail the influence of communism on Russia and China. For Russia, has communism now been successfully replaced with democracy and capitalism? In China, has the system strayed so far from Marxism that it can hardly be seen as communism today?

IMPORTANT TERMS AND CONCEPTS

bourgeoisie
central planning
Communist Manifesto
co-optation
democratic centralism
Maoism
market-based socialism
Marxism
Marxism-Leninism
nomenklatura
proletariat
revolution of the proletariat
social mobility
"vanguard of the revolution"

GOVERNMENT AND POLITICS IN THE RUSSIAN FEDERATION

AUTHORITARIAN OLIGARCHY, ILLIBERAL DEMOCRACY, OR BUDDING LIBERAL DEMOCRACY?

Between 1945 and 1991 global politics was defined by intense competition between two superpowers: the Soviet Union and the United States. The competition encompassed almost all areas of the world and affected a broad range of economic, political, social, and cultural patterns. As a result, when the Soviet Union surprisingly and suddenly collapsed in 1991, the reverberations were heard everywhere. In the wake of its demise, its component republics broke apart, leaving the Russian Federation as the largest piece, with a population cut in half, but with a land space that allowed it to remain the largest country in the world.

The first president of the Russian Federation was **Boris Yeltsin**, a former member of the old Soviet Politburo who declared the end of the old Soviet-style regime. The "**shock therapy**" reforms that he advocated pointed the country in the direction of democracy and a free-market economy. Yet Yeltsin was an uneven leader, often ill or under the influence of alcohol, who reverted to authoritarian rule whenever he was lucid. A small group of family members and advisers took control from the weakened president, and they ran the country as an **oligarchy**, granting themselves favors and inviting economic and political corruption. However, despite this development, a new constitution was put in place in 1993, and regular, competitive elections have taken place since then.

A new president, **Vladimir Putin**, was elected in 2000 and 2004 without serious conflict, but many observers are still wary of the continuing influence of the oligarchy. Putin has often acted aggressively in containing the oligarchs' political and economic powers, and has followed a clear path toward increasing centralization of power since he came into power. As the election of 2008 approached, Putin followed the Constitution by indicating that he would step down after two terms, but many signs point toward his immense control over who his successor will be. Is Putin's presidency itself a signal that Russia is again becoming an authoritarian state and that its fling with democracy is now over?

Modern Russia, then, is a very unpredictable country. Its historic roots deeply influence every area of life, and Russia has almost no experience with democracy and a free market. Is liberal democracy finally taking hold in Russia, or is the new regime just a smoke and mirrors imitation of the old historic authoritarianism that has characterized Russia for centuries? Or perhaps it is possible that Russia is settling in as an illiberal democracy, with direct elections and other democratic structures in place, but with little hope of strengthening the democratic principles of civil liberties and rights, rule of law, and independence of the judiciary. No one knows at this point, but Russian history and political culture leave room for all three paths. Slavic roots provide a strong tendency toward autocratic rule, but the desire to modernize and compete for world power has been apparent since the late 17th century, and Russia is certainly influenced by the recent democratization of so many other countries of the world.

SOVEREIGNTY, AUTHORITY, AND POWER

For most of the 20th century, public authority and political power emanated from one place: the Politburo of the Communist Party. The Politburo was a small group of men who climbed the ranks of the party through **nomenklatura**, an ordered path from local party soviets to the "commanding heights" of leadership. When the Soviet Union dissolved, its authority and power vanished with it, leaving in place a new government structure with questionable legitimacy. Still, the political culture and historical traditions of Russia are firmly entrenched and have shaped the genesis of the new regime, and undoubtedly will determine the nature of its future.

LEGITIMACY

In these early years of the 21st century, the legitimacy of the Russian government is at very low ebb, partly because the regime change is so recent, and partly because the change appears to be a drastic departure from the past. However, there is growing evidence that the system has stabilized since Vladimir Putin was first elected president in 2000. It is unclear at this point how far Putin might retreat from democratic practices to reestablish some of the old authoritarianism from Russia's traditional political culture.

Historically, political legitimacy has been based on strong, autocratic rule, first by centuries of **tsars**, and then by the firm dictatorship of party leaders during the 20th century. Under communist rule, **Marxism-Leninism** provided the legitimacy base for the party, with its ideology of **democratic centralism**, or rule by a few for the benefit of the many. Although it theoretically only supplemented Marxism-Leninism, **Stalinism** in reality changed the regime to **totalitarianism**, a more complete, invasive form of strong-man rule than the tsars ever were able to implement. After Stalin, two reformers – Nikita Khrushchev and Mikhail Gorbachev – tried to loosen the party's stranglehold on power, only to facilitate the downfall of the regime.

In its attempt to reconstruct the country's power base, the **Constitution of 1993** provided for a strong president, although the power of the position is checked by popular election and by the lower house of the legislature, the **Duma.** The institution of the presidency only dates back to the late 1980s, but the Duma actually existed under the tsars of the late 19th century. Yeltsin attempted to strengthen the Constitution's legitimacy by requiring a referendum by the people to endorse its acceptance. In its short history, the Constitution's legitimacy was seriously tested by attempted coups and intense conflict between President Yeltsin and the Duma. However, the 2000 presidential transition from Yeltsin to Putin went smoothly, an accomplishment that may indicate that the Constitution may be more resilient than it seemed to be a few years ago. Under Putin government operations have stabilized significantly.

HISTORICAL INFLUENCES ON POLITICAL TRADITIONS

Several legacies from Russian history shape the modern political system:

- **Absolute, centralized rule** – From the beginning, Russian tsars held absolute power that they defended with brutality and force. One reason for their tyranny was based on geography: the Russian plain was overrun and conquered by a series of invaders, including the Huns, Vikings, and Mongols. The chaos caused by these takeovers convinced Russian leaders of the importance of firm, unchallenged leadership in keeping their subjects under control. Centralized power also characterized the Communist regime of the 20th century. Some observers believe that Vladimir Putin currently may be steering the country back to this style of leadership.

- **Extensive cultural heterogeneity** – Until the 17th century Russia was a relatively small inland culture, but even then, the numerous invasions from earlier times meant that the area was home to people of wide cultural diversity. This **cultural heterogeneity** was intensified as Russia rapidly expanded its borders, until by the end of the 19th century, the empire stretched from the Baltic Sea to the Pacific Ocean. Since then, the borders of Russia have been in an almost constant state of change, so that ethnicities have been split, thrown together with others, and then split apart again. The name "Russian Federation" reflects the diversity, with countless "republics" and "autonomous regions" based on ethnicity, but with borders impossible to draw because of the blend and locations of people. This heterogeneity has always been a special challenge to Russian rulers.

- **Slavophile v. westernizer** – In the mid-20th century, American diplomat George Kennan identified this conflicting set of political traditions as a major source of problems for Russia. The slavophile ("lover of slavs") tradition has led to a pride in slavic customs, language, religion, and history that causes Russia to resist outside influence. This tendency to value isolation was challenged first by **Tsar Peter the Great** in the late 17th and early 18th century. He used the western model to "modernize" Russia with a stronger army, a navy, an infrastructure of roads and communication, a reorganized bureaucracy, and a **"Window on the West."** The window was St. Petersburg, a city built by Peter on newly conquered lands on the Baltic Sea. His efforts to build Russia's power were followed by those of **Catherine the Great** of the late 18th century, so that by the time of her death, Russia was seen as a major empire. However, their efforts set in place a conflict, since the affection for slavic ways did not disappear with the changes.

- **Revolutions of the 20th century** – The long, autocratic rule of the tsars suddenly and decisively came to an end in 1917 when **Vladimir Lenin's Bolsheviks** seized power, and renamed the country the Union of Soviet Socialist Republics. Communist leaders replaced the tsars, and they ruled according to socialist principles, although the tendency toward absolute, centralized rule did not change. The old social classes, however, were swept away, and the new regime tried to blend elements of westernization (industrialization, economic development, and technological innovation) with those of the slavophile (nationalism, resistance to Western culture and customs). A second revolution occurred in 1991, when the USSR dissolved, and its fifteen republics became independent nations. The Russian Federation, born in that year, is currently struggling to replace the old regime with a new one.

POLITICAL CULTURE

Russia's political culture has been shaped by its geographic setting, cultural orientation, and conflicting attitudes toward the state.

GEOGRAPHIC SETTING

Geographically, Russia is the largest country in the world and encompasses many different ethnicities and climates. Its republics and regions border the Black Sea in the Southwest, the Baltic Sea in the Northwest, the Pacific to the East, the Arctic Ocean to the North, and China to the south. Its borders touch many other nations with vastly different political cultures and customs. Russia is also one of the coldest countries on earth, partly because of northern latitude, but also because so many of its cities are inland. Ironically for a country of its size, warm water ports are few, and its history has been shaped by the desire to conquer countries that block Russian access to the sea. Russia has many natural resources, including oil, gas, and timber, but much of it is locked in Siberia, frozen and very difficult to extract. However, in recent years these resources have been developed, and have fueled significant economic growth.

EASTERN ORTHODOXY

Early in its history, Russians cast their lot with the flourishing city of Constantinople, establishing trade routes in that direction, and adopting the Eastern Orthodox religion. As Constantinople's influence waned, the influence of Western Europe increased, but Russia's orientation meant that it did not share the values generated by the Renaissance, Reformation, Scientific Revolution, and Enlightenment. Instead of individualism, Russians came to value a strong state that could protect them from their geographic vulnerabilities. In contrast to Russian **statism**, the West developed a taste for a **civil society**, or spheres of privacy free from control by the state. Eastern Orthodoxy also was inextricably linked to the state, so the principle of separation of church and state never developed. Even when the Communist state forbade its citizens to practice religion, the acceptance of government control remained.

EQUALITY OF RESULT (contrasted to equality of opportunity)

The Communist regime instilled in the Russian people an appreciation for equality, a value already strong in a country of peasants with similar living standards. Russian egalitarianism has survived the fall of the Soviet Union, and most Russians resent differences of wealth or income. This **"equality of result"** is very different from western **"equality of opportunity"** that sees "getting ahead" as a sign of initiative, hard work, and talent. As a result, the Russian political culture is not particularly conducive to the development of capitalism.

SKEPTICISM ABOUT POWER

Despite their dependence on government initiative, Russian citizens can be surprisingly hostile toward their leadership. Mikhail Gorbachev found this out the hard way when he initiated *glasnost* – a new emphasis on freedom of speech and press – in the 1980s. He received torrents of complaints from citizens that almost certainly contributed to the breakup of the Soviet Union. Today surveys show that citizens have little faith in the political system, although people seem to have much more confidence in Putin than in any other individual leaders or institutions. Since he has come into power, Putin's approval ratings have remained between 70 and 80 percent, but no other public officials have comparable popularity, including governors of regions, army generals, Duma members, or the police. The Russian people also appear to have little confidence in nongovernmental leaders, such as entrepreneurs, bankers, and media personalities.

THE IMPORTANCE OF NATIONALITY

Even though cultural heterogeneity has almost always been characteristic of the Russian political culture, people tend to categorize others based on their nationality, and they often discriminate against groups based on long-held stereotypes. Russians generally admire the Baltic people for their "civility"and sophistication, but they sometimes express disdain for the Muslim-Turkic people of Central Asia. In return, governments in those areas have passed laws discouraging Russians from remaining within their borders. Anti-Semitism was strong in tsarist Russia, and today some nationalists blame Jews for Russia's current problems.

POLITICAL AND ECONOMIC CHANGE

In contrast to Britain, Russia has almost always had difficulty with gradual and ordered change. Instead, its history reflects a resistance to change by reform and a tendency to descend into chaos or resort to revolution when contradictory forces meet. The most successful tsars, such as Peter the Great and Catherine the Great, understood the dangers of chaos in Russia, and often resorted to force in order to keep their power. The 19th century tsars faced the infiltration of Enlightenment ideas of democracy and individual rights, and those that tried reforms that allowed gradual inclusion of these influences often failed. For example, Alexander II, who freed Russian serfs and experimented with local assemblies, was assassinated by revolutionaries in 1881. The forces that led to his assassination later blossomed into full-blown revolution, the execution of the last tsar, and the establishment of a communist regime. Likewise, the late 19th century tsars' attempts to gradually industrialize Russia were largely unsuccessful, but Joseph Stalin's Five-Year Plans that called for rapid, abrupt economic change led to the establishment of the Soviet Union as one of two superpowers that dominated the world for a half century after the conclusion of World War II. In the late 20th century, Mikhail Gorbachev's attempts to reform the political and economic systems failed, and change again came abruptly with a failed coup d'etat, and the sudden collapse of the Soviet Union.

Russia's history is characterized by three distinct time periods:

- **A long period of autocratic rule by tsars** – Tsars ruled Russia from the 14th to the early 20th century. Control of Russia was passed down through the Romanov family from the 17th century on, but transitions were often accompanied by brutality and sometimes assassination.

- **20th century rule by the Communist Party** – Communist rule began in 1917 when Vladimir Lenin's Bolsheviks seized control of the government after the last tsar, Nicholas II, was deposed. The regime toppled in 1991 when a failed coup from within the government created chaos.

- **An abrupt regime change to democracy and a free market in 1991** – President Boris Yeltsin put western-style reforms in place to create the Russian Federation.

The two transitions between time periods were sparked by revolution and quick, dramatic change. The Slavic influence has brought some continuity to Russia's history, but in general change has rarely been evolutionary and gradual. Instead, long periods of authoritarian rule have been punctuated by protest and violence.

TSARIST RULE

The first tsars were princes of Moscow, who cooperated with their 13th century Mongol rulers, and were rewarded for their assistance with land and power. But when Mongol rule weakened, the princes declared themselves "tsars" in the tradition of the "Caesars" of ancient Rome. The tsars were autocratic from the beginning, and tightly controlled their lands in order to protect them from other invasions and attacks. The tsars also headed the **Russian Orthodox Church,** so that they were seen as both political and religious leaders. Early Russia was isolated from Western Europe by its orientation to the Eastern Orthodox world, and long distances separated Russian cities from major civilizations to the south and east.

WESTERN INFLUENCE

In the late 17th and early 18th centuries, **Tsar Peter the Great** introduced western technology and culture in an attempt to increase Russia's power and influence. From his early childhood, he was intrigued by the West, and he became the first tsar to travel to Germany, Holland, and England. There he learned about shipbuilding and other types of technology. He brought engineers, carpenters, and architects to Russia, and set the country on a course toward world power. **Catherine the Great**, who originally came from Germany, ruled Russia during the late 18th century, and managed to gain warm water access to the Black Sea, an accomplishment that had eluded Peter. Both looked to the West to help develop their country, but neither abandoned absolute rule. Catherine read widely, and was very interested in Enlightenment thought, but she checked any impulses she had to apply them to her rule. Instead, she became an **enlightened despot**, or one who ruled absolutely, but with the good of the country in mind. Tsars after Peter and Catherine alternated between emphasizing Slavic roots and tolerating western style reform, although none of them successfully responded to the revolutionary movement growing within their country during the 19th century.

NINETEENTH CENTURY TSARS

Russia was brought into direct contact with the West when Napoleon invaded in 1812. Alexander I successfully resisted the attack, but at great cost to the empire. Western thought also influenced Russian intellectuals who saw no room for western political institutions to grow under the tsars' absolutism. Their frustration erupted in the **Decembrist Revolt of 1825**, which was crushed ruthlessly by Nicholas I. By mid-century the Russian defeat in the **Crimean War** convinced many of the tsar's critics that Russian ways were indeed backward and in need of major reform. Nineteenth century tsars reacted to their demands by sending the secret police to investigate and by exiling or executing the dissenters.

Of all the 19th century tsars, the only one who seriously sponsored reform was Alexander II. However, even though he freed Russia's serfs and set up regional *zemstvas* (assemblies), the increasingly angry *intelligentsia* did not think his actions went far enough. Alexander II was assassinated in 1881 by his critics, and his son Alexander III reacted by undoing the reforms and intensifying the efforts of the secret police.

THE REVOLUTION OF 1917, LENIN, AND STALIN

The most immediate cause of the Revolution of 1917 was Russia's ineffectiveness in fighting the Russo-Japanese War and World War I. Tsar Nicholas II was indeed in the wrong place at the wrong time, but he also was a weak ruler who had no control over the armies. The first signs of the revolution were in 1905, when riots and street fighting broke out in protest to Russian losses in the war with Japan. The tsar managed to put that revolution down, but the state finally collapsed in 1917 in the midst of World War I. Russian soldiers were fighting without guns or shoes, and mass defections from the war front helped send the state into chaos.

LENIN AND THE BOLSHEVIKS

By the 1890s some of the revolutionists in Russia were **Marxists** who were in exile, along with other dissidents. However, according to Marxism, socialist revolutions would take first place not in Russia, but in capitalist countries like Germany, France, and England. At the turn of the century, Russia was still primarily an agricultural society with little industrial development. In his 1905 pamphlet *What Is To Be Done*, **Vladimir Lenin** changed the meaning of Marxism when he argued for **democratic centralism**, or a "vanguard" leadership group that would lead the revolution in the name of the people. Lenin believed that the situation in Russia was so bad that the revolution could occur even though it was a non-industrialized society. Lenin's followers came to be called the **Bolsheviks**, and they took control of the government in late 1917. Russia was then renamed the Union of Soviet Socialist Republics.

By 1918 a civil war had broken out between the **White Army**, led by Russian military leaders and funded by the Allied Powers, and the **Red Army** led by Lenin. The Reds won, and in 1920 Lenin instituted his **New Economic Policy**, which allowed a great deal of private ownership to exist under a centralized leadership. The plan brought relative prosperity to farmers, but it did not promote industrialization. Would Lenin have moved on to a more socialist approach? No one knows, because Lenin died in 1924 before his plans unfolded and before he could name a successor. A power struggle followed, and the "Man of Steel" that won control led the country to the heights of totalitarianism.

STALINISM

Stalin vastly changed Lenin's democratic centralism (also known as **Marxism-Leninism).** Stalin placed the Communist Party at the center of control, and allowed no other political parties to compete with it. Party members were carefully selected, with only about 7% of the population actually joining it. Communists ran local, regional, and national governments, and leaders were identified through *nomenklatura*, or the process of party members selecting promising recruits from the lower levels. Most top government officials also belonged to the **Central Committee**, a group of 300 party leaders that met twice a year. Above the Central Committee was the **Politburo**, the heart and soul of the Communist Party. This group of about twelve men ran the country, and their decisions were carried out by government agencies and departments. The head of the Politburo was the **general secretary**, who assumed the full power as dictator of the country. Joseph Stalin was the general secretary of the Communist Party from 1927 until his death in 1953.

Collectivization and Industrialization

Stalin's plan for the U.S.S.R. had two parts: **collectivization and industrialization**. Stalin replaced the NEP with "**collective farms**" that were state run and supposedly more efficient. Private land ownership was done away with, and the farms were intended to feed workers in the cities who contributed to the industrialization of the nation. Some peasants resisted, particularly those that owned larger farms. These **kulaks** were forced to move to cities or to labor camps, and untold numbers died at the hands of government officials.

With the agricultural surplus from the farms, Stalin established his first **Five Year Plan**, which set ambitious goals for production of heavy industry, such as oil, steel, and electricity. Other plans followed, and all were carried out for individual factories by **Gosplan,** the Central State Planning Commission. Gosplan became the nerve center for the economy, and determined production and distribution of virtually all goods in the Soviet Union.

Stalinism, then, is this two-pronged program of collectivization and industrialization, carried out by central planning, and executed with force and brutality.

Stalin's Foreign Policy

During the 1930s Stalin's primary focus was internal development, so his foreign policy was intended to support that goal. He advocated "socialism in one country" to emphasize his split with traditional Marxism, and he tried to ignore the fascist threat from nearby Germany and Italy. Stalin signed a non-aggression pact with Nazi Germany in 1939, only to be attacked by Germany the following year. Russia then joined sides with the Allies for the duration of World War II, but tensions between east and west were often apparent at conferences, and as soon as the war ended, the situation escalated into the Cold War. These significant shifts in foreign policy all accommodated his main goal: the industrial development of the USSR.

The Purges

Joseph Stalin is perhaps best known for his purges: the execution of millions of citizens, including up to one million party members. He became obsessed with disloyalty in the party ranks, and he ordered the execution of his own generals and other members of the Politburo and Central Committee. Stalin held total power, and by the time of his death in 1953, many speculated that he had gone mad. His successor, Nikita Khrushchev, set about to reform Stalinism by loosening its totalitarian nature and publicly denouncing the purges.

REFORM UNDER KHRUSHCHEV AND GORBACHEV

After Stalin died in 1953, a power struggle among top Communist Party leaders resulted in **Nikita Khrushchev** being chosen as party secretary and premier of the USSR. In 1956 he gave his famous **secret speech,** in which he revealed the existence of a letter written by Lenin before he died. The letter was critical of Stalin, and Khrushchev used it to denounce Stalin's rules and practices, particularly the purges that he sponsored. This denouncement led to **deStalinization,** a process that led to reforms, such as loosening government censorship of the press, decentralization of economic decision-making, and restructuring of the collective farms. In foreign policy, Khrushchev advocated "peaceful coexistence," or relaxation of tensions between the United States and the Soviet Union. He was criticized from the beginning for the suggested reforms, and his diplomatic and military failure in the Cuban Missile Crisis ensured his loss of control. Furthermore, most of his reforms did not appear to be working by the early 1960s. He was replaced by the much more conservative **Leonid Brezhnev,** who ended the reforms and tried to cope with the increasing economic problems that were just under the surface of Soviet power.

After Brezhnev died in 1982, he was eventually replaced in 1985 by a reformer from a younger generation, **Mikhail Gorbachev.** Gorbachev was unlike any previous Soviet leader in that he not only looked and acted more "western," but he also was more open to western-style reforms than any other, including Khrushchev. Gorbachev inherited far more problems than any outsider realized at the time, and many of his reforms were motivated by shear necessity to save the country from economic disaster. His program was three-pronged:

- *Glasnost* – This term translates from the Russian as "openness," and it allowed more open discussion of political, social and economic issues as well as open criticism of the government. Although this reform was applauded by western nations, it caused many problems for Gorbachev. After so many years of repression, people vented hostility toward the government that encouraged open revolt, particularly among some of the republics that wanted independence from Soviet control.

- **Democratization** – Gorbachev believed that he could keep the old Soviet structure, including Communist Party control, but at the same time insert a little democracy into the system. Two such moves included the creation of 1) a new Congress of People's Deputies with directly elected representatives and 2) a new position of "President" that was selected by the Congress. The reforms did bring a bit of democracy. However, many of the new deputies were critical of Gorbachev, increasing the level of discord within the government.

- *Perestroika* – This economic reform was Gorbachev's most radical, and also his least successful. Again, he tried to keep the old Soviet structure, and modernize from within. Most significantly, it transferred many economic powers held by the central government to private hands and the market economy. Specific reforms included authorization of some privately owned companies, penalties for under-performing state factories, leasing of farm land outside the collective farms, price reforms, and encouragement of joint ventures with foreign companies.

None of Gorbachev's reforms were ever fully carried out because the Revolution of 1991 swept him out of office.

A FAILED COUP AND THE REVOLUTION OF 1991

In August 1991 "conservatives" (those that wanted to abandon Gorbachev's reforms) from within the Politburo led a coup d'etat that tried to remove Gorbachev from office. The leaders included the vice-president, the head of the KGB (Russian secret police), and top military advisers. The coup failed when popular protests broke out, and soldiers from the military defected rather than support their leaders. The protesters were led by **Boris Yeltsin**, the elected president of the Russian Republic and former Politburo member. Yeltsin had been removed from the Politburo a few years earlier because his radical views offended the conservatives. Yeltsin advocated more extreme reform measures than Gorbachev did, and he won his position as president of the Russian Republic as a result of new voting procedures put in place by Gorbachev.

Gorbachev was restored to power, but the USSR only had a few months to live. By December 1991 eleven republics had declared their independence, and eventually Gorbachev was forced to announce the end of the union, which put him out of a job. The fifteen republics went their separate ways, but Boris Yeltsin emerged as the president of the largest and most powerful republic, now renamed the Russian Federation.

THE RUSSIAN FEDERATION: 1991-PRESENT

Once the Revolution of 1991 was over, Boris Yeltsin proceeded with his plans to create a western-style democracy. The old Soviet structure was destroyed, but the same problems that haunted Gorbachev were still there. The **Constitution of 1993** created a three-branch government, with a president, a prime minister, a lower legislative house called the **Duma**, and a **Constitutional Court**. Conflict erupted between Yeltsin and the Duma, and the Russian economy did not immediately respond to the "**shock therapy**" (an immediate market economy) that the government prescribed. Yeltsin also proved to be a much poorer president than he was a revolutionary leader. His frequent illnesses and alcoholism almost certainly explain the erratic behavior that led him to hire and fire prime ministers in quick succession. Yeltsin resigned in the months before the election of 2000, and Prime Minister Vladimir Putin became acting president. Although Putin supported Yeltsin's reforms, he was widely seen as a more conservative leader who many hoped would bring stability to the newly formed government. As his presidency has progressed, many believe that Putin has retreated significantly from the commitments that Yeltsin made to the establishment of a democratic system.

MILESTONES IN RUSSIAN POLITICAL DEVELOPMENT

988 C.E. - Russian Tzar Vladimir I converted to Orthodox Christianity, setting Russia on a different course of development from Western Europe.

1613 The Romanov family came to power and ruled until 1917.

1689 - 1725 Peter the Great ruled Russia, bringing the dynamic of "slavophile vs. westernizer" to Russian political development.

1762 - 1796 Catherine the Great, the second great westernizer, solidified and expanded Peter's reforms, though she still ruled with an iron hand, as all Russian tsars did.

1917 The last tsar was deposed, and the Bolshevik Revolution put Vladimir Lenin in control of the U.S.S.R.

1917-1921 The Russian civil war raged as many factions inside and outside Russia fought to oust Lenin from power. Lenin solidified his power in 1921.

1927-1953 Joseph Stalin ruled the U.S.S.R., reinterpreting the meaning of communism and instituting his programs of collectivization and industrialization.

1991 A coup against General Secretary Mikhail Gorbachev failed, but also instigated a process that led to the collapse of the Soviet Union.

1993 The new Russian Constitution put in place the current regime.

CITIZENS, SOCIETY AND THE STATE

Russian citizens are affected by many contradictory influences from their political culture. When questioned, most say that they support the idea of a democratic government for Russia, although many do not believe that one exists today. However, they also like the idea of a strong state and powerful political leaders, characteristics that help to explain the popularity of Vladimir Putin as president.

CLEAVAGES

The Russian Federation has many societal cleavages that greatly impact policymaking, including nationality, religion, social class, and rural vs. urban divisions.

NATIONALITY

The most important single cleavage in the Russian Federation is **nationality**. Although about 80% are Russians, the country includes sizeable numbers of Tatars, Ukrainians, Armenians, Chuvashes, Bashkis, Byelorussians, and Moldavians. These cleavages determine the organization of the country into a "federation," with "autonomous regions," republics, and provinces whose borders are based on ethnicity. Like the breakaway republics of 1991, many would like to have their independence, although most have trade benefits from the Russian government that induce them to stay within the Federation. A notable exception is **Chechnya,** a primarily Muslim region in the Caucasus that has fought for years for their freedom. The Russian government has had considerable difficulty keeping Chechnya a part of Russia, and the independence movement there is still very strong. In recent years, Chechens have been involved in terrorist acts, including the 2004 seizure of a school in southern Russia that resulted in gunfire and explosions that killed more than 350 people, many of them children. Almost certainly, other regions within Russia's borders are watching, and the government knows that if Chechen rebels are successful, other independence movements may break out in the country. In an effort to gain legitimacy for the Russian government in Chechnya, a referendum was held to vote on a new constitution for the region. The constitution was approved by the Chechen voters, even though it declared that their region was an "inseparable part" of Russia.

RELIGION

Tsarist Russia was overwhelmingly Russian Orthodox, with the tsar serving as spiritual head of the church. In reaction, the Soviet Union prohibited religious practices of all kinds, so that most citizens lost their religious affiliations during the twentieth century. Boris Yeltsin encouraged the Russian Orthodox Church to reestablish itself, partly as a signal of his break with communism, but also as a reflection of old Russian nationalism. Today most ethnic Russians identify themselves as Russian Orthodox, but they are still largely nonreligious, with only a small percentage regularly attending church services.

The growing acceptance of the church was demonstrated in 2007, when the Russian Church Abroad reunited with the Russian Orthodox Church. The Russian Church Abroad had split after the Bolshevik Revolution in 1917, vowing never to return as long as the "godless regime" was in power. In a meeting in 2003 in New York, Putin met with leaders of the church to assure them "that this godless regime is no longer there...You are sitting with a believing president." (*New York Times*, May 17, 2007). After the reunion in 2007 Moscow still retained ultimate authority in appointments and other church matters.

Other religions are represented in small percentages – Roman Catholic, Jews, Muslim and Protestant. Since the current regime is so new and political parties so uncertain, no clear pattern has emerged that indicate political attitudes of religious v. nonreligious citizens. However, in the past Russia has generally followed a pragmatic combination of authoritarianism and flexibility toward minorities.

RELIGION AND ETHNIC GROUPS IN RUSSIA	
RELIGION	**ETHNIC GROUPS**
Russian Orthodox 15 - 20%	Russian 79.8%
Muslim 10 - 15%	Tatar 3.8%
Other Christian 2%	Ukrainian 2%
note: estimates are of practicing worshipers; Russia has large	Chuvash 1.1%
numbers of non-practice believers and non-believers, a legacy of Soviet rule	Other 12.1%

One pattern worth noting is the rapid rise in the Muslim share of the population in recent years. Russia has more Muslims than any other European state except Turkey, and some estimates show as many as 20 million Muslims in the country. Muslims are concentrated in three areas:

1. **Moscow** – Muslims form a large share of laborers who have migrated to Moscow in recent years to find work.

2. **The Caucasus** – In this area between the Black Sea and the Caspian Sea, many ethnicities (including Chechens) are Muslim. This area is often seen as a hot spot of trouble (along with Palestine, Kashmir, and Bosnia) for Muslims. The repression of Chechens, as well as intermittent violence in the entire region, has been the biggest issue for Putin as he has tried to cultivate Russia's role in global Muslim affairs.

3. **Bashkortostan and Tatarstan** – Muslim relations with Russians are generally calmer in these two regions than in the Caucasus. Tatarstan's Muslim president, Mintimer Shaimiev, has accompanied Mr. Putin around the Middle East, as the president tries to restructure Russia's image as a country supportive of Islam.

MAIN REGIONS WITH MUSLIM POPULATIONS

Moscow

Tatarstan nad
Bashkortostan

Caucasus

SOCIAL CLASS

The Soviet attempts to destroy social class differences in Russia were at least partially successful. The old noble/peasant distinction of tsarist Russia was abolished, but was replaced by another cleavage: members of the Communist Party and nonmembers. Only about 7% of the citizenry were party members, but all political leaders were recruited from this group. Economic favors were granted to party members as well, particularly those of the Central Committee and the Politburo. However, egalitarian views were promoted, and the ***nomenklatura*** process of recruiting leaders from lower levels of the party was generally blind to economic and social background. Today Russian citizens appear to be more egalitarian in their political and social views than people of the established democracies.

Many observers of modern Russia note that a new socio-economic class may be developing within the context of the budding market economy: entrepreneurs that have recently amassed fortunes from new business opportunities. Although the fortunes of many of these newly rich Russians were wiped away by the 1997 business bust, others survived and new ones have emerged since then. Boris Yeltsin's government contributed to this class by distributing huge favors to them, and many believe that a small but powerful group of entrepreneurs sponsored the presidential campaign of Vladimir Putin in 2000. In the Putin era, oligarchs have come under fire for various alleged and real illegal activities, particularly the underpayment of taxes in the businesses they acquired. Vladimir Gusinsky (MediaMost) and Boris Berezovsky were both effectively exiled, and the most prominent, Mikhail Khodorkovsky (Yukos Oil), was arrested in October 2003, sentenced to eight years in prison, with his company trying to protect itself from being dismantled.

RURAL VS. URBAN

Industrialization since the era of Joseph Stalin has led to an increasingly urban population, with about 73% of all Russians now living in cities, primarily in the western part of the country. The economic divide between rural and urban people is wide, although recent economic woes have beset almost all Russians no matter where they live. City dwellers are more likely to be well educated and in touch with western culture, but the political consequences of these differences are unclear in the unsettled current political climate.

BELIEFS AND ATTITUDES

In the old days of the Soviet Union, citizens' beliefs and attitudes toward their government were molded by Communist Party doctrines. At the heart of this doctrine was **Marxism**, which predicted the demise of the capitalist west. This belief fed into Russian nationalism and supported the notion that the Russian government and way of life would eventually prevail. The ideals of the revolutionary era of the early 20th century envisioned a world transformed by egalitarianism and the elimination of poverty and oppression. As **Stalinism** set in, the ideals shifted to pragmatic internal development, and many of the old tendencies toward absolutism and repression returned. The collapse of the Soviet Union brought out much hostility toward the government that is reflected in the attitudes of Russian citizens today.

- **Mistrust of the government** - Political opinion polls are very recent innovations in Russian politics, so information about citizens' attitudes and beliefs toward their government is scarce. However, the limited evidence does reflect a great deal of alienation toward the political system. Most polls show that people support democratic ideals, including free elections and widespread individual civil liberties and rights. However, most do not trust government officials or institutions to convert these ideals to reality. Alienation is also indicated by a low level of participation in interest groups, including trade unions and other groups that people belonged to in the days of the Soviet Union. An interesting bit of contradictory evidence, though, is the high level of approval that President Vladimir Putin has enjoyed. Other Russian public officials do not share his popularity.

- **Statism** - Despite high levels of mistrust in government, Russian citizens still expect the state to take an active role in their lives. For most of Russian history, citizens have functioned more as subjects than as participants, and the central government of the Soviet Union was strong enough to touch and control many aspects of citizens' lives. Today Russians expect a great deal from their government, even if they have been disappointed in the progress of reform in recent years.

- **Economic beliefs** - Boris Yeltsin's market reforms created divisions in public opinion regarding market reform. Nearly all parties and electoral groups support the market transition, but those with more favorable opinions of the old Soviet regime are less enthusiastic. At the other end of the spectrum are those that support rapid market reform, including privatization and limited government regulation. The latter approach was favored by Yeltsin, and his "shock therapy" marketization was blamed by his critics for the steep economic decline that characterized the 1990s.

- **Westernization** - Political opinion follows the old divide of **slavophile vs. westernizer.** Some political parties emphasize nationalism and the defense of Russian interests and Slavic culture. These parties also tend to favor a strong military and protection from foreign economic influence. On the other hand, reform parties strongly support the integration of Russia into the world economy and global trade.

Economic beliefs and attitudes toward the west also shape attitudes about whether or not the modern regime should integrate elements of the old Soviet government into its policymaking. Some citizens are nostalgic about the "good old days" when everyone had a guaranteed income, and they are most likely to support the Communist Party that still exists within the competitive election system. Some observers are seeing a generational split between those that remember better times under Soviet power, and those that have come of age during the early days of the Russian Federation.

POLITICAL PARTICIPATION

Russian citizens did actually vote during Soviet rule in the 20th century. In fact, their voting rate was close to 100% because they faced serious consequences if they stayed home. However, until Gorbachev brought about reforms in the late 1980s, the elections were not competitive, and citizens voted for candidates that were hand picked by the Communist leadership. Gorbachev created competitive elections in the Soviet Union, but because no alternate political parties existed yet, voter choice was limited to the designated party candidate vs. anyone from within party ranks that wanted to challenge the official candidate. In some cases, this choice made a real difference, because Boris Yeltsin was elected as an "alternate candidate" to be president of the then Russian Republic.

Since 1991 voter turnout in the Russian Federation has been fairly high: higher than in the United States, but somewhat lower than turnout rates in Britain and France. Political alienation is reflected in the 50.3% rate in the 1993 Duma elections, but those elections followed a failed attempt by the Duma to take over the country. Voter turnout in the Duma election in December 2003 was just under 56%. Meanwhile, voter turnouts have been declining in recent presidential elections, with almost 75% of eligible citizens voting in the first presidential election in 1991, and less that 65% voting in 2004.

CIVIL SOCIETY

Despite the relatively high voter turnouts, participation in other forms of political activities is relatively low. Part of this lack of participation is due to a relatively undeveloped **civil society**, or private organizations and associations outside of politics. For example, most Russians don't attend church on a regular basis, nor do they belong to sports or recreational clubs, literary or other cultural groups, charitable organizations, or labor unions. Only about 1% report belonging to a political party. On the other hands, Russians are not necessarily disengaged from politics. Many report that they regularly read newspapers, watch news on television, and discuss politics with family and friends.

Civil society appears to be growing in Russia. Before the 1917 Revolution, little civil society existed because of low economic development, authoritarianism, and feudalism. Soviet authorities argued that only the party could and should represent the people's interests, and so state-sponsored organizations appeared in a **state corporatist** arrangement with the government clearly in control of channeling the voice of the people. The Russian Orthodox Church was brought tightly under control of the Communist Party. With the advent of glasnost in the 1980s, however, civil society slowly began to emerge, and since that time many organizations have formed to express points of view on many different issues, including the environment, ethnicity, gender, human rights, and health care. Despite the proliferation of these groups, the government has placed severe restrictions on their activities, especially on groups that are openly critical of the government's policies. Rather than directly attacking the groups, the government has used a number of tactics to weaken them, such as investigating sources of income, making registration with the authorities difficult, and police harassment.

RUSSIAN YOUTH GROUPS

In recent years Vladimir Putin has created a handful of youth movements to support the government. The largest is **Nashi,** and others are the Youth Guard, and Locals. All are part of an effort to build a following of loyal, patriotic young people and to defuse any youthful resistance that could emerge during the sensitive presidential election of 2008. Nashi has organized mass marches in support of Mr. Putin and staged demonstrations over foreign policy issues that resulted in the physical harassment of the British and Estonian ambassadors. For example, after Estonia relocated a Soviet-era war memorial in April 2007, Nashi laid siege to the Estonian Embassy in Moscow, throwing rocks, disrupting traffic, and tearing down the Estonian flag. Members of the group attacked the Estonian ambassador, and her guards had to use pepper spray to defend her.

Nashi's opponents deride the organization as a modern "transmission belt" (p. 36) version of Komsomol, the youth wing of the Communist Party of the Soviet Union. Nashi receives grants from the government and large state-run businesses, so critics of the group see it as an arm of an increasingly authoritarian state.

POLITICAL INSTITUTIONS

Russian history includes a variety of regime types, but the tradition is highly authoritarian. The reforms that began in the early 1990s are truly experimental, and only time will tell whether democracy and a free market economy will take root. Even if they do, the nature of the regime must take into account Russian political culture and traditions. Current political parties, elections, and institutions of government are all new, and their functions within the political system are very fluid and likely to change within the next few years. However, the Russian Federation has survived its first few rocky years, and many experts believe that at least some aspects of Russian government and politics are beginning to settle into a pattern.

Even though the Soviet Union was highly centralized, it still maintained a **federal government structure**. The Russian Federation has retained this model, and the current regime consists of eighty-nine regions, twenty-one of which are ethnically non-Russian by majority. Each region is bound by treaty to the Federation, but not all – including Chechnya – have signed on. Most of these regions are called "republics," and because the central government was not strong under Yeltsin, many ruled themselves almost independently. In the early 1990s, several republics went so far as to make claims of sovereignty that amounted to near or complete independence. Many saw the successful bid of the former Soviet states for independence as role models, and they believed that their own status would change as well. Chechnya's bid for independence and the war that followed are good examples of this sentiment. Some regions are much stronger than others, so power is devolved unequally across the country, a condition called **asymmetric federalism.**

 Vladimir Putin has cracked down on regional autonomy recently, ordering the army to shell even Chechnya into submission. Several measures that Putin has imposed are:

- **Creation of super-districts** – In 2000 seven new federal districts were created to encompass all of Russia. Each district is headed by a presidential appointee, who supervises the local authorities as Putin sees fit.

- **Removal of governors** - A law allows the president to remove a governor from office that refuses to subject local law to the national constitution.

- **Appointment of governors** - Putin further centralized power in Moscow in late 2004 with a measure that ended direct election of the eighty-nine regional governors. Instead, the governors now are nominated by the president, and then confirmed by regional legislatures.

- **Changes in the Federation Council** – Originally the Federation Council (the upper legislative house) was comprised of the governors and Duma heads of each region. In 2002 a Putin-backed change prohibited these officials from serving themselves, although they were still allowed to appoint council members.

As a result of all these changes, the "federation" is highly centralized.

LINKAGE INSTITUTIONS

Groups that link citizens to government are still not strong in Russia, a situation that undermines recent attempts to establish a democracy. Political parties were highly unstable and fluid during the 1990s, and since Putin's election in 2000, more and more power has been concentrated in his party, so that after the parliamentary elections of late 2003 and presidential elections of early 2004, no strong opposing political parties were in existence. Interest groups have no solid footing in civil society since private organizations are weak, and the media has come more and more under government control.

PARTIES

Most established democracies had many years to develop party and electoral systems. However, Russians put theirs together almost overnight after the Revolution of 1991. Many small, factional political parties ran candidates in the first Duma elections in 1993, and by 1995, 43 parties were on the ballot. Many of the parties revolved around a particular leader or leaders, such as the "Bloc of General Andrey Nikolaev and Academician Svyaloslav Fyodorov," the "Yuri Boldyrev Movement," or "Yabloko," which is an acronym for its three founders. Others reflected a particular issue, such as the "Party of Pensioners," "Agrarian Party of Russia," or "Women of Russia." By 1999 the number of parties who ran Duma candidates had shrunk to 26, but many of the parties were new ones, including Vladimir Putin's Unity Party. Needless to say, with these fluctuations going on, citizens have had no time to develop party loyalties, leadership in Russia continues to be personalistic, and political parties remain weak and fluid.

Within this context, the most influential parties in the 2003 Duma elections and the 2004 presidential elections were United Russia and the Communist Party of the Russian Republic. All other parties received only small percentages of the vote.

United Russia

The party was founded in April 2001 as a merger of Fatherland All-Russia Party, and the Unity Party of Russia. The Unity Party was put together by oligarch Boris Berezovsky and other entrepreneurs to support then Prime Minister Vladimir Putin in the presidential election of 2000. The merger put even more political support behind Putin. United Russia won 221 of the 450 Duma seats in the election of 2003, although this figure underestimates the party's strength since many minor parties are Putin supporters or clients. Putin, running as United Russia's candidate, won the presidential election of 2004 with 71% of the vote and no serious challengers from any other political parties. Ideologically, United Russia is hard to define except that it is pro-Putin.

The Communist Party of the Russian Federation (CPRF)

The Communist Party of the old Soviet Union survives today as the second strongest party in the Duma, even though they have not yet won a presidential election. After the election of 1995, they held 157 of the Duma's 450 members, and even though they lost seats in the 1999 election, the party remained an important force in Russian politics. However, the party's support dropped significantly in the parliamentary elections of 2003, winning only 12.6% of the vote and 51 of the 450 Duma seats. The party's leader, **Gennady Zyuganov**, came in second in the 1996 and 2000 presidential elections, but his percentage in the second round fell from 40.3% in 1996 to 29.21% in 2000. Zyuganov dropped out of the presidential election of 2004, and in July 2004, a breakaway faction led by Vladimir Tikhonov weakened the party further.

The CPRF is not exactly like the old Communist Party, but it is far less reformist than other parties are. Zyuganov opposed many reforms during the Gorbachev era, and he continues to represent to supporters the stability of the old regime. The party emphasizes centralized planning and nationalism, and implies an intention to regain territories lost when the Soviet Union broke apart.

Reformist Parties

Russia has two parties that have been consistently reformist, although both of them are in jeopardy of disappearing from the political scene before the next election.

- **Yabloko** has survived all elections since 1993, and it has been consistently reformist. Its name is an acronym for its three founders, but "yabloko" also means "apple" in Russian. It has taken the strongest stand for pro-democracy, and it generally does best among intellectuals who have supported reform since the days of Gorbachev rule. The leader – Grigori Yavlinski – came in third in the Russian presidential election of 2000, but he received only 5.8% of the vote. The party gained only 4.4% of the vote in the parliamentary elections of 2003, making the party ineligible for seats under proportional representation. They won only 4 seats in the Duma.

- **Union of Right Forces** is not "rightist" in orientation. The name only implies that they are "right" in the sense of understanding the truth. It emphasizes the development of a free market, and backs further privatization of industry. They had 29 representatives in the Duma before the election of 2003, but like Yabloko, they received less than 5% of the vote, and currently have only 3 seats in the Duma.

Liberal Democrats

This misnamed party is by far the most controversial. It is headed by **Vladimir Zhirinovsky** who has made headlines around the world for his extreme nationalist positions. He regularly attacks reformist leaders, and particularly disliked Yeltsin. He has implied that Russia under his leadership would use nuclear weapons on Japan, and he makes frequent anti-Semitic remarks (despite his Jewish origins).

He has also brought the wrath of Russian women by making blatantly sexist comments. His party was reformulated as "Zhirinovsky's bloc" for the 2000 presidential election, when he received only 2.7% of the vote. The party did pick up seats in the 2003 Duma elections, receiving about 11% of the total vote, as well as 37 seats.

Overall, since 1993 ideological parties have faded in importance and have been replaced by **parties of power**, or parties strongly sponsored by economic and political powerholders. For example, United Russia is Putin's party, created by powerful oligarchs to get him elected. As long as Putin is in power, United Russia will be, too, and if he is able to orchestrate who his successor will be, the party of power will probably remain the voters' choice.

ELECTIONS

The Russian political system supports three types of national votes:

- **Referendum** – The Constitution of 1993 allowed the president to call for national referenda by popular vote on important issues. Even before the Constitution was written, Boris Yeltsin called for a referendum on his job performance. The people clearly supported his reforms, but his majorities were not overwhelming. The second referendum was held later in the year, and the people voted in favor of the new Constitution. A regional referendum was held in Chechnya in 2003 to approve a constitution for the area. The constitution was approved, including the phrase that declared Chechnya to be an "inseparable part" of Russia.

- **Duma elections** – Russian citizens have gone to the polls four times to elect Duma representatives (1993, 1995, 1999, and 2003). The Duma has 450 seats, half of which are elected by proportional representation, and the other half by single-member districts. Parties must get at least 5% of the total vote to get any seats according to proportional representation, but many of the single-member district seats are held by local power brokers with no major party affiliation. Since 1993 parties have merged and disappeared, so that only a few have survived to the present. Elections follow a two-round pattern, with the top two candidates competing in a runoff two weeks after the first round.

- **Presidential elections** – Presidential elections also follow the two-round model that the Duma has. In 2000 Putin received 52.94% of the vote, so no run-off election was required, since he captured a majority on the first round. Communist Gennady Zyuganov received 29.21%, and no other candidates garnered more than 5.8%. Some observers have questioned the honesty of elections, particularly since the media obviously promoted Yeltsin in 1996 and Putin in 2000. A 2001 law seriously restricted the right of small, regional parties to run presidential candidates, so critics questioned how democratic future presidential elections might be. The presidential election of 2004 added credence to the criticism, since Vladimir Putin won with 71% of the vote, again requiring no run off. His closest competitor was Nikolay Kharitonov, who ran for the Communist Party, and received less than 14% of the vote.

INTEREST GROUPS

Of course, interest groups were only allowed in the Soviet Union under **state corporatism**, controlled by the government. Decision-making took place within the Central Committee and the Politburo, and if any outside contacts influenced policy, they generally were confined to members of the Communist Party. When market capitalism suddenly replaced centralized economic control in 1991, the state-owned industries were up for grabs, and those that bought them for almost nothing were generally insiders (members of the *nomenklatura)* who have since become quite wealthy. This collection of **oligarchs** may be defined loosely as an interest group because they have been a major influence on the policymaking process during the formative years of the Russian Federation.

THE OLIGARCHY

The power of the oligarchy became obvious during the last year of Boris Yeltsin's first term as President of the Federation. The tycoons were tied closely to members of Yeltsin's family, particularly his daughter. Together they took advantage of Yeltsin's inattention to his presidential duties, and soon monopolized Russian industries and built huge fortunes. One of the best-known oligarchs is **Boris Berezovsky,** who admitted in 1997 that he and six other entrepreneurs controlled over half of the Russian GNP. Berezovsky's businesses had giant holdings in the oil industry and in media, including a TV network and many newspapers. He used the media to insure Yeltsin's reelection in 1996, and he and the "family" clearly controlled the presidency. When Yeltsin's ill heath and alcoholism triggered events that led to his resignation in 2000, Berezovsky went to work with other oligarchs to put together and finance the Unity Party. When Unity's presidential candidate Vladimir Putin easily won the election with more than 50% of the vote in the first round, it looked as if the oligarchs had survived Yeltsin's demise.

Putin, however, has shown resistance to oligarchic control. He has clashed with the entrepreneurs on several occasions, and when television magnate Vladimir Gusinsky harshly criticized Putin's reform plans, Gusinsky was arrested for corruption and his company was given to a state-owned monopoly. Both Berezovsky and Gusinsky are now in exile, but they still have close political and economic connections in Russia. In October 2003, Mikhail Khodorvsky, the richest man in Russia and chief executive officer of Yukos Oil Company, was arrested as a signal from Putin that the Russian government was consolidating power. The government slapped massive penalties and additional taxes on Yukos, forcing it into bankruptcy. The other oligarchs heeded the warning and largely withdrew from political activities, leaving Putin in control but probably with a narrower base of support from economic leaders.

STATE CORPORATISM

Under Putin's leadership **state corporatism,** where the state determines which groups have input into policymaking, has become well established. The Russian government has established vast, state-owned holding companies in automobile and aircraft manufacturing, shipbuilding, nuclear power, diamonds, titanium, and other industries. If companies appear to be too independent or too rich the government has not forced owners to sell, but has cited legal infractions (such as with Yukos) to force sales. Either government-controlled companies, or companies run by men seen as loyal to Mr. Putin, are the beneficiaries. Another term for such an arrangement is **insider privatization.**

STATE CORPORATISM IN RUSSIA

State Owned Company	Chairman	Benefits
Gazprom (natural gas)	Dmitri A. Medvedev (deputy prime minister)	Sibneft oil company Sakhalin II oil company (controlling stakes) Yukos Oil assets
Rosneft (oil)	Igor I. Sechin (presidential deputy chief of staff)	the Yuganskneftegaz oil fields (Yukos assets) Refineries, oil fields from Yukos
Russian Technology (weapons trader)	Sergey V. Chemezov (former KGB colleague of Putin)	Avtovaz, Russia's largest car maker VSMPO, a titanium aircraft parts maker
United Aircraft Corporation	Sergei B. Ivanov (first deputy prime minister)	Company created in 2006 by presidential decree

Reference: The New York Times, **July 8, 2007.** The chart also reflects Russia's **patron-client system**, where individuals in power give favors to subordinates, in return for political support.

THE RUSSIAN MAFIA

A larger and even more shadowy influence than the oligarchs is known as the "mafia," but this interest group controls much more than underworld crime. Like the oligarchs, they gained power during the chaotic time after the Revolution of 1991, and they control local businesses, natural resources, and banks. They thrive on payoffs from businesses ("protection money"), money laundering, and deals that they make with Russian government officials, including members of the former KGB. They have murdered bankers, journalists, businessmen, and members of the Duma.

The huge fortunes made by the oligarch and mafia offend the sensibilities of most Russian citizens, who tend to value **equality of result** (p. 104), not equality of opportunity. In Russia's past, lawlessness has been dealt with by repressive, authoritarian rule, and these groups represent a major threat to the survival of the new democracy.

THE RUSSIAN MEDIA

During a joint press conference with Vladimir Putin in early 2005, two Russian reporters challenged comments by U.S. President George Bush about the lack of a free press in Russia. Of course, the reporters were hand picked to accompany Putin on his trip to the United States, but they argued that the Russian media often criticizes the government. It is true that newspapers and television stations are now privately owned in Russia, although the state controls many of them. There are also many instances of reporters commenting on political actions and decisions, but how much real freedom they have is not clear. One example occurred when the Kremlin used a state-controlled company to take over the only independent television network, NTV. When the ousted NTV journalists took over a different channel, TV-6, the state shut it down. Russian media circles also were suspicious of the alleged poisoning of Anna Politkovskaya, one of the most outspoken critics of the government's policies in Chechnya. In March 2007 correspondent Ivan Safronov, who worked for the business daily *Kommersant*, was killed in a fall from the window of his Moscow apartment.

The status of freedom of the press in Russia is illustrated by media coverage of the school seizure at Beslan in 2004. As the tragedy unfolded on a Friday, two of Russia's main TV channels did not mention what was happening until an hour after explosions were first heard at the school. When state-owned Russia TV and Channel One finally reported it, they returned to their regularly scheduled programs. However, NTV, which is owned by state-controlled Gazprom, did have rolling coverage for three hours, even though it started late.

State corporatism appears to be impacting the media business, just as it has oil, gas, aircraft building, and auto companies. For example, in May 2007 the Russian Union of Journalists was evicted from its headquarters in Moscow to make space for the Russia Today television channel. According to the general secretary of the RUJ, the eviction was based on an order from President Vladimir Putin to accommodate the expansion plans of the state-owned English-language channel, which aims to promote a positive image of Russia abroad.

INSTITUTIONS OF GOVERNMENT

The structure of the government was put in place by the Constitution of 1993. It follows a **semi-presidential model** (p. 11) , borrowing from both presidential and parliamentary systems, and the resulting hybrid government is meant to allow for a strong presidency, but at the same time place some democratic checks on executive power. Its brief history has been stormy, but it is too early to say whether the difficulties centered on Yeltsin's ineffective presidency, or if they reflect inherent flaws within the system. The relationships among the branches have stabilized, but in Putin's administration, the executive has clearly dominated the other branches, and Putin has commanded the executive branch.

THE PRESIDENT AND PRIME MINISTER

The executive branch separates the **head of state** (the president) from the **head of government** (the prime minister). Unlike the Queen's role in British politics, the president's position is far from ceremonial. Although the Constitution provided for a strong presidency, under Putin the president has come to dominate the prime minister.

Russian voters directly elect the president for a four-year term, with a limit of two terms. Since Russian political parties are in flux, anyone who gets a million signatures can run for president. In 1996, 2000, and 2004, many candidates ran on the first ballot, and in 2000 and 2004 Putin won without a second-round vote. The president has the power to:

- **Appoint the prime minister and cabinet** - The Duma must approve the prime minister's appointment, but if they reject the president's nominee three times, the president may dissolve the

Duma. In 1998, Yeltsin replaced Prime Minister Kiriyenko with Viktor Chernomyrdin, and the Duma rejected him twice. On the third round – under threat of being dissolved – they finally agreed on a compromise candidate, Yevgeni Primakov. Putin was prime minister when he ran for president, and when he became president, he appointed Mikhail Kasyanov as prime minister. Kasyanov served for four years, and was eventually replaced by Mikhail Fradkov, who was prime minister until September 2007, when Putin dismissed him and appointed cabinet official Victor Zubkov. The appointment was widely seen as an indication that Putin favors Zubkov to succeed him as president.

- **Issue decrees that have the force of law** – The president runs a cabinet that has a great deal of concentrated, centralized power. For example, Putin created the state-owned United Aircraft Corporation by decree, a decision that the legislature had no control over. According to the **Constitution,** the Duma has no real power to censure the cabinet, except that they may reject the appointment of the prime minister.

- **Dissolve the Duma** – This power was tested even before the Constitution was put in place. In 1993 Yeltsin ordered the old Russian Parliament dissolved, but the conservative members staged a coup, and refused to leave the "White House." (the parliament building). He ordered the army to fire on the building until the members gave up, but the chaos of the new regime was revealed to the world through the images of a president firing on his own parliament. No such chaos has occurred under Putin.

Russia has a prime minister as well as a president. There is no vice-president, so if a president dies or resigns before his term is up, the prime minister becomes acting president. This situation occurred in 1999 when Prime Minister Vladimir Putin took over presidential duties when Yeltsin resigned. Prime ministers are not appointed because they are leaders of the majority party (as they are in Great Britain); instead most have been career bureaucrats chosen for their technical expertise or loyalty to the president.

A BICAMERAL LEGISLATURE

So far, the Russian legislature has proved to be only a very weak check on executive power. The lower house, the **Duma**, has 450 deputies, half by **proportional representation,** and half from **single-member districts**. The Duma passes bills, approves the budget, and confirms the president's political appointments. However, these powers are very limited, since the president may rule by decree, and the Duma's attempts to reject prime ministers has failed. In another confrontation with Yeltsin, the Duma tried to use their constitutional power to impeach him, but the process is so cumbersome that it failed. Although the Duma has been controlled by Putin because his party (United Russia) has almost half the seats, it still wields some power in the drafting of legislation. Most legislation originates with the president or prime minister, just as it does in Great Britain and most other parliamentary systems, but the Duma debates bills that must pass the deputies' vote before they become laws.

The upper house, called the **Federation Council**, consists of two members from each of the 89 federal administrative units. Since 2002 one representative is selected by the governor of each region and another by the regional legislature. The Federation Council serves the purpose that most upper houses do in bicameral federalist systems: to represent regions, not the population as such. However, like most other upper houses in European governments, it seems to only have the power to delay legislation. If the Federation Council rejects legislation, the Duma may override the Council with a two-thirds vote.

On paper, it also may change boundaries among the republics, ratify the use of armed forces outside the country, and appoints and removes judges. However, these powers have not been used yet.

THE JUDICIARY

No independent judiciary existed under the old Soviet Union, with courts and judges serving as pawns of the Communist Party. The Constitution of 1993 attempted to build a judicial system that is not controlled by the executive by creating a **Constitutional Court**. The Court's nineteen members are appointed by the president and confirmed by the Federation Council, and it is supposed to make sure that all laws and decrees are constitutional. The Constitution also created a Supreme Court to serve as a final court of appeal in criminal and civil cases. It is too soon to tell if they will be effective, but both have been actively involved in policymaking, although their independence from the executive is questionable. One problem is that most prosecutors and attorneys were trained under the Soviet legal system, so the judiciary currently suffers from a lack of expertise in carrying out the responsibilities outlined in the constitution.

Vladimir Putin came into office with a mission to revive the great period of law reform under the tsars, including jury trial, planned for all regions except Chechnya by 2007. Russia brought in procedural codes for criminal and civil rights, and spent a great deal of money on law reform. However, the system is still very much in transition, and corruption is a serious problem. The advent of juries is a real change, but the presumption of innocence is far from a reality. The independence of the judiciary is still not apparent, especially since no courts have challenged Putin in his pursuit of the oligarchs and the dismantling of their empires.

THE MILITARY

The army was a very important source of Soviet strength during the Cold War era from 1945 to 1991. The Soviet government prioritized financing the military ahead of almost everything else. The armed forces at one time stood at about 4 million men, considerably larger than the United States combined forces. However, the military usually did not take a lead in politics, and generals did not challenge the power of the Politburo. Even though some of the leaders of the attempted coup of 1991 were military men, the armed forces themselves responded to Yeltsin's plea to remain loyal to their government.

Under the Russian Federation, the army shows no real signs of becoming a political force. It has suffered significant military humiliation, and many sources confirm that soldiers go unpaid for months and have to provide much of their own food. Even as early as 1988, under Gorbachev, Soviet forces had to be withdrawn in disgrace from Afghanistan, and in 1994-1996, Chechen guerillas beat the Soviet forces. More recently, the army partially restored its reputation by crushing Chechen resistance in 1999-2000.

One prominent former general, **Alexander Lebed**, gained a political following before the election of 1996, and Yeltsin had to court his favor in order to win reelection. However, most political leaders have been civilians, so a military coup appears to be unlikely in the near future. Even so, some observers are wary of a military takeover, especially considering the tentative nature of the current "democracy."

Recently Russia's army has reasserted its old vigor, with Putin's 2007 announcement that, for the first time in 15 years, the Russian Air Force would begin regular, long-range patrols by nuclear-capable bombers again. The move was seen by some observers as one of several signs that Russia is rising in strength and wishes to assert itself internationally again.

PUBLIC POLICY AND CURRENT ISSUES

These first few years of the Russian Federation have been very difficult ones, characterized by a great deal of uncertainty regarding the regime's future.   Any regime change creates legitimacy issues, but Russia's case has been extreme, with public policy directed at some very tough issues and seemingly intractable problems.

THE ECONOMY

The Soviet Union faced many challenges in 1991, but almost certainly at the heart of its demise were insurmountable economic problems. Mikhail Gorbachev enacted his **perestroika reforms,** primarily consisting of market economy programs inserted into the traditional centralized state ownership design of the Soviet Union. These plans were never fully implemented, partly because dissent within the Politburo led to the attempted coup that destroyed the state.

Today leaders of the Russian Federation face the same issue: How much of the centralized planning economy should be eliminated, and how should the market economy be handled? Yeltsin's "shock therapy" created chaotic conditions that resulted in a small group of entrepreneurs running the economy. In 1997 the bottom fell out of the economy when the government defaulted on billions of dollars of debts. The stock market lost half of its values, and threatened to topple other markets around the globe. Meanwhile, the Russian people suffered from the sudden introduction of the free market. Under the Soviet government, their jobs were secure, but in 1997 the unemployment rate soared. The ruble – once pegged by the government at $1.60 – lost its value quickly, so that by early 2002, it took more than 30,000 rubles to equal a dollar. The oligarchs and mafia members prospered, but almost everyone else faced a new standard of living much worse than what they had had before.

Since 1997, the Russian economy has steadily improved, slightly during 1999 and 2000, particularly in the new areas of privatized industries, and then more clearly since then. In 2004 the economy showed strong indications of recovery, with an annual growth of about 7 percent. The standard of living is rising even faster, although real incomes improved more rapidly in neighboring countries, such as the Ukraine. For example, very few people, rich or poor, have running hot water for several weeks in the summer in Moscow because the plants and network of pipelines shut down for maintenance every year. Many people are still disillusioned with the new regime, and question the wisdom of current policymakers.

Today Russia's economy is fueled by their huge oil and gas reserves, and the corporations (mostly state run) that own them. With recent increases in oil and gas prices, these companies have prospered, and the value of the ruble is rapidly increasing against the dollar and the euro. However, if oil prices should fall, Russia's economy will certainly suffer. To prepare for that eventuality, Russia is putting oil money into a Stabilization Fund as reserves for state spending.

FOREIGN POLICY

The Soviet Union held hegemony over huge portions of the world for much of the 20th century, and when it broke apart in 1991, that dominance ended. The 1990s were a time of chaos and humiliation for Russia, as Yeltsin had to rely on loans from its old nemesis, the United States, to help shake its economic doldrums. As the 21st century began, the new president, Vladimir Putin, set out to redefine Russia's place in the world, a two-dimensional task that required a new interpretation of the country's relationship with the west, as well as its role among the former Soviet States.

Relations with the near-abroad

The weak **Confederation of Independent States** unites the fifteen former republics of the Soviet Union, and Russia is the clear leader of the group. However, the organization has little formal power over its members, and Russia's motives are almost always under strict scrutiny by the other countries. Still, trade agreements bind them together, although nationality differences keep the members from reaching common agreements. These nationality differences also threaten the Federation itself, with the threat of revolution from Chechnya spreading to other regions. In short, the CIS is a long way from being a regional power like the European Union, and many experts believe that the confederation will not survive.

One of the most controversial recent moves of the Russian government in the near-abroad was Putin's involvement in the 2004 presidential elections in the Ukraine. According to challenger Viktor Yushchenko, President Putin promised heavy financing and political advisors for Prime Minister Viktor Yanukovich's campaign for the presidency. Putin himself went to the Ukraine twice to campaign for Yanukovich. Popular protests broke out after Yanukovich won, with claims that the election was fraudulent. The elections were held again, and Yushchenko's victory in this round further strained relations with the near-abroad.

Another controversy erupted between Russia and Estonia in 2007 when the Estonian government removed a Soviet-era statue from a public place in its capital, Tallinn. The Estonian move met with a reaction from ethnic Russians living in Estonia, with hundreds of them attacking the main theater and the Academy of Arts in the capital. Events took a strange turn when computers went down all over Estonia the day after the protests. The Estonians accused Russia of orchestrating the computer attacks, and young protesters in Moscow reacted by attacking Estonia's embassy with eggs and harassing the Estonian ambassador. The old ethnicities of the culturally heterogeneous Soviet Union are still at odds, even though they are no longer united under one central government.

Relations with the West

The biggest adjustment for Russia is the loss of its superpower status from the Cold War era. The United States emerged as the lone superpower in 1991, and the two old enemies – Russia and the United States – had to adjust their attitudes toward one another. U.S. Presidents George H. Bush and Bill Clinton both believed that it was important to maintain a good working relationship with Russia. They also knew that the economic collapse of Russia would have disastrous results for the world economy. Both presidents sponsored aid packages for Russia, and they also encouraged foreign investment in the country's fledgling market economy. The United States and the other G-7 political powerhouses of Europe welcomed Russia into the organization, now known as the G-8, acknowledging the political importance of Russia in global politics. Russia supported France in blocking the UN Security Council's approval of the U.S.-sponsored war on Iraq in early 2003. Whether the move was a wise one is yet to be seen, but it does indicate Russia's willingness to assert its point of view, even if it opposes that of the United States. Russia is currently negotiating for membership in the World Trade Organization (WTO), a powerful body responsible for regulating international trade, settling trade disputes, and designing trade policy through meetings with its members. If Russia's bid to join the WTO is successful, it would almost certainly be a milestone in its integration with the international economic community.

Russia's relations with countries of the west and the near-abroad are defined more and more strongly by the clout of their oil and gas industries. In an ongoing dispute about gas lines that cross Ukraine, Belarus, and other nearby countries, Russia's state-run gas company, Gazprom, has institute gas price hikes that have been met by stiff resistance. In 2006, Gazprom reduced pressure in the Ukrainian pipeline system so that Ukrainian gas customers had no gas to use, even for basics, such as heating their homes. Europeans were affected because the pipelines eventually provide gas to them, and their governments demanded action from Putin's government until the pressure was restored.

Russia's relationship with Great Britain was strained in 2006 because of an espionage controversy in which a Russian businessman, Andrei Lugovoi, was accused of poisoning a former KGB officer and a Kremlin critic. The man became ill in Britain and was hospitalized there, and in a complicated case that involved British espionage as well, Britain demanded the extradition of Lugovoi from Russia to Britain so that he could stand trial there. When Russia stalled, relations between the two countries soured.

After the September 11th terrorist attacks, Putin's solidarity with the United States seemed to mark the beginning of a new era in Russian-American relations. However, in recent times, Putin has flexed his muscles with the U.S. as well. In Munich in February 2007 accused the U.S of overstepping its national borders and exhibiting a disdain for international law. Although he gave no specifics, his speech rankled Americans and Europeans alike, although U.S. President George Bush did not immediately make an issue of it.

TERRORISM

Just as has happened in the United States and Britain, Russia has had a number of acts of terror in recent years, with the Beslan school siege in southern Russia in 2004 being the most well known. Just prior to Beslan, a suicide bombing occurred near a subway station in Moscow, and bombs went off in two Russian airplanes almost simultaneously. As the government tried to break the Beslan siege by militants, 360 people died, including many children. President Putin responded with a reform package to boost security. In an emergency gathering of regional and national leaders in late 2004, Putin argued that only a tighter grip from the central government would foil terrorists whose aim it was to force the country's disintegration. He laid out not just security measures, but also a sweeping political reform – top officials (including regional governors) would no longer be directly elected, but would be selected by the president, and then approved by regional legislatures. The Duma approved the president's plan later in the year.

RE-CENTRALIZATION OF POWER IN THE KREMLIN?

Some critics believe that Putin's reforms for the selection of regional governors is more than a response to terrorism, but is part of a re-centralization of power in the Kremlin. Putin's party now has almost 50% of the seats in the Duma, and his government has taken important steps toward controlling the power of the oligarchs. The Kremlin now controls major television stations, as well as the Russian gas giant Gazprom. It is not clear whether these moves mark the beginning of the end of democratic experimentation in Russia, or simply a reaction to terrorism similar to those of the U.S. and British governments after major attacks in those countries.

DEVELOPMENT OF A CIVIL SOCIETY

The notion of civil society starts with the acceptance of two areas of life: a public one that is defined by the government, and a private one, in which people are free to make their own individual choices. In a country with a strong civil society, people follow rules, operate with a degree of trust toward others, and generally have respectful dealings with others even if the government is not watching. Even though these ideals may not always be met, citizens are aware of both the rule of law in the public realm and their own privacy that exists outside it. Democracy and capitalism both depend on civil society for their successful operation.

Russians do not necessarily share the assumptions that civil society rests on: the inherent value of life, liberty, and property. Instead, they have been much more influenced by traditions of **statism** – have a strong government or die. Their history began with this truth – survival amidst the invasions across the Russian plains and the rebellions of the many ethnicities depends on a strong, protective government. In the twentieth century, Russia became a superpower in the same way – through a strong, centralized government. Is it possible for stability, power, and prosperity to return to Russia through a democratic state and a capitalist economy?

In many ways the answer to that question tests the future of democracy as a worldwide political model. Were John Locke and other Enlightenment philosophers correct in their assumptions that it is in "human nature" to value freedom above equality? That people "naturally" have the right to own property and to live private lives? If so, can these values thrive among a people who have traditionally valued government protection and equality? So far, the spread of democracy has taken many forms. If it takes hold in the Russian Federation, it is indeed a hardy, versatile, and potentially global philosophy.

IMPORTANT TERMS AND CONCEPTS

asymmetric federalism
Berezovsky, Boris
bolsheviks
boyars
Catherine the Great
Central Committee
civil society in Russia
collective farms, collectivization
Confederation of Independent States
conflict in Chechnya
Constitution of 1993
Constitutional Court
Crimean War
CPRF
cultural heterogeneity in Russia
Decembrist Revolt

decrees
democratic centralism
de-Stalinization
Duma
equality of result in Russia
federal government structure
Federation Council
Five Year Plans
general secretary
glasnost
Gorbachev, Mikhail
Gorbachev's three-pronged reform plan
Gosplan
head of government, head of state
Khrushchev, Nikita
kulaks
Lebed, Alexander
Lenin, Vladimir
Liberal Democrats
mafia
Marxism-Leninism
Mensheviks
nationality
near abroad
New Economic Policy
nomenklatura
oligarchy
perestroika
Peter the Great
politburo
proportional representation in Russia
Putin, Vladimir
Red Army/White Army
Russian Orthodox Church
secret speech
semi-presidential model
"shock therapy"
slavophile vs. westernizer
Stalinism
state corporatism
statism in Russia
totalitarianism
tsars
United Russia Party
"Window on the West"
Yobloko
Yeltsin, Boris

zemstras
Zhirinovsky, Vladimir
Zyuganov, Gennady

MULTIPLE-CHOICE QUESTIONS
THE RUSSIAN FEDERATION

1. Theoretically, Russia could be considered to be an illiberal democracy instead of an authoritarian state if it has

    a) free, regular, and competitive elections
    b) rule of law
    c) civilian control of the military
    d) a well-developed civil society
    e) individual civil rights and liberties

2. In the Soviet Union elite recruitment took place through

    a) the old aristocracy
    b) elite universities
    c) consultation with oligarchs
    d) *zemstvas*
    e) *nomenklatura*

3. When Boris Yeltsin put the Russian Constitution of 1993 to a referendum, he was trying to

    a) pass responsibility to his subordinates
    b) legitimize the Constitution
    c) weaken the supporters of democracy
    d) set up a federalist government
    e) undermine the sovereignty of neighboring states

4. The "slavophile v. westernizer" characteristic of Russia's political culture indicates that the political culture is

    a) ethnically homogeneous
    b) consensual
    c) subject to revolutions
    d) conflictual
    e) resistant to absolute rulers

5. The well-established tradition of statism in Russia indicates that the country will have a difficult time developing

    a) obedience to law
    b) equality of opportunity
    c) rule of law
    d) economic prosperity
    e) civil society

6. Russians are generally skeptical about their government and highly critical of their political leaders. A fact that contradicts this tendency is that

   a) Russian rulers are generally authoritarian
   b) Vladimir Putin has very high approval ratings
   c) leaders of the Russian federation have been more popular than leaders of the USSR
   d) governors of regions are more popular than national leaders
   e) Russians tend to admire elected representatives to the Duma more than they trust government bureaucrats.

7. Democratic centralism was (is) a key ideology that defined the legitimacy of

   a) Russia before Peter the Great
   b) Russia between Peter the Great and the Revolution of 1917
   c) the USSR
   d) the government under Boris Yeltsin
   e) the government under Vladimir Putin

8. Collectivization and industrialization were key platforms for the programs of

   a) 19th century tsars
   b) Vladimir Lenin
   c) Joseph Stalin
   d) Mikhail Gorbachev
   e) Boris Yeltsin

9. The policy of *glasnost* proved to be a dangerous policy for the Soviet Union because it

   a) encouraged open discussion and criticism of the government
   b) democratized the institutions of government
   c) infused capitalism into the economy
   d) allowed for emigration to other countries
   e) allowed the military to have policymaking power

10. Britain has experienced violence in Northern Ireland, and Russia has experienced violence in Chechnya. Both conflicts are examples of cleavages based on

    a) social class
    b) rural vs. urban
    c) regional differences
    d) ideology
    e) ethnicity

11. Both Britain and Russia have seen significant demographic increases in their percentages of

    a) Catholics
    b) Sub-Saharan Africans
    c) Southeast Asians
    d) Scandinavians
    e) Muslims

12. In contrast to presidential elections during the 1990s, the presidential elections of 2000 and 2004 were

    a) more competitive
    b) less competitive
    c) less controlled by oligarchs
    d) less interesting to the Russian public
    e) more corrupt

13. Compared to Great Britain, Russia's civil society is

    a) growing less rapidly
    b) less regulated by the government
    c) more dominated by intellectual groups
    d) less well developed
    e) more likely to support popular elections

14. Which of the following is an accurate comparison of Russia's and Britain's government structures?

    a) Russia is a unitary state; Britain is a democratic state.
    b) Russia is a confederal state; Britain is a federalist state.
    c) Britain and Russia are both unitary states.
    d) Britain is a unitary state; Russia is a federalist state.
    e) Britain and Russia are both federalist states.

15. Which of the following of Russia's political parties is MOST clearly a party of power?

    a) United Russia
    b) The Communist Party of the Russian Federation
    c) Yabloko
    d) Union of Right Forces
    e) Liberal Democratic Party

16. Which of the following types of elections take place in BOTH Britain and Russia?

   I. referenda
   II. presidential elections
   III. elections to a national legislature

   a) I only
   b) I and III only
   c) II only
   d) II and III only
   e) I, II, and III

17. The arrangement in Russia where the businesses and companies that participate in the policy-making process are controlled by the government is called

   a) the socialist market economy
   b) pluralism
   c) democratic centralism
   d) neo-corporatism
   e) state corporatism

18. Which of the following is an accurate statement about the Russian media?

   a) All media outlets are owned by the central government.
   b) Most media outlets are privately owned, and the government has very little control over them.
   c) Most media outlets are owned by private individuals, but the government regulates them.
   d) Most media outlets are owned by private individuals, but the government seriously restricts freedoms of press and speech.
   e) More media outlets are owned by the central government than not, but private companies are allowed to compete with government-sponsored companies.

19. Which of the following is an accurate comparison of the British and Russian prime ministers?

   a) Both prime ministers are the heads of government.
   b) Both prime ministers are the heads of state.
   c) The British prime minister is the head of government; the Russian prime minister is the head of state.
   d) The Russian prime minister is the head of government; the British prime minister is the head of state.
   e) Neither prime minister is head of government nor head of state.

20. The main purpose of the Federation Council, according to the Russian Constitution, is to

   a) adjudicate disputes between the Duma and the president
   b) represent individual citizens in the national legislature
   c) represent regions in the national legislature
   d) advise the president on foreign policy
   e) check the powers of the regional governments

21. Which of the following is NOT a power of the Duma?

    a) It may reject the president's nomination for prime minister.
    b) It may pass legislation.
    c) It must confirm the president's nominations to the Constitutional Court.
    d) It must approve the budget.
    e) It may impeach the president.

22. The main responsibility of the Constitutional Court, according to the Russian Constitution, is to

    a) serve as the highest court of appeals
    b) decide the constitutionality of laws and presidential decrees
    c) reform civil and criminal law
    d) define common law
    e) check the power of the regional governors

23. Which of the following do the British and Russian military have in common?

    a) Both are major sources of recruitment for political leaders.
    b) Neither actively participates in the policymaking process.
    c) Both are much stronger and better equipped than they were twenty years ago.
    d) Both consider the United States military its biggest foe.
    e) Neither has been well-funded by the central government in recent years.

24. Which of the following is an accurate statement about the current Russian economy?

    a) The oil and gas industries are making very little money.
    b) Compared to the 1990s, the economy is much weaker now.
    c) The Russian ruble is much stronger against the euro and the dollar than it was in 2002.
    d) Russian standards of living are higher than those in neighboring countries.
    e) The Russian economy is no longer controlled by the central government.

25. Which of the following is an accurate comparison of the Confederation of Independent States and the European Union?

    a) Both organizations have a common currency.
    b) Neither organization is dominated by a single member country.
    c) Both organizations have their own parliaments.
    d) Member states of both organizations are bound by trade agreements.
    e) Neither organization has its own court of justice.

26. Russia currently belongs to all of the following supranational organizations EXCEPT:

    I. Confederation of Independent States
    II. United Nations
    III. G-8
    IV. World Trade Organization

    a) I only
    b) I and II only
    c) I, II, and III only
    d) I and IV only
    e) I, II, and III only

27. Russia's recent assertiveness with western countries is BEST explained by

    a) insecurity as a result of its recent economic collapse
    b) competition with the west for influence in less developed countries of the world
    c) its technological superiority
    d) the growing clout of its oil and gas industries
    e) its fear of terrorist attack

28. Recently President Putin announced that regional governors would no longer be directly elected, but would be selected by the president. The incident that provoked his announcement was the

    a) siege of the Beslan school
    b) poisoning of a Russian spy in Britain
    c) resistance by Ukraine to higher gas prices
    d) building of U.S. missile sites in Central Asia
    e) Iraq War

29. President Putin has taken all of the following moves to centralize power in the presidency EXCEPT:

    a) taken control of the oil and gas industries through Gazprom
    b) taken control of major television stations
    c) gained power to remove governors from office
    d) gained the power to nominate regional governors
    e) insisted on running for a third term of office

30. "Shock therapy" is the method for jump-starting the Russian economy used by

    a) Joseph Stalin
    b) Nikita Khrushchev
    c) Mikhail Gorbachev
    d) Boris Yeltsin
    e) Vladimir Putin

FREE-RESPONSE QUESTION
THE RUSSIAN FEDERATION

The nature of political change in British political development over time contrasts greatly with the nature of political change over time in Russian political development.

a) Define reform, revolution, and coup d'etat as types of political and/or economic change.

b) Using the concepts of reform, revolution, and coup d'etat, discuss the nature of political change over time in British political development.

c) Using the concepts of reform, revolution, and coup d'etat, discuss the nature of political change over time in Russian political development.

GOVERNMENT AND POLITICS IN CHINA

"Let China sleep. For when China wakes, it will shake the world."
Napoleon Bonaparte

Ancient China was arguably one of the strongest, richest empires in existence - so much so that her rulers saw little value in contacting anyone else in the world. Even though China's power was much diminished by the era of Napoleon, his words describing China as a sleeping giant prophesied the China of the early 21st century – a great civilization on the rise again.

Since western countries first began exploring the world several centuries ago, they have tended to either ignore or exploit China in world politics. And yet the presence of China is deeply felt, sometimes promising riches and cooperation, and other times threatening competition and destruction. Today China stands as one of the few remaining communist nations, with no signs of renouncing communism. China is by some standards a less developed country, but on the other hand the country is emerging as a major world power, partly because of recent dramatic improvements in GNP and standards of living. China no longer sleeps. Its leaders now claim membership in the World Trade Organization, travel frequently to other countries, and take active part in the United Nations. The world increasingly comes to China for its vast array of products, and China often is going outside its borders for investments, labor supplies, and raw materials. Its steady move toward capitalism has led some to argue that democratization will follow, yet the government remains highly authoritarian, providing evidence that marketization and democracy do not always go hand in hand.

SOVEREIGNTY, AUTHORITY, AND POWER

Until the 20th century China's history was characterized by **dynastic cycles** – long periods of rule by a family punctuated by times of "chaos", when the family lost its power and was challenged by a new, and ultimately successful, ruling dynasty. Power was determined by the **mandate of heaven,** or the right to rule as seen by the collective ancestral wisdom that guided the empire from the heavens above. For many centuries public authority rested in the hands of the emperor and an elaborate bureaucracy that exercised this highly centralized power. After a time of chaos in the early 20th century, communist leader Mao Zedong took over China in 1949, bringing in a new regime whose values often disagreed with traditional concepts of power. How different is the new China from the old? Have the changes brought instability, or have they successfully transformed the country into a modern world power?

China's political structures reflect many modern influences, but the weight of tradition has shaped them in unique ways. For example, China is technically governed by a constitution that grants formal authority to both party and state executive and legislative offices. However, the country is still governed by an authoritarian elite that is not bound by rule of law. As long as the rulers are above the law, the constitution will not be a major source of legitimacy for the state.

LEGITIMACY

Under dynastic rule, Chinese citizens were subjects of the emperor. Legitimacy was established through the mandate of heaven, and power passed from one emperor to the next through hereditary connections within the ruling family. As long as things went well, the emperor's authority was generally accepted, but when problems occurred and the dynasty weakened, rival families challenged the throne, claiming that the emperor had lost the mandate. Legitimacy was not for peasants to determine, although popular rebellions and unrest in the countryside served as signs that the emperor was failing.

The Revolution of 1911 gave birth to the Chinese Republic, with western-educated **Sun Yat-sen** as its first president. The new regime was supposed to be democratic, with legitimacy resting on popular government. However, regional warlords challenged the government, much as they always had done in times of political chaos. Emerging from the mayhem was Mao Zedong, with his own version of authority, an ideology known as **Maoism**. The People's Republic of China was established in 1949, and Mao led the Communist Party as the new source of power until his death in 1976.

Inspired by Marxism, Maoism was idealistic and egalitarian, and even though it endorsed centralized power exercised through the top leaders of the party, it stressed the importance of staying connected to the peasants through a process called **mass line.** Mass line required leaders to listen to and communicate with ordinary folks, and without it, the legitimacy of the rulers was questionable.

Since Mao's death, the **Politburo** of the Communist Party remains the legitimate source of power in China, but the leadership has come under a great deal of criticism in recent years. The Party is said to be corrupt and irrelevant, holding authoritarian power over an increasingly market-based economy. In truth, rebellions against the party have flared up throughout PRC history, but the rumblings have been louder and more frequent since the Tiananmen incident in 1989. How serious a threat these criticisms are to the current regime is a matter of some debate, and current Communist leaders show no signs of loosening the party's hold on the government and the economy.

One important source of power in the People's Republic of China has been the military. The military played an important role in the rise of the Communist Party, and it is represented in the government by the **Central Military Commission**. The head of this commission plays an important role in policy-making. For example, long-time leader Deng Xiaoping was never general secretary of the Communist Party, but he directed the Central Military Commission.

HISTORICAL TRADITIONS

Despite the fact that the last dynasty (the Qing) fell in the early 20th century, many traditions from the dynastic era influence the modern political system:

- **Authoritarian power** – China's borders have changed over time, but it has long been a huge, land-based empire ruled from a central place by either an emperor or a small group of people. Chinese citizens have traditionally been subjects of, not participants in, their political system. Despite the many dynastic rulers in China's history, the ruling family was always subject to attack from regional warlords who challenged their right to the mandate of heaven. This tendency toward decentralization is apparent in the modern regime as a centralized politburo attempts to control its vast population and numerous policies and problems.

- **Confucianism** – This philosophy has shaped the Chinese political system since the 6th century B.C.E. It emphasized the importance of order and harmony, and encouraged Chinese citizens to submit to the emperor's power, and reinforced the emperors' responsibility to fulfill his duties conscientiously. This aspect of Confucianism may be tied to **democratic centralism**, or the communist belief in a small group of leaders who rule for the good of the people. Confucianism is still a major influence on Chinese society today as it contradicts the egalitarian ideology of communism with its central belief in unequal relationships and mutual respect among people of different statuses, especially within families.

- **Bureaucratic hierarchy based on scholarship** – The emperors surrounded themselves with highly organized bureaucracies that formed an elite based on Confucian scholarship. Government jobs were highly coveted and extremely competitive, with only a small percentage of candidates mastering the examination system. The exams were knowledge-based, and bureaucrats had to be well-versed in Confucianism and related philosophies. A major social separation in Ancient China was between a large peasant population and the bureaucratic elite.

- **The "Middle Kingdom"** – Since ancient times, Chinese have referred to their country as *zhong-guo*, meaning "Middle Kingdom", or the place that is the center of civilization. Foreigners were seen as "barbarians" whose civilizations are far inferior to China's, not just in terms of power, but also in terms of ethics and quality of life. All countries are ethnocentric in their approaches to others, but China almost always assumed that no one else had much to offer them. After the empire's 19th century weakness was exploited by the imperialist powers, these traditional assumptions were challenged, but not destroyed.

- **Communist ideologies** - The 20th century brought the new influence of Maoism that emphasized the "right thinking" and moralism of Confucianism, but contradicted the hierarchical nature of the old regime with its insistence on egalitarianism. The late 20th century brought Deng Xiaoping Theory, a practical mix of authoritarian political control and economic privatization.

CONFUCIANISM AND MAOISM

CONFUCIANISM	MAOISM
Mandate of Heaven (responsibility of ruler to the people)	Democratic Centralism (responsibility of ruler to the people)
Vision of an ideal society based on harmony and obedience	Vision of ideal society based on self reliance and struggle
Hierarchical social and political organization; rulers and subjects have unequal positions	Egalitarian social structure; mass line between rulers and subjects
Emphasis on loyalty to family	Emphasis on loyalty to the state, Mao

POLITICAL CULTURE

China's political culture is multi-dimensional and deep, shaped by geographical features and by the many eras of its history: dynastic rule, control by imperialist nations and its aftermath, and communist rule.

GEOGRAPHIC INFLUENCES

Today China has the largest population of any country on earth, and its land surface is the third largest, after Russia and Canada. Some of its important geographical features include:

- Access to oceans/ice free ports

- Many large navigable rivers

- Major geographical/climate splits between north and south

- Geographic isolation of the western part of the country

- Mountain ranges, deserts, and oceans that separate China from other countries

Population concentrations in China. The vast majority of the population live in urban areas in the east, with many cities located along rivers and in coastal areas. Large stretches of mountains and deserts make the western and northern parts of the country less habitable.

These geographic features have shaped Chinese political development for centuries. China's location in the world and protective mountain ranges allowed the Chinese to ignore the rest of the world whenever they wanted to until the 19th century. The rugged terrain of the western part of the country has limited population growth there. The large navigable rivers and good harbors of the east have attracted population, so that the overwhelming majority of people in China have lived in these areas for centuries. Differences in climate and terrain have also created a cultural split between the north and the south.

HISTORICAL ERAS

1. **Dynastic rule** - The political culture inherited from centuries of dynastic rule centers on **Confucian values**, such as order, harmony, and a strong sense of hierarchy - "superior" and "subservient" positions. China has traditionally valued scholarship as a way to establish superiority, with mandarin scholars filling bureaucratic positions in the government. China's early relative isolation from other countries contributes to a strong sense of cultural identity. Related to Chinese identity is a high degree of ethnocentrism - the sense that China is central to humanity (the "middle kingdom") and superior to other cultures. Centuries of expansion and invasion have brought many other Asian people under Chinese control, resulting in long-standing tensions between "Han" Chinese and others groups. A modern example is Tibet, where a strong sense of Tibetan ethnicity has created resistance to Chinese control.

2. **Resistance to imperialism** - During the 19th century China's strong sense of cultural identity blossomed into nationalism and persistent attempts by imperialist nations - such as Britain, France, Germany, and Japan - to exploit China's natural resources and people. This nationalism was secured by the Revolution of 1911, and the hatred of the **"foreign devils"** has led China to be cautious and suspicious in her dealings with capitalist countries today.

3. **Maoism** - Mao Zedong was strongly influenced by Karl Marx and Vladimir Ulyanov (Lenin), but his version of communism is distinctly suited to China. Whereas Lenin emphasized the importance of a party vanguard to lead the people to revolution and beyond, Mao resisted the inequality implied by Lenin's beliefs. He believed in the strength of the peasant, and centered his philosophy on these central values:

- **Collectivism** - The good of the community is valued above that of the individual. This belief suited the peasant-based communities that have existed throughout Chinese history, but scholars (valued by the old culture) have often been drawn to individualism.

- **Struggle and activism** - Mao encouraged the people to actively pursue the values of socialism, something he understood would require struggle and devotion.

- **Mass line** - Mao conceptualized a line of communication between party leaders, members, and peasants that would allow all to struggle toward realization of the goals of a communist state. The mass line involved teaching and listening on everyone's part. Leaders would communicate their will and direction to the people, but the people in turn would communicate through the mass line their wisdoms to the leaders.

- **Egalitarianism** - Hierarchy was the key organizing principle in Chinese society before 1949, and Mao's emphasis on creating an egalitarian society was in complete opposition.

- **Self-reliance** - Instead of relying on the elite to give directions, people under Maoist rule were encouraged to rely on their own talents to contribute to their communities.

  4. Deng Xiaoping Theory - "It doesn't matter whether a cat is white or black, as long as it catches mice." This famous 1962 statement by Deng reflects his practical approach to solving China's problems. In other words, he didn't worry too much about whether a policy was capitalist or socialist as long as it improved the economy. The result of his leadership (1978-1997) was a dramatic turnaround of the Chinese economy through a combination of socialist planning and the capitalist free market. His political and social views, however, remained true to Communist tradition - the party should supervise all, and no allowances should be made for individual freedoms and/or democracy.

THE IMPORTANCE OF INFORMAL RELATIONSHIPS

Especially among the political elite, power and respect depend not so much on official positions as on who has what connections to whom. During the days of the early PRC, these ties were largely based on reputations established during the **Long March**, a 1934-1936 cross-country trek led by Mao Zedong as Chiang Kai-shek's nationalist army pursued his communist followers. Today those leaders are dead, but **factions** of their followers still compete for power, and informal relationships define each change in leadership. This informal network – a version of a **patron-client system** – is not apparent to the casual outside observer. As a result, whenever new leaders come to power, such as the 2003 transition, it isn't easy to predict how policymaking will be affected. However, an important principle is to study their relationships with past leaders. For example, it is a significant that **Hu Yaobang**, a reformer whose death was mourned by the students that led the Tiananmen Square protest in 1989, mentored **Hu Jintao**, the current general secretary of the CCP. Also important is the fact that, before he died, Deng Xiaoping designated Hu Jintao as his "4th generation" successor.

POLITICAL AND ECONOMIC CHANGE

Like Russia, China is an old civilization with a long, relatively stable history that experienced massive upheavals during the 20th century that resulted in regime changes. Unlike Russia, however, China rose to regional hegemony (control of surrounding countries) very early in its history and has ranked as one of the most influential political systems in the world for many centuries. Russia's history as a great power is much shorter than China's.

Until the 19th century **dynastic cycles** explained the patterns of political and economic change in China. A dynasty would seize power, grow stronger, and then decline. During its decline, other families would challenge the dynasty, and a new one would emerge as a sign that it had the mandate of heaven. This cycle was interrupted by the Mongols in the 13th century, when their leaders conquered China and ruled until the mandate was recaptured by the Ming who restored Han Chinese control. The Manchu were also a conquering people from the north, who established the Qing (or "pure") dynasty in the 17th century. This last dynasty toppled under European pressure in the early 20th century.

Change during the first half of the 20th century was radical, violent, and chaotic, and the result was a very different type of regime: communism. Did European intrusions and revolutions of the 20th century break the Chinese dynastic cycles forever? Or is this just another era of chaos between dynasties? It is hard to imagine that dynastic families might reappear in the 21st century or beyond, but Chinese political traditions are strong, and they almost certainly will determine what happens next in Chinese political development.

CHANGE BEFORE 1949

China's oldest cultural and political traditions have long provided stability and longevity for the empire/country. These traditions come from the dynastic rule that lasted for many centuries. However, in recent years two disruptive influences - control by imperialistic nations (19th century) and revolutionary upheavals (20th century) have threatened that stability and provide challenges to modern China.

CONTROL BY IMPERIALISTIC NATIONS

During the 19th century, the weakened Qing Dynasty fell prey to imperialistic nations - such as England, Germany, France, and Japan - who carved China into "**spheres of influence**" for their own economic gain. This era left many Chinese resentful of the "**foreign devils**" that they eventually rebelled against.

REVOLUTIONARY UPHEAVALS

Major revolutions occurred in China in 1911 and 1949, with many chaotic times in between. Three themes dominated this revolutionary era:

- **Nationalism** - The Chinese wished to recapture strength and power from the imperialistic nations that dominated them during the 19th century. The Revolution of 1911 - led by **Sun Yat-sen** - was a successful attempt to reestablish China as an independent country.

- **Establishing a new political community** - With the dynasties gone and the imperialists run out, what kind of government would modern China adopt? One answer came from **Chiang Kai-shek**, who founded the **Nationalist Party (Guomindang)** and the other from **Mao Zedong**, the founder of the Chinese Communist Party.

- **Socioeconomic development** - A major challenge of the 20th century has been the reestablishment of a strong economic and social fabric after the years of imperialistic control. During the 1920s, the newly formed Soviet Union served as a model for policymaking, but the Nationalists broke with them in 1928. Chiang Kai-shek became the president of China, and Mao Zedong and his communists were left an outlaw party.

THE LEGEND OF THE LONG MARCH

Strength for Mao's Communist Party was gained by the Long March - the 1934-36 pursuit of Mao's army across China by Chiang and his supporters. Chiang was trying to depose his rival, but his attempt to find and conquer Mao had the opposite effect. Mao eluded him until finally Chiang had to turn his attentions to the invading Japanese. Mao emerged as a hero of the people, and many of his loyal friends on the March lived to be prominent leaders of the People's Republic of China after its founding in 1949.

THE FOUNDING OF THE PEOPLE'S REPUBLIC OF CHINA – 1949-1966

The Japanese occupied China during World War II, but after the war ended, the forces of Chiang and Mao met in civil war, and Mao prevailed. In 1949 Chiang fled to Taiwan, and Mao established the People's Republic of China under communist rule.

The People's Republic of China was born from a civil war between the Nationalists under Chiang Kai-shek and the Communists under Mao Zedong. After many years of competitive struggle, Mao's army forced Chiang Kai-shek and his supporters off the mainland to the island of Taiwan (Formosa). Mao named his new China the "People's Republic of China," and Chiang claimed that his headquarters in Taiwan formed the true government. The "**Two Chinas**", then, were created, and the PRC was not to be recognized as a nation by the United Nations until 1972.

The early political development of the PRC proceeded in two phases:

 1) **The Soviet model** (1949-1957) - The Soviet Union had been supporting Mao's efforts since the 1920s, and with his victory in 1949, they began pouring money and expertise into the PRC. With this help, Chairman Mao and the Chinese Communist Party (CCP) quickly turned their attention to some of the country's most glaring social problems.

- **Land reform -** This campaign redistributed property from the rich to the poor and increased productivity in the countryside.

- **Civil reform -** The regime set about freeing people from opium addiction, and women's legal rights were greatly enhanced. For example, they allowed women to free themselves from un-happy arranged marriages. These measures helped to legitimize Mao's government in the eyes of the people.

- **Five-Year Plans -** Between 1953 and 1957, the CCP launched the first of its Soviet-style Five-Year Plans to nationalize industry and collectivize agriculture, implementing steps toward socialism.

 2) **The Great Leap Forward** (1958-1966) - Mao changed directions in 1958, partly in an effort to free China from Soviet domination. The spirit of nationalism is a force behind Mao's policy here, and he was still unhappy with the degree of inequality in Chinese society. The Great Leap Forward was a utopian effort to transform China into a radical egalitarian society.   Its emphasis was mainly economic, and it was based on four principles:

- **All-around development -** not just heavy industry (as under Stalin in the USSR), but almost equal emphasis on agriculture.

- **Mass mobilization -** an effort to turn the sheer numbers of the population into an asset - better motivation, harder work, less unemployment.

- **Political unanimity and zeal -** an emphasis on party workers running government, not bureau-crats. **Cadres -** party workers at the lowest levels - were expected to demonstrate their party devotion by spurring the people on to work as hard as they could.

- **Decentralization -** encouraged more government on the local level, less central control. The people can do it!

The Great Leap Forward did not live up to its name. Mao's efforts ran counter to the traditional political culture (bureaucratic centralism), and the people lacked skills to contribute to industrialization. Some bad harvests conjured up fears of the loss of the mandate of heaven.

THE CULTURAL REVOLUTION – 1966-1976

Between 1960 and 1966, Mao allowed two of his faithful - Liu Shaoqi and **Deng Xiaoping** - to implement market-oriented policies that revived the economy. but Mao was still unhappy with China's progress toward true egalitarianism. And so he instituted the Cultural Revolution - a much more profound reform in that it encompassed political and social change, as well as economic. His main goal was to purify the party and the country through radical transformation. Important principles were:

- **the ethic of struggle**

- **mass line**

- **collectivism**

- **egalitarianism**

- **unstinting service to society** (see p. 141)

A primary goal of the Cultural Revolution was to remove all vestiges of the old China and its hierarchical bureaucracy and emphasis on inequality. Scholars were sent into the fields to work, and universities and libraries were destroyed. Emphasis was put on elementary education - all people should be able to read and write - but any education that created inequality was targeted for destruction.

Mao died in 1976, leaving his followers divided into factions:

- **Radicals** - Led by Mao's wife, Jiang Qing, one of the "**Gang of Four**," the radicals supported the goals of the Cultural Revolution.

- **Military** - Always a powerful group because of the long-lasting 20th century struggles that required an army, the military was led by Lin Biao, who died in a mysterious airplane crash in 1971.

- **Moderates** - Led by **Zhou Enlai,** moderates emphasized economic modernization and limited contact with other countries, including the United States. Zhou influenced Mao to invite President Richard Nixon to China in 1972. He died only a few months after Mao.

Members of these factions were not only tied to one another through common purposes, but also through personal relationships, illustrating the importance of informal politics throughout Chinese history.

DENG XIAOPING'S MODERNIZATIONS (1978-1997)

The Gang of Four was arrested by the new CCP leader, Hua Guofeng, whose actions helped the moderates take control. Zhou's death opened the path for new leadership from the moderate faction. By 1978, the new leader emerged - Deng Xiaoping. His vision drastically altered China's direction through **"Four Modernizations"** invented by Zhou Enlai before his death - **industry, agriculture, science, and the military**. These modernizations have been at the heart of the country's official policy ever since. Under Deng's leadership, these policies have helped to implement the new direction:

- **"Open door" trade policy** - Trade with everyone was encouraged, including capitalist nations like the U.S. that will boost China's economy.

- **Reforms in education** - Higher academic standards and expansion of higher education and research reversed the policy of the Cultural Revolution.

- **Institutionalization of the Revolution** - Revolutionary goals were reconciled with restoring the legal system and bureaucracy of the Old China, decentralizing the government, modifying elections, and infusing capitalism.

CITIZENS, SOCIETY AND THE STATE

As leadership of the country has passed from Mao to Deng to **Jiang Zemin** and then **Hu Jintao**, the relationship of Chinese citizens to the state has changed profoundly. Under Maoism, virtually no civil society was allowed, and the government controlled almost every facet of citizens' lives. With a transition to a market based economy, important transformations are occurring in citizen-state relationships.

Party leaders realize that most citizens no longer see communist ideology as central to their lives. As a result, the Chinese Communist Party now appeals to patriotism and the traditional pride in being Chinese. The message is that China's economic resurgence in recent years is a reemergence of the great ancient Chinese Empire, and now under communist leadership. For example, the party-state does all it can to tout its leading role in China's economic achievements, winning the 2008 Summer Olympics for Beijing, and returning Hong Kong to Chinese control.

ETHNIC CLEAVAGES

China's ethnic population is primarily **Han Chinese**, the people that historically formed the basis of China's identity, first as an empire, and eventually as a country. China's borders have long included other ethnicities, primarily through conquest and expansion of land claims in Asia. Minority groups now comprise only about eight percent of the PRC's population, but their **"autonomous areas"** (such as **Tibet** and **Xinjiang**) make up more than 60 percent of China's territory and have a long history of resistance to the Chinese government. There are 55 officially recognized minority groups, and no one minority is very large. Even so, the Chinese government has put a great deal of time and effort into its policies regarding ethnic groups.

Most minorities live on or near China's borders with other countries, and most of their areas are sparsely populated. For example, Mongols live in both Mongolia and China, and Kazakhs live in both the Kazakh Republic and China. Because dissidents are a long way from areas of dense population, China is worried that they may encourage independence, or join with neighboring countries. Tibet – with its long history of separate ethnic identity – has been especially problematic since the Chinese army conquered it in the early days of the PRC.   The former government of Tibet never recognized Chinese authority, and some Tibetans today campaign for independence. A second group that has shown increasing unrest is the **Uighurs**, who live in Xingjiang, very close to the borders with Afghanistan and Pakistan and the Central Asian states of the former Soviet Union. Uighur militants want to create a separate Islamic state and have sometimes used violence to support their cause. In the post-September 11 world, the Chinese have become very concerned with these Muslim dissidents.

Even though the percentages are not high, China does have about 100 million citizens who are members of minorities groups, a huge number by anyone's calculations. Generally, the government's policy has been to encourage economic development and suppress expressions of dissent in ethnic minority areas. Most of China's minorities are in the five autonomous regions of Guangxi, Inner Mongolia, Ningxia, Tibet, and Xinjiang. The Chinese constitution grants autonomous areas the right of self-government in some matters, such as cultural affairs, but their autonomy is in fact very limited. Ethnic dissent continues into the present, although many groups appear to be content to be part of the Chinese empire.

Even among the Han Chinese there is great linguistic diversity, although they have shared a written language for many centuries. Since its inception the Communist regime has tried to make Mandarin the official language of government and education. For example, in early 2006 China stepped up its repression of Shanghainese, a language which, in its various forms, is native to close to 100 million people, especially around Shanghai, China's largest city. Rules required most people in the public sector, including teachers and members of the broadcast media, to use Mandarin when addressing the public. Despite restrictions such as this, dialects remain embedded in Chinese society, and demonstrate the difficulty that the centralized state has in imposing its will on its huge territorial space.

URBAN-RURAL CLEAVAGES

An increasingly important divide in Chinese society is between rural and urban areas. Most of China's tremendous economic growth over the past few decades has taken place in cities. As a result, the gap between urban and rural incomes has grown to the point that some observers have redefined the meaning of "two Chinas" – this time, a rural and an urban one. The divide is not just economic, but also includes social life style differences that form the basis of growing resentments across the countryside. One result has been an upsurge in protests in rural areas, where some believe that the government is not looking out for their interests. For example, a few years ago in Hunan Province, thousands of angry farmers marched on the township government headquarters to protest excessive taxes and corruption of local officials. Shortly afterward, nine people suspected of being leaders of the protests were arrested. In reaction to this discontent, Prime Minister **Wen Jiabao** announced in 2006 a new government emphasis on **"a new socialist countryside,"** a program to lift the lagging rural economy. He recognized the following year that the rural poor had an array of problems not shared by urban residents.

POLITICAL PARTICIPATION

According to Chinese tradition before 1949, citizens are subjects of government, not participants in a political system. The communist state redefined political participation by creating a relationship between the Communist Party and citizenship, and by shaping the economic relationship between citizens and the government. Nevertheless, old traditions that governed personal ties and relationships still mold China's political processes and influence the actions and beliefs of elites and citizens alike. In recent years popular social movements that support democracy, religious beliefs, and community ties over nationalism have influenced Chinese politics and helped to define China's relationships with other countries.

PARTY AND PARTICIPATION

The **Chinese Communist Party** (CCP) is the largest political party in the world in terms of total formal membership, with about 58 million members at the turn of the century. However, as was true in the USSR, its members make up only a small minority of the country's population. Only about eight percent of those over eighteen (the minimum age for joining the party) are members of the CCP. Only those that are judged to be fully committed to the ideals of communism and who are willing to devote a great deal of time and energy to party affairs may join. Party membership is growing, with new members recruited largely from the CCP's **Youth League.** Almost 70 million Chinese youths belonged to the Youth League by 2005.

The economic reforms begun by Deng Xiaoping paved the way for a milestone transition in the backgrounds of party members. During the Maoist era (before 1976) revolutionary **cadres** whose careers depended on party loyalty and ideological purity led the CCP at all levels. Most cadres were peasants or factory workers, and few were intellectuals or professionals. Since Deng's reforms, **"technocrats,"** people with technical training who have climbed the ladder of the party bureaucracy, have led the party increasingly. All seven members of the current Standing Committee have academic and professional backgrounds in technical fields, and five of them were trained as engineers. Today less than 40 percent of party members come from the peasantry, although peasants still make up the largest single group within the CCP. The fastest growing membership category consists of officials, intellectuals, technicians, and other professionals. Women make up about 20 percent of the membership and only about 4 percent of the Central Committee.

A significant change in party membership came in 2001 with the decision to allow capitalists to become members. In a repudiation of Maoist principles, President Jiang Zemin argued that the CCP ought to represent not just workers and peasants but business interests as well. According to some estimates, between a quarter and a third of all Chinese entrepreneurs are CCP members, a fact that significantly alters the traditional concept of "cadre."

THE GROWTH OF CIVIL SOCIETY

In recent years the control mechanisms of the party have loosened as new forms of associations appear, like Western-style discos and coffeehouses. Communications through cell phones, fax machines, TV satellite dishes, and internet have made it more difficult for the party-state to monitor citizens.

An important new development is the growth of **civil society** – the appearance of private organizations that may or may not directly challenge the authority of the state but focus on social problems, such as the environment, AIDS, and legal reform. For example, recently activist organizations have protested government-sponsored dam projects that would flood the farmland of millions of peasants. The government is trying to harness water power for further industrial development, and even though the protestors will probably not block the projects, the very existence of these groups represents a major change.

Activists had virtually no say in the Chinese political system until the 1990s when Beijing allowed **nongovernmental organizations (NGOs)** to register with the government. Today China has thousands of NGOs, ranging from ping-pong clubs to environmentalist groups. A key test of China's tolerance is religion. Today Christianity and Buddhism are rebounding, after years of communist suppression of religion. Despite these changes, the government still keeps close control of these groups, with their 1999-2001 crackdown on the religious movement **Falon Gong** a good example of the party's limited tolerance of activities outside the political realm.

PROTESTS

The **Tiananmen Square massacre** of 1989 showed the limits of protest in China. Massive repression was the government's message to its citizens that democratic movements that defy the party leadership will not be tolerated. In recent years, religious groups, such as Falon Gong, have staged major protests, but none have risen to the level of conflict apparent in 1989. Village protests have made their way into the news, and thousands of labor strikes have been reported. Some observers believe that protests will pose serious threats to the party in the near future.

POLITICAL INSTITUTIONS

China's political regime is best categorized as **authoritarian**, one in which decisions are made by political elites – those that hold political power – without much input from citizens. Leaders are recruited through their membership in the Communist Party, but personal relationships and informal ties to others are also important in deciding who controls the regime. However, this authoritarian regime has the same problem that emperors of past dynasties had – how to effectively govern the huge expanse of land and large population from one centralized place. As China has moved away from a command economy toward a market economy, this centralization has become even more problematic in recent years. As a result, a major feature of economic decision-making is now **decentralization**, or devolution of power to subnational governments. Local governments often defy or ignore the central government by setting their own tax rates or building projects without consulting the central government.

The political framework of the People's Republic of China is designed to penetrate as many corners of the country as possible through an elaborately organized Chinese Communist Party (CCP). As in the old Soviet Union, party personnel control government structures. Unlike the Soviet Union, however, the CCP also integrates its military into the political hierarchy. Political elites are often recruited from the military, and the head of the Central Military Commission is among the most powerful leaders in China.

THE CHINESE COMMUNIST PARTY (CCP)

Despite the many changes that China has experienced in recent years, the Chinese Communist Party is still at the heart of the political system. The party bases its claim to legitimacy not on the expressed will of the people but on representation of the historical best interests of all the people. Society is best led by an elite vanguard party with a superior understanding of the Chinese people and their needs (democratic centralism).

THE ORGANIZATION OF THE CCP

The **Chinese Communist Party** (CCP) is organized hierarchically by levels - village/township, county, province, and nation. At the top of the system is the supreme leader (Deng Xiaoping's phrase was "the core"), who until 1976 was Chairman Mao Zedong. The title "chairman" was abandoned after Mao's death, and the head of the party is now called the "general secretary." The party has a separate constitution from the government's constitution of 1982, and its central bodies are:

- **National Party Congress -** This body consists of more than 2000 delegates chosen primarily from congresses on lower levels. It only meets every five years, so it is obviously not important in policymaking. It usually rubberstamps decisions made by the party leaders, although in recent years it has acted somewhat more independently. Its main importance remains its power to elect members of the Central Committee.

- **Central Committee** - The Committee has about 340 members (some of whom are alternates) that meet together annually for about a week. They carry on the business of the National Party Congress between sessions, although their size and infrequent meetings limit their policymaking powers. Their meetings are called **plenums**, and they are important in that they are gatherings of the political elites, and from their midst are chosen the Politburo and the Standing Committee.

- **Politburo/Standing Committee** - These most powerful political organizations are at the very top of the CCP structure. They are chosen by the Central Committee, and their decisions dictate government policies. The Politburo has 24 members, and the Standing Committee - chosen from the Politburo membership - has only 7. They meet in secret, and their membership reflects the balance of power among factions and the relative influence of different groups in policymaking.

NON-COMMUNIST PARTIES

Even though China effectively has a one-party system, the CCP does allow the existence of eight "democratic" parties. Each party has a special group that it draws from, such as intellectuals or businessmen. Their total membership is about a half million, and they are tightly controlled by the CCP. They do not contest the CCP for control of the government, but they do serve an important advisory role to the party leaders. Some members even attain high government positions, but organizationally these parties serve only as a loyal non-opposition. Attempts to establish independent democratic parties outside CCP control have been squashed, with the party doling out severe prison sentences to the independent-minded leaders.

ELECTIONS

The PRC holds elections in order to legitimize the government and the CCP. The party controls the commissions that run elections, and it reviews draft lists of proposed candidates to weed out those it finds politically objectionable. The only direct elections are held at the local level, with voters choosing deputies to serve on the county people's congresses. The people's congresses at higher levels are selected from and by the lower levels, not directly by the people. Since the 1980s the party has allowed more than one candidate to run for county positions, and most candidates are nominated by the people. One move toward democracy has occurred at the village level, where local officials are no longer appointed from above, but are chosen in direct, secret ballot elections.

THE POLITICAL ELITE

Mao Zedong's place in Chinese history was sealed by the Long March of 1934-36. He emerged from the ordeal as a charismatic leader who brought about great change. His compatriots that made the journey with him became known as the "Old Guard," a group of friends that networked with one another for many years through *guanxi*, or personal connections. These personal connections are still the glue that holds Chinese politics together today.

China, like the USSR, recruits its leaders through ***nomenklatura,*** a system of choosing cadres from lower levels of the party hierarchy for advancement based on their loyalty and contributions to the well-being of the party. However, Chinese leaders communicate with one another through a **patron-client network** called ***guanxi.*** These linkages are similar to "old boys' networks" in the West, and they underscore the importance of person career ties between individuals as they rise in bureaucratic or political structures. Besides bureaucratic and personal ties, *guanxi* is based on ideology differences and similarities, and as a result, has been the source of factions within the party. *Guanxi* is also pervasive at the local level, where ordinary people link up with village leaders and lower party officials.

FACTIONALISM

 Factionalism in the years before Mao's death in 1976 is demonstrated in the splits among the radicals (led by Jiang Qing and the Gang of Four), the military under Lin Biao, and the reformers under Zhou Enlai. All three men (Mao, Lin, and Zhou) were part of the "Old Guard" that went on the Long March in the 1930s, but by 1976, all were dead. Deng Xiaoping emerged as the new leader of China, partly because he was able to unite the factions in a course toward economic reform.

Even before Deng's death in 1997, however, factional strife was apparent within the leadership, most notably during the 1989 Tiananmen Square incident. In general, the factions have split in at least three ways:

- **Conservatives -** Although all factions supported economic reform, conservatives worry that perhaps the power of the party and the central government has eroded too much. They are particularly concerned about any movement toward democracy and generally support crackdowns on organizations and individuals who act too independently. Their most prominent leader has been **Li Peng,** the former premier and chair of the National People's Congress. His retirement in 2003 leaves the leadership of this faction in doubt.

- **Reformers/open door -** This faction supports major capitalist infusion into the PRC's economy and generally promotes an open door trade policy. These leaders have pushed for membership in the World Trade Organization and have courted the U.S. to grant "most-favored trading" status to China. They don't necessarily support democratic reform, but their focus is on economic growth and development, so their political attitudes tend to be pragmatic. Two important leaders of the reformers were **Jiang Zemin** - the PRC President and CCP General Secretary until 2003 - and **Zhu Rongji** - the former governor of the central bank and the PRC Premier until 2003. The current president, **Hu Jintao,** and prime minister, **Wen Jiabao,** have allied with this faction so far.

- **Liberals -** This faction has been out of power since the 1989 Tiananmen Square incident, but they are generally more accepting of political liberties and democratic movements than are the other factions. They support economic and political reform. The two most famous leaders of this faction are **Hu Yuobang** - whose death started the protests in 1989 - and **Zhao Ziyang** - the Premier and General Secretary who was ousted for being too sympathetic with the Tiananmen protestors. Hu Yuobang was the mentor of China's current president, Hu Jintao, but so far he has shown no support for democratic movements.

The factions follow the process of ***fang-shou*** - a tightening up, loosening up cycle - a waxing and waning of the power of each. In some ways, the cycle is similar to the old dynastic cycle, when ruling families were challenged when they lost the mandate of heaven. Part of the current dominance of the reformers has to do with the lingering influence of Deng Xiaoping, who designated before his death in 1997 that Jiang Zemin would be the "3ʳᵈ generation" (after Mao and Deng) leader, and Hu Jintao would be the "4ᵗʰ generation" leader.

CORRUPTION

The combination of *guanxi* and the economic boom of the past twenty years has brought about rampant corruption within the Chinese economic and political system. Bribes are common, and corruption is widely regarded as a major problem. President Jiang Zemin acknowledged in 1997, "The fight against corruption is a grave political struggle vital to the very existence of the party and the state...If corruption cannot be punished effectively, our Party will lose the support and confidence of the people." In 2004 the Communist Party's Central Committee published a policy paper that warned its members that corruption and incompetence could threaten its hold on power. The anti-corruption statement bears the mark of President Hu Jintao, who has responded to popular perception of widespread corruption among party members. Under his watch, thousands of officials have recently been punished for corruption, although the problem continues to plague the regime.

In 2007 the Chinese government was embarrassed by international publicity about tainted food, health products, and drugs that were making their way through the world market. In reaction, the head of Beijing's most powerful food and drug regulating agency was arrested, imprisoned, and eventually executed. In his confession he acknowledged that he had accepted gifts and bribes valued at more than $850,000 from eight drug companies that sought special favors. Because the Chinese media hardly ever report corruption cases without official approval, many speculated that this arrest was meant to be a warning from the government. In another case, the press did not report the arrest of the deputy head of a state-run lottery in 2006 for several months. An audit in 2005 found that the lottery had diverted about $72 million from lottery funds, with a good chunk of it ending up as bonuses for agency staff.

INTEREST GROUPS

Organized interest groups and social movements are not permitted to influence the political process unless they are under the party-state authority. The party-state tries to preempt the formation of independent groups by forming mass organizations in which people may express their points of view within strict limits. These mass organizations often form around occupations or social categories. For example, most factory workers belong to the All-China Federation of Trade Unions, and women's interests are represented in the All-China Women's Federation. In urban areas, the party maintains social control through **danwei** - social units usually based on a person's place of work. People depend on the units for their jobs, income, and promotion, but also for medical care, housing, daycare centers, and recreational facilities.

Despite the ever-present control of the state, in the last 15 years China has gone from having virtually no independent groups of any kind to more than 300,000 nongovernmental organizations, by official count. But that probably understates the true number. Counting unregistered groups, some estimates place the number as high as two million. Still, their impact on the policymaking process is not clearly felt. For example, in 2007 China's legislature passed a new labor law to protect workers, requiring employers to provide written contracts and restricting the use of temporary laborers to help give more employees long-term job security. However, the law also enhanced the power of the All-China Federation of Trade Unions, a monopoly union for the Communist Party. It is an official state organization charged with overseeing workers, and it alone was given the power to collectively bargain for wages and benefits. Workers are not allowed to form independent unions.

These organizations and the state's relationship with them reflect **state corporatism** (p. 36), as well as the logic of Lenin's democratic centralism Most organizations are created, or at least approved, by the state, and many have government officials as their leaders. In yet another demonstration of corporatism, the state only allows one organization for any given profession or activity. In cases where two groups with similar interests exist in a community, local officials will force them to merge or will disband one in favor of the other. This practice prevents competition between the associations and limits how many associations are allowed to exist, making it easier for the state to monitor and control them.

INSTITUTIONS OF GOVERNMENT

The political structure of the People's Republic of China can best be seen as three **parallel hierarchies** that are separate yet interact with one another:

- **The Communist Party**

- **The state or government**

- **The People's Liberation Army.**

The party dominates the three yet the organizations are separate. The relationship between the party and the government is controlled by the principle of **dual role** - *vertical* supervision of the next higher level of government and *horizontal* supervision of the Communist Party at their own level.

The organization of party and state are similar on paper to those of the former USSR, largely because the PRC's structure was designed by the Soviets during the period between 1949 and 1958. In reality, China's policymaking is governed more directly by factions and personal relationships.

THE STRUCTURE OF THE GOVERNMENT

The government structure of the People's Republic of China has three branches - a legislature, an executive, and a judiciary. But all branches are controlled by the party, so they are not independent, nor does a system of checks and balances exist. All top government positions are held by party members, as are many on the lower levels.

The People's Congresses

Government authority is formally vested in a system of people's congresses, which begins with a **People's National Congress** at the top and continues in hierarchical levels down through the provincial, city, and local congresses. Theoretically they are the people's legislatures, but in reality they are subject to party authority. The National People's Congress chooses the president and vice president of China, but there is only one party-sponsored candidate for each position. Although the Congress itself has little power, its meetings are important to watch because the Politburo's decisions are formally announced then. For example, during the 10th National People's Congress in 2003, China's new president and general secretary (**Hu Jintao**) and chief of Parliament (**Wu Bangguo**) were announced. Although their appointments were widely known before the meeting began (partly because their leadership had been announced at the 2002 CCP meeting), the PNC meeting was the chosen format for introducing the new leaders to the world.

Executive/Bureaucracy

The **president** and **vice president** serve five-year terms, are limited to two terms, and must be at least 45 years old. The positions are largely ceremonial, though senior party leaders have always held them. Currently, Hu Jintao is both the president and the general secretary of the CCP.

The **premier** is the head of government, formally appointed by the president, but again, the position is always held by a member of the Standing Committee. Zhu Rongji held this position from 1998 to 2003, and the current premier is Wen Jiabao. He directs the State Council, which is composed of ministers who direct the many ministries and commissions of the bureaucracy. These are controlled by the principle of **dual role.**

 The bureaucracy exists on all levels - national, provincial, county, and local. These lower level positions are held by **cadres,** people in positions of authority who are paid by the government or party. Many are both government officials and party members, but not all. In all, about 30 million cadres around China see that the leaders' policies are carried out everywhere.

The Judiciary

China has a four-tiered "**people's court**" system, organized hierarchically just as the people's congresses are. A nationwide organization called the "**people's procuratorate**" provides public prosecutors and defenders to the courts.

During the Cultural Revolution the judicial system came under attack as a bastion of elitism and reform, and the law was subjected to the leaders. In recent decades, the judiciary has been revitalized, and more than 100,000 new judges and lawyers have been trained. New law codes have also been instituted. However, no structure exists for judicial review, and the judicial system remains subservient to the party hierarchy. Laws have been applied selectively to punish political opponents or to provide examples to others.

The criminal justice system works swiftly and harshly, with a conviction rate of more than 99% of all cases that come to trial. Prison terms are long and subject to only cursory appeal. Hundreds, perhaps thousands of people have been executed during periods of government-sponsored anti-crimes campaigns. Human rights organizations criticize China for its extensive use of the death penalty.

THE PEOPLE'S LIBERATION ARMY (PLA)

"Political power grows out of the barrel of a gun."

Mao Zedong

The military grew hand in hand with communism, as Mao's famous statement reflects. The **People's Liberation Army** encompasses all of the country's ground, air, and naval armed services. The army is huge, with about 3 million active personnel and about 12 million reserves, yet in proportion to its population, the Chinese military presence is smaller than that of the United States. China has about 2.4 military personnel for every 1000 people, whereas the U.S. has 6.1. Military spending is only about four percent of that of the U.S., although many analysts suspect that the government underestimates the military budget. Despite these statistics, China's military budget has been growing at double-digit rates for years, with an estimated 18% rise estimated for 2007. In early 2007 a missile was sent into space to destroy an old weather satellite, indicating the growing military sophistication of the PLA.

The military has never held formal political power in the People's Republic of China, but it has been an important influence on politics and policy. All of the early political leaders were also military leaders. For example, Mao and the other members of the "Old Guard", led the Long March of the 1930s primarily by military moves.

The second half of Mao's famous quote above is less often quoted:

> "Our principle is that the party commands the gun, and the gun must never be allowed to command the party."

Clearly, the military has never threatened to dominate the party. It is represented in the government by the **Central Military Commission**, which has been led by many prominent party leaders, including Deng Xiaoping.

The Tiananmen crisis in 1989 greatly harmed the image of the PLA, since the military was ordered to recapture the square and do so with brutal force. But the PLA continues to play an important role in

Chinese politics. Two of the 24 members of the Politburo are military officers, and PLA representatives make up over 20 percent of the Central Committee membership. In 2003, Jiang Zemin's retention of his position as head of the Central Military Commission despite his stepping down as president, indicates that he still had significant policymaking power. When President Hu Jintao replaced Jiang in 2004, the shift signaled that the transition of power was complete, and that Hu now has full control of the parallel hierarchies.

POLICYMAKING AND POLITICAL ISSUES

Since the beginning of Deng Xiaoping's rule in 1979, policymaking in China has centered on reconciling centralized political authority with marketization and privatization of the economy. Many political scientists who have assumed that democracy and capitalism always accompany one another have waited for China to democratize, an event that has yet to occur. After all, that pattern occurred in the countries that industrialized first, and the fall of the Soviet Union confirmed the notion that authoritarian states cannot be capitalistic. China has defied these theorists, and perhaps is finding its own path to economic prosperity.

POLICYMAKING PROCESS: *FANG-SHOU*

Deng Xiaoping's carefully balanced blend of socialist central planning with a capitalist market economy has not been without its critics. The tensions within the system - both economic and political - are evidenced in *fang-shou*, a letting go, tightening-up cycle evidenced even under Mao in his reaction to the Hundred Flowers Movement. The cycle consists of three types of actions/policies - economic reform, democratic movements (letting go), and a tightening-up by the CCP. With each new economic reform, liberal factions react with a demand for political reforms, which the Party responds to with force.

POLICY ISSUES

Policy issues are numerous, but they may be put into three categories: democracy and human rights issues, economic issues, and foreign policy and international trade issues.

DEMOCRACY AND HUMAN RIGHTS

The Chinese leaders that came to power after Deng's death in 1997 have not strayed significantly from Deng's path of economic reform and resistance to political reform. Jiang Zemin was the General Secretary of the CCP from 1989-2003 and the President from 1993 to 2003, but he did not consolidate his power until after Deng's death in 1997. Zhu Rongji - Premier from 1998 to 2003 and former governor of the central bank - also emerged as an influential leader. Jiang was often criticized for being a weak leader and did not have the same stature as Deng or Mao - the two men who dominated China during the second half of the 20th century. Hu Jintao, leader since 2003, for the most part has also held to the path defined by Deng.

Despite the continuing tensions between economic and political policy, some democratic reforms can be seen:

- Some input from the National People's Congress is accepted by the Politburo.

- More emphasis is placed on laws and legal procedures.

- Village elections are now semi-competitive, with choices of candidates and some freedom from the party's control.

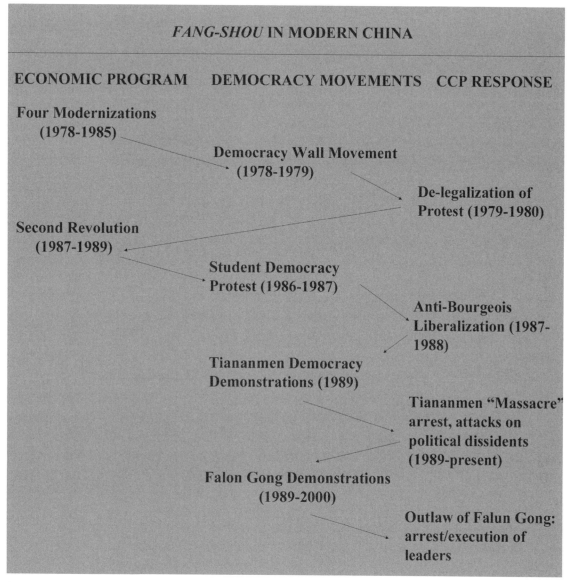

FANG-SHOU IN MODERN CHINA

| ECONOMIC PROGRAM | DEMOCRACY MOVEMENTS | CCP RESPONSE |

Four Modernizations (1978-1985)

Democracy Wall Movement (1978-1979)

De-legalization of Protest (1979-1980)

Second Revolution (1987-1989)

Student Democracy Protest (1986-1987)

Anti-Bourgeois Liberalization (1987-1988)

Tiananmen Democracy Demonstrations (1989)

Tiananmen "Massacre" arrest, attacks on political dissidents (1989-present)

Falon Gong Demonstrations (1989-2000)

Outlaw of Falun Gong: arrest/execution of leaders

Tensions in China's political economy. The process of fang-shou gives some insight into how the Chinese government has managed the tensions between capitalism and democracy. The two rounds of economic reform shown (The Four Modernizations and the Second Revolution) were each followed by democracy movements that were repressed by the government. Although Falon Gong is a religious, not a democratic movement, it too was repressed by the government.

The Tiananmen Crisis began as a grief demonstration for the death of Hu Yaobang - a liberal who had earlier resigned from the Politburo under pressure from the conservatives. Most of the original demonstrators were students and intellectuals, but other groups joined them, and the wake turned into democratic protests. They criticized corruption and demanded democratic reforms, and hundreds of thousands joined in. Protests erupted all over China, and Tiananmen became the center of international attention for almost two months. How would the Politburo react?

The answer came with guns, as Deng sent the People's Liberation Army to shut down the protests, using whatever means necessary. The army shot its way to the square, killing hundreds of protesting citizens.

They recaptured control, but the fatalities and arrests began a broad new wave of international protests from human rights advocates. Unofficial estimates of fatalities range from 700 to several thousands.

Since then, China has been under a great deal of pressure from international human rights organizations to democratize their political process and to abide by human rights standards advocated by the groups. Deng Xiaoping showed little impulse to liberalize the political process, as did the government that followed under Jiang Zemin, at least publicly. Factional disagreements are kept from the public eye, yet all evidence indicates that Hu Jintao is following the same path.

The Rule of Law

The principle of **rule of law**, almost always associated with liberal democracies, is based on the belief that rulers should not have absolute power over their subjects, and that their actions should be constrained by the same principles that control ordinary citizens. From the communist point of view, law is part of politics that the bourgeoisie uses to suppress the proletariat. Communist leaders, then, have never acknowledged rule of law as a legitimate principle. For example, during the Cultural Revolution, in an effort to bring about his dream of a new egalitarian society, Mao Zedong set about to destroy the old legal codes of dynastic China. However, since 1978 legal codes have begun to revive, partly because the new economic growth and investments have required that consistent regulations be in place that allow China to trade internationally and attract foreign companies.

Criminal law, almost nonexistent in 1978, has also developed because of the new opportunities for bribery, theft, and inside stock market trading created by the economic boom. As a result, **procuratorates**, officials who investigate and prosecute official crimes, were recreated from earlier days, and they have played a role in Hu Jintao's crackdown on corruption within the Communist Party. The 1982 Constitution, theoretically at least, commits the party to the authority of law. Today the Chinese state is more constrained by law and Chinese citizens freer by law from political whim than ever before. However, this trend does not change the fact that Chinese justice is harsh by the standards of most other nations, and the death penalty is often enforced for smuggling, rape, theft, bribery, trafficking in women and children, and official corruption.

Civil Rights and Liberties

Since the protests at Tiananmen Square in 1989, the status of civil rights and liberties in China has been widely debated. Many people believed that because Hu Jintao was mentored by Zhao Ziyang and Hu Yaobang (leaders of the liberal faction), that he would promote more individual freedoms in China. For example, Hu and Premier Wen Jiabao took the lead in reversing the party's cover-up of the deadly SARS outbreak, pledging greater accountability and transparency in government. However, by 2005, Hu showed few signs of changing the government's basic political policies toward individual civil liberties and rights. For example, he has adopted new measures to regulate discussions on university internet sites. Several dissident writers who have criticized the government have been arrested, and a professor who posted highly critical comments of the government on the internet was dismissed from Beijing University. Hu has also called for "ideological education" in universities, a phrase that is reminiscent of the Maoist era.

ECONOMIC POLICY

From 1949 to 1978, China followed a communist political economic model: a command economy directed by a central government based on democratic centralism. Mao Zedong called this policy the "**iron rice bowl**," or cradle-to-grave health care, work, and retirement security. The state set production quotas and distributed basic goods to consumers. When this model failed, Deng Xiaoping began a series of economic reforms that make up the **socialist market economy** – gradual infusion of capitalism while still retaining state control.

Agricultural policy

- **The people's communes -** During the early days of the PRC - in an effort to realize important socialist goals - virtually all peasants were organized into collective farms of approximately 250 families each. During the Great Leap Forward, farms were merged into gigantic **people's communes** with several thousand families. These communes were one of the weakest links in Mao's China, with production and rural living standards showing little improvement between 1957 and 1977. Many communes were poorly managed, and peasants often didn't see the need to work hard, contrary to Mao's hopes of developing devotion through the mass line.

- **Household responsibility system -** In the early 1980s, Deng dismantled the communes and replaced them with a **household responsibility system**, which is still in effect today. In this system individual families take full charge of the production and marketing of crops. After paying government taxes and contract fees to the villages, families may consume or sell what they produce. Food production improved dramatically, and villages developed both private farming and industry.

"Private Business"

In 1988 the National People's Congress officially created a new category of **"private business"** under the control of the party. It included urban co-ops, service organizations, and rural industries that largely operate as capitalist enterprises. The importance of China's state sector has gradually diminished, although private industry remains heavily regulated by the government. Price controls have been lifted, and private businesses have grown by leaps and bounds since the 1980s, and are far more profitable and dynamic than are the state-owned ones.

The fastest growing sector of the Chinese economy is rooted in **township and village enterprises** (TVEs), rural factories and businesses that vary greatly in size, and are run by local government and private entrepreneurs. Although they are called collective enterprises, they make their own decisions and are responsible for their profits and losses. The growth of the TVE system has slowed the migration of peasants to the cities, and has become the backbone of economic strength in the countryside.

Economic Problems

The reforms have brought several important economic problems:

- **Unemployment and inequality** – Under Maoism, everyone was guaranteed a job, but marketization has brought very high rates of unemployment to China today. The Chinese leadership hopes that the booming economy will eventually take care of the unemployed, once the economy has had time to adjust to the reforms. Economic growth has also made some people very rich, and has barely affected others. As a result, economic inequality has increased significantly. The growing inequality has created a **floating population** of rural migrants seeking job opportunities in cities. As cities grow larger, crime rates have increased and infrastructures are strained, leaving urban residents with the tendency to blame the new migrants for their problems.

- **Inefficiency of the state sector** – Over the years the state-owned sector of the economy has gradually declined so that today almost three-fourths of industrial production is privately owned. The state sector is still large, however, and it is plagued by corruption, inefficiency, and too many workers. Without state subsidizes these industries would almost surely fail, bringing about even higher unemployment rates, so the government has continued to support them.

- **Pollution** – As China has industrialized, air and water pollution have become increasingly serious problems. Beijing and Shanghai have some of the most polluted air in the world, and sulfur dioxide and nitrogen oxides emitted by China' coal-fired power plants fall as acid rain on the neighboring countries of South Korea and Japan. Experts once thought China would overtake the United States as the world's leading producer of greenhouse gases by 2010, but now the International Energy Agency believes that will happen before 2008. The issue is a real dilemma for the government because China is still a poor country in many ways, and to reduce industrial output could ruin the economic progress of the past few decades. However, evidence that China's air and water are unhealthy for the population is mounting. The government has set targets for energy efficiency and improved air and water quality, but so far they have gone unmet.

- **Product Safety** – In 2007 Chinese factories were caught exporting poisonous pharmaceutical ingredients, dangerous toys, bogus pet food, faulty tires, and unhealthy shellfish. An international outcry followed, and the government has been pressured to do something about it. A big part of the problem lies with the tension between central government authority and capitalism. In order to allow the market economy to grow, authority has been decentralized, so that local officials have gained a great deal of decision-making power. As a result, the central government has lost direct control over production, and some faulty products have made their way into the international market.

FOREIGN POLICY AND INTERNATIONAL TRADE

Since 1998 Chinese foreign policy has undergone profound changes that have brought the country closer into the mainstream of international politics. China still resists pressure from other countries to improve its human rights record, and Chinese leaders continue to threaten to invade Taiwan now and again. However, especially in the areas of trade, China has integrated itself into the world community in almost unprecedented ways. It is quickly replacing Japan as the most powerful economy in Asia, and is now Asia's central economy that affects all others. Chinese-Japanese relations have been problematic since the late 19th century when Japan began to rise as a world power, generally at China's expense. Both countries are particularly sensitive about Japan's invasion of China during World War II, and formal relations were called off for several months in 2006 because the Japanese prime minister visited a controversial war memorial. Now the two countries are on speaking terms again, but tensions still remain. China also has trading partners all over the world, and that trade is an integral part of the growing economy.

Foreign Policy Under Mao

Until Mao's death in 1976, the PRC based its foreign policy on providing support for third world revolutionary movements. It provided substantial development assistance to a handful of the most radical states. Examples are Korea and Vietnam. Under Mao, China's relationship with the USSR changed dramatically in the late 1950s from one of dependence to independence.

During the 1920s and 1950s, the USSR gave large amounts of money, as well as technical and political advice to China. The countries broke into rivalry during the late 1950s when Mao decided that the Soviets had turned their backs on Marx and revolution. The Great Leap Forward and the Cultural Revolution affirmed China's independent path from Moscow's control.

US/Chinese Relations

The chill in China/USSR relationships encouraged the U.S. to eye the advantages of opening positive interactions with China. As long as Mao was in control, his anti-capitalist attitudes - as well as U.S. containment policy - meant that the countries had no contacts until the early 1970s. Then, with Mao sick and weak, reformist Zhou Enlai opened the door to western contact. President Nixon and Secretary of State Henry Kissinger engineered negotiations, and Nixon's famous 1972 visit to China signaled a new era. Relations opened with a ping-pong match between the two countries, but after Deng Xiaoping's leadership began in 1978, his open door policy helped lead the way to more substantial contact. Today the U.S. imports many more products from China than it exports, and is concerned about the imbalance between exports and imports. The U.S. has pressured China to devalue its currency and to crack down on illegal exports, but so far, China has resisted the currency adjustment, and the illegal exports continue to be a problem.

International Trade and Business Today

Another integral part of the economic reform of the past quarter century has been the opening of the Chinese economy to international forces. Four **Special Economic Zones (SEZs)** were established in 1979. In these regions, foreign investors were given preferential tax rates and other incentives. Five years later fourteen more areas became SEZs, and today foreign investments and free market mechanisms have spread to most of the rest of urban China.

Since 1978 China's trade and industry have expanded widely. With this expansion has come a rapidly growing GDP, entrepreneurship, and trade with many nations. A wealthy class of businessmen has emerged, and Chinese products have made their way around the world. China is now a member of the World Trade Organization, and it has "most favored nation status" for trading with the U.S. A monumental recognition of China's new economic power came in 1997, when the British officially "gave" the major trading city of Hong Kong back to Chinese control.

Deng Xiaoping emphasized economic reform, but he continued to believe that the Party should be firmly in command of the country. In general, he did not support political reforms that included democracy and/or more civil liberties for citizens. Freedoms and incentives were granted to entrepreneurs, but they have operated largely under the patron-client system (*guanxi*).

Hong Kong

In 1997 the British ceded control of Hong Kong to mainland China under a "**one country, two systems**" agreement signed by Britain and China in 1984. Under this policy, Hong Kong would be subject to Chinese rule, but would continue to enjoy "a high degree of autonomy," meaning that it would maintain its capitalist system, legal system, and way of life. Since the handover, Beijing authorities have been less heavy-handed than feared, and Hong Kong today enjoys the same civil liberties as under British rule.

Some problems surfaced in 2003 when Tung Chee-hwa, chief executive of the Hong Kong Special Administration region, spearheaded a move to sell government-owned public housing and business properties without consultation with the partially elected legislature. The incident spilled over into a half a million protestors marching the streets to protest Beijing's lack of movement toward wider popular representation and an elected governor. Hu chastised Tung for his actions, and even though tensions still remain, no protests have reemerged on the same scale as those in 2003.

Taiwan

The island of Taiwan was the destination of Chiang Kai-shek after being driven from mainland China by Mao Zedong in 1949. Since post World War II, Taiwan has claimed to be the Republic of China, separate from the People's Republic of China ruled by the Communist Party. Taiwan's autonomy was protected by the United States in a Cold War tactic against Communist China, and until the 1970s, Taiwan was recognized by western nations as the sole legitimate representative of China. However, in 1971, Taiwan lost its membership in the United Nations, and its seat on the Security Council went to the People's Republic of China. In 1979, the United States recognized mainland China diplomatically. Today only a few countries recognize Taiwan's sovereignty.

In recent years, the Chinese government has made its claim to Taiwan clear. Chinese leaders assert the belief that Taiwan is historically and legitimately a part of China and should be returned to its control. The Taiwanese government does not agree, but political parties in Taiwan are split in their attitudes about how to respond to China's claims. One point of view is that Taiwan should stand up to, or even defy China, but an alternate sentiment is that Taiwan should try to reconcile its differences with its giant neighbor. The fact that China is Taiwan's biggest trade partner has encouraged the Taiwanese leadership to explore the possibility of strengthening the island's ties to the mainland.

Will China continue to expand its international contacts and its free market economy? If so, will tensions increase between economic and political sectors of the country? During the 20th century many countries have struggled to define the relationship between free market economies and political leadership styles. Most obviously, the Soviet Union collapsed rather than reconcile market liberalization with centralized political power. Will the same thing happen to China, or will their policy of introducing market principles gradually work out in the end? This challenge and many more await answers from Hu Jintao and his leadership team.

IMPORTANT TERMS AND CONCEPTS

"3rd generation leader", "4th generation leader"
autonomous regions
cadres
Central Committee
Central Military Commission
Chiang Kai-shek
collectivism
Chinese Communist Party (CCP)
Confucianism
The Cultural Revolution
danwei

decentralization
democratic centralism
Deng Xiaoping Theory
dual role
dynastic cycles
egalitarianism
ethic of struggle
factions, factionalism
fang-shou
floating population
foreign devils"
Four Modernization
free market socialism
"Gang of Four"
guanxi
The Great Leap Forward
Han Chinese
hegemony
household responsibility system
Hu Jintao
Hu Yaobang
iron rice bowl
Jiang Zemin
Li Peng
The Long March
mandate of heaven
Mao Zedong
Maoism
mass line
mass mobilization
"Middle Kingdom" (*zhongguo*)
Nationalist Party (Goumindang)
National Party Congress
"a new socialist countryside"
nomenklatura
Non-governmental organizations (NGOs)
"one country, two systems"
parallel hierarchies
patron client system in China
People's Courts, procuratorate
People's Liberation Army
People's National Congress
plenums
politburo/standing committee
political elites

"private business"
rule of law in China
self-reliance
socialist market economy
Special Economic Zones (SEZs)
state corporatism
Sun Yat-sen
technocrats
township and village enterprises (TVEs)
"Two Chinas"
unstinting service
Wen Jiabao
Youth League
Zhao Ziyang
zhongguo

MULTIPLE-CHOICE QUESTIONS
CHINA

1. Which of the following is a formal source of sovereignty, authority, and power, but in reality has little bearing on policymaking in China today?

   a) the Constitution of 1982
   b) Deng Xiaoping Theory
   c) democratic centralism
   d) *guanxi*
   e) *zhongguo*

2. A similarities between Confucianism and Maoism is that both

   a) have a vision of an ideal society based on harmony and obedience
   b) emphasize a hierarchical social and political organization
   c) emphasize loyalty to the family
   d) refer to a mass line between rulers and subjects
   e) emphasize the responsibility of ruler to the people

3. Which of the following is an accurate statement regarding geographic influences on China's political system?

   a) China does not have good access to oceans and ice free ports.
   b) China's population is concentrated along river valleys and coastal areas in the east.
   c) China has very few navigable rivers for a country its size.
   d) Most of China's land space is relatively flat and fertile, with few mountains and deserts.
   e) As large as China is, the climate is remarkable similar all over.

4. Which of the following Maoist values emphasizes communication between party leaders, members, and peasants?

   a) collectivism
   b) struggle and activism
   c) mass line
   d) egalitarianism
   e) self-reliance

5. "It doesn't matter whether a cat is white or black, as long as it catches mice."

The phrase above describes

   a) Maoism
   b) mandate of heaven
   c) Chinese nationalism
   d) Deng Xiaoping Theory
   e) parallel hierarchies

6. The modern day political effects of The Long March of 1934-1936 are most clearly manifested in

   a) patron-clientelism
   b) ethnocentrism
   c) parallel hierarchies
   d) *fang-shou*
   e) free market socialism

7. Which of the following is an accurate comparison of political and economic change in China and Russia?

   a) Both countries were world powers in ancient times.
   b) China rose to regional hegemony before Russia did.
   c) Russia rose to the position of a world power in the 20ᵗʰ century after China did.
   d) Both countries have been characterized by drastic, revolutionary, violent change throughout their histories.
   e) Neither country was powerful or economically prosperous before the 19ᵗʰ century.

8. In what way were patterns of political and economic change altered significantly in China during the 19ᵗʰ century?

   a) Dynastic cycles were broken by invaders from Central Asia.
   b) Dynastic cycles began longer and more stable.
   c) A Chinese warlord toppled the empire, ending it forever.
   d) Europeans established spheres of influence in China.
   e) Communist rulers established a new style of regime.

9. In the period between 1958 and 1966, Chinese communist policy differed from Russian communist policy in that Chinese policy put more emphasis on

   a) Five-Year Plans
   b) industrialization
   c) development of the agricultural sector
   d) centralization of authority
   e) collectivization

10. The primary goal of the Chinese Cultural Revolution was to

   a) seize power from Mao Zedong
   b) establish a communist regime in China
   c) improve economic productivity
   d) establish military rule in China
   e) purify the party and the country through radical transformation

(Questions 11 and 12 are based on the following chart):

THE GINI INDEX FOR SELECTED COUNTRIES 2006*

Norway	.26
Canada	.33
United Kingdom	.36
New Zealand	.36
Russia	.40
United States	.41
Iran	.43
Nigeria	.44
China	.45
Mexico	.50

*A low Gini coefficient indicates more equal income or wealth distribution, while a high Gini coefficent indicates unequal income or wealth distribution. "0" corresponds to perfect equality (everyone has the same income), and "1" corresponds to complete inequality (one person has all the income; everyone else has zero income).

11. What does the chart tell us about China's economy in relation to other countries on the chart?

    a) Chinese income is more equally distributed than it is in most of the other countries.
    b) Chinese income inequality is greater than it is in most of the other countries.
    c) Chinese GDP per capita is higher than it is in most of the other countries.
    d) Chinese GDP per capita is lower than it is in most of the other countries.
    e) China's industrial production is higher than it is in most of the other countries.

12. Which of the following factors is MOST CLEARLY connected to the comparison that you noted in #11?

    a) centralization of power
    b) factionalization
    c) marketization/privatization
    d) collectivism
    e) danwei

13. All of the following are accurate statements about China's ethnic minorities EXCEPT:

   a) Most live on or near China's borders.
   b) Most live in sparsely populated areas.
   c) An independence movement is active in Tibet.
   d) Few of China's ethnic minorities are Muslim.
   e) China has officially recognized many ethnic minority groups.

14. Wen Jiabao's "new socialist countryside" program is meant to address the issue of

   a) ethnic group unrest
   b) linguistic diversity
   c) urban-rural cleavages
   d) north-south regional differences
   e) hostility of non-party members toward the CCP

15. Which of the following is a significant change in membership of the CCP in recent years?

   a) Fewer technocrats are leaders of the party.
   b) The percentage of party members in the Chinese population has increased.
   c) Membership is now open to Chinese non-nationals.
   d) Most party members now come from the peasantry.
   e) Capitalists may now be party members.

16. The proliferation of nongovernmental organizations (NGOs) in China is an indication that

   a) civil society is growing
   b) civil liberties and rights are now respected
   c) rule of law is strengthening
   d) a competitive party system is developing
   e) the CCP is more tolerant of protests

17. The most significant factor in the continuing decentralization of policymaking in China is

   a) weak leadership
   b) democratization
   c) marketization/privatization
   d) *guanxi*
   e) state corporatism

18. The most important center of policymaking in China is the

   a) National Party Congress
   b) People's National Congress
   c) Central Committee
   d) State Council
   e) Standing Committee of the Politburo

19. Which of the following is an accurate statement about elections in China?

I. The president and vice president are directly elected.
II. The representatives to the People's National Congress are directly elected.
III. The deputies to the county people's congresses are directly elected.
IV. Local officials are directly elected.

a) I only
b) I and II only
c) II and III only
d) II, III, and IV only
e) III and IV only

20. China and the USSR both conduct(ed) elite recruitment through

a) direct popular election
b) *nomenklatura*
c) horizontal supervision
d) plenums
e) procuratorates

21. Which faction has controlled the politburo since the death of Deng Xiaoping in 1997?

a) radicals
b) conservatives
c) military
d) reformers/open door
e) liberals

22. 1st generation is Mao Zedong, 2nd generation is Deng Xiaoping, 3rd generation is Jiang Zemin, 4th generation is

a) Zhao Ziyang
b) Hu Jintao
c) Wen Jiabao
d) Zhu Rongji
e) Hu Yuobang

23. The two biggest factors in creating the high level of corruption evident in the Chinese political culture are the economic boom and

a) *guanxi*
b) *fang-shou*
c) *nomenklatura*
d) globalization
e) *danwei*

24. Interest groups interact with the government in both Russia and China in a system best described as

    a) state corporatism
    b) neocorporatism
    c) pluralism
    d) democratic centralism
    e) liberalism

25. Which of the following dominates the parallel hierarchies of Chinese political institutions?

    a) State Council
    b) People's Liberation Army
    c) Central Military Commission
    d) The People's National Congress
    e) The Chinese Communist Party

26. Which of the following countries formally divides its executive into two positions: the head of government and the head of state?

    I.   Great Britain
    II. Russia
    III. China

    a) I only
    b) I and II only
    c) II and III only
    d) I and III only
    e) I, II, and III

27. Which of the following countries bases its legal and judicial systems on common law?

    I.   Great Britain
    II. Russia
    III. China

    a) I only
    b) I and II only
    c) I and III only
    d) II and III only
    e) I, II and III

28. Which of the following is a major difference between the Russian and Chinese military?

a) The Russian military is better financed than the Chinese military.
b) The Russian military is larger than the Chinese military.
c) The technology of the Chinese military is superior to the technology of the Russian military.
d) The Chinese military takes an active role in policymaking; the Russian military does not.
e) The Russian military puts more emphasis on their air force than the Chinese military does.

29. Which of the following is the MOST important factor in the revival of legal codes in modern day China?

a) decentralization
b) marketization/privatization
c) patron-clientelism
d) the Cultural Revolution
e) the iron rice bowl

30. "One country, two systems" is a reference to Chinese policy toward

a) Taiwan
b) Special Economic Zones
c) Hong Kong
d) Tibet
e) urban-rural issues

FREE-RESPONSE QUESTION
CHINA

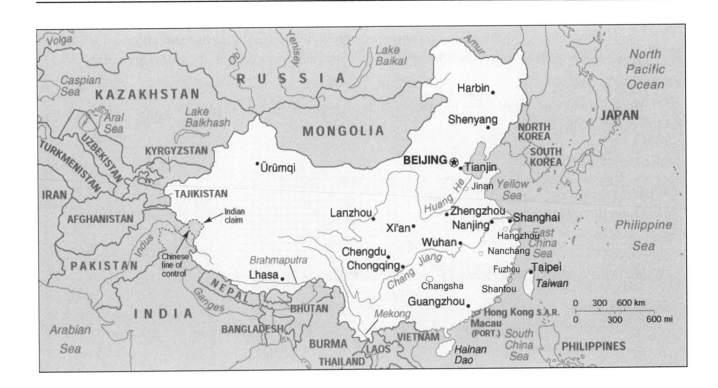

China is the most populous country in the world with the 3rd largest land space, after Russia and Canada.

(a) Describe one population pattern in China displayed on the map above.

(b) Using the population pattern that you described in (a), identify and explain two implications of the population pattern for policymaking in China.

NEWLY INDUSTRIALIZING AND LESS DEVELOPED COUNTRIES

So far, we have investigated countries that represent two types of political systems – advanced democracies and communist and post-communist countries. However, the vast majority of countries in the world have had neither liberal-democratic nor communist regimes. They are often categorized by political scientists and other observers as "less developed countries," or LDCs. Formerly they were known as "third world countries," but since the Cold War ended in the early 1990s, the term is obsolete. Their very categorization invites students to overlook the vast differences that exist among them. LDCs exist on most continents, and they have a wide array of ethnicities, racial characteristics, political cultures, and political economies.

What do these countries have in common? Most obviously, they all struggle with economic issues, including poverty, low GNPs, trade dependency, and weaknesses in infrastructure. And, despite a wide variety of government types, most LDCs are currently developing fragile democracies. Many are still ruled by dictators, military leaders, or hereditary monarchs, but most absolute rulers have been challenged in some way by democratic movements.

TWO CATEGORIES

We will begin by dividing this huge category of countries in two: **newly industrializing countries** and **less developed countries.** During the last few decades, some countries, mostly in Asia and parts of Latin America, have experienced both economic growth and democratization. As a result, they now exhibit many characteristics of advanced democracies, including relative political and social stability. An example is South Korea, a country that only fifty years ago was a relatively poor agricultural country. During the late 20th and early 21st century, South Korea developed into one of the world's largest economies and also experimented with democratic institutions. The process that it experienced is sometimes called **compressed modernity** – rapid economic and political change that transformed the country into a stable nation with democratizing political institutions, a growing economy, and an expanding web of nongovernmental institutions. In this book, newly industrializing countries are represented by Mexico, a country that has experienced this compressed modernity over the past 30 years or so, and Iran, that has partially industrialized but has not democratized as Mexico has.

Less developed countries form a larger category than newly industrializing countries, and we will examine Nigeria as an example. Nigeria has experienced political and economic change, but it has not developed distinct characteristics of advanced democracies. It has experienced economic difficulties, political instability, and authoritarian rule during the past few decades.

ECONOMIC DEVELOPMENT

Economic development by itself cannot explain the differences among the countries that the AP Comparative Government and Politics Course focuses on. One way to measure economic development is by using **purchasing power parity (PPP),** a statistical tool that estimates the buying power of income across different countries by using prices in the United States as a benchmark. It is generally a better indicator than **Per Capita Gross National Product (GNP),** which merely divides the total market value of all goods and services produced by the population of the country. PPP takes into consideration the fact that some countries are more expensive to live in than others, and it is usually expressed as a per capita figure.

COMPARATIVE PPP	
Country	**PPP (in U.S. dollars)**
United Kingdom	$31,800
Russia	$12,200
China	$7,700
Mexico	$10,700
Iran	$8,700
Nigeria	$1,500

Source: *The CIA World Factbook*, 2006 estimates

Clearly, our three countries in this section (Mexico, Nigeria, and Iran) vary widely in terms of PPP, with Nigeria falling far behind any other countries on the chart. One notable variation is the size of PPP in the United Kingdom compared to any of the others. For comparison's sake, the highest PPP in the world is that of Luxembourg at $71,400, followed by Bermuda at $69,000, and Jersey at $57,000 (The U.S. is $44,000). Virtually all of the top PPP countries are advanced democracies. However, the variations among communist, post-communist, newly industrializing, and less developed countries are huge.

Another way to consider economic development is by examining economic sectors:

- **The primary sector (agriculture)** is the part of the economy that draws raw materials from the natural environment. The primary sector – agriculture, raising animals, fishing, forestry, and mining - is largest in low-income, pre-industrial nations.

- **The secondary sector (industry)** is the part of the economy that transforms raw materials into manufactured goods. This sector grows quickly as societies industrialize, and includes such operations as refining petroleum into gasoline and turning metals into tools and automobiles.

- **The tertiary sector (services)** is the part of the economy that involves services rather than goods. The tertiary sector grows with industrialization and comes to dominate **post-industrial societies,** or countries where most people are no longer employed in industry. Examples of tertiary jobs include construction, trade, finance, real estate, private services, government, and transportation.

Because the sectors represent necessary economic activities, most countries have some people employed in all three. However, the percentages vary widely, especially if you compare percentages of people employed in each sector.

COMPARATIVE LABOR FORCES BY ECONOMIC SECTOR			
Country	Primary (Agriculture)	Secondary (Industry)	Tertiary (Services)
United Kingdom	1.4%	18.2%	80.4%
Russia	10.8%	29.1%	60.1%
China	25%	24%	31%
Mexico	18%	24%	58%
Iran	30%	25%	45%
Nigeria	70%	10%	20%

Source: *CIA World Factbook*, 1999-2006 estimates

By comparing economic sectors, the United Kingdom is the best example of a post-industrial society, with only 1.4% of its population engaged in agriculture, and 72.7% in services. Even though Russia's PPP was fairly low ($12,200), Russia appears to have moved into post-industrialism as well. Likewise, Mexico has moved away from agriculture (18%) toward services (58%), as has Iran to a lesser extent. Despite its recent economic boom, 25% of China's population is still employed in agriculture, and Nigeria, along with its sagging PPP ($1,500) has the largest percentage of its people (70%) employed in the primary sector.

THEORIES OF ECONOMIC DEVELOPMENT

What factors explain the lack of economic development in LDCs, and what is in store for their future? Their condition is often referred to as **neocolonialism,** or an unequal relationship in a world in which new indirect forms of imperialism are at play. Two conflicting theories have guided political scientists in answering these questions:

- **Westernization model** – According to this theory, Britain was the first country to begin to develop its industry. The Industrial Revolution was spurred by a combination of prosperity, trade connections, inventions, and natural resources. Once started, the British model spread to other European nations and the United States, who prospered because they built on British ingenuity and economic practices. By extension, any country that wants its economy to grow should study the paths taken by the industrial nations, and logically they too can reap the benefits of modernization, or "westernization." According to this model, the biggest obstacle for LDCs is tradition because holding on to old values can hinder progress.

- **Dependency theory** – In contrast to the westernization model, dependency theory holds that economic development of many countries in the world is blocked by the fact that industrialized nations exploit them. How can a country develop when its resources (natural and human) are controlled by a handful of prosperous industrialized countries? Dependency theory is an outgrowth of Marxism, which emphasizes exploitation of one social class of the other. The same dynamic is at work in assessing relationships among countries. Problems, then, cannot be solved by westernization, but must be addressed by establishing independence. In reaction to this theory, many LDCs have experimented with forms of socialism with the intent of nationalizing industry and narrowing the gap between the rich and the poor.

Most political scientists today do not adhere to one theory or the other, but instead take a pluralist approach: a country's problems have many sources, and no one formula will work for all. Many LDCs today have "mixed" economies – with some elements of capitalism and some of socialism – and they take a variety of approaches in trying to solve their problems. Political leaders are influenced by both theories, with left-leaning governments usually preferring dependency theory, and more conservative governments looking to westernization as a model.

ECONOMIC POLICIES IN THE LESS-DEVELOPED WORLD

Two distinct types of economic policies have been applied throughout the less-developed world in an effort to jump-start their economies:

- **Import substitution** is based on the belief that governments in poorer countries must create more positive conditions for the development of local industries. If these countries are to compete successfully with the advanced industrialized democracies, the governments must restrict imports by setting quotas or imposing heavy import taxes. The reasoning is that people then will have to buy locally, and that demand will stimulate the growth of domestic businesses. Eventually these businesses will develop the ability to compete in the international market because they will have built the capital and the infrastructure necessary for success. Beginning in the 1930s, import substitution was used widely in Latin America, and later in parts of Africa, and Asia.

- **Export-oriented industrialization** has been used by the so-called **"Asian tigers"** – Hong Kong, South Korea, Taiwan, and Singapore – whose economies boomed starting in the 1960s. This strategy seeks to directly integrate the country's economy into the global economy by concentrating on economic production that can find a place in international markets. The countries have watched the "product life cycle" that follows stages: first an innovator country produces something new; next that country moves on to other innovations. Meanwhile, other countries think of ways to make the first product better and cheaper, and export it back to the innovator country. For example, Asian countries have prospered from this strategy with automobiles and electronics in their trade with the United States.

POLITICAL DEVELOPMENT

As we explored briefly in the introductory review chapter of this book, a major political trend of the 20th and early 21st centuries is **democratization,** or the process of developing a political system in which power is exercised either directly or indirectly by the people. Characteristics of liberal democracies include regular competitive elections, civil liberties, rule of law, neutrality of the judiciary, open civil society, and civilian control of the military. It is true that most countries that have high PPPs and developed tertiary sectors are also liberal democracies. However, does this correlation mean that economic development cannot occur without democratization? If not, then Russia's recent move toward centralized authority is not a good sign for the future of the Russian economy. China has experienced an almost unprecedented economic boom since 1978, but the political system is still authoritarian. Does this situation spell trouble for China's current political regime? The answers to these questions are uncertain, but they have tremendous implications for the countries that we will study in this section. For example, might it be correct to categorize Iran as a "less developed country" because it has an authoritarian government? Economically its PPP is a relatively healthy $8,700, and 45% of its people are employed in the tertiary sector. These statistics imply stronger economic development than China. Our categories are imperfect, partly because no one knows for sure if postindustrial societies are by necessity democracies.

In the pages that follow, three very different countries illustrate some of the common characteristics and issues facing newly industrialized and less developed countries today. In the late 20th century Mexico was declared by some observers to be a poster child for the benefits of westernization, only to have their economy come crashing down with the oil bust of the early 1980s. Since then, the economy has improved, but the country is still riddled with political and economic problems. Nigeria, as Africa's most populous nation, illustrates the perils of new democracies, especially in countries with strong military traditions. Iran represents a part of the world where democracy has very little foothold. However, countries of Southwest Asia have asserted themselves in many ways in recent years, and they have profoundly affected the balance of power among nations of the world.

IMPORTANT TERMS AND CONCEPTS

"Asian tigers"
compressed modernity
democratization
dependency theory
economic sectors: primary, secondary, tertiary
export-oriented industrialization
GNP per capita
import substitution
PPP
westernization model

GOVERNMENT AND POLITICS IN MEXICO

Not too many years ago, many observers considered Mexico to be a model for LDCs (less developed countries) around the world. The "**Mexican miracle**" described a country with a rapidly increasing GNP in orderly transition from an authoritarian to a democratic government. Then, the economy soured after oil prices plummeted in the early 1980s, the peso took a nosedive, and debt mounted during the decade. Ethnic conflict erupted in the mid-1990s when the Zapatistas took over the capital of the southern state of Chiapas and refused to be subdued by the Mexican army. On the political front, the leading presidential candidate was assassinated, and top political officials were arrested for bribery, obstructing justice, and drug pedaling. Next, under new leadership, Mexico surprised the world by recovering some financial viability through paying back emergency money they borrowed from the United States. In 2000, under close scrutiny by western democracies, Mexico held an apparently honest, competitive presidential election, and confirmed the emergence of a competitive electoral system. Then, just as pundits were declaring Mexico's path to capitalism and liberal democracy a successful one, the contentious presidential election of 2006 threatened to rock the government's legitimacy to its core.

Despite its uncertain path, Mexico may be seen as a representative for the category of "newly industrializing countries." Its purchasing power parity ($10,700 per year) is fairly high, and about 58% of its workers are employed in the service sector. This "developing" nation called Mexico is full of apparent contradictions that make its politics sometimes puzzling, but always interesting and dynamic. Mexico is generally described economically as a developing country and politically as a "transitional democracy."   In both cases it is at an "in-between" stage when compared with other countries globally, but the transition has had its surprises, and its successes and challenges may well serve as beacons for other nations to follow.

SOVEREIGNTY, AUTHORITY, AND POWER

Like many other Latin American countries, Mexico's sources of public authority have fluctuated greatly over the centuries. From the time that the Spanish arrived in the early 16th century until independence was won in 1821, Mexico was ruled by a viceroy, or governor put in place by the Spanish king. The rule was centralized and **authoritarian**, and it allowed virtually no participation by the indigenous people. After Mexican independence, this ruling style continued, and all of Mexico's presidents until the mid-20th century were military generals. The country was highly unstable in the early 20th century, and even though a constitution was put into place, Mexico's presidents dictated policy until very recent years.   Significant economic growth characterized the late 20th century, followed by democratization that is currently reshaping the political system.

LEGITIMACY

Most Mexican citizens consider their government and its power legitimate. An important source of legitimacy is the **Revolution of 1910-1911,** and Mexicans deeply admire revolutionary leaders throughout their history, such as Miguel Hidalgo, Benito Juarez, Emilio Zapata, Pancho Villa, and Lazaro Cardenas. Revolutions in general are seen quite positively, and charisma is highly valued as a leadership characteristic.

The revolution was legitimized by the formation of the **Institutional Revolutionary Party (PRI)** in 1929. The constitution that was written during that era created a democratic, three-branch government, but PRI was intended to stabilize political power in the hands of its leaders. PRI, then, served as an important source of government legitimacy until other political parties successfully challenged its monopoly during the late 20th century. After the election of 2000, PRI lost the presidency and one house of Congress, and by 2006, the party held only a minority of seats in both houses of the legislature, and the presidency again was won by a non-PRI candidate. Today, sources of public authority and political power appear to be changing rapidly. However, some characteristics carry through from one era to the next.

HISTORICAL TRADITIONS

Mexico's historical tradition may be divided into three stages of its political development – colonialism, the chaos of the 19th and early 20th century, and the emphasis on economic development during its recent history.

- **Authoritarianism** – Both from the colonial structure set up by Spain and from strong-arm tactics by military-political leaders such as Porfirio Diaz, Mexico has a tradition of authoritarian rule. Currently, the president still holds a great deal of political power, although presidential authority has been questioned in the past few years.

- **Populism** – The revolutions of 1810 and 1910 both had significant peasant bases led by charismatic figures that cried out for more rights for ordinary Mexicans, particularly Amerindians. The modern Zapatista movement is a reflection of this historical tradition, which is particularly strong in the southern part of the country.

- **Power plays/divisions within the elite** – The elites who led dissenters during the Revolutions of 1810 and 1910, the warlords/caudillos of the early 20th century, and the *politicos vs. tecnicos* of the late 20th century are all examples of competitive splits among the elite. Current party leaders are often at odds, as displayed during the election crisis of 2006. Presidential candidate Andres Manuel Lopez Obrador's challenge of the election results threatened to destroy fragile democratic structures, although the crisis appeared to have passed by 2007.

- **Instability and legitimacy issues** – Mexico's political history is full of chaos, conflict, bloodshed, and violent resolution to political disagreements. As recently as 1994, a major presidential candidate was assassinated. Even though most Mexicans believe that the government is legitimate, the current regime still leans toward instability.

POLITICAL CULTURE

SENSE OF NATIONAL IDENTITY

Mexicans share a strong sense of national identification based on a common history, as well as a dominant religion and language.

- **The importance of religion** – Until the 1920s, the Catholic Church actively participated in politics, and priests were often leaders of populist movements. During the revolutionary era of the early 20th century, the government developed an anti-cleric position, and today the political influence of the church has declined significantly. However, a large percentage of Mexicans are devout Catholics, and their beliefs strongly influence their political values and actions.

- **Patron-clientelism** – This system of cliques based on personal connections and charismatic leadership has served as the glue that has held an agrarian Mexico together through practicing "you scratch my back, I'll scratch yours." The network of **camarillas** (patron-client networks) extends from the political elites to vote-mobilizing organizations throughout the country. **Corruption** is one by-product of patron-clientelism. Democratization and industrialization have put pressure on this system, and it is questionable as to whether or not modern Mexico can continue to rely on patron-clientelism to organize its government and politics. The defeats of PRI for the presidency in 2000 and 2006 are indications that clientelism may be on the decline, but corporatism still plays a big role in policymaking.

- **Economic dependency** – Whether as a Spanish colony or a southern neighbor of the United States, Mexico has almost always been under the shadow of a more powerful country. In recent years Mexico has struggled to gain more economic independence.

GEOGRAPHIC INFLUENCE

Mexico is one of the most geographically diverse countries in the world, including high mountains, coastal plains, high plateaus, fertile valleys, rain forests, and deserts within an area about three times the size of France.

Some geographical features that have influenced the political development of Mexico are:

- **Mountains and deserts** – Because large mountain ranges and vast deserts separate regions, communication and transportation across the country are often difficult. Rugged terrain also limits areas where productive agriculture is possible. Regionalism, then, is a major characteristic of the political system.

- **Varied climates** - Partly because of the terrain, but also because of its great distance north to south, Mexico has a wide variety of climates - from cold, dry mountains to tropical rain forests.

- **Natural resources** - Mexico has an abundance of oil, silver, and other natural resources, but has always struggled to manage them wisely. These resources undoubtedly have enriched the country (and the United States), but they have not brought general prosperity to the Mexican people.

- **A long** (2000-mile-long) **border with the United States** – Relationships, including conflicts over migration and dependency issues, between the two countries are inevitable.

- **106 million people** - Mexico is the most populous Spanish-speaking country in the world, and among the ten most populous of all. Population growth has slowed to about 1.8 percent, but population is still increasing rapidly.

- **Urban population** – Mexico has urbanized rapidly, as people have moved to cities from rural areas. Today about 3/4 of the population lives in cities of the interior or along the coasts. Mexico City is one of the largest cities in the world, with about 18 million inhabitants living in or close to it. The shift from rural to urban population during the late 20th century disrupted traditional Mexican politics, including the patron-client system.

POLITICAL AND ECONOMIC CHANGE

Mexican history dates back to its independence in 1821, but many influences on its political system developed much earlier. Over time, Mexico has experienced authoritarian governments first under the colonial control of Spain, and then under military dictatorships during the 19th century. The 19th century also saw populist movements influenced by democratic impulses, accompanied by violence, bloodshed, and demagoguery. During the first decades of the 20th century, an intensification of violence sank the country into chaos, and the political system was characterized by serious instability and rapid turnover of political authority. Stability was regained by resorting to authoritarian tactics that remained in place until the latter part of the century. In recent years, Mexico has shown clear signs of moving away from authoritarianism toward democracy.

Economic changes in Mexico have been no less dramatic. For most of its history, Mexico's economy was based on agriculture, along with other primary sector activities such as mining. However, Mexico was strongly influenced by the industrialization of its northern neighbor, the United States, starting in the late 1800s. Under the dictatorship of Porfirio Diaz, U.S. business interests were encouraged to develop in Mexico, and a strong dependency on the U.S. economy was put in place. Mexican nationalists have reacted against U.S. participation in the Mexican economy at various times since those days, so that anti-U.S. sentiments have become one dynamic of political and economic interactions. During the late 20th century, Mexico industrialized rapidly, with its rich natural resource of oil serving as the wind that drove the economic expansion. Mexico has struggled since then to break its dependency on one product, especially after the sudden drop in oil prices during the early 1980s sent the Mexican economy into a tailspin. Today Mexico has moved from an agricultural society to an industrial one, and even in some ways toward post-industrialism.

We will divide our study of historical influences into three parts:

* **Colonialism**
* **Independence until the Revolution of 1910**
* **The 20th century after the revolution**

COLONIALISM

From 1519 to 1821 Spain controlled the area that is now Mexico. The Spanish placed their subjects in an elaborate social status hierarchy, with Spanish born in Spain on top and the native Amerindians on the bottom. Colonialism left several enduring influences:

* **Cultural heterogeneity** - When the Spanish arrived in 1519 the area was well populated with natives, many of whom were controlled by the Aztecs. When the conquistador Hernan Cortes captured the Aztec capital of Tenochtitlan, the Spanish effectively took control of the entire area. Even though status differences between native and Spanish were clearly drawn, the populations soon mixed, particularly since Spanish soldiers were not allowed to bring their families from Spain to the New World. Today about 60 percent of all Mexicans are **mestizo** (a blend of the two peoples), but areas far away from Mexico City - particularly to the south - remain primarily Amerindian.

- **Catholicism** - Most Spaniards remained in or near Mexico City after their arrival, but Spanish Catholic priests settled far and wide as they converted the population to Christianity. Priests set up missions that became population centers, and despite the differences in status, they often developed great attachments to the people they led.

- **Economic dependency** - The area was controlled by Spain, and served the mother country as a colony, although the territory was so vast that the Spanish never realized the extent of Mexico's natural resources.

INDEPENDENCE/NEW COUNTRY (1810-1911)

As part of a wave of revolutions that swept across Latin America in the early 1800s, a Mexican parish priest named **Miguel Hidalgo** led a popular rebellion against Spanish rule in 1810. After eleven years of turmoil (and Father Hidalgo's death), Spain finally recognized Mexico's independence in 1821. Father Hidalgo, though of Spanish origins, was seen as a champion of the indigenous people of Mexico. He still symbolizes the political rights of the peasantry, and statues in his memory stand in public squares all over the country. However, stability and order did not follow independence, with a total of thirty-six presidents serving between 1833 and 1855.

THE NEW COUNTRY

Important influences during this period were:

- **Instability and legitimacy issues** - When the Spanish left, they took their hierarchy with them, and reorganizing the government was a difficult task.

- **Rise of the military** - The instability invited military control, most famously exercised by Santa Anna, a military general and president of Mexico.

- **Domination by the United States** - The U.S. quickly picked up on the fact that her neighbor to the south was in disarray, and chose to challenge Mexican land claims. By 1855, Mexico had lost half of her territory to the U.S. What is now Texas, New Mexico, Arizona, California, Utah, and part of Colorado fell under U.S. control after the Treaty of Guadalupe Hidalgo was signed in 1848.

- **Liberal vs. conservative struggle** - The impulses of the 1810 revolution toward democracy came to clash with the military's attempt to establish authoritarianism (as in colonial days). The Constitution of 1857 was set up on democratic principles, and a liberal president, **Benito Juarez,** is one of Mexico's greatest heroes. Like Father Hidalgo, Juarez was very popular with ordinary Mexican citizens, but unlike Hidalgo, he was a military general with a base of support among elites as well. Conservatism was reflected in the joint French, Spanish, and English takeover of Mexico under Maximilian (1864-1867.) His execution brought Juarez back to power, but brought no peace to Mexico.

"THE PORFIRIATO" (1876-1911)

Porfirio Diaz - one of Juarez's generals - staged a military coup in 1876 and instituted himself as the president of Mexico with a promise that he would not serve more than one term of office. He ignored that pledge and ruled Mexico with an iron hand for 34 years. He brought with him the *cientificos*, a group of young advisors that believed in bringing scientific and economic progress to Mexico. Influences of the "**Porfiriato**" are:

- **Stability** - With Diaz came an end to years of chaos, and his dictatorship brought a stable government to Mexico.

- **Authoritarianism** - This dictatorship allowed no sharing of political power beyond the small, closed elite.

- **Foreign investment and economic growth** - The *cientificos* encouraged entrepreneurship and foreign investment - primarily from the United States - resulting in a growth of business and industry.

- **Growing gap between the rich and the poor** - As often happens in developing countries, the introduction of wealth did not insure that all would benefit. Many of the elite became quite wealthy and led lavish life styles, but most people in Mexico remained poor.

Eventually even other elites became increasingly sensitive to the greed of the Porfirians and their own lack of opportunities, and so Diaz' regime ended with a coup from within the elite, sparking the Revolution of 1910.

1910 - PRESENT

The Revolution of 1910 marked the end of the "Porfiriato" and another round of instability and disorder, followed by many years of attempts to regain stability.

THE CHAOS OF THE EARLY 20TH CENTURY

In 1910 conflict broke out as reformers sought to end the Diaz dictatorship. When Diaz tried to block a presidential election, support for another general, Francisco Madero - a landowner from the northern state of Coahuila - swelled to the point that Diaz was forced to abdicate in 1911. So the Revolution of 1910 began with a movement by other elites to remove Diaz from office. Their success set off a period of warlordism and popular uprisings that lasted until 1934.

The influences of this era include:

- **Patron-client system -** In their efforts to unseat Diaz, **caudillos -** political/military strongmen from different areas of the country - rose to challenge one another for power. Two popular leaders - **Emiliano Zapata** and **Pancho Villa** - emerged to lead peasant armies and establish another dimension to the rebellion. Around each leader a **patron-client** system emerged that encompassed large numbers of citizens. Many caudillos (including Zapata and Villa) were assassinated, and many followers were violently killed in the competition among the leaders.

- **Constitution of 1917 -** Although it represents the end of the revolution, the Constitution did not bring an end to the violence. It set up a structure for democratic government - complete with three branches and competitive elections - but political assassinations continued into the 1920s.

- **Conflict with the Catholic Church** - The **Cristeros Rebellion** broke out in the 1920s as one of the bloodiest conflicts in Mexican history, with hundreds of thousands of people killed, including many priests. Liberals saw the church as a bastion of conservatism and put laws in place that forbid priests to vote, put federal restrictions on church-affiliated schools, and suspended religious services. Priests around the country led a rebellion against the new rules that contributed greatly to the chaos of the era.

- **The establishment of PRI** - Finally, after years of conflict and numerous presidential assassinations, President Calles brought caudillos together for an agreement in 1929. His plan - to bring all caudillos under one big political party - was intended to bring stability through agreement to "pass around" the power from one leader to the next as the presidency changed hands. Each president could only have one six-year term (**sexenio**), and then must let another leader have his term. Meanwhile, other leaders would be given major positions in the government to establish their influence. This giant umbrella party - **PRI (**Institutional Revolutionary Party) - "institutionalized" the revolution by stabilizing conflict among leaders.

COMPARATIVE REVOLUTIONS
EARLY 20TH CENTURY

Country	Motivations	Characteristics	Outcomes
Russia (1917)	Defeat authoritarian government; carry forward Marxist ideology	Led by Vladimir Lenin, Bolsheviks; violent, sudden change; carried out in middle of World War I	Four years of civil war; triumph of Marxism-Leninism; one-party state
China (1911)	Drive out "foreign devils"; defeat authoritarian, weak government; assert nationalism	regional warlordism, violent, sudden change; chaotic, competing forces	Years of chaos; two competing forces; triumph of Maoism; one-party state
Mexico (1910)	Defeat authoritarian government; break dependency on foreign governments; elite power struggle	began as a conflict among elites; joined by populist forces; sudden, violent change; chaotic competing forces	Years of violence, instability; elites "umbrellaed" under PRI for stability; one-party state

Origins of one-party states. Although the early 20th century revolutions of Russia, China, and Mexico had some very different motivations, characteristics, and outcomes, they had a few things in common, including the outcome of a one-party state.

THE CARDENAS UPHEAVAL - 1934 - 1940

When Calles' term as president was up, **Lazaro Cardenas** began a remarkable sexenio that both stabilized and radicalized Mexican politics. Cardenas (sometimes called "the Roosevelt of Mexico" by U.S. scholars) gave voice to the peasant demands from the Revolution of 1910, and through his tremendous charisma, brought about many changes:

- **Redistribution of land** - Land was taken away from big landlords and foreigners and redistributed as *ejidos* - collective land grants - to be worked by the peasants.

- **Nationalization of industry** - Foreign business owners who had been welcomed since the time of Diaz were kicked out of the country, and much industry was put under the control of the state. For example, **PEMEX -** a giant government-controlled oil company - was created.

- **Investments in public works -** The government built roads, provided electricity, and created public services that modernized Mexico.

- **Encouragement of peasant and union organizations** - Cardenas welcomed the input of these groups into his government, and they formed their own camarillas with leaders that represented peasants and workers on the president's cabinet.

- **Concentration of power in the presidency -** Cardenas stabilized the presidency, and when his sexenio was up, he peacefully let go of his power, allowing another caudillo to have the reins of power.

The strategy of state-led development that Cardenas followed is called **import substitution industrialization.** ISI employs high tariffs to protect locally produced goods from foreign competition, government ownership of key industries, and government subsidies to domestic industries.   Since there was relatively little money in private hands to finance industrialization, the government took the lead in promoting industrialization. Although including peasant and union organizations in the policymaking process is a populist touch, the Cardenas government is still an example of **state corporatism**, with the president determining who represents different groups to the government.

THE EMERGENCE OF THE *TECNICOS* AND THE PENDULUM THEORY

Six years after Cardenas left office, Miguel Aleman became president, setting in place the **Pendulum Theory**. Aleman rejected many of Cardenas' socialist reforms and set Mexico on a path of economic development, again encouraging entrepreneurship and foreign investment. He in turn was followed by a president who shifted the emphasis back to Cardenas-style reform, setting off a back-and-forth effect - socialist reform to free-market economic development and back again. As Mexico reached the 1970s the pendulum appeared to stop, and a new generation of *tecnicos* - educated, business-oriented leaders - appeared to take control of the government and PRI with a moderate, free-market approach to politics. In many ways, the pendulum was swinging between modernization and dependency theories (see p. 175-176), with the government eventually settling on modernization theory. By the 1980s, Mexico had settled into **neoliberalism**, a strategy that calls for free markets, balanced budgets, privatization, free trade, and limited government intervention in the economy.

By the 1950s, Mexico was welcoming foreign investment, and the country's GNP began a spectacular growth that continued until the early 1980s. This "**Mexican Miracle**" - based largely on huge supplies of natural gas and oil - became a model for less developed countries everywhere. With the "oil bust" of the early 1980s, the plummeting price of oil sank the Mexican economy and greatly inflated the value of the peso. Within PRI, the division between the *"politicos"* - the old style caciques who headed camarillas - and the *tecnicos* began to grow wider.

CITIZENS, SOCIETY, AND THE STATE

For many years Mexican citizens have interacted with their government through an informal web of relationships defined by patron-clientelism. Because the camarillas are so interwoven into the fabric of Mexican politics, most people have had at least some contact with the government during their lifetimes. However, interactions between citizens and government through clientelism generally have meant that the government has had the upper hand through its ability to determine which interests to respond to and which to ignore. The role of citizens in the Mexican political system is changing as political parties have become competitive and democracy seems to be taking root, yet the old habits of favor-swapping are engrained in the political culture.

CLEAVAGES

Cleavages that have the most direct impact on the political system are social class, urban v. rural, mestizo v. Amerindian, and north v. south. These cleavages are often **crosscutting**, with different divisions emerging as the issues change, but in recent years they have often **coincided** (see p. 24) as urban, middle class mestizos from the north have found themselves at odds with rural, poor Amerindians from the south.

- **Urban v. rural** - Mexico's political structure was put into place in the early 20th century – a time when most of the population lived in rural areas. PRI and the patron-client system were intended to control largely illiterate peasants who provided political support in exchange for small favors from the *politicos*. Today Mexico is more than 75% urban, and the literacy rate is about 90%. Urban voters are less inclined to support PRI, and they have often been receptive to political and economic reform.

- **Social class** – Mexico's Gini coefficient is .50 (2006 estimate), which means that economic inequality is very high, (higher than any of the other five countries in this course). In 2002 the poorest 10% of the population earned about 1.6% of Mexico's income while the wealthiest 10 percent earned 35.6%. This economic divide translates into higher infant mortality rates, lower levels of education, and shorter life expectancies among the poor. In very recent years Mexico's middle class has been growing, even in poorer sections of the country. Some are from the **informal economy** (businesses not registered with the government), and others from new industries or service businesses. Middle and upper class people are more likely to support PAN, and are more likely to vote than the poor, especially as PRI-style patron-client ties unwind.

- **Mestizo v. Amerindian** – The main ethnic cleavage in Mexico is between **mestizo** (a blend of Europe and Amerindian blood) and Amerindian. Only about 10% of Mexicans actually speak an indigenous language, but as many as 30% think of themselves as Amerindian. Amerindians are more likely to live in marginalized rural areas and to live in poverty. This cleavage tends to define social class, with most of Mexico's wealth in the hands of mestizos.

- **North v. south** – In many ways, northern Mexico is almost a different country than the area south of Mexico City. The north is very dry and mountainous, but its population is much more prosperous, partly because many are involved in trade with the United States. The north has a substantial middle class with relatively high levels of education. Not surprisingly, they are generally more supportive of a market-based economy. The south is largely subtropical, and its people are generally less influenced by urban areas and the United States. Larger numbers are Amerindian, with less European ethnicity, and their average incomes are lower than those in the north. Although their rural base may influence them to support PRI, some southerners think of the central government as repressive. The southernmost state of Chiapas is the source of the Zapatista Movement, which values the Amerindian heritage and seeks more rights for natives.

One recent change worth noting is that the incomes of the poorest half of the population are growing faster than the average. Poverty levels as defined by the government have fallen, and income distribution is becoming less unequal. For example, Mexico's Gini coefficient has dropped from more the .54 in 2002 to .50 in 2006. If significant numbers of the poor begin making enough money to move them into the middle class, cleavages that define political behavior will certainly be affected. Likewise, if job opportunities in the **formal sector** (businesses recognized by the government) spread into new regions of the country as the economy grows, regional and ethnic divisions may also change.

POLITICAL PARTICIPATION

Political participation in Mexico has been characterized by revolution and protest, but until recently, Mexican citizens were generally subjects under authoritarian rule by the political elite. Citizens sometimes benefited from the elaborate patronage system, but legitimate channels to policymakers were few. Today, citizens participate through increasingly legitimate, regular elections.

THE PATRON-CLIENT SYSTEM

Traditionally, Mexican citizens have participated in their government through the informal and personal mechanisms of the **patron-client system**. Since the formation of PRI in 1929, the political system has emphasized compromise among contending elites, behind-the-scenes conflict resolution, and distribution of political rewards to those willing to play by the informal and formal rules of the game.

The patron-client system keeps control in the hands of the government elite, since they have the upper hand in deciding who gets favors and who doesn't. Only in recent years have citizens and elites begun to participate through competitive elections, campaigns, and interest group lobbying.

Patron-clientelism has its roots in warlordism and loyalty to the early 19th century **caudillos.** Each leader had his supporters that he - in return for their loyalty - granted favors to. Each group formed a **camarilla,** a hierarchical network through which offices and other benefits were exchanged. Until the election of 2000, within PRI most positions on the president's cabinet were filled either by supporters or by heads of other camarillas that the president wanted to appease. Peasants in a camarilla received jobs, financial assistance, family advice, and sometimes even food and shelter in exchange for votes for PRI.

Despite trends toward a modern society, the patron-client system is still very important in determining the nature of political participation. Modernization tends to break up the patron-client system, as networks blur in large population centers, and more formal forms of participation are instituted. However, vestiges of the old patron-client system were at work in the controversy surrounding the 2006 presidential election, with the losing candidate Andres Manuel Lopez Obrador accusing the winning candidate's PAN party of election fraud. Polls indicate that between a quarter and a third of voters believed Obrador, since decades of one-party rule had sustained fraudulence under the patron-client system. As a result, many Mexicans still deeply distrust government officials and institutions.

PROTESTS

When citizen demands have gotten out of hand, the government has generally responded by not only accommodating their demands, but by including them in the political process through **co-optation.** For example, after the 1968 student protests in Mexico City ended in government troops killing an estimated two hundred people in **Tlatelolco Plaza,** the next president recruited large numbers of student activists into his administration. He also dramatically increased spending on social services, putting many of the young people to work in expanded antipoverty programs in the countryside and in urban slums.

Social conditions in Mexico lie at the heart of the Chiapas rebellion that began in 1994. This poor southern Mexican state sponsored the **Zapatista uprising**, representing Amerindians that felt disaffected from the more prosperous mestizo populations of cities in the center of the country. The Chiapas rebellion reminded Mexicans that some people live in appalling conditions with little hope for the future. Indeed, the average length of schooling is still under five years nationwide, and only about half of the eligible students are enrolled in secondary schools.

Another major protest erupted in 2006 in Oaxaca, a neighboring state to Chiapas in the south. The unrest began as a teachers' strike in the state capital, but when local police tried to break it up, other activists joined in, the police lost control, and the demonstrations went on for months. The protests focused on Ulises Ruiz, the governor of Oaxaca State, one of the few PRI candidates to win gubernatorial elections in 2004. Activist groups demanded his resignation, claiming that his election was fraudulent and criticizing Ruiz for ruling with an iron hand. Eventually President **Vicente Fox** sent a national police force to Oaxaca to shut down the demonstrations, but activists vowed to continue their struggle to remove Ruiz from office. Since Fox' action took place during his last month in office, he left it to his successor, **Felipe Calderon**, to deal with the unruly state.

VOTER BEHAVIOR

Before the political changes of the 1990s, PRI controlled elections on the local, state, and national levels. Voting rates were very high because the patron-client system required political support in exchange for political and economic favors. Election day was generally very festive, with the party rounding up voters and bringing them to the polls. Voting was accompanied by celebrations, with free food and entertainment for those that supported the party. Corruption abounded, and challengers to the system were easily defeated with "tacos," or stuffed ballot boxes.

Despite PRI's control of electoral politics, competing parties have existed since the 1930s, and once they began pulling support away from PRI, some distinct voting patterns emerged. Voter turnout was probably at its height in 1994, when about 78% of all eligible citizens actually voted. This is up from 49% in 1988, although any comparisons before 1988 have to be considered in light of corruption, either through fraudulent voting or simply the announcement from PRI of inflated voter participation rates. Voter rates have declined since 1994, but a respectable 64% of those eligible actually voted in the election of 2000, and 60% in the election of 2006.

Some factors that appeared to influence voter behavior in the presidential election of 2006 were:

- **Region** – Regional differences were quite dramatic, with 47% of the voters in the north choosing PAN candidate Felipe Calderon, 27% choosing PRI candidate Roberto Madrazo, and 24% selecting Andres Manuel Lopez Obrador. In contrast, 40% of voters in the south selected Obrador, 29% chose Madrazo, and 27% chose Madrazo. Obrador also picked up many votes (44%) in the central part of the country around Mexico City, where he served as mayor before running for president.

- **Education** – The higher the amount of education, the more likely voters were to vote for the PAN candidate Felipe Calderon, with about 42% of all voters with college educations voting for Calderon. However, PRD on the left had significant support, with Andres Manuel Lopez Obrador garnering 38% among the college-educated. In contrast, only 14% of those with university educations voted for Roberto Madrazo (the PRI candidate).

- **Income** – Income also made a difference, with 50% of upper income voters choosing PAN's Calderon, compared to 30% for Obrador, and 14% for Madrazo.

CIVIL SOCIETY

Despite the fact that PRI formed an umbrella party over elites in the years that it ruled, Mexico has always had a surprising number of groups who have refused to cooperate. These groups have formed the basis for a lively civil society in Mexico, which also has provided an atmosphere where public protests have been acceptable. PRI practiced **state corporatism,** with the state mediating among different groups to ensure that no one group successfully challenged the government. PRI formally divided interest groups into three sectors: labor, peasants, and the middle class ("popular"), with each dominated by PRI-controlled groups. However, The Confederation of Employers of the Mexican Republic (a labor group) was an autonomous group that vocally and publicly criticized the government.

PRI's downfall started in civil society with discontented businessmen who were not incorporated into the government's system. This group was behind the formation of PAN in 1939, and though the party did not successfully challenge PRI for many years, PAN's 2000 presidential candidate – Vicente Fox – emerged to successfully challenge PRI partly because he had the backing of powerful business interests. With the narrow PAN victory in 2006, business interests again benefitted, so PRI's old state corporatism clearly has been broken up. What will emerge in its place is now the question – state corporatism, neocorporatism (where interests, not the government controls), or pluralism (independent interests have input, but don't control).

POLITICAL INSTITUTIONS

Mexico is a country in economic and political transition. As a result, it is difficult to categorize its regime type. For many years its government was highly authoritarian, with the president serving virtually as a dictator for a six-year term. Mexico's economy has also been underdeveloped and quite dependent on the economies of stronger nations, particularly that of the United States. However, in recent years Mexico has shown strong signs of economic development, accompanied by public policy supportive of a free market economy. Also, the country's political parties are becoming more competitive, and the dictatorial control of PRI has been soundly broken by elections since 1997. Although the political structures themselves remain the same as they were before, significant political and economic reforms have greatly altered the ways that government officials operate.

REGIME TYPE

Traditionally, Mexico has had a **state corporatist structure** - central, authoritarian rule that allows input from interest groups outside of government. Through the camarilla system, leaders of important groups, including business elites, workers, and peasants, actually served in high government offices. To-day political and economic reforms appear to be leading toward a more open structure, but corporatism is still characteristic of policymaking. Is the modern Mexican government authoritarian or democratic? Is the economy centrally controlled, or does it operate under free market principles? The answers are far from clear, but the direction of the transition is toward **liberal democracy** and capitalism.

"DEVELOPED," "DEVELOPING," OR "LESS DEVELOPED"?

Categorizing the economic development of countries can be a tricky business, with at least four different ways to measure it:

- **GNP per capita** - This figure is an estimate of a country's total economic output divided by its total population, converted to a single currency, usually the U.S. dollar. This measure is often criticized because it does not take into account what goods and services people can actually buy with their local currencies.

- **PPP -** Purchasing Power Parity - This measure takes into account the actual cost of living in a particular country by figuring what it costs to buy the same bundle of goods in different countries. Mexico's figure is $10,700 per year.

- **HDI -** Human Development Index - The United Nations has put together this measure based on a formula that takes into account the three factors of longevity (life expectancy at birth), knowledge (literacy and average years of schooling), and income (according to PPP). Mexico's literacy rate is 92.4% for men, and 89.6% for women, and life expectancy is 72.8 for men and 78.5 for women.

- **Economic dependency -** A less developed country is often dependent on developed countries for economic support and trade. Generally speaking, economic trade that is balanced between nations is considered to be good. A country is said to be "developing" when it begins relying less on a stronger country to keep it afloat financially.

- **Economic inequality** – The economies of developing countries usually benefit the rich first, so characteristically the gap between the rich and poor widens. This trend is evident in Mexico with its high Gini coefficient of .50.

No matter which way you figure it, Mexico comes out somewhere in the middle, with some countries more developed and some less. Since these indices in general are moving upward over time for Mexico, it is said to be "developing."

A TRANSITIONAL DEMOCRACY

Politically, Mexico is said to be in transition between an authoritarian style government and a democratic one. From this view (modernization theory), democracy is assumed to be a "modern" government type, and authoritarianism more old-fashioned. Governments, then, may be categorized according to the degree of democracy they have. How is democracy measured? Usually by these characteristics:

- **Political accountability** - In a democracy, political leaders are held accountable to the people of a country. The key criterion is usually the existence of regular, free, and fair elections.

- **Political competition** - Political parties must be free to organize, present candidates, and express their ideas. The losing party must allow the winning party to take office - peacefully.

- **Political freedom** - The air to democracy's fire is political freedom - assembly, organization, and political expression, including the right to criticize the government.

- **Political equality** - Signs of democracy include equal access to political participation, equal rights as citizens, and equal weighting of citizens' votes.

Mexico - especially in recent years - has developed some democratic characteristics, but still has many vestiges of its authoritarian past, as we have seen. Another often used standard for considering a country a democracy is the longevity of democratic practices. If a nation shows *consistent* democratic practices for a period of 40 years or so (a somewhat arbitrary number), then it may be declared a stable democracy. Mexico does not fit this description.

LINKAGE INSTITUTIONS

Even before the trend toward democratization took hold during the late 20th century, Mexico's political parties, interest groups, and mass media all worked to link Mexican citizens to their government in significant ways. This linkage took place under the umbrella of PRI elite rulers so that a true, independent civil society did not exist. However as democratization began and civil society developed, the structures were already in place, so that activating democracy was easier than it would have been otherwise.

POLITICAL PARTIES

For most of the 20th century, Mexico was virtually a one-party state. Until 2000 all presidents belonged to PRI, as did most governors, representatives, senators, and other government officials. Over the past twenty years or so other parties have gained power, so that today competitive elections are a reality, at least in many parts of Mexico.

The three largest parties in Mexico today are:

1) **PRI** - The *Partido Revolucionario Institucional* was in power continuously from 1920 until 2000, when an opposition candidate finally won the presidency. PRI was founded as a coalition of elites who agreed to work out their conflicts through compromise rather than violence. By forming a political party that encompassed all political elites, they could agree to trade favors and pass power around from one cacique to another. The party is characterized by:

   - **A corporatist structure** - Under the PRI dominated government, interest groups were woven into the structure of the party. The party had the ultimate authority, but other voices were heard by bringing interest groups under the broad umbrella of the party. This structure is not democratic, but it allowed input into the government from party-selected groups whose leaders often held cabinet positions. Particularly after the Cardinas sexenio (1934-

1940), peasant and labor organizations were represented in the party and held positions of responsibility, but these groups are carefully selected and controlled by the party.

- **Patron-client system** - The party traditionally gets its support from rural areas where the patron-client system is still in control. As long as Mexico remained rural-based, PRI had a solid, thorough organization that managed to garner overwhelming support. Until the election of 1988, there was no question that the PRI candidate would be elected president, with 85-90% victories being normal.

2) **PAN** - The National Action Party, or PAN, was founded in 1939, making it one of the oldest opposition parties. It was created to represent business interests opposed to centralization and anti-clericism (PRI's practice of keeping the church out of politics.) PAN is strongest in the north, where the tradition of resisting direction from Mexico City is the strongest. PAN's platform includes

- Regional autonomy
- Less government intervention in the economy
- Clean and fair elections
- Good rapport with the Catholic Church
- Support for private and religious education

PAN is usually considered to be PRI's opposition to the right. PAN's candidates won the presidency in 2000 and 2006, and since the 2006 election, it has more deputies and senators in the legislature than any other party.

3) **PRD** - The Democratic Revolutionary Party, or PRD, is generally thought of as PRI's opposition on the left. Their presidential candidate in 1988 and 1994 was **Cuauhtemoc Cardenas**, the son of Mexico's famous and revered president Lazaro Cardenas. He was ejected from PRI for demanding reform that emphasized social justice and populism, and he responded by switching parties. In 1988 Cardenas won 31.1% of the official vote, and PRD captured 139 seats in the Chamber of Deputies (out of 500). Many observers believe that if the election had been honest, Cardenas actually would have won.

PRD has been plagued by a number of problems that have weakened it since 1988. They have had trouble defining a left of center alternative to the market-oriented policies established by PRI. Their leaders have also been divided on issues, and have sometimes publicly quarreled. The party has been criticized for poor organization, and Cardenas is not generally believed to have the same degree of charisma as did his famous father. PRD's new standard-bearer is **Andres Manuel Lopez Obrador**, the popular mayor of Mexico City that barely lost the presidential election in 2006 to PAN candidate Felipe Calderon. The party also made significant gains in the legislative elections of 2006.

ELECTIONS

Citizens of Mexico directly elect their president, Chamber of Deputy representatives, and senators, as well as a host of state and local officials. Although the parties have overlapping constituencies, typical voter profiles are:

- PRI - small town or rural, less educated, older, poorer

- PAN - from the north, middle-class professional or business, urban, better educated (at least high school, some college), religious (or those less strict about separation of church and state)

- PRD - younger, politically active, from the central states, some education, small town or urban; drew some middle-class and older voters in 2006

Elections in Mexico today tend to be most competitive in urban areas, but more competition in rural areas could be seen in both the presidential and legislative elections of 2006. Under PRI control, elections were typically fraudulent, with the patron-client system encouraging bribery and favor swapping. Since 1988, Mexico has been under pressure to have fairer elections. Part of the demands have come from a more urban, educated population, and some have come from international sources as Mexico has become more and more a part of world trade.

The election of 2000 brought the PAN candidate, **Vicente Fox**, into the presidency. PAN captured 208 of the 500 deputies in the lower house (Chamber of Deputies), but PRI edged them out with 209 members. 46 of the 128 senators elected were from PAN, as opposed to 60 for PRI. The newly created competitive electoral system has encouraged coalitions to form to the left and right of PRI, and the split in votes may be encouraging gridlock, a phenomenon unknown to Mexico under the old PRI-controlled governments.

COMPARATIVE PARTY SYSTEMS

	BRITAIN	RUSSIA	MEXICO
Type of system	multi-party system	multi-party system	multi-party system
relationship to the legislature	2 parties dominate the legislature	1 party dominates the legislature	3 parties well-represented in the legislature
relationship to the executive	1 party dominates the executive	1 party dominates the executive	unclear pattern, appears competitive
Types of parties	parties on the left, center, and right; regional parties relatively strong	parties of power common; party in the previous one-party system is still competitive.	parties on left and right; party in the previous one-party system is still competitive.

The Elections of 2006

When the votes were counted in the presidential election on July 2, 2006, PAN candidate Felipe Calderon and PRD candidate Andres Manuel Lopez Obrador were virtually tied for the lead, with PRI candidate Roberto Madrazo trailing far behind. The official vote tally put Calderon ahead by about 230,000 votes out of 41.5 million votes cast, about a half percentage point difference. Obrador challenged the results as fraudulent and demanded a recount. The election tribunal investigated his allegations, and for more than two months the election was held in the balance until the tribunal gave its report. In early August the tribunal ordered recounts on only about 9% of the precincts, not the full recount demanded by Obrador. In early September, the tribunal announced that the recount did not change the outcome, despite some errors in math and some cases of fraud. During the entire process Obrador held rallies for supporters, and he refused to accept the tribunal's decision, claiming that the election was "stolen" by a broad conspiracy between business leaders and the government. He encouraged his supporters to protest, and he claimed to be the legitimate president. Obrador's challenge drew strength from well established traditions from the political culture - populism and dissent among the elites – but by 2007 the crisis appeared to have passed.

The legislative elections of 2006 changed the power balance as PRI lost heavily in both houses, PAN received modest gains in the Chamber of Deputies, and PRD gained many seats in both houses.

Electoral System

The president is elected through the **"first past the post"** (plurality) system with no run-off elections required. As a result, the current Mexican president, **Felipe Calderon**, was elected with only a little more than a third of the total popular votes. Members of congress are elected through a dual system of "first-past-the-post" and **proportional representation**. Proportional representation was increased in a major reform law in 1986, a change that gave power to political parties that have challenged PRI's control. Each of Mexico's 31 states elects three senators. Two of them are determined by majority vote, and the third is determined by whichever party receives the second highest number of votes. Also, thirty-two senate seats are determined nationally through a system of proportional representation that divides the seats according to the number of votes cast for each party. In the lower house (the Chamber of Deputies), 300 seats are determined by plurality within single-member districts, and 200 seats are chosen by proportional representation.

INTEREST GROUPS AND POPULAR MOVEMENTS

The Mexican government's corporatist structure generally responds pragmatically to the demands of interest groups through accommodation and **co-optation**. As a result, political tensions among major interests have rarely escalated into the kinds of serious conflict that can threaten stability. Where open conflict has occurred, it has generally been met with efforts to find a solution. Because private organizations have been linked for so long to the government, Mexico's development of a separate civil society has been slow.

In the past 30 years or so, business interests have networked with political leaders to protect the growth of commerce, finance, industry and agriculture. Under **state corporatism,** these business elites have become quite wealthy, but they were never incorporated into PRI. However, political leaders have listened to and responded to their demands. Labor has been similarly accommodated within the system. Wage levels for unionized workers grew fairly consistently between 1940 and 1982, when the economic crisis prompted by lowering oil prices caused wages to drop. The power of union bosses is declining, partly because unions are weaker than in the past, and partly because union members are more independent. Today with PAN in control of the presidency business interests may exhibit more characteristics of **neocorporatism,** but PAN does not control the legislature, and there is no clear evidence that businesses are controlling the government.

One powerful interest group is the Educational Workers' Union, Latin America's largest trade union. It has long had the power to negotiate salaries for teachers each year, and many see it as a neocorporatist group that has a great deal of power over government decisions in education.

In rural areas, peasant organizations have been encouraged by PRI, particularly through the **ejido** system that grants land from the Mexican government to the organizations themselves. Since the 1980s these groups have often demanded greater independence from the government, and have supported movements for better prices for crops and access to markets and credit. They have joined with other groups to promote better education, health services, and environmental protections.

Urban popular movements also abound in Mexico, with organizations concerned about social welfare spending, city services, neighborhood improvements, economic development, feminism, and professional identity. As these groups have strengthened and become more independent, the political system has had to negotiate and bargain with them, transforming the political culture and increasing the depth of civil society.

THE MEDIA

As long as PRI monopolized government and politics in Mexico, the media had little power to criticize the government or to influence public opinion. The government rewarded newspapers, magazines, and radio and television stations that supported them with special favors, such as access to newsprint or airwaves. The government also subsidized the salaries of reporters, writers, and media personalities that strongly supported PRI initiatives. A considerable amount of revenue came from government-placed advertisements, so few media outlets could afford to openly criticize the government.

The media began to become more independent starting in the 1980s at the same time that PRI began losing its hold in other areas. Today there are several major television networks in the country, and many people have access to international newspapers and networks, such as CNN and BBC. Several news magazines now offer opinions of government initiatives, just as similar magazines do in the United States. One indication of freedom of the press came early in the Fox administration when the media publicized "Toallagate", a scandal involving the purchase of some significantly overpriced towels for the president's mansion. The Mexican press also criticized President Fox for his *"Comes y te vas"* (eat and leave) instructions to Fidel Castro after a United Nations gathering, so as not to offend U.S President George W. Bush with Castro's presence. So, for better or for worse, Mexican citizens now have access to a much broader range of political opinions than they ever had before.

GOVERNMENT INSTITUTIONS

Mexico is a **federal republic**, though under PRI domination the state and local governments had little independent power and few resources. Historically, the executive branch with its strong presidency has had all the power, while the legislature and judiciary followed the executive's lead, rubber-stamping executive decisions. Though Mexico is democratic in name, traditionally the country has been authoritarian and corporatist. Since the 1980s, the government and its citizens have made significant changes, so that more and more Mexico is practicing democracy.

According to the Constitution of 1917, Mexican political institutions resemble those of the U.S. The three branches of government theoretically check and balance one another, and many public officials - including the president, both houses of the legislature, and governors - are directly elected by the people. In practice, however, the Mexican system is very different from that of the United States. The Mexican constitution is very long and easily amended, and the government can best be described as a **strong presidential system**.

THE EXECUTIVE

A remarkable thing happened in the presidential election of 2000. The PRI candidate did not win. Instead, **Vicente Fox**, candidate for the combined PAN/PRD parties won with almost 43 percent of the vote. He edged out Francisco Labastida, the PRI candidate, who garnered not quite 36 percent. This election has far-reaching implications, since the structure of the government had been built around the certainty that the PRI candidate would win. This election may mark the end of patron-clientelism and the beginning of a true democratic state. The election of **Felipe Calderon** in 2006 secured PAN's control of the presidency, but since he only received about 36% of the vote – only .5% more than PRD's Obrador – he has had to build a coalition cabinet.

Since the formation of PRI, policymaking in Mexico had centered on the presidency. The president - through the patron-client system - was virtually a dictator for his **sexenio**, a non-renewable six-year term. The incumbent always selected his successor, appointed officials to all positions of power in the government and PRI, and named PRI candidates for governors, senators, deputies, and local officials. Until the mid 1970s, Mexican presidents were considered above criticism, and people revered them as symbols of national progress and well-being. As head of PRI, the president managed a huge patronage system and controlled a rubber stamp Congress. The president almost always was a member of the preceding president's cabinet. Despite recent changes, the Mexican president remains very powerful.

During his sexenio, Vicente Fox had to manage a new Mexico without the supporting patron-client system of PRI behind him. His predecessor, Ernesto Zedillo had responded to pressure to democratize by relinquishing a number of the traditional powers of the presidency. For example, Zedillo announced that he would not name his PRI successor (the candidate in 2000), but that the party would make the decision.   Even so, President Fox inherited a job that most people still saw as all-powerful, and they often blamed him for failing to enact many of his promised programs, despite the fact that he did not have a strong party in Congress or many experienced people in government.

THE BUREAUCRACY

Almost 1 1/2 million people work in the federal bureaucracy, most of them in Mexico City. More government employees staff the schools, state-owned industries, and semi-autonomous agencies of the government, and hundreds of thousands of bureaucrats fill positions in state, and local governments. Officials are generally paid very little, but those at high and middle levels have a great deal of power. Under PRI control, all were tied to the patron-client system and often accepted bribes and used insider information to promote private business deals.

Under PRI, the **para-statal** sector – composed of semiautonomous or autonomous government agencies – was huge. These companies often produce goods and services that in other countries are carried out by private individuals, and the Mexican government owned many of them. The best-known para-statal is **PEMEX**, the giant state-owned petroleum company. After the oil bust of the early 1980s, reforms trimmed the number of para-statals, and the number has continued to dwindle, so that many of them are now privately owned. President Fox pushed for privatization of PEMEX, but did not succeed.

LEGISLATURE

The Mexican legislature is bicameral, with a 500-member **Chamber of Deputies** and a 128-member **Senate**. All legislators are directly elected - 300 deputies from **single-member districts**, 200 by **proportional representation**, and 3 senators from each of 31 states and the federal district (Mexico City), with the remaining senators selected by proportional representation. Although legislative procedures look very similar to those of the United States, until the 1980s the legislature remained under the president's strict control.

PRI's grip on the legislature slipped earlier than it did on the presidency. The growing strength of opposition parties, combined with legislation that provided for greater representation of minority parties (proportional representation) in Congress, led to the election of 240 opposition deputies in 1988. After that, presidential programs were no longer rubber stamped, but were open to real debate for the first time. President Salinas' reform programs, then, were slowed down, and for the first time, the Mexican government experienced some gridlock. In 1997 PRI lost a majority in the Chamber of Deputies when 261 deputies were elected from opposition parties. The election of 2000 gave PRI a bare plurality – but far from a majority - in both houses. In the election of 2003, the pattern held, with voters selecting 224 PRI deputies, to 149 for PAN and 97 for PRD. In the election of 2006, PRI's support slipped in both houses, PAN gained some seats in the Chamber of Deputies, and PRD made big gains in both houses.

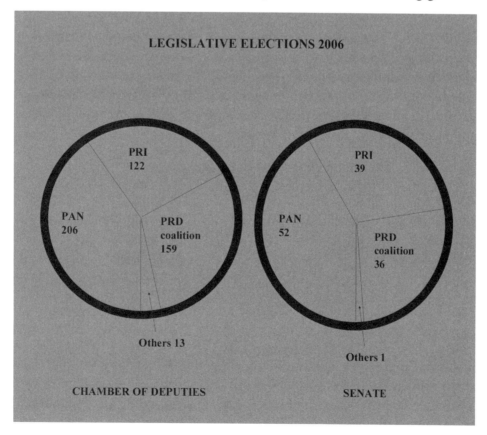

The number of women in both houses of the legislature has risen significantly in recent years to 113 of 500 (22.6%) deputies and 22 of 128 (17.2%) senators. The main reason for this change is the implementation of a 1996 election law that required political parties to sponsor women candidates. Parties must run at least 30% women for both lists for the proportional representation election, as well as candidates for the single-member districts/states. In an effort to regain some of its lost clout, PRI has exceeded the requirements by instituting a 50% quota for its candidates. So far, no major party has fielded a female candidate for the presidency, although a minor party – Social-Democratic and Farmers – ran Patricia Mercado in 2006.

As a competitive multiparty system begins to emerge, the Mexican Congress has become a more important forum for various points of view. PRI candidates are facing more competitive elections in many locales, and the number of "safe seats" is declining. The legislature challenged Fox on a number of occasions, but whether or not a true system of checks and balances is developing is still unclear.

JUDICIARY

A strong judicial branch is essential if a country is to be ruled by law, not by the whim of a dictator. Mexico does not yet have an independent judiciary, nor does it have a system of judicial review. Like most other non-English speaking countries, it follows code law, not common law (see p. 15). Even though the Constitution of 1917 is still in effect, it is easily amended and does not have the same level of legitimacy as the U.S. Constitution does.

Mexico has both federal and state courts, but because most laws are federal, state courts have played a subordinate role. If states continue to become more independent from the central government, the state courts almost certainly will come to play a larger role.

The **Supreme Court** is the highest federal court, and on paper it has judicial review, but in reality, it almost never overrules an important government action or policy. Historically, then, the courts have been controlled by the executive branch, most specifically the president. As in the United States, judges are officially appointed for life. In practice, judges resign at the beginning of each sexenio, allowing the incoming president to place his loyalists on the bench as well as in the state houses, bureaucratic offices, and party headquarters.

But change is in the wind. The administration of **Ernesto Zedillo** (1994-2000) tried to strengthen the courts by emphasizing the rule of law. Increasing interest in human rights issues by citizens' groups and the media has added pressure to the courts to play a stronger role in protecting basic freedoms. Citizens and the government are increasingly resorting to the courts as a primary weapon against corruption, drugs, and police abuse. President Zedillo often refused to interfere with the courts' judgments, and Vicente Fox promised to work for an independent judiciary, although the results were disappointing to many people. The strength of the judiciary is limited by the general perception that judges are corrupt, especially at the local level, where many decisions are made.

MILITARY

Military generals dominated Mexican politics throughout the 19th century and into the early 20th century. The military presided over the chaos, violence, and bloodshed of the era following the Revolution of 1910, and it was the competitiveness of their generals that caused PRI to dramatically cut back their political power. Although all presidents of Mexico were generals until the 1940s, they still acted to separate the military from politics. Even critics of PRI admit that gaining government control of the military is one of the party's most important accomplishments. Over the past fifty years, the military has developed into a relatively disciplined force with a professional officer corps.

Much credit for de-politicizing the military belongs to Plutarco Calles and Lazaro Cardenas, who introduced the idea of rotating the generals' regional commands. By moving generals from one part of the country to another, the government kept them from building regional bases of power. And true to the old patron-client system, presidents traded favors with military officers - such as business opportunities - so that generals could enjoy economic, if not political power.

The tendency to dole out favors to the military almost certainly has led to the existence of strong ties between military officers and the drug trade. In recent years, the military has been heavily involved in efforts to combat drug trafficking, and rumors abound about deals struck between military officials and drug barons. Such fears were confirmed when General Jesus Gutierrez Rebollo, the head of the anti-drug task force, was arrested in February 1997 on accusations of protecting a drug lord.

POLICIES AND ISSUES

Mexican government and politics has changed dramatically since the 1980s. Today Mexico has taken serious steps toward becoming a democracy, and the economy has shown signs of improvement since the collapse of 1982. The country is trying to move from being a regionally vulnerable area to a globally reliable one. Still, stubborn problems remain. PRI has been entangled with the government so long that creating branches that operate independently is a huge task. The gap between the rich and poor is still wide in Mexico, despite the growth of the middle class in the north. And Calderon faces a big challenge in shaping Mexico's relationship with the United States. How does Mexico retain the benefits of trade and cooperation with its neighbor to the north, and yet steer its own independent course?

THE ECONOMY

Mexico's economic development has had a significant impact on social conditions in the country. Overall, the standard of living has improved greatly since the 1940s. Rates of infant mortality, literacy, and life expectancy have steadily improved. Health and education services have expanded, despite severe cutbacks after the economic crisis of 1982.

"THE MEXICAN MIRACLE"

Between 1940 and 1960 Mexico's economy grew as a whole by more than 6 percent a year. Industrial production rose even faster, averaging nearly 9 percent for most of the 1960s. Agriculture's share of total production dropped from 25 percent to 11 percent. while that of manufacturing rose from 25 percent to 34 percent. All this growth occurred without much of the inflation that has plagued many other Latin American economies.

Problems

- **A large gap between the rich and the poor** was a major consequence of the rapid economic growth. Relatively little attention was paid to the issues of equality and social justice that had led to the revolutions in the first place. Social services programs were limited at best. From 1940 to 1980 Mexico's income distribution was among the most unequal of all the LDCs, with the bottom 40 percent of the population never earning more than 11 percent of total wages. Today inequality has lessened slightly, but it is still an important issue.

- **Rapid and unplanned urbanization** accompanied the growth. The Federal District, Guadalajara, and other major cities became urban nightmares, with millions of people living in huge shantytowns with no electricity, running water, or sewers. Poor highway planning and no mass transit meant that traffic congestion was among the worst in the world. Pollution from cars and factories makes Mexico City's air so dirty that it is unsafe to breathe.

The Crisis

In its effort to industrialize, the Mexican government borrowed heavily against expectations that oil prices would remain high forever. Much of the rapid growth was based on the oil business, especially since Mexico's production began increasing just as that of OPEC countries was decreasing during the early 1970s. When the price of oil plummeted in 1982, so did Mexico's economy. By 1987, Mexico's debt was over $107 billion, making it one of the most heavily indebted countries in the world. The debt represented 70 percent of Mexico's entire GNP.

REFORM

President Miguel de la Madrid began his sexenio in 1982 with all of these economic problems before him. He began a dramatic reform program that reflected the values of the new *tecnico* leaders. This program continued through the presidencies of Salinas and Zedillo, and it has brought about one of the most dramatic economic turnarounds in modern history.

- **Sharp cuts in government spending** - According to agreements with the International Monetary Fund, the World Bank, the U.S. government, and private banks, Mexico began an austerity plan that greatly reduced government spending. Hundreds of thousands of jobs were cut, subsides to government agencies were slashed, and hundreds of public enterprises were eliminated.

- **Debt reduction** - Mexico's debt still continues to be problematic, although the U.S. spearheaded a multinational plan to reduce interest rates on loans and allow more generous terms for their repayment. Mexico still pays an average of about $10 billion a year in interest payments.

- **Privatization** - In order to allow market forces to drive the Mexican economy, Madrid's government decided to give up much of its economic power. Most importantly, the government privatized many public enterprises, especially those that were costing public money. President Salinas returned the banks to the private sector in 1990. By the late 1980s a "mini silicon valley" was emerging in Guadalajara where IBM, Hewlett-Packard, Wang, and other tech firms set up factories and headquarters. Special laws - like duty-free importing of components - and cheap labor encouraged U.S. companies to invest in Mexican plants.

Still, the problems persist today, particularly those of income inequality, urban planning, and pollution. As a businessman, Vicente Fox made a campaign promise to oversee a 7% annual growth in the Mexican economy during his sexenio, but his hopes fell short. Between 2001 and 2003, Mexico's economic slowdown can be partially explained by the U.S. recession that began in 2000. In 2004, the economy grew by 4.1%, but an estimated 40% of the Mexican population was still below the poverty line. A bright spot is that today the poor are doing better than they were a few years ago. One reason is a government anti-poverty program, **Oportunidades,** which includes free benefits and pensions for those not covered by jobs in the formal economy.

FOREIGN POLICY

The crisis that began in 1982 clearly indicated that a policy of encouraging more Mexican exports and opening markets to foreign goods was essential. In the years after 1982 the government relaxed restrictions on foreign ownership of property and reduced and eliminated tariffs. The government courted foreign investment and encouraged Mexican private industry to produce goods for export. Mexico's foreign policy is still more concerned with the United States than with any other country, but in recent years Mexican leaders have asserted themselves in iternational forums, such as the United Nations and the World Trade Organization.

DRUG TRAFFICKING

Drug trafficking between Mexico and the United States has been a major problem for both countries for many years. The drug trade has spawned corruption within the Mexican government, so that officials have often been bribed to look the other way or even actively participate in the trade. The depth of drug-related problems was evident in early 2005, when the government staged a raid on its own maximum-security prison, *La Palma*, in an effort to regain control of the prison from drug lords who had engineered the murder of a prominent fellow inmate. Fox vowed to stamp out the corruption and some major arrests were made, but the problem remained far from resolved at the end of his sexenio.

When Felipe Calderon took office he stepped up the war on drugs, sending troops and federal agents into areas where gangs control local officials. He also promised to remake the nation's police departments, root out corrupt officers, and support legislation that makes it possible for the local police to investigate drug rings. The immediate reaction has been one of the worst waves of drug-related violence ever. The number of brutal murders, often of policemen, has increased significantly. One cause of the violence is a fierce competition between two competing drug rings that want exclusive control of very lucrative smuggling routes between Mexico and the United States.

IMMIGRATION POLICY

Early in his term, Vicente Fox pushed hard to solve tensions between the United States and Mexico regarding immigration policy. Fox proposed a bold immigration initiative that included a guest worker program, amnesty for illegal immigrants, an increase in visas issued, and movement to an eventual open border. The plan would have allowed Mexicans to work legally in the U.S., while amnesty for illegal immigrants would have eventually offered a green card as well as legal citizenship to over three million undocumented Mexicans living in the U.S. In exchange, Fox pledged to tighten the Mexican border to prevent additional illegal immigration. President George W. Bush responded positively to Fox's initiatives, but the plan fell through after the September 11, 2001 attacks in the United States. President Bush reevaluated the security risks involved with Fox's plan, and the whole thing unraveled within weeks, and only recently has come to life again.

In late 2006 President Bush signed a bill providing for construction of 700 miles of added fencing along the Mexico/United States border that he called "an important step toward immigration reform." Bush had wanted a more comprehensive bill that provided for a guest worker program, as well as the possibility of eventual citizenship for many illegal immigrants, but those measures were opposed by Republicans in the legislature. Felipe Calderon sternly denounced the U.S. construction of the wall, comparing it to the "huge mistake" the Russians made in building the Berlin Wall in 1961. Calderon has promised to emphasize the improvement of the Mexican economy to take away the incentive for people to immigrate to the United States.

MAQUILADORA AND NAFTA

A manufacturing zone was created in the 1960s in northern Mexico just south of the border with the United States. Workers in this *maquiladora* district have produced goods primarily for consumers in the U.S., and a number of U.S. companies have established plants in the zone to transform imported, duty-free components or raw materials into finished industrial products. Industrialization of the zone was promoted by the North American Free Trade Agreement (NAFTA), a treaty signed in 1995 by Mexico, the United States, and Canada, that eliminated barriers to free trade among the three countries. Today hundreds of thousands of workers are employed in the *maquiladora* district, accounting for over 20 percent of Mexico's entire industrial labor force. U.S. companies have been criticized for avoiding employment and environmental regulations imposed within the borders of the U.S., hiring young women for low pay and no benefits who work in buildings that are environmentally questionable.

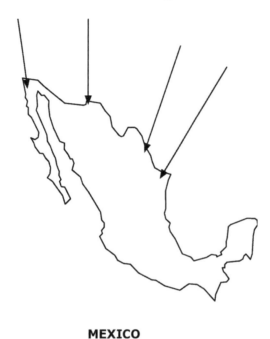

MEXICO

The *maquiladoras* district. This trade zone exists in northern Mexico not far from the U.S. border.

Since the mid-1980s, Mexico has entered into many trade agreements and organizations in order to globalize its economy and pay its way out of debt:

- **GATT/WTO -** In 1986, Mexico joined the General Agreement on Tariffs and Trade (GATT), a multilateral agreement that attempts to promote freer trade among countries. The World Trade Organization was created from this agreement.

- **NAFTA** - The North American Free Trade Agreement was signed by Mexico, Canada, and the United States. Its goal is to more closely integrate the economies by eliminating tariffs and reducing restrictions so that companies can expand into all countries freely. Mexico hopes to stimulate its overall growth, enrich its big business community, and supply jobs for Mexicans in new industries. U.S. firms gain from access to inexpensive labor, raw materials, series and tourism, as well as new markets to sell and invest in. Mexico runs the risk of again being overshadowed by the United

States, but hopes that the benefits will outweigh the problems. President Fox generally supported freer flow of labor and goods between Mexico and its northern neighbors, although some of his advisers were more skeptical of NAFTA. Unlike the agreement among member nations of the European Union, the NAFTA agreement currently does not allow free flow of labor across borders.

ETHNIC REBELLIONS

In his first year in office, Fox made several efforts to negotiate with the **Zapatistas** to settle their dispute with the government. The **EZLN** (Zapatista National Liberation Front) began in 1994 in the southern state of Chiapas in protest to the signing of the NAFTA treaty. They saw the agreement as a continuation of exploitation by voracious landowners and corrupt PRI bosses. Their army captured four towns, including a popular tourist destination, and they demanded jobs, land, housing, food, health, education, independence, freedom, democracy, justice and peace. Their rebellion has spread, and Zapatista supporters wear black ski masks to hide their identity from the government.

The Zapatista rebellion was based on ethnicity - the Amerindian disaffection for the mestizo, urban-based government. It has since spread to other areas and ethnicities, and it represents a major threat to Mexico's political stability. The 2006 uprising in Oaxaca is another indication that hostilities toward the rich and the government are still quite strong in the south, particularly toward PRI leaders.

DEMOCRACY

Part of the answer to Mexico's economic and foreign policy woes lies in the development of democratic traditions within the political system. Mexico's tradition of authoritarianism works against democratization, but modernization of the economy, the political value of populism, and democratic revolutionary impulses work for it. One of the most important indications of democracy is the development of competitive, clean elections in many parts of the country.

The **CFE (Federal Election Commission)** was created as an independent regulatory body to safeguard honest and accurate election results. Although it was dominated by PRI in its early years, in recent elections it appears to be operating as it should. Some election reforms include

- Campaign finance restrictions - laws that limit contributions to campaigns

- Critical media coverage, as media is less under PRI control

- International watch teams, as Mexico has tried to convince other countries that elections are fair and competitive

- Election monitoring by opposition party members

The 1994 campaign for the presidency got off to a very bad start when PRI candidate Luis Donaldo Colosio was assassinated in Tijuana. PRI quickly replaced him with Ernesto Zedillo, but the old specters of violence and chaos threatened the political order. The incumbent president's brother was implicated in the assassination, and high officials were linked to drug trafficking. Despite this trouble, Zedillo stepped up to the challenge, and PRI won the election handily. Many observers believe that the elections of 1994 and 2000 have been the most competitive, fair elections in Mexico's history. The election of 2000 broke all precedents when a PAN candidate - Vicente Fox - won the presidency, finally displacing the 71-year dominance of PRI. The controversial election of 2006 was clearly competitive, but it also threatened to tear the fragile base of democracy apart. Obrador questioned the very legitimacy of the process, and the strong support he received from his followers is evidence that instability is still a part of the Mexican political system. However, the fact that the election tribunal followed the process set by law is a step toward becoming a liberal democracy. Even more significant is the eventual acceptance by most Mexican citizens of its decisions, evidence that the country has successfully passed through the crisis.

What will the future bring? Will Mexico be able to sustain a strong, stable economy? Will the political system emerge from its peasant-based patron-client system and authoritarianism as a modern democracy? Will more social equality be granted to peasants and city workers? Many observers await the answers to these questions, including people in less developed countries that look to Mexico as an example of development. More powerful countries - particularly the United States - realize that international global politics and economies are tied to the successes of countries like Mexico. Despite the instabilities of its past, Mexico does have strong traditions, a well-developed sense of national pride, many natural resources, and a record of progress, no matter how uneven.

IMPORTANT TERMS AND CONCEPTS

Amerindians
Amigos de Fox
Calderon, Felipe
camarillas
Cardenas, Cuauhtemoc
Cardenas, Lazaro
caudillos
Chamber of Deputies, Senate
Chiapas rebellion
co-optation
corporatism (state and neo)
Cristeros Rebellion
dependency
Diaz, Porfirio
ejidos
election reform (in Mexico)
EZLN
Father Hidalgo
Federal Election Commission
formal, informal economic sectors
Fox, Vicente
GATT
GNP per capita
HDI
import substitution
Juarez, Benito

mestizos
"Mexican Miracle"
NAFTA
neoliberalism
Obrador, Andres Manuel Lopez
Oportunidades
para-statals
patron-client system
PEMEX
pendulum theory
plurality (first past the post)/proportional representation electoral systems
politicos
Porfiriato
proportional representation in Mexico
PAN
PPP
PRD
PRI
Santa Anna
sexenio
technicos
Villa, Pancho
WTO
Zapata, Emiliano
Zapatistas
Zedilla, Ernesto

MULTIPLE-CHOICE QUESTIONS
MEXICO

1. Left-leaning political leaders of Mexico have often promoted policies based on

   a) modernization theory
   b) compressed modernity
   c) dependency theory
   d) neocolonialism
   e) neoliberalism

2. Compared to the other core countries, Mexico's purchasing power parity (PPP) is

   a) lower than Britain only
   b) lower than Britain and Russia only
   c) lower than Britain, Russia, and China only
   d) higher than Nigeria only
   e) higher than Nigeria and Iran only

3. All of the following are accurate descriptions of strong historical traditions in Mexico EXCEPT:

   a) authoritarianism
   b) populism
   c) divisiveness among elites
   d) instability
   e) reliance on common law

4. Which of the following countries have strong patterns of patron-clientelism in their political cultures?

   I. Britain
   II. Russia
   III. China
   IV. Mexico

   a) I and III only
   b) II and III only
   c) III and IV only
   d) II, III, and IV only
   e) I, II, III, and IV

5. During which era in its history did Mexico begin to move clearly toward neoliberalism AND liberal democracy?

   a) early 19th century
   b) late 19th century
   c) early 20th century
   d) mid-20th century
   e) late 20th century

6. A strong cleavage in Mexican society between European and Amerindian began with Spanish occupation in the late 16th century. Europeans that bridged that cleavage were usually

   a) priests
   b) military generals
   c) bureaucrats
   d) peasant
   e) city workers

7. The style of government during the Porfiriato is best described as

   a) authoritarian
   b) liberal
   c) neocorporatist
   d) theocratic
   e) rational-legal

8. Which of the following was a common characteristic of the Russian, Chinese, and Mexican revolutions of the early 20th century?

   a) All were ideological.
   b) All resulted in the overthrow of a strong, authoritarian government.
   c) All resulted eventually in one-party states.
   d) All put charismatic leaders strongly in control of the government.
   e) All were focused on driving westerners from the country.

9. All of the following were reforms from the sexenio of Lazaro Cardenas EXCEPT:

   a) ejidos
   b) export-oriented industrialization
   c) nationalization of industry
   d) inclusion of peasant and union organizations in policymaking
   e) investments in public works

10. The division between *tecnicos* and *politicos* among PRI leaders developed because of disagreements about

a) democratization
b) the term limits for the presidency
c) economic development
d) drug trafficking prevention programs
 e) immigration policies

(Questions 11 and 12 are based on the following charts):

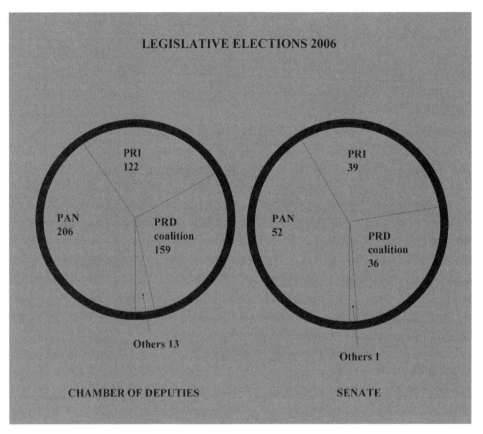

11. The patterns of party affiliations in Mexico's legislature shown in the chart BEST support the prediction that in the near future the government will experience

a) gridlock
b) domination by PAN
c) domination by the president
d) conflict between the Chamber of Deputies and the Senate
e) less competitive elections

12. Which of the following accurately compares changes in patterns of party affiliations in Mexico's legislature between 2003 and 2006?

    a) PRI lost seats in the Chamber of Deputies, but gained seats in the Senate.
    b) PAN gained seats in the Chamber of Deputies, but lost seats in the Senate.
    c) PAN lost seats in both houses.
    d) PRD gained seats in both houses.
    e) PRI gained seats in both houses.

13. Which of the following accurately compares north and south in Mexico?

    a) The north is less prosperous.
    b) Voters in the north are more likely to vote for PAN.
    c) People that live in the north are more likely to be Amerindian.
    d) People that live in the south are more supportive of a market-based economy.
    e) The north is more prone toward ethnic-based protests.

14. Which of the following accurately describes voter participation rates in Mexican presidential elections?

    a) The voter rate reached its height in 1994, and has declined in the two elections since.
    b) Voter rates in recent elections have been significantly lower than they were before 1988.
    c) Voter rates have been consistently low over the past few elections.
    d) Voter rates are lower for presidential elections than they are for local elections.
    e) Voter rates were higher than usual in the elections of 2000 and 2006.

15. In comparison to interest groups in China's civil society, interest groups in Mexico's civil society have been more likely to

    a) agree with the government
    b) stay out of the policymaking process
    c) solicit peasants as members
    d) support the government
    e) refuse to cooperate with the government

16. Mexico has a high Gini coefficient of .50, which means that the country

    a) is developing
    b) has a middling HDI score
    c) has a great deal of inequality
    d) is an illiberal democracy
    e) has a middling GNP per capita

17. One reason that Mexico cannot yet be declared a stable democracy is that the country does not

    a) hold regular, competitive elections
    b) show consistent democratic practices for at least 40 years
    c) have a free press
    d) have a market economy
    e) allow private interest groups to form

18. All of the following are accurate statements about PRD EXCEPT:

    a) it is generally seen as PRI's opposition on the left
    b) it has been plagued by poor organization
    c) it is less likely to support a market economy than PAN
    d) it generally has more support in the north than in the south
    e) it made significant gains in the legislative elections of 2006

19. Which of the following countries directly elect both a president and representatives to a legislative body?

    I. Britain
    II. Russia
    III. China
    IV. Mexico

    a) I only
    b) II only
    c) I, II, and III only
    d) II and IV only
    e) I, II, and IV only

20. Which of the following countries combines a plurality (first-past-the-post) electoral system with proportional representation?

    I. Britain
    II. Russia
    III. China
    IV. Mexico

    a) I only
    b) II only
    c) I, II, and III only
    d) II and IV only
    e) I, II, and IV only

21. Which of the following government programs is MOST representative of a socialist ideology?

    a) the ejido system
    b) the NAFTA agreement
    c) maquiladora
    d) debt reduction plan
    e) import substitution industrialization

22. The presidential election of 2000 brought about a significant change in the Mexican political system because

    a) the violent assassination of the PRI candidate created instability
    b) the PRI candidate received almost no votes
    c) the vote was so close that a runoff election had to be held
    d) a non-PRI candidate won
    e) a president was re-elected, ending the tradition of a one-term head of state

23. A good example of a Mexican para-statal is

    a) NAFTA
    b) Educational Workers' Union
    c) PEMEX
    d) The Federal Election Commission
    e) The Confederation of Employers of the Mexican Republic

24. The main reason that an increasing number of women have been elected recently to the Mexican legislature is

    a) less emphasis on *machismo* in Mexican political culture
    b) an election law that requires political parties to sponsor women candidates
    c) change to the electoral system to include proportional representation
    d) the decline in PRI power
    e) the growing political influence of the U.S.

25. The Mexican Supreme Court has the power to

    a) exercise judicial review, on paper and in reality
    b) remove senators and deputies from their posts for ethical reasons
    c) hear appeals from those accused on crime, but not to exercise judicial review
    d) exercise judicial review, on paper but not in reality
    e) dismantle lower courts and appoint new judges

26.   A major change in the Mexican military since the mid-twentieth century is that it

a) no longer has policymaking power
b) is not as well financed as before
c) has more powerful generals than before
d) is much less corrupt than before
e) is much less professional than before

27. Which of the following has NOT been a major problem for the economy since the early 1980s?

a) overreliance on one product for export
b) high national debt
c) a large gap between and rich and the poor
d) lack of monetary assistance from other countries
e) rapid and unplanned urbanization

28. Most accusations of corruption among Mexican police officers stems from their involvement in

a) unlawful arrests
b) international terrorist organizations
c) immigration disputes
d) the oil industry
e) drug trafficking

29. Russia is to the Chechen rebellion as Mexico is to the

a) Crisneros rebellion
b) Revolution of 1910
c) 1969 protests at the Mexico City Olympics
d) "Mexican Miracle"
e) Zapatista Rebellion

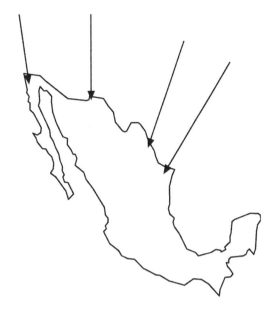

MEXICO

30. The arrows on the map above point out Mexico's

    a) areas of strongest support for PRI
    b) areas of strongest support for PRD
    c) the locations of the strongest camarilla
    d) maquiladora district
    e) areas of strength for the Catholic Church

FREE-RESPONSE QUESTION
MEXICO

(a) Describe three specific economic problems that Mexico has had since 1982.

(b) For each economic problem you identified in (a), describe a policy reaction that the government has had to the problem.

GOVERNMENT AND POLITICS IN IRAN

> "This is the voice of Iran, the voice of the true Iran,
> the voice of the Islamic Revolution."

> Iran National Radio
> February 11, 1979

This dramatic announcement came on Iran's national radio the first evening after the coup d'etat that deposed Muhammad Reza Shah, who had followed his father in ruling Iran with an iron fist for more than half a century. The announcement struck fear into the hearts of many westerners who today see the 1979 Revolution in Iran as the beginning of a great conflict between the West and Islamic civilizations. According to this line of reasoning, the events of 1979 started a great fundamentalist movement that spread throughout the Islamic world and eventually culminated in the September 11, 2001 attacks on the World Trade Towers and the Pentagon in the United States. For some political scientists, Samuel Huntington foresaw this situation in his 1993 article in *Foreign Affairs* magazine called, "The Clash of Civilizations."

This view of Iran's role in modern world politics, however, ignores the complexities of Iran's political culture. Iran's identity is steeped in thousands of years of history that not only includes a deep attachment to Islam, but also a popular revolution in the early 20th century that resulted in a western-style constitution that was intact until 1979. These influences are still at odds today, and they shape the major challenges that face the political system. Is democracy incompatible with Islam, or is true Islam actually based in popular support? The first impulse leads Iran toward a **theocracy,** or a government ruled strictly by religion, and the second leads the country toward **secularization**, or the belief that religion and government should be separated. These political questions are complicated by Iran's developing economy that squarely places it in the global market, but is heavily reliant on one product. Iran is the second largest oil producer in the Middle East and the fourth largest in the world. Should these resources be controlled by clerics, or do economic matters require an expertise outside the realm of religious leaders?

In many ways, Iran is a unique addition to the AP Comparative Government and Politics course because it is the only one of the six countries that currently is governed as a theocracy. However, Iran shares a characteristic with Russia, China, Mexico, and Nigeria in its possession of that all-important modern resource – oil. Like Mexico, its economy may be labeled "developing" rather than "less developed," as is the case for Nigeria. China also may be seen as having a rapidly "developing" economy. Similar to all the other five countries, Iran's political system is multi-faceted, and cannot be boiled down simply to a monolithic representation of the Islamic world.

SOVEREIGNTY, AUTHORITY, AND POWER

An early Iranian concept of sovereignty can be traced to the days of the ancient Achemenian Empire (called Persia by the Greeks) that existed as the world's largest empire from its founding by Cyrus in the 6th century B.C.E. till its defeat some 200 years later. Iran's greatest rival was ancient Greece, and the two civilizations couldn't have been more different. Greece was divided into quarreling city-states and its economy and transportation was heavily reliant on the sea. In contrast, Iran emerged from the dry lands north of the Persian Gulf and spread its power through highly centralized military leadership by land as far as the Aegean Sea, where its interests conflicted with those of the Greeks. The clash between two great civilizations may be seen as the first act of a drama that has played out over the centuries: West vs. East. Ironically, both civilizations were conquered by a Macedonian, Alexander the Great, but Alexander's affinity for the Greeks led him to spread their culture to lands that he conquered. Less well known is the fact that Alexander much admired the Persian political structure, and left it largely in place as he conquered their lands.

The Persian sovereigns were always hereditary military leaders who very much enjoyed the trappings of royalty. One king, Darius, built a magnificent capital at Persepolis, and joined his new city to many parts of the ancient world by an intricate system of roads that carried his armies all over and allowed people from many lands to pay tribute to him. His title was "The Great King, King of Kings, King in Persia, King of countries," and he referred to everyone, even the Persian nobility, as "my slaves." The king's authority was supported by a strong military as well as a state-sponsored religion, **Zoroastrianism**.

Although none of the rulers of empires that followed were able to centralize power so successfully as the Achemenians did, the stage was set for the authoritarian state. Zoroastrianism did not survive as a major religion, but it continued to be sponsored by rulers for centuries, including those of the Sassanid Dynasty (226-651 C.E.)

THE IMPORTANCE OF SHIISM

From the 7th to 16th centuries C.E., the geographical region of Iran had little political unity, and experienced numerous invasions, including that of the Arabs, who brought Islam to the area. What emerged was a new glue that held the Persians together – not political, but religious in nature. As a result, even when their caliphate (an Islamic empire put in place by the Arabs) was defeated by the mighty Mongols in the 13th century, the religion survived the chaos as the invaders converted to the religion of the conquered. Despite the changes in political leadership over the years, the religion of Islam has continued to be a vital source of identity for the Iranians.

The brand of Islam that distinguishes Iran from its neighbors today – **Shiism** – was established as the state religion in the 16th century by **Ismail**, the founder of the Safavid Empire. Ismail and his *qizilbash* ("redheads," because of their colorful turbans) were supporters of this sect of Islam that had quarreled bitterly with **Sunni** Muslims for centuries. The division originated after the religion's founder, Muhammad, died without a designated heir, a significant problem since his armies had conquered many lands. The Sunnis favored choosing the caliph (leader) from the accepted leadership (the Sunni), but the Shiites argued that the mantle should be hereditary, and should pass to Muhammad's son-in-law, Ali. When Ali was killed in the dispute, the Shiite opinion became a minority one, but they kept their separate identity, and carried the belief that the true heirs of Islam were the descendants of Ali. These heirs, called **imams**, continued until the 9th century, when the 12th descendant disappeared as a child, only to become known as the "**Hidden Imam.**"

When Ismail established Iran as a Shiite state in the 16th century, he distinguished it as different from all Sunni states around him, a characteristic that still exists today. He gave political legitimacy to the belief that the "Hidden Imam" would eventually return, but until he did, the rulers of Iran stood in his place as the true heirs of Islam.

LEGITIMACY IN THE MODERN STATE

To a remarkable extent, these historical influences still shape the modern state. Authoritarian leaders played an important role in the 20th century as the **Pahlavi** shahs ("King of Kings," or "shah in shah") ruled from 1925 to 1979. Their attempts to secularize the state, though, were undone by a charismatic leader – the **Ayatollah Ruhollah Khomeini** – who personified the union of political and religious interests from ancient days. His appeal may be likened to that of Ismail – the protector of the "true faith" that unites the Shiite religion with the power of the state. The Ayatollah was hailed as the "Leader of the Revolution, Founder of the Islamic Republic, Guide of the Oppressed Masses, Commander of the Armed Forces, and Imam of the Muslim World" – titles that blend the historical influences into the persona of one very powerful religious/political leader.

The Ayatollah Khomeini led the **Revolution of 1979**, an event that transformed the legitimacy of the state, anchoring it once again in principles of Shiism. The most important document that legitimizes the state today is the **Constitution of 1979**, along with its amendments of 1989, written during the last months of the Ayatollah Khomeini's life. The document and its 40 amendments is a highly complex mixture of theocracy and democracy. Its preamble reflects the importance of religion for the legitimacy of the state, affirming faith in God, Divine Justice, the Qur'an, the Prophet Muhammad, the Twelve Imams, and the eventual return of the Hidden Imam. Khomeini's doctrine of **jurist's guardianship** (which we'll define later) is included along with the other "divine principles."

In recent years two conflicting ideas – sovereignty of the people and divinely inspired clerical rule – have created a crisis of legitimacy in Iran. During the presidency of **Muhammad Khatami** (1997-2005), reformers who supported a democratic government came to the forefront, but with the election of **Mahmoud Ahmadinejad** in 2005, the conservatives who endorsed a theocracy took control. As a result, the rift between these two forces – reformers and conservatives – has illustrated the issue of just how a theocracy can also function as a democracy. The conflict is reflected in differences among clerics in the seminaries of **Qom** (a city south of Tehran) in their interpretations of the true meaning of jurist's guardianship.

POLITICAL CULTURE

Although the Safavid Empire was followed by centuries of weak political organization in Iran, Shiism continued as an important unifying thread to the political culture. However, the dynasty that followed - the Qajars - did not claim the imam's mantle, so Shiite clerical leaders came to be the main interpreters of Islam, and a separation between religion and politics developed. Although the Qajars were never very strong, they did not succumb to European imperialism, and they ruled until the 20th century. These complex historical influences – with roots in ancient times – have formed a multi-faceted political culture characterized by:

- **Authoritarianism, but not totalitarianism** – Beginning with the Safavid Empire, the central political leaders did not control all areas of individuals' lives. While the leaders claimed to be all-powerful, in reality they were not, and people became accustomed to paying attention to local officials and/or to leading their own lives within civil society.

- **Union of political and religious authority** – From the days of the ancient Persians, political and religious leaders were often one and the same. However, starting with the rule of the Qajars

(1794-1925), the two types of authority were separated, only to be brought back together by the Revolution of 1979.

- **Shiism and *sharia* as central components** – Today almost 90% of all Iranians identify themselves as Shiite, a fact that links citizens to the government, which is officially a theocracy. Islamic law, the *sharia*, is an important source of legitimacy that the modern government particularly emphasizes.

- **Escape from European colonization** – Unlike most countries of Asia, Africa, and South America, Iran was never officially colonized by Europeans during the imperialist era of the 18th and 19th centuries. Although the area was heavily affected by European power moves, imperialism did not have the same direct impact on Iran that it had on Mexico and Nigeria.

- **Geographic limitations** – A great deal of Iran's land space is unusable for agriculture, with a vast central desert plain, and mountains to the north and northeast. Such geographic restrictions caused the early Persians to seek better lands to the west by expansion and conquest. In modern day, the population of Iran is unevenly distributed, with most living in cities and in the northwest, where the most arable land is located.

- **The influence of ancient Persia** – Differences between Iran and neighboring countries is not only based on Shiite vs. Sunni Islam. Even after the Arabs invaded Iran, the people continued to speak Persian rather than Arabic, and many of their other cultural habits remained as well, including distinctive architecture, literary works, poetry, and decorative arts (such as "Persian rugs"). This identity shapes Iranian nationalism today.

POLITICAL AND ECONOMIC CHANGE

Not surprisingly, with Iran's long, complex history, political and economic change has taken many forms, including both evolution and revolution. Politically, Iran established itself as the first large empire in world history - a military powerhouse with strong leaders and centralized governing structures. Despite the continuity of religious and political union, a gradual separation of religion from politics resulted in declining centralization of political power over time before the 20th century. The 20th century saw two revolutions: one in 1905-1909 that set democratic impulses in place, and one in 1979 that reunified religion with politics into the modern theocracy.

Economically, Iran has both suffered and benefited from natural resources. A lack of arable land has meant that the agricultural basis of the empires was never secure, and geographical location also caused Iran to emphasize trade by land. When world commerce turned to sea-based powers beginning in the 16th century, Iran was marginalized. Although Iran maintained its independence during the age of European imperialism, it did not prosper until its greatest modern natural resource was discovered. However, oil has brought its own set of economic problems to Iran – that of managing this necessary commodity for industrialization in such a way that it benefits not only the state but its people as well.

We will follow political and economic change through four eras: The Safavids (1501-1722); The Qajars (1794-1925); the Pahlavis (1925-1979); and the Islamic Revolution and Republic (1979-the Present).

THE SAFAVIDS (1501-1722)

As discussed in the previous section, modern Iran traces its Shiite identity to the **Safavid Empire** that began in the 16th century. By the mid-17th century, the Safavids had succeeded in converting nearly 90% of their subjects to Shiism. Sunnism has survived to modern day among ethnic groups along the borders: Kurds in the northwest, Turkmen in the northeast, Baluchis in the southeast, and Arabs in the southwest. Despite their religious fervor, the Safavids tolerated the Sunnis, as well as smaller numbers of Jews, Zoroastrians, and Christians. They shared with other Muslim rulers a special regard for **People of the Book** – monotheistic people who subjected their lives to holy books similar to the Qur'an. They respected all these religions because they had their own books: Jews, the Torah; Christians, the Bible; and Zoroastrians, the Avesta.

The Safavids ruled from Isfahan, a Persian-speaking city, and most of their bureaucrats were Persian scribes. However, the Safavids had serious economic constraints. Trade routes from Iran to the ancient Silk Route had broken up, and world trade had shifted to the Indian and Atlantic Oceans. Isfahan was far inland with little access to sea-based trade, and agricultural production was hampered by lack of arable land. These economic problems affected the Safavids' ability to rule, since they did not have money for a large bureaucracy or a standing army. As a result, they had to rely largely on local rulers to keep order and collect taxes. In theory, the Safavids claimed absolute power, but in reality they lacked a central state and had to seek the cooperation of semi-independent local leaders. Geographic features fragmented the empire, particularly the mountains, and many clerics lived safely outside the reach of the government. As a result of both political and economic factors, the monarchy became separated from society and had lost a great deal of their power by 1722.

THE QAJARS (1794-1925)

The Safavid Empire ended when Afghan tribesmen invaded Isfahan in 1722. Iran was in disarray for more than a half century, until the land was finally conquered by another Turkish group, the **Qajars.** The Qajars moved the capital to Tehran, and they retained Shiism as the official state religion. However, the Qajar rule marked an important political change. Whereas the Safavids claimed to be the descendants of the Twelve Imams, the Qajars obviously could not tie their legitimacy to such a link. As a result, the Shia clerical leaders could claim to be the main interpreters of Islam, and the separation between government and religion widened significantly.

Economically and politically Iran's power eclipsed during the 19th century. The Qajars ruled during the era of European imperialism, and they suffered land losses to the north and northwest to the growing power of Russia. They sold oil-drilling rights in the southwest to Britain, and they borrowed heavily from European banks to meet their considerable court expenses. By the end of the 19th century, the shah had led the country into serious debt, and many Iranians were upset by his lavish lifestyle.

These problems encouraged the **Constitutional Revolution of 1905-1909.** The revolution began with business owners and bankers demonstrating against the Qajars' move to hand over their customs collections to Europeans. Although the Qajars were attempting to settle their debts, the middle class was fed up, particularly because they suspected that the shah would sacrifice paying domestic debts in order to repay European loans. In 1906 the merchants and local industrialists, affected by British liberalism, demanded a written constitution from the shah. The British, who had many business interests in Iran, encouraged the shah to concede, particularly since Iran did not have an army to effectively put down an insurrection.

The Constitution of 1906 was modeled after western ones, and included such democratic features as:

- Direct elections
- Separation of powers
- Laws made by an elected legislature
- Popular sovereignty
- A Bill of Rights guaranteeing citizens equality before the law, protections for those accused of crimes, and freedom of expression

The revolution sparked a debate about separation of religion from the government – the trend that the Qajars themselves had initiated. The constitution retained the monarchy, but it created a strong legislature to balance executive power. The new assembly was called the *Majles*, and seats were guaranteed to the "People of the Book": Jews, Christians, and Zoroastrians. The *Majles* not only had the authority to make and pass laws, but it also controlled cabinet ministers, who reported to the legislature, not the shah.

The Constitution of 1906 did not turn away from Shiism completely. Shiism was declared the official state religion, and only Shiites could hold cabinet positions. The constitution also created a **Guardian Council** of clerics that had the power to veto any legislation passed by the *Majles*.

These political reforms could do nothing, however, for Iran's economic woes. World events of the early 20th century led to Iran's division into three parts, with one piece for themselves, but another piece occupied by Russia, and another by Britain during World War I. By 1921 Iran was in political and economic disarray, with quarreling factions polarizing the *Majles* into an ineffective ruling body. The country was ready for a strong leader to deliver them from complete chaos.

THE PAHLAVIS (1925-1979)

The Cossack Brigade had been one of the few areas of strength in the latter days of the Qajars, since it was the only force that resembled a real army. The brigade's commander, Colonel **Reza Khan**, carried out a successful coup d'etat against the weakened political state in 1921, and declared himself shah-in-shah in 1925, establishing his own **Pahlavi** dynasty, using a name of an ancient language from Iran's glorious past.

Under Reza Shah, the *Majles* lost its power, and authoritarian rule was reestablished in Iran. He ruled with absolute authority until he turned over power to his son, **Muhammad Reza Shah** in 1941. Despite the fact that the Pahlavis reestablished order in Iran, the democratic experimentation resulting from the Constitution of 1906 was not forgotten, and the second shah had to confront some democratic opposition. One group that challenged the shah was the communist **Tudeh** (Masses) **Party** that gained most of its support from working class trade unions. A second group was the **National Front**, led by **Muhammad Mosaddeq**, whose life influenced many later political leaders in Iran. The National Front drew its support from middle class people who emphasized Iranian nationalism. Mosaddeq advocated nationalizing the British-owned company that monopolized Iran's oil business, and he also wanted to take the armed forces out from under the shah's control. Mosaddeq was elected prime minister in 1951, and his power grew so that the shah was forced to flee the country in 1953. Mosaddeq's career was cut short when the British struck back by sponsoring an overthrow of Mosaddeq, and restoring the shah to full power again. The U.S., ever mindful of keeping Soviet power contained in these Cold War days, helped the British to reinstall the shah. As a result, many Iranians came to see Britain and the U.S. as supporters of autocracy, and the shah as a weak pawn of foreign powers.

Economically, Iran was transformed into a **rentier state** under the Pahlavis because of the increasing amount of income coming in from oil. A rentier economy is heavily supported by state expenditure, while the state receives rent from other countries. Iran received an increasing amount of income by exporting its oil and leasing out oil fields to foreign countries. The income became so great by the 1970s that the government no longer had to rely on internal taxes for its support, but paid most of its expenses through oil income. In short, the government didn't need the people anymore. Iran was quickly transformed into a one-product economy, and was heavily dependent on oil to keep the government afloat. Even though the shah did adopt **import substitution industrialization** (p. 176) by encouraging domestic industries to provide products that the population needed, by 1979, oil and its associated industries made up a large percentage of Iran's GNP, and provided 97% of the country's foreign exchange.

THE WHITE REVOLUTION

During their rule, the two Pahlavi shahs built a highly centralized state, the first since the ancient days of the Persian Empire. The state controlled banks, the national radio-television network, and most importantly, the National Iranian Oil Company. The armed forces grew into the fifth largest army in the world by 1979, and came to include a large navy and air force as well. The central bureaucracy gained control of local governments, and the *Majles* became a rubber-stamp legislature that let the shah rule as he pleased. Whereas Iran remained a religious state, its courts became fully secularized, with a European-style judicial system and law codes in place. Most controversial of all was the shah's **White Revolution** (so named because it was meant to counter communist, or "red" influences) that focused on land reform, with the government buying land from large absentee owners and selling it to small farmers at affordable prices. The purpose was to encourage farmers to become modern entrepreneurs with irrigation canals, dams, and tractors. The White Revolution secularized Iran further by extending voting rights to women, restricting polygamy, and allowing women to work outside the home.

PATRONAGE AND THE RESURGENCE PARTY

Both Pahlavi shahs bolstered their own personal wealth first by seizing other people's property, and eventually through establishing the tax-exempt **Pahlavi Foundation**, a patronage system that controlled large companies that fed the pocketbooks of the shah and his supporters. In 1975 Muhammad Reza Shah announced the formation of the **Resurgence Party**, and declared Iran to be a one-party state with him as its head. He replaced the Islamic calendar with a new one, and claimed two new titles: "Guide to the New Great Civilization," and "Light of the Aryans." The shah also dared to create a Religious Corps, whose duty it was to teach Iranian peasants "true Islam."

THE ISLAMIC REVOLUTION AND THE REPUBLIC (1979-Present)

Great revolutions have shaken the world in many places since the late 18th century, and the causes and consequences of Iran's 1979 revolution are in some ways very similar to those in Russia, China, and Mexico in the 20th century. However, Iran's revolution is unique in that it was almost completely religious in nature. The dominant ideology was religion, whereas revolutions in Russia and China revolved around communism. Although the Catholic Church was very much involved in the revolutionary era (early 20th century) in Mexico, the Church did not direct the military, and PRI quickly sidelined the Church once the party gained control of the country. In Iran, the dominant ideology was Shiism, and the most important revolutionary leader was a cleric, who in turned ruled Iran for ten years following the revolution. Perhaps most significantly, Iran's revolution resulted in the establishment of a **theocracy**, while other revolutions generally were against religious control of the government.

COMPARATIVE RULING FAMILIES: IRAN

SAFAVIDS (1501-1722)	QAJARS (1794-1925)	PAHLAVIS (1925-1979)
Characteristics		
Converted Iranians to Shiism	Turkish invaders	Overthrew a representative
Tolerated "People of the Book"	Ruled from Tehran	government;
Ruled from Isfahan	Retained Shiism, but lost	Centralized power in shah
Relied on local rulers	hereditary claims to 12 Imams	Increasing oil income:
Rulers claimed to be	Dominated by other countries;	creation of the rentier state
descendants of the 12 Imams	Loved luxury; fell into debt	Contact with the West
		Secularization of Iran
		Corruption; shah's personal
		enrichment
Influences on modern political system		
Almost 90% of Iranians today	Loosened Shiite influence	Reinforced authoritarian
are Shiite	Tradition of trade/contact	rule; led to resistance to
Tradition of isolation	with others	totalitarianism
Authoritarianism, not	Authoritarianism, not	Modern corruption issues
totalitarianism	totalitarianism	in government, economy
Foundations for a theocracy	Foundations for secularism,	Increased secularization led
	separation between religious	to reestablishment of a
	and political leaders	theocracy
	Failures of regime led to	
	the creation of a representative	
	government	

The Creation of a Conflictual Political Culture. Between 1501 and 1979 Iran was ruled by three families that shaped the modern day clash between the conflicting political goals of authoritarianism, democracy, and theocracy.

The shah's behavior disturbed Iranians largely because from many people's points of view, he overstepped the bounds of the political culture in three ways:

- He was perceived as being totalitarian, not just authoritarian, as shahs before the Pahlavis had been. Not unlike Porfirio Diaz in Mexico, the shah set about to create a patrimonial state, with patron-clientelism in place, but without any real input from interest groups. As a result, true corporatism did not develop.

- He broke the balance between the secular and the religious state by secularizing Iran too much and too fast, certainly from the point of view of the clergy.

- His ties to the west (particularly the United States) offended Iranian nationalists as well as the clergy.

In many ways, the shah created a divide in the political culture, with one side supporting modernization in the sense of establishing closer ties to the West, and the other side staunchly defending traditional ways, in particular Shiism. An elite of clerics rose to oppose the shah, lead a revolution, and eventually take over the government.

One more ingredient for the success of the revolution was the charisma of its leader, the **Ayatollah Ruhollah Khomeini**. He not only defended Islamic **fundamentalism**, which emphasized literal interpretation of Islamic texts, social conservatism, and political traditionalism, but he also articulated resentments toward the elite and the United States. His depiction of the United States as the "Great Satan" puzzled Americans, but resonated with many frustrated people in Iran. The Ayatollah gave new meaning to an old Shia term *velayat-e-faqih* **(jurist's guardianship)**. The principle originally gave the senior clergy (including himself) broad authority over the unfortunate people (widows, orphans, mentally unstable) in the society, but Khomeini claimed that the true meaning of jurist's guardianship gives the clergy authority over the entire Shia community.

THE REVOLUTION BEGINS

Revolutions generally need a spark to begin the crisis. Although discontent had been building for a long time, two factors brought the situation to explode in revolution:

- Oil prices decreased by about 10% in the late 1970s at the same time that consumer prices increased about 20% in Iran. According to the theory of the **revolution of rising expectations,** revolutions are most likely to occur when people are doing better than they once were, but some type of setback happens. Iran fits this classic model in the early days of 1979.

- The United States put pressure on the shah to loosen his restraints on the opposition. President Jimmy Carter was a big promoter of human rights around the globe, and the shah's tight control on Iranian civil society was worrisome to his administration. However, in this situation, when the shah let his opponents speak, it encouraged others to voice their frustrations

Once the reins loosened, many groups supported the revolution – political parties, labor organizations, professional associations, bazaar (merchant) guilds, college students, and oil workers. In late 1978, hundreds of unarmed demonstrators were killed in a central square in Tehran, and oil workers went on strike, paralyzing the oil industry. Anti-regime rallies were attracting as many as 2 million protestors. It is important to note that the rallies were organized and led by the clerics, but were broadly supported by people from many sectors of society. Although Khomeini was in exile in Paris, audiotapes of his speeches were passed out freely at the rallies, where people called for the abolition of the monarchy. The shah fled the country at the beginning of February 1979, and his government officially ended on February 11 with the famous announcement from the national television-radio station quoted at the beginning of this chapter.

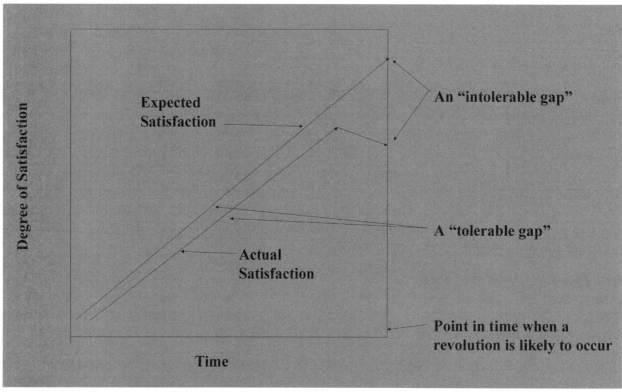

Revolution of Rising Expectations. In this chart the line that dips represents a a drop in a standard of living that had been going up for some time. However, expectations rise along with living standards, and when the drop occurs, people are more likely to support a revolution.

(Source: James Davies, "Toward a Theory of Revolution," *The American Sociological Review,* February 1962)

The Founding of the Islamic Republic

In late April 1979, a national referendum was held, and the Iranian people officially voted out the monarchy and established the Islamic Republic in its place. A constitution was drawn up late in the year by the **Assembly of Religious Experts**, a 73-man assembly of clerics elected directly by the people. The constitution gave broad authority to Khomeini and the clergy, although Prime Minister Mehdi Bazargan strongly objected. Bazargan advocated a presidential republic that would be based in Islam, but would be democratic in structure. However, Khomeini's constitution was presented to the people in the midst of the U.S. hostage crisis, a time of high hostility toward Americans. The result was not surprising: 99% of the electorate endorsed it, even though only 75% of the eligible voters actually voted.

Once the constitution was endorsed, the Shia leaders launched the **Cultural Revolution** with goals that were very similar to Mao Zedong's goals as he led China's Cultural Revolution in 1966. The Cultural Revolution in Iran aimed to purify the country from not only the shah's regime, but also from secular values and behaviors, particularly those with western origins. The universities were cleared of liberals and staffed with faculty who supported the new regime. The new government suppressed all opposition, including almost all groups from civil society, and many were executed in the name of "revolutionary justice."

Post-Khomeini – 1989-Present

Until the Ayatollah Khomeini's death in 1989, the clerics consolidated and built their power. Their success was cemented by several important factors that brought them popular support:

- World petroleum prices rebounded, so Iran's economy improved accordingly. The government was able to afford social programs for the people, such as modern improvements for housing and medical clinics.

- Iraq (under Saddam Hussein) invaded Iran in 1980, beginning a war between the two countries that continued throughout the decade. The people rallied around the government in response to this threat.

- Khomeini's **charismatic authority** (p. 14) remained strong, and the power of his presence inspired faith in the government.

Khomeini's death in 1989 marked the beginning of a new era for the Republic. His successor, **Ali Khamenei,** does not have the same magnetism of personality, nor does he have the academic credentials that Khomeini had, facts that have encouraged some scholars in Qom to question the legitimacy of the theocracy. The Iran-Iraq War ended in 1988, and world oil prices fell again during the 1990s. Most importantly, many in the population began to criticize the authoritarian rule of the clerics, and to advocate a more democratic government.

In many ways the conflict between theocratic and democratic values has played itself out during the presidencies of **Mohammad Khatami** (1997-2005) and **Mahmoud Ahmadinejad** (2005-Present). Although both are clerics, Khatami was a reformist who aimed to end the freeze in relations between Iran and the West, particularly the United States. Khatami believed in a "dialogue among civilizations" that fostered positive relationships with other countries, not just a cessation of hostilities. Although he never advocated changing theocratic political structures, reformers became a strong presence in both the *Majles* and the executive branch. In contrast, Ahmadinejad is a conservative who has antagonized western countries, although he has not isolated himself from them. He has asserted theocratic values, and has appealed to Iranian nationalism to solidify his **white** (bloodless) **coup** of the reformists.

CITIZENS, SOCIETY, AND THE STATE

Iranian citizens have had little direct experience with democracy, but they generally do understand the importance of civil society. Until the Pahlavi shahs of the 20th century, the authoritarian rulers had very little power to reach into citizens' everyday lives. Local officials were a presence, to be sure, and religious law, *sharia,* set strict rules for behavior. The democratic experiment after the Constitution of 1906 did create an elected legislature, the *Majles*, but the new government was so unable to solve the country's problems that chaos followed, inviting authoritarian rule to return with the Pahlavis.

CLEAVAGES

Major divisions in Iranian society are based on:

- **Religion** – Almost 90% of Iranians are Shia Muslims, but almost 10% are Sunni, and 1% are a combination of Jews, Christians, Zoroastrian, and Baha'i. Although the constitution recognizes religious minorities and guarantees their basic rights, many religious minorities have left the country since the founding of the Republic in 1979. The **Baha'i** faith, which many Shiites believe to be an unholy offshoot of Islam, has been a particular object of religious persecution. Their leaders have been executed, imprisoned, and tortured, their schools closed, and their community property taken by the state. Many Baha'i have immigrated to Canada, as have a large number of Jews and Armenian Christians. The constitution does not mention Sunnis, and so their rights are often unclear.

- **Ethnicity** – Ethnicity is closely tied to religion, but other cultural differences distinguish minorities in Iran. 51% may be considered Persian, speaking Persian (Farsi) as their first language; 24% are Azeri; 8% are Gilaki and Mazandarani; 7% are Kurds; 3% are Arabi; and the remaining percentages are a mixture of other groups. Many Azeris live in the northwest close to the former Soviet republic of Azerbaijan, creating a worry for the Iranian government that the Azeris will want to form a larger state by taking territory away from Iran. The Azeris do not speak Persian, but they are strongly Shiite, and the Supreme Leader that followed Khomeini in 1989 – Ali Khameini – is Azeri. Kurds and Arabs tend to be Sunni Muslim, so the religious cleavage is reinforced by ethnicity.

- **Social class** – The peasantry and lower middle class are sources of support for the regime, partly because they have benefited from the government's social programs that have provided them with electricity and paved roads. However, middle and upper-middle class people are largely secularized, and they tend to be highly critical of the clerics and their control of the society. Many middle class people have not fared well economically during the years since the Republic was founded. As a result, their cultural and political views of secularism are reinforced by their economic problems, creating discontent and opposition to the regime.

- **Reformers v. conservatives** – A fundamental cleavage in the political culture since the founding of the Republic has to do with a debate about the merits of a theocracy v. a democracy. The conservatives want to keep the regime as it is, under the control of clerics and *sharia* law, and the reformers would like to see more secularization and democracy. Most reformers do not want to do away with the basic principles of an Islamic state, but they display a wide array of opinions about how much and where secularization and democracy should be infused into the system.

CIVIL SOCIETY

A major source of unhappiness with the rule of the Pahlavi shahs was the government's incursion into private lives of citizens – the civil society. However, civil society has not been restored under the current regime, and this fact tends to create discontent, especially among middle class people. The Shia revolutionary elites launched a campaign that may be compared to Mao's Cultural Revolution in that they sought to enforce values of the Islamic state on the general population. University professors with reputations for western preferences were fired and replaced with people that clearly supported the regime. Other professionals quietly left the country to seek refuge in western nations. However, the desire to preserve civil society did not disappear – it was too large an influence on the political culture before the takeover by Reza Shah in the early 1920s.

Under the presidency of **Muhammad Khatami** (1997-2005), Iranians experienced the so-called **"Tehran spring"** – a period of cautious political liberalization, with a loosening of freedom of speech and press, a more open economy, and a friendlier stance towards the outside world. However, the Iranian president has only limited powers, and the reforms were limited by more conservative elements in the government. Since **Mahmoud Ahmadinejad** became president in 2005, the government has closed down newspapers, banned and censored books and websites, and no longer tolerates the peaceful demonstrations and protests of the Khatami era. Prominent scholars have been arrested, including Haleh Esfandiari, the director of the Woodrow Wilson Center in Washington, D.C. Dr. Esfandiari had dual citizenship (the U.S. and Iran), but was arrested in 2007 while visiting her mother in Tehran. She was imprisoned for more than three months before being released to return to the United States.

One indication that civil society is alive and well in Iran may be found among Iran's growing number of young people. Demographically, the young have grown in proportion to old at very dramatic rates, partly because of the Republic's encouragement of large families during the first years after it was founded. Many are the sons and daughters of disillusioned middle class professionals, and they appear to be very attracted to western popular culture – music, dress, cars, and computers. The regime under Khatami showed some signs of tolerating this behavior, but under Ahmadinejad there has been a crackdown against western dress, with arrests of women who show too much hair under their headscarves or wear makeup.

POLITICAL PARTICIPATION

 Despite the fact that guarantees for civil liberties and rights were written into the 1979 constitution, the Islamic Republic from the beginning closed down newspapers, labor unions, private organizations, and political parties. Due process principles were ignored as many were imprisoned without trials. Political reformers were executed, and others fled the country. The regime also banned demonstrations and public meetings.

PROTESTS AND DEMONSTRATIONS

The Republic's actions against public demonstrations did not curtail them, particularly on college campuses. In 1999, protests erupted in universities all across the country when the government shut down a reformist newspaper. In late 2002, similar demonstrations broke out among students when the courts ruled a death sentence for a reformist academic. In Iran in the summer of 2003, student demonstrations escalated into mass protests over the privatization of the university system. The protestors called for the overthrow and even death of Iran's religious and political leaders. Thousands were arrested over 4 days of protest in June. Because more than half of all Iranians alive today have been born since the Revolution of 1979, these youthful protesters may be a force for change in the future. Factory workers also tend to participate in rallies against the government. Their concerns are high unemployment rates, low wages, and unsatisfactory labor laws. Since Ahmadinejad became president in 2005, the government has renewed its crackdown on protests and demonstrations. For example, in January 2007 security forces attacked striking bus drivers in Tehran and arrested hundreds of them. Two months later police beat hundreds of men and women who had assembled to commemorate International Women's Day.

WOMEN AND THE POLITICAL SYSTEM

One of the most frequently heard criticisms of Iran by westerners is the regime's treatment of women. The veil has become a symbol of oppression, but probably more for westerners than for Iranian women themselves. The wearing of veils predates the birth of Islam as a religion in the 7th century, and women of many other religions in Southwest Asia have also worn veils. However, traditionally women in Islamic cultures have stayed home, with little education or opportunity to work outside the home. 20th century Iran is something of an exception because women have had better access to education. Educated women harbor particular resentments toward the regime. Their educations have led them to expect better job opportunities and more political rights than they have been granted. Judges usually interpret the *sharia* narrowly, so that women are often considered to be wards of their male relatives. However, today more than half of all college students are women, and they are also well represented as doctors and government employees.

The Islamic Republic calls its policy toward women "**equality-with-difference,**" meaning that divorce and custody laws now follow Islamic standards that favor males. Women must wear scarves and long coats in public, and they cannot leave the country without the consent of male relatives. Occasional stonings of women for adultery have also taken place, though the government recently issued a ban on them. However, women are allowed education and entrance to at least some occupations. Women now constitute about 33% of the total labor force.

WOMEN IN NATIONAL PARLIAMENTS

Country	Lower House % Women	Upper House % Women
China	20.3%	___*
Iran	4.1%	___*
Mexico	22.6%	17.2%
Nigeria	6.4%**	7.3%
Russia	9.8%	3.4%
United Kingdom	19.7%	18.9%

* No directly comparable upper house
**2003 figure; data from 2007 election not available

Source: *Women in National Parliaments*, www.ipu.org

Iranian women are not well represented in the *Majles*, as the chart above shows. Mexico's large representation is partly due to the recent parity laws that require political parties to run women candidates for office. Nigeria's low representation is probably reflective of traditional society there, although President Obasanjo made it a part of his reelection campaign in 2003 to include more women in his cabinet and top bureaucratic positions.

POLITICAL INSTITUTIONS

The political system of Iran is unlike any other in the world today in that it blends a theocracy with a democracy. The theocracy is represented in the national government by a position called the **Supreme Leader,** and governmental bodies called the **Guardian Council** and the **Expediency Council.** The president, The **Assembly of Religious Experts**, and the national assembly (the *Majles*) are democratically elected. Linkage institutions are in various stages of development, and tend to be fluid in nature.

LINKAGE INSTITUTIONS

The constitution guarantees citizens the right to organize and to express themselves, so some institutions that link people to the government have developed. Some organizations, such as interest groups and the press, had developed long before 1979 and continue till today. Others, like political parties, had to begin all over again.

POLITICAL PARTIES

The constitution provides for political parties, but the government did not allow them until Muhammad Khatami's election as president in 1997. Since then, multiple parties have formed, with most of them organized around personalities, not issues.

A number of new parties appeared for the *Majles* elections of 2004 and the presidential elections of 2005, and only a few carried over from previous elections, so current parties are highly unstable and very likely to change in the near future. However, some of the current parties are:

- **The Iranian Militant Clerics Society** is a left wing pro-reform party led by Muhammad Khatami, president of the Republic from 1997 to 2005. Several other prominent politicians belong to this party, including a former *Majles* speaker, and a vice-president. Their candidate for president in 2005, Mehdi Karroubi, came in third in the first round and so did not advance to the second round.

- **The Islamic Iran Participation Front** is a reformist party led by Muhammad Khatami's brother, Muhammad Reza Khatami. The party was founded in 1998 with the motto, "Iran for all Iranians." This party did well in the 2000 *Majles* election, but the Guardian Council barred many of its candidates from running in 2004, so their representation slipped considerably.

- **The Executives of Construction Party** was founded by several members of former President **Akbar Hashemi Rafsanjani**'s cabinet. The party is considered one of the most important supporters of Rafsanjani and his politics. Rajsanjani was a second round contender in the presidential election, and he currently heads the Expediency Council and the Assembly of Religious Experts.

- **The Islamic Society of Engineers** is a member of the conservative alliance, and its most famous member is the current president of the Republic, Mahmoud Ahmadinejad, who won the presidential election of June 2005. However, the society did not support him as their candidate; they supported Ali Larijani instead, who lost in the first round of the election.

A number of reformist parties – including the Iranian Militant Clerics Society, and the Islamic Iran Participation Front – formed an alliance called the **Khordad Front** in the presidential election of 2000, winning reelection for reformer Muhammad Khatami. The Second Khordad Front did not survive the Guardian Council's banning of many reformist candidates for the Majles election of 2004, when 70% of the seats went to conservative candidates. In 2005 the conservative presidential candidate Mahmoud Ahmadinejad won, with the reformers splitting their votes among several candidates.

Many political parties of former dissidents are now in exile but still active. The Liberation Movement, a moderate Islamic party, was established by Mehdi Bazargan (Khomeini's first prime minister) in 1961, but was banned in 2002 as a subversive organization. The National Front, headed by the shah's dissident Prime Minister Mossadeq in the 1950 was banned in the late 1980s. Other parties in exile are the **Mojahedin**, a guerilla organization that fought the shah's regime; the **Fedayin**, a Marxist guerilla group that modeled itself after Latin American hero Che Guevara; and **Tudeh**, a communist party.

The party system reflects **factionalism,** or the splintering of the political elites based not just on points of view, but also on personalities. Since parties are fluid and weak, they are not vehicles for discussing policymaking alternatives. Instead, factions tend to coalesce before elections and then break apart if their candidates are chosen. Defeated factions tend to stay together between elections in hopes of reversing their fortunes in the next election.

ELECTIONS

On the national level, citizens over the age of eighteen (minimum age changed in early 2007 from fifteen to eighteen) may vote for members of the Assembly of Religious Experts, representatives to the *Majles*, and the president of the Republic. The Republic is a highly centralized regime, although citizens may also vote for officials on the local level. Elections to the *Majles* and the presidency are conducted according to plurality, or winner-take-all, and no proportional representation is used. However, elections consist of two rounds, so that one of the two contenders left in the second round will get a majority of the votes.

The *Majles* Election of 2004

The first round elections to the *Majles* were held on February 20, 2004, but they took place after the Council of Guardians banned thousands of candidates from running, mainly from the reformist parties. Particularly hard hit was the Islamic Iran Participation Front. Out of a possible 285 seats (5 seats are reserved for religious minorities), reformist parties could only introduce 191 candidates. Some reformists refused to vote, and the official turnout was only about 51%. Not surprisingly, conservative candidates won about 70% of the seats.

The Presidential Election of 2005

The constitution provides that presidents may not run for more than two terms of office, so President Khatami had to step down in 2005. The Guardian Council disqualified about 1000 candidates, leaving only seven to run, some with the support of a party, and some not. The results of the first round were very close, with two candidates going on to the second round: **Akbar Hasemi Rafsanjani,** a former president known for his moderate and pragmatic views (21% of the vote); and **Mahmoud Ahmadinejad**, the conservative major of Tehran (19.5% of the vote). Ahmadinejad won in the second round with almost 62% of the vote, since Rafsanjani was not able to organize the reformist vote behind him. Ahmadinejad is known for his populist views, and he announced after his victory that he meant for prosperity to be shared among all classes, not just the elite.

INTEREST GROUPS

Since political parties are ill defined in Iran, it is often difficult to draw the line between parties and interest groups. A large number of groups have registered with the government, including an Islamic

Association of Women and a Green Coalition. The parties in exile, such as the National Front, the Liberation Movement, and the Mojahedin also have members still in Iran that work for their benefit.

An important interest group for factory workers is called **Workers' House**, that operates with the help of its affiliated newspaper, *Kar va Kargar* (*Work and Worker*). Their political party, Islamic Labor Party, backed Khatami in the 2000 election, but their coalition with other reform parties was broken up by the Guardian Council's banning of reformist candidates in 2004 (*Majles* election), and 2005 (presidential election). Workers' House holds a May Day rally most years, and in 1999 their rally turned into a protest when workers marched to parliament to denounce conservatives for watering down labor laws. When bus drivers joined the protest, most of central Tehran was shut down. A bus drivers' protest was shut down by the government also in 2007.

Few interest groups have formed for business because private businesses have been crowded out since the Revolution of 1979, when many were taken over by the government. Agriculture, internal trade and distribution are mostly in private hands, but the government controls between 65% and 80% of the economy.

MASS MEDIA

Over 20 newspapers were shut down shortly after the Revolution in 1979, and by 1981 an additional seven were closed. In 1981 the *Majles* passed a law making it a criminal offense to use "pen and speech" against the government. In more recent years, some of the restrictions have been lifted. The Rafsanjani government permitted some debate in the press on controversial issues during the 1990s, and the Khatami administration issued permits to dozens of new publications, apparently hoping to establish an independent press. However, freedom of the press is still a major issue between conservatives and reformists, and the large-scale student demonstrations in 1999 were sparked by newly imposed restrictions on the media. Shortly after the 2000 *Majles* elections, when many reformists were elected, the outgoing *Majles* approved a press control law, which the Council of Guardians ruled could not be overturned by the new legislature. Some 60 pro-reform newspapers were shut down by 2002.

Radio and television are government-run by the Islamic Republic of Iran Broadcasting (IRIB), but many newspapers and magazines are privately owned. Compared with other regimes in the region, the Iranian press has more freedom to criticize the government. Iran's elite is well educated, and many of these publications cater to their needs as professional journals, sports magazines, and publications for the fine arts, cinema, and health care. Most are nonpolitical, however. A semipublic institution whose directors are appointed by the Supreme Leader runs the country's two leading newspapers, *Ettela'at* and *Kayhan*.

GOVERNMENT INSTITUTIONS

Iran is a highly centralized state, but it is divided administratively into provinces, districts, subdistricts, and local areas. The Islamic constitution promises elected councils on each level of administration, and it also requires governors and other regional officials (who are all appointed) to consult local councils. No steps were taken to hold council elections until 1999 when President Khatami insisted on holding nationwide local elections. The election resulted in a landslide for reformists, presenting a challenge for the conservative clergy. Local elections in December 2006 supported candidates critical of Mahmoud Ahmadinejad, reflecting a weakness in the president's popularity.

The government structure of Iran is complex, but the most important thing to remember is that it is an attempt to blend theocratic ideals with democratic ones. Every structure has a purpose in terms of one or both of these principles.

JURIST'S GUARDIANSHIP

The Supreme Leader, the Guardian Council, the Assembly of Religious Experts, and the Expediency Council do not fit into a three-branch arrangement of government institutions. All three have broad executive, legislative, and judicial powers that allow them to supersede all other positions and bodies. They abide by the Ayatollah Khomeini's overarching principle of ***velayat-e-faqih* (jurist's guardianship)** in that they have all-encompassing authority over the whole community based on their ability to understand the *sharia* and their commitment to champion the rights of the people.

The Supreme Leader

This position at the top of Iran's government structure was clearly meant to be filled by the Ayatollah Ruhollah Khomeini, the leader of the 1979 Revolution. The Supreme Leader was seen as the imam of the whole community, and he represents the pinnacle of theocratic principles of the state. The constitution specifically put Khomeini in the position for life, and stated that after his death, his authority would pass to a leadership council of two or three senior clerics. This did not occur when Khomeini died in 1989 because his followers did not trust the clerics, so instead they selected as Supreme Leader **Ali Khamenei**, a cleric of the middle rank who had none of Khomeini's formal credentials. Khamenei also was appointed for life, and continues as Supreme Leader to the present.

The constitution gives the Supreme Leader many powers. First and foremost, he is the *faqih*, or the leading Islamic jurist to interpret the meaning of religious documents and *sharia,* Islamic law. He links the three branches of government together, may mediate among them, and is charged with "determining the interests of Islam." His many powers include:

- Elimination of presidential candidates
- Dismissal of the president
- Command of the armed forces
- Declaration of war and peace
- Appointment and removal of major administrators and judges
- Nomination of six members of the Guardian Council
- Appointment of many non-governmental directors, such as the national radio-television network and semi-public foundations

Although the dual executive positions of the Iranian government may be categorized as **head of state** (the Supreme Leader) and **head of government** (the president), the Supreme Leader holds ultimate power, and is far from a figurehead.

The Guardian Council

A body that also represents theocratic principles is the Guardian Council, which consists of twelve male clerics. Six are appointed by the Supreme Leader, and the other six are nominated by the chief judge and approved by the *Majles*. Bills passed by the *Majles* are reviewed by the Guardian Council to ensure that they conform to the *sharia*, and the council also has the power to decide who can compete in elections. In 2004 and 2005 they disqualified 1000s of candidates for both the *Majles* and the presidential elections.

Together the Supreme Leader and the Guardian Council exercise the principle of **jurist's guardianship**, making sure that the democratic bodies always adhere to Islamic beliefs and laws.

The Assembly of Religious Experts

In 1989 a smaller Assembly of Religious Experts was expanded to be a 86-man house directly elected by the people every four years. The Assembly is given the responsibility, along with the Supreme Leader and the Guardian Council, of broad constitutional interpretation. One of the new Assembly's first actions was to elect Ali Khamenei as Khomeini's replacement as Supreme Leader. The Assembly also reserved the right to dismiss him if he was unable to fill Khomeini's shoes. So far, that has not happened. The Assembly's members were required to have a seminary degree equivalent to a master's degree, but in 1998 revisions were made that allowed nonclerics to stand for the Assembly, but the candidates are still subject to approval by the Guardian Council.

In 2007 former President **Hashemi Rafsanjani** was picked as chairman of the Assembly, a move that could pose a challenge to Mahmoud Ahmadinejad, and possibly even Supreme Leader Khamenei. Rafsanjani, a moderate, was Ahmadinejad's main opponent in the presidential election of 2005, and he also tends to side with pro-democracy reformers who believe the government's authority is derived from popular elections.

The Expediency Council

Because the Guardian Council can overturn decisions and proposals for law made by the *Majles*, the two bodies often argued fiercely during the days of the early republic, so Khomeini created a body to referee their disputes. It began as a council with thirteen clerics, including the president, the chief judge, the speaker of the *Majles*, and six jurists from the Guardian Council. The Expediency Council eventually passed some compromise bills, and was institutionalized by the 1989 constitutional amendments. Today it consists of 32 members, and it has many more powers than it had originally. For example, it now may originate its own legislation. Not all of its members today are clerics, but they are still appointed by the Supreme Leader (Ali Khamenei). Collectively they are the most powerful men in Iran. Former President **Hashemi Rafsanjani** is currently head of the Expediency Council, a position he holds in addition to chairing the Assembly of Religious Experts.

THE EXECUTIVE

Iran does not have a presidential system, so the head of the executive branch does not have the same authority as presidents in countries that have a presidential system, such as the U.S., Mexico, and Nigeria. However, the president does represent the highest official representing democratic principles in Iran.

The President and the Cabinet

The president is the chief executive and the highest state official after the Supreme Leader. He is directly elected every four years by Iranian citizens, and he is limited to two consecutive terms in office. Although he is democratically elected, the constitution still requires him to be a pious Shiite that upholds Islamic principles.

Some of the president's powers include:

- Devising the budget
- Supervising economic matters
- Proposing legislation to the *Majles*
- Executing policies
- Signing of treaties, laws, and agreements
- Chairing the National Security Council
- Selecting vice presidents and cabinet ministers
- Appointing provincial governors, town mayors, and ambassadors

All of the six presidents of the Islamic Republic have been clerics, except for one: Abol-Hasan Bani-Sadr, who was ousted in 1981 for criticizing the regime as a dictatorship.

The cabinet conducts the real day-to-day work of governance. Practically all new laws and the budget are initiated and devised by cabinet members, and then submitted to the *Majles* for approval, modification, or rejection.

The Bureaucracy

The president heads a huge bureaucracy that has expanded over the years to provide jobs for college and high school graduates. It has doubled in numbers since 1979. Some of the newer ministries include: Culture and Islamic Guidance, that censures the media; Intelligence, that serves as the chief security organization; Heavy Industry, that manages nationalized factories; and Reconstruction, that expands social services and sees that Islam extends into the countryside. The clergy dominate the bureaucracy, just as the presidency. The most senior ministries – Intelligence, Interior, Justice, and Cultural and Islamic Guidance – are headed by clerics, and other posts are often given to their relatives.

Semipublic Institutions

These groups are theoretically autonomous, but they are directed by clerics appointed personally by the Supreme Leader. They are generally called "foundations," with such names as the "Foundation for the Oppressed," the "Martyrs Foundation," and the "Foundation for the Publication of Imam Khomeini's Works." They are tax exempt and are reputed to have a great deal of income. Most of the property they supervise was confiscated from the pre-1979 elite.

THE LEGISLATURE (The *Majles)*

For most of its recent history Iran has had a **unicameral legislature**, the *Majles,* although in some ways the Assembly of Religious Experts has functioned as an upper house since 1989, when its membership was expanded to 86 elected representatives. Both the *Majles* and the Assembly are directly elected by the people.

The *Majles* was first created by the Constitution of 1906, when it was part of Iran's early 20th century experiment with democracy. The *Majles* survived the turmoil of its early days as well as the dictatorship of the Pahlavi shahs, and was retained as the central legislative body by the Constitution of 1979. Although the 1989 constitutional amendments weakened the *Majles* in relationship to the presidency, it is still an important political institution with significant powers. Some of those powers are:

- Enacting or changing laws (with the approval of the Guardian Council)
- Interpreting legislation, as long as they do not contradict the judicial authorities
- Appointing six of the twelve members of the Guardian Council, chosen from a list drawn up by the chief judge
- Investigating the cabinet ministers and public complaints against the executive and judiciary
- Removing cabinet ministers, but not the president
- Approving the budget, cabinet appointments, treaties, and loans

The *Majles* has 290 seats, all directly elected through single member districts by citizens over the age of fifteen. The election of 2000 saw many reformists fill the seats through a coalition of reformist parties called the **Khordad Front**. They won 80 percent of the vote in a campaign that drew over 70 percent of the electorate. Many supporters of secular parties, all banned from the campaign, voted for the reformers, since they saw them as better alternatives to the religious conservatives. Before the 2004 elections, the Guardian Council banned many reformist candidates from entering the race, and the result was an overwhelming victory for the conservatives. Significantly, control of the *Majles* flip-flopped dramatically from the hands of the reformers to the religious conservatives.

THE JUDICIARY

Two very important things to remember about Iran's judiciary are: 1) Two distinct types of law govern: *sharia* and *qanun*; and 2) the principle of jurist's guardianship means that the Supreme Leader, the Guardian Council, and the Assembly of Religious Experts have the final say regarding interpretation of law.

Two types of law are:

- *Sharia*, or Islamic law, was built up over several centuries after the death of the religion's founder, Muhammad, in the 7th century. *Sharia* is considered to be the foundation of all Islamic civilization, so its authority goes far beyond Iran's borders. It has incorporated the ideas of many legal scholars, and captures what many Muslims believe to be the essence of Muhammad himself. Overall, *sharia* is meant to embody a vision of a community in which all Muslims are brothers and sisters and subscribe to the same moral values. The very foundations of Iran's political system rest in the belief that *sharia* supersedes all other types of law, and its interpretation is the most important of all responsibilities for political and religious leaders. The principle of jurist's guardianship reflects reverence for *sharia*, and much of the legitimacy of the Supreme Leader is based in his ultimate authority as the interpreter of this sacred law.

- *qanun* - Unlike *sharia*, *qanun* has no sacred basis, but instead is a body of statutes made by legislative bodies. In Iran, *qanun* are passed by the *Majles*, and they have no sacred meaning. *Sharia*, then, is divine law derived from God, and *qanun* is law made by the people's elected representatives. Of course, *qanun* must in no way contradict *sharia*, so it becomes the responsibility of the *Majles* to pass responsible *qanun*, but an important job for the Guardian Council (and ultimately the Supreme Leader) is to review the work of the legislature and to apply the interpretation of *sharia* to all laws passed.

In a very different way than we have seen it applied in other countries, judicial review does exist in Iran. However, ultimate legal authority does not rest in the constitution, but in *sharia* law itself. Because *sha-*

ria is so complex, its interpretation is not an easy task, and it has been applied in many different ways. In Iran, the Ayatollah Khomeini's importance in shaping the political system is that his interpretation of *sharia* came to be the standard that influenced all leaders that followed him - Supreme Leader Khamenei, the six presidents, and all other high officials. In other words, a core principle of the present-day regime is to accommodate Islam to a constitutional framework, as provided by the Constitution of 1979.

The Islamic Republic Islamized the judiciary code by interpreting *sharia* very strictly. They passed the Retribution Law, which permitted families to demand "blood money" (compensation to the victim's family from those responsible for someone's death), and mandated the death penalty for a whole range of activities, including adultery, homosexuality, drug dealing, and alcoholism. The law also set up unequal legal treatment of men and women, and Muslim and non-Muslim. The government also banned interest rates on loans, condemning them as "usury," which implies that people in need of loans are taken advantage of by the lenders.

THEOCRATIC AND DEMOCRATIC ELEMENTS IN IRAN'S GOVERNMENT STRUCTURE

Structure/Position	Theocratic Characteristics	Democratic Characteristics
Supreme Leader	Jurist guardianship; ultimate interpreter of sharia; appointed for life	
Guardian Council	Jurist guardianship; interpreter of shari'a; six members selected by the Supreme Leader	Six members selected by the *Majles,* which is popularly elected; indirect democratic tie
Assembly of Religious Experts	Jurist guardianship; interpreter of *sharia*	Directly elected by the people
Expediency Council	Appointed by the Supreme Leader; most members are clerics	Not all members are clerics
Majles	Responsibility to uphold *sharia*	Directly elected by the people; pass *qanun* (statutes)
Judiciary	Courts held to *sharia* law; subject to the judicial judgments of the Supreme Leader, Guardian Council	Court structure similar to those in democracies; "modern" penalties, such as fines and imprisonment

Although Khomeini argued that the spirit of *sharia* calls for local judges to pronounce final decisions, the regime did realize that a centralized judicial system was needed to tend to matters of justice in an orderly fashion. The regime retained the court structure from the shah's government, keeping the appeals system, the hierarchy of state courts, and the central government's right to appoint and dismiss judges. Furthermore, the interpretation of the *sharia* has broadened gradually, so that the harsh corporal punishments outlined in the Retribution Law are rarely carried out today. Modern methods of punishment are much more common than harsh public retributions, so that most law breakers are fined or imprisoned rather than flogged in the town square.

THE MILITARY

Immediately after the 1979 Revolution the Ayatollah Khomeini established the **Revolutionary Guard,** an elite military force whose commanders are appointed by the Supreme Leader. The shah had built up the regular army, navy, and air forces, and so the Revolutionary Guard was created as a parallel force with its own budgets, weapons, and uniforms, to safeguard the Republic from any subterfuge within the military. The Supreme Leader is the commander in chief, and also appoints the chiefs of staff and the top commanders of the regular military. According to the Constitution, the regular army defends the borders, while the Revolutionary Guard protects the republic. Both regular armed forces and the Revolutionary Guard were greatly taxed during the war with Iraq that finally ended in 1988.

Iran currently has about 540,000 active troops, making it the eighth largest military in the world. Much about the military is kept secret but its advanced abilities and technologies have been shown through the building of long-range missiles. The Revolutionary Guard remains an important political force, with its own ministry, army, navy, and air-force units, and appears to have a great deal of say in Iran's nuclear program. The Guard is becoming increasingly independent, and takes an active role in policymaking. A large number of former Guards sit in the *Majles*, and men with close links to the Guard control principal media outlets, such as the state broadcaster and the powerful Ministry for Islamic Guidance and Culture. In 2004 the Guard showed its strength by deciding on its own authority to close down the airport in Tehran, on the grounds that a national security threat was present. The Guard's engineering arm, known as Ghorb, has been granted big state projects, such as a new section of the Tehran metro.

PUBLIC POLICY

The policymaking process in Iran is highly complex because laws can originate in many places (not just the legislature), and can also be blocked by other state institutions. Also, policies are subject to change depending on factional control.

POLICYMAKING FACTIONS

The leaders of the Revolution of 1979 and their supporters agreed on one thing: they wanted the shah to abdicate. Most people also wanted the Ayatollah Khomeini to lead the country after the shah left. After that, the disagreements began and continue until this day. Two types of factions are:

- **Conservative vs. reformist** – By and large, these factions are created by the often contradictory influences of theocracy and democracy. **Conservatives** uphold the principles of the regime as set up in 1979, with its basis in strict *sharia* law with a minimum of modern modifications. They are wary of influence from western countries and warn that modernization may threaten the tenets of Shiism that provide the moral basis for society, politics, and the economy. They support the right and responsibility of clerics to run the political system, and they believe that political and religious decisions should be one and the same. **Reformists**, on the other hand, believe that the political system needs significant reform, although they disagree on exactly what the reforms should be. They are less wary of western influence, and tend to advocate some degree of international involvement with countries of the west. Most reformers support Shiism and believe it to be an important basis of Iranian society, but they often support the idea that political leaders do not necessarily have to be clerics.

- **Statists vs. free-marketers** – This rift cuts across conservatives and reformers, and has taken different meanings over the years. Basically, though, the **statists** believe that the government should take an active role in controlling the economy – redistributing land and wealth, eliminating unemployment, financing social welfare programs, and placing price ceilings on consumer goods. We have seen this point of view at work in Mexico under Lazaro Cardenas during the 1930s, and in Russia and China under communism. Statists are not necessarily communists (and few in Iran are), but the same philosophy directed the economy of the Soviet Union with its Five-Year Plans, and continues to direct China's "socialist market economy." On the other hand, the **free-marketers** want to remove price controls, lower business taxes, encourage private enterprise, and balance the budget. In many ways they believe in the same market principles that guide the United States, but they envision it working within the context of the theocratic/democratic state.

These factional disputes have often brought about gridlock and instability, such as the flip-flop that occurred in the *Majles* between the election of 2000 and 2004 from reformist to conservative control. The disputes among the factions have led many of Iran's best and brightest to leave the country, and have deprived the reformists in particular of some potentially good leadership. Factions have also led to confusion on the international scene as well. For example, after the September 11, 2001 attacks in the United States, President Khatami almost immediately extended his condolences to the American people. However, Supreme Leader Ali Khamenei forbid any public debate about improving relations with the United States, and also implied that Americans had brought the situation on themselves.

THE IMPORTANCE OF QOM

The legitimacy of the modern Iranian theocracy has its roots in Qom, a desert city about 60 miles south of Tehran. It was from Qom that Ayatollah Khomeini began to denounce the shah, and it was there that he set up his government after returning from exile in France. It is a city of seminaries, and the scholars that inhabit them help to define the very foundation of Iranian society. Ironically, despite the fact that Khomeini's doctrine of *velayat-e-faqih* was devised in Qom, many scholars there are not entirely comfortable with the theocratic state. Their debate frames the factionalism of Iranian politics.

From some perspectives, the only rightful union of religion and politics will occur when the Twelfth Imam (see p. 216) returns from hiding. Until then, these scholars say, men of religion should be careful not to get involved in politics, and no one has special authority to guide society during this period called "occultation" between the disappearance and the return of the twelfth imam. Therefore, *velayat-e-faqih* is invalid, because it endows the Supreme Leader – and other government structures – with divine authority. President Khatami's reform movement drew heavily on the views of clerics that see politics as an experimental, man-made activity that Islam should respect. Of course, other religious scholars – the conservatives - agree with the doctrine of *velayat-e-faqih* and the divine authority that it implies, and their points of view are very influential in the reversal of the Khatami reforms under President Ahmadinejad.

ECONOMIC ISSUES

The factional disagreements within the political elite are apparent in Iran's struggles with economic policymaking. On the international scene in 2002, a bill was drafted in the *Majles* that would have permitted foreigners to own as much as 100 percent (up from 48%) of any firm in the country. Not surprisingly, the bill came from the reformists. Predictably, the bill was not approved by the Guardian Council, a reflection of the tug of war between reformists and conservatives. Domestically, most Iranian leaders want improved standards of living for the people, but conservatives are cautious about the influence of secular prosperity on devout Shiism.

Oil has created a vertical divide in the society, particularly among the elites. On one side are elites with close ties to the oil state. On the other side is the traditional sector of the clergy. It was this divide that was clearly evident during the Revolution of 1979, and despite the fact that the clerics won, the secularists have not gone away. Almost no one denies the benefits that oil has brought to Iran. Money from the rentier state that grew under Muhammad Reza Shah helped to build the economic infrastructure and fuel the growth of a middle class. By the 1970s Iran was clearly an industrializing country with increasing prosperity, and its economy was integrated into the world economy.

The Ayatollah Khomeini famously stated that **"economics is for donkeys,"** disdaining the importance of economics for policymakers and affirming the superiority of religious, rather than secular leaders. Even conservatives today don't deny the importance of economic policy decisions, but the factions don't agree on whether or not secularists should be allowed to make policy. The main economic problem plaguing the Islamic Republic has been the instability in the price of oil. The country suffered greatly when oil prices plunged in the early 1980s, rebounded somewhat, and then dropped again in the 1990s. Prices stayed relatively low until the end of the century. Since then, oil prices have rebounded, and the Iranian economy has benefited.

The management of the economy has been criticized, especially under President Ahmadinejad. He was elected based on his promises to provide government subsidies for consumers, and government expenditures on subsidies increased to about 25% of Iran's GDP in 2005-2006. The programs include food, housing, and bank credit, and perhaps most controversially, gasoline. Gasoline costs about $.11 a liter, a price so low that domestic refiners refuse to raise production to meet demand, so Iran has to import about 40% of its oil. This situation encourages oil smuggling to neighboring countries, and corruption among the quasi-state companies that deal in oil products.

FOREIGN AFFAIRS

Iran's international profile has been raised considerably by President Mahmoud Ahmadinejad, whose statements and actions have been quite controversial. He became the most polarizing head of government in the Muslim world when he declared the Holocaust a "myth," and argued that Israel should be "wiped away." Since then he has threatened to retaliate against American interests "in every part of the world" if the U.S. were to attack Iran. His 2006 letter to George W. Bush inviting him to a televised discussion about their differences was openly published in newspapers, and although Bush declined,

Ahmadinejad received a great deal of international publicity for his gesture. He holds regular press conferences with western journalists, and he travels widely. Yet the stance that he generally takes is to defend Iran against the rest of the world, particularly the west, reinforcing the historical perception of Iran as an isolated country.

The attitudes toward supranational organizations such as the United Nations, the World Bank, and the World Trade Organization are mixed. Iran's application to join the WTO in 1996 failed in part because of the difficulties in making foreign investments within the country's borders. Their application also failed because the United States opposed it, so these hostilities between the two countries have reverberated into many areas of international economic policy. Iran's most important international membership is probably in OPEC (Organization for Petroleum Exporting Countries) that controls the price of oil exported from its member states.

NUCLEAR ENERGY

> "States like these [Iran, Iraq, and North Korea], and their terrorist allies, constitute an axis of evil, arming to threaten the peace of the world. By seeking weapons of mass destruction, these regimes pose a grave and growing danger. They could provide these arms to terrorists, giving them the means to match their hatred. They could attack our allies or attempt to blackmail the United States."

> U.S. President George W. Bush
> State of the Union Address
> January 29, 2002

President Bush's "**axis of evil**" statement quoted above created a stir of controversy regarding Iran's international relations with western countries. Iran's nuclear program goes back many decades, but this program has been under serious scrutiny by western nations since the attacks on the United States on September 11, 2001. Iran has maintained that the purpose of its nuclear program was for the generation of power, not for use as weapons. However, in August 2002, a leading critic of the regime revealed two secret nuclear sites, a uranium enrichment facility in Natanz and a heavy water facility in Arak. Late in 2003, the U.S. insisted that Iran be "held accountable" for allegedly seeking to build nuclear arms in violation of international treaties, including the Nuclear Non-Proliferation Treaty that Iran had signed. Then in November 2004, Iran's chief nuclear negotiator announced that Iran had temporarily suspended the uranium enrichment program after pressure from the European Union. This dispute boiled over in August 2005, when the International Atomic Energy Agency announced that Iran had broken seals on one of its nuclear sites – seals that had been placed there by the United Nations in 2004. In 2006 Britain, France, and Germany offered Iran trade, civil-nuclear assistance, and a promise of talks with America if it stopped enriching the uranium that could produce the fuel for a bomb. When Iran refused, diplomacy led in December 2006 to the imposition of formal economic sanctions by the United Nations' Security Council.

Iran's complex political culture and internal factional debates make it very difficult to predict its future. Oil continues to fill the government's coffers with income, but the economy's dependence on one product is worrisome to economists and politicians alike. Iran's unique political system is a bold experiment, and tests the question as to whether or not it is possible for a theocracy to be democratic. A major theme in government and politics that Iran's case raises is the relationship between religion and politics. Is a democracy possible without separating the two into different spheres? Does the state benefit from being based in religious principles that are meant to guide human life in general? On the other hand, does religion increase tensions in the relationship between citizens and state so that the government loses its objectivity and essential fairness to its citizens? For these reasons and more, the evolution of Iran's political system is interesting to watch and vital to understand.

IMPORTANT TERMS AND CONCEPTS

Ahmadinejad, Mahmoud
Assembly of Religious Experts
"axis of evil"
Baha'i
Constitution of 1979
constitutional revolution of 1905-09
Cultural Revolution
"economics is for donkeys"
equality-with-difference
The Executives of Construction Party
faqih
fundamentalism
Guardian Council
head of state, head of government
Hidden Imam
imams
import substitution industrialization
Iranian Militant Clerics Society
The Islamic Iran Participation Front
The Islamic Society of Engineers
Ismail
jurist's guardianship (*velayat-e-faqih*)
Khamenei, Al
Khatami, Muhammad
Khomeini, Ayatollah Ruhollah
Khordad Front
Majles
Majles Election of 2004
Mosaddeq, Muhammad
Muhammad Reza Shah
National Front
qanun
Qajar Empire
Qom
Pahlavi Foundation
the Pahlavis
People of the Book

Persian Empire
presidential election of 2005
Rafsanjani, Akbar Hasemi
reformers v. conservatives
rentier state
Resurgence Party
Revolution of 1979
revolution of rising expectations
Revolutionary Guards
Reza Shah
Safavid Empire
secularization
sharia
Shiism
statists v. free-marketers
Sunni Muslims
Supreme Leader
"Tehran spring"
theocracy
Tudeh Party
white coup
White Revolution
Workers' House
Zoroastrianism

MULTIPLE-CHOICE QUESTIONS
IRAN

1. Iran's ancient traditions rooted in the Achemenian Empire include all of the following concepts of sovereignty EXCEPT:

   a) union of religious and political power
   b) king's power supported by the military
   c) centralization of political power
   d) rule by religious clerics
   e) authoritarian rule

2. In recent years a crisis in political legitimacy in Iran has occurred between two conflicting ideas – sovereignty of the people and

   a) sovereignty of the monarch
   b) divinely inspired clerical rule
   c) outside interference by other countries
   d) charismatic authority of the president
   e) the power of judicial review

3. Which of the following characteristics have shaped the political cultures of Russia, China, Mexico, and Iran?

   a) authoritarianism
   b) Shiism
   c) union of political and religious authority
   d) escape from European colonization
   e) little arable land

4. Which of the following countries did NOT have a major internal revolution in the 20th century?

   a) Great Britain
   b) Russia
   c) China
   d) Mexico
   e) Iran

5. Iran traces its identity with Shiism to the

   a) Achemenian Empire
   b) Safavids
   c) Qajars
   d) Pahlavis
   e) Revolution of 1979

(Questions 6 and 7 are based on the following table):

WOMEN IN NATIONAL PARLIAMENTS

Country	Lower House % Women	Upper House % Women
China	20.3%	___*
Iran	4.1%	___*
Mexico	22.6%	17.2%
Nigeria	6.4%**	7.3%
Russia	9.8%	3.4%
United Kingdom	19.7%	18.9%

* No directly comparable upper house
**2003 figure; data from 2007 election not available

6. According to the table, which of the following is the BEST description of women's participation in the Iranian legislature?

   a) Women are well represented.
   b) Women are represented more fairly than they are in Mexico and Nigeria.
   c) Women are seriously under-represented.
   d) Women are represented more fairly than they are in Russia and China.
   e) Women are represented equally well in Iran and Great Britain.

7. In which of the following areas of life are women in Iran BEST represented?

   a) property ownership
   b) political representation
   c) religious leadership
   d) employment
   e) university enrollment

8. The first written constitution for Iran came about as a direct result of the

   a) conquest of the Safavids
   b) Revolution of 1905-1909
   c) rise of the Pahlavis
   d) Revolution of 1979
   e) death of the Ayatollah Khomeini

9. The government position/organization that has had the power to veto laws passed by the *Majles* since 1906 is the

   a) Supreme Leader
   b) Guardian Council
   c) Assembly of Religious Experts
   d) Expediency Council
   e) President

10. During which era did Iran become a rentier state?

   a) rule of the Safavids
   b) rule of the Qajars
   c) the time immediately following the Revolution of 1905-1909
   d) rule of the Pahlavis
   e) rule of Ayatollah Ruhalla Khomeini

11. The Revolution of 1979 was different from 20th century revolutions in Russia and China because it resulted in a(n)

   a) religious state
   b) dictatorship
   c) one party state
   d) ideological government
   e) failed state

12. The Islamic fundamentalism that the Ayatollah Khomeini that was basic to the 1979 revolution was characterized by all of the following EXCEPT:

   a) resentments toward the United States
   b) literal interpretation of Islamic texts
   c) liberalism
   d) political traditionalism
   e) resentments toward the Iranian elite

13. Iran's Constitution of 1979 differed from the Constitution of 1909 because it (the Constitution of 1979) put more emphasis on

   a) divinely inspired clerical rule
   b) democratic electoral processes
   c) the legislative processes
   d) the rule of law
   e) civil rights and liberties

14. Which of the following Iranian political leaders has been MOST associated with liberal reforms?

   a) Mahmoud Ahmadinejad
   b) Ali Khamenei
   c) Muhammad Khatami
   d) Ruhollah Khomeini
   e) Asbar Hasemi Rafsanjani

15. Which of the following is a mismatch between country and ethnic minority group?

   a) Iran/Azeri
   b) Russia/Chechen
   c) China/Han
   d) Mexico/Amerindian
   e) Britain/Pakistani

16. Which of the following is an accurate description of the change in civil society between Khatami's presidency (1997-2005) and Ahmadinejad's presidency (2005-present)?

   a) Civil society has been maintained at a high level.
   b) Civil society has been restored to its pre-1997 high levels.
   c) Civil society has expanded for men, but not for women.
   d) Civil society has expanded for older people, but not for younger people.
   e) Civil society has been more restricted under Ahmadinejad than under Khatami.

17. The theocracy is most directly represented in the national government by the Supreme Leader, the Expediency Council, and the

   a) president
   b) Majles
   c) Assembly of Religious Experts
   d) cabinet
   e) Guardian Council

18. The political party system in Iran is characterized by

   a) a strong party in power
   b) two large parties
   c) one party
   d) factional splits
   e) numerous stable parties

19. Which of the following countries include proportional representation in their electoral systems?

I. Britain
II. Russia
III. Mexico
IV. Iran

a) I and II only
b) II and III only
c) II, III, and IV only
d) III and IV only
e) I, II, III, and IV

20. Which of the following countries have federalist political systems?

I. Britain
II. Russia
III. Mexico
IV. Iran

a) I and II only
b) II and III only
c) II, III, and IV only
d) III and IV only
e) I, II, III, and IV

21. Which of the following has the power to remove the Supreme Leader from office?

a) Guardian Council
b) Expediency Council
c) Assembly of Religious Experts
d) Majles
e) the president

22. Which of the following countries has a president?

I. Britain
II. Russia
III. China
IV. Mexico
V. Iran

a) I, II, and IV only
b) II, IV, and V only
c) II, III and V only
d) II, III, IV and V only
e) I, II, III, IV, and V

23. Foundation for the Oppressed, Martyrs Foundation, and the Foundation for the Publication of Imam Khomeini's Works are all examples of

    a) departments in the bureaucracy
    b) private interest groups
    c) controversial organizations not endorsed by the government
    d) groups supervised by the *Majles*
    e) semipublic institutions

24. Which of the following is LEAST likely to be a cleric?

    a) the Supreme Leader
    b) the president
    c) a member of the Guardian Council
    d) a member of the Expediency Council
    e) a member of the *Majles*

25. The body of statutes with no sacred basis in the Iranian system is called

    a) *sharia*
    b) *faqih*
    c) *velayat-e-faqih*
    d) Baha'i
    e) *qanun*

26. In Iran ultimate legal authority rests in

    a) *sharia* law
    b) *qanun*
    c) the Constitution of 1979
    d) the Supreme Court
    e) the *Majles*

27. In which of the following countries does the military currently take an active role in policy-making?

    I.   Russia
    II. China
    III. Mexico
    IV. Iran

    a) I and III only
    b) I and IV only
    c) II and III only
    d) II and IV only
    e) II, III, and IV only

28. The belief that the government should take an active role in controlling the economy is called

    a) capitalism
    b) statism
    c) liberalism
    d) conservatism
    e) fundamentalism

29. Political discussions that occur in Qom take place mainly among

    a) religious scholars
    b) government officials
    c) international business leaders
    d) revolutionary Guards
    e) justices and judges

30. The Ayatollah Khomeini's attitude toward economic policy can best be described as

    a) liberal
    b) laissez faire
    c) disdainful
    d) erratic
    e) controlling

FREE-RESPONSE QUESTION - IRAN

The political cultures of the Russian Federation and Iran may both be described as conflictual.

(a) Describe one basic conflict at work within the Russian political culture.

(b) Explain one political consequence of the conflict you identified in (a) for the modern Russian political system.

(c) Describe one basic conflict at work within the Iranian political culture.

(d) Explain one political consequence of the conflict you identified in (c) for the modern Iranian political system.

GOVERNMENT AND POLITICS IN NIGERIA

As Nigeria goes, so goes the rest of sub-Saharan Africa."

a common saying

The quote above reflects both the importance of Nigerian political and economic issues as well as the vulnerability of its political system. With its history of tradition-based kingdoms, colonialism, military dictatorships, and disappointing steps toward democracy, Nigeria faces daunting problems, and it is anyone's guess as to what the future holds. Its importance lies partly in the fact that it is Africa's most populous state, with about 140 million citizens, making it one of the largest countries in the world. Nigeria, like many of its neighbors, is a study in contrasts. Its political traditions include strong democracy movements, coupled with a susceptibility to totalitarian military rule. It has vast resources, including one of the largest oil deposits in the world, but 60 percent of its people live in poverty, with a PPP per capita of about $1500 a year. Nigeria is also a microcosm of worldwide religious tensions, with its population split almost evenly between Islam and Christianity. Yet this division masks an even greater challenge to the nation state: the lack of a coherent national identity that binds together the many ethnicities encompassed within its borders. Most recently, the government's legitimacy was rocked to its core by the flagrantly fraudulent national elections of 2007, which observers declared to be even more flawed than previous elections.

Is it possible for Nigeria to somehow reconcile its tradition-based and colonial past with the present needs of a modern nation? Will Nigeria's fledgling democracy survive? Will its leaders successfully harness the political muscle of the military and learn to better manage the country's resources? Finally, is it possible for the country to stay together, even though its people identify more with their individual ethnic groups than with their nation of Nigeria? An examination of these questions, with answers that are far from certain, will help us to understand the dynamics of all these issues not only in Nigeria, but in lands far beyond.

SOVEREIGNTY, AUTHORITY, AND POWER

Citizens of all countries have differing opinions about how political power should be distributed and how the government should be structured. However, in Nigeria the differences run far deeper than in most other countries. Even though it has been an independent nation since 1960, neither its leaders nor its citizens agree on the basics of who should rule and how. This dilemma is known as the **"national question"** of how the country should be governed, or even if Nigeria should remain as one nation. The issue is magnified by regional disagreements and hostilities and by the tendency to solve problems by military force and authoritarian leaders, not by mutual agreements.

CONSTITUTIONALISM

Nigeria's first constitution was written in 1914, but since then, eight more constitutions have been written, with the last one introduced in 1999 and heavily amended since. Nigerian constitutions represent attempts to establish a basic blueprint for the operation of the government, but none have lasted for any length of time. As a result, **constitutionalism,** or the acceptance of a constitution as a guiding set of principles, has eluded Nigeria. Military and civilian leaders alike have felt free to disobey and suspend constitutional principles, or to toss out older constitutions for those more to their liking. Without constitutionalism, the "national question" has been much harder to answer.

LEGITIMACY

The fact that Nigeria is a relatively young country, gaining its independence in 1960, means that establishing the government's legitimacy is a challenging priority. The "national question" is at the heart of the country's legitimacy problems. Nigeria has strong impulses toward **fragmentation**, or the tendency to fall apart along ethnic, regional, and religious lines. Its history is full of examples of ethnic and religious conflicts, economic exploitation by the elite, and use of military force. Ironically, the military is one of the few truly national organizations in Nigeria, so despite the problems that it has posed for democracy, it is also a source of stability in an unstable country. That stability lends legitimacy to the military's right to rule, and explains why, despite the fact that the last two presidents of Nigeria have been civilians, one (**Olusegun Obasanjo**) was formerly a military general. Most major candidates for the presidency in recent years have also been drawn from the military, although President **Umaru Yar'Adua**, elected in 2007, has a non-military background.

The legitimacy of the Nigerian government is currently at very low ebb, with many citizens having little or no trust in their leaders' abilities to run an efficient or trustworthy state. Part of the problem lies in the different political impulses originating in contradictory influences from Nigeria's past. As a British colony, Nigerians learned to rely on the western traditions of **rule of law**, in which even those that govern are expected to obey and support laws. On the other hand, almost since independence was granted in 1960, Nigerian leaders have used military might to enforce their tentative, personalized authority. These military strong men generally adhered to no discernible rule of law. The corruption associated with **General Ibrahim Babangida**, who ruled from 1985 to 1993, and **General Sani Abacha** (1993-1998) alienated citizens even further. Many people questioned why they should pay taxes when their hard-earned money went straight to the generals' bank accounts. This corruption has tainted civilian rule as well, so that most Nigerians are very skeptical about their government. Yet democratic movements have continued throughout the years, so there is a certain hope beneath the cynicism on the surface.

A generation ago novelist Chinua Achebe wrote, "The trouble with Nigeria is simply and squarely a failure of leadership," a statement that strikes at the heart of the country's legitimacy crisis. The deeply flawed election of 2007 reinforced Achebe's statement, as it became apparent that the state and national leaders were selected amidst widespread vote rigging, intimidation, fraud, and violence. The international criticisms of the election, as well as the frustration and skepticism of the Nigerian people, are a strong challenge to the legitimacy of the new president, Umaru Yar'Adua.

POLITICAL TRADITIONS

Nigerian political traditions run deep and long. Kingdoms appeared as early as 800 C.E., and historical influences may be divided into three eras:

THE PRECOLONIAL ERA (800-1860)

Centralized states developed early in the geographic area that is now Nigeria, especially in the northern savanna lands. Transportation and communication were easier than in the southern forested area, and the north also needed government to coordinate its need for irrigation of crops. Influences from this era include:

- **Trade connections** – The Niger River and access to the ocean allowed contact and trade with other civilizations. Also, trade connections were established across the Sahara Desert to North Africa.

- **Early influence of Islam** – Trade with the north put the early Hausa and other groups in contact with Arabic education and Islam, which gradually replaced traditional customs and religions, especially among the elite. Islamic principles, including the rule of religious law (*sharia*), governed politics, emphasizing authority and policymaking by the elite. All citizens, especially women, were seen as subordinate to the leaders' governance.

- **Kinship-based politics** – Especially among the southern people, such as the Tiv, political organization did not go far beyond the village level. Villages were often composed of extended families, and their leaders conducted business through kinship ties. This political organization contrasts greatly with the tendency toward larger states in the north.

- **Complex political identities** – Unfortunately for those trying to understand Nigeria's political traditions, the contrast between centralized state and local governance is far from clear-cut. Even in the south, some centralized kingdoms merged (such as **Oyo** and **Ife**), and many small trading-states emerged in the north.

- **Democratic impulses** – One reason why the people of Nigeria today still value democracy despite their recent experiences is that the tradition goes back a long way. Among the **Yoruba** and **Igbo** especially, the principle of accountability was well accepted during the pre-colonial period. Rulers were expected to seek advice and to govern in the interest of the people. If they did not, they were often removed from their positions. Leaders were also seen as representatives of the people, and they were responsible for the good of the community, not just their own welfare.

THE COLONIAL ERA (1860-1960)

Colonialism came much later to Africa than to many other parts of the world, but its impact was no less important. In contrast to Mexico that gained independence in 1821, Nigeria only broke with its colonial past in 1960. As a result, Nigeria has had much less time to develop a national identity and political stability. Ironically, even though they brought the rule of law with them, the British also planted influences that worked against the democratic patterns set in place in Nigeria during the pre-colonial period.

- **Authoritarian rule** – The British ruled indirectly by leaving chiefs and other natives in charge of governments designed to support British economic interests. In order to achieve their goals of economic domination, the British strengthened the authority of the traditional chiefs, making them accountable only to the British. This new pattern resulted in the loosening of the rulers' responsibility to the people.

- **The interventionist state** – The colonialists trained the chiefs to operate their governments in order to reach economic goals. Whereas in Britain individual rights and free market capitalism check the government's power, no such checks existed in Nigeria. This practice set in place the expectation that citizens should passively accept the actions of their rulers.

- **Individualism** – Capitalism and western political thought emphasizes the importance of the individual, a value that generally works well in Britain and the United States. However, in Nigeria it released a tendency for chiefs to think about the personal benefits of governance, rather than the good of the whole community.

- **Christianity** – The British brought their religion with them, and it spread throughout the south and west, the areas where their influence was the strongest. Since Islam already was well entrenched in the north, the introduction of Christianity created a split between Christian and Muslim dominated areas.

- **Intensification of ethnic politics** – During the colonial era, ethnic identities both broadened and intensified into three groups: the **Hausa-Fulani, Igbo,** and **Yoruba.** This process occurred partly because the British pitted the groups against one another in order to manage the colony by giving rewards (such as education and lower-level bureaucratic jobs) to some and not to others. Another factor was the anti-colonial movement that emerged during the 20th century. Independence leaders appealed to ethnic identities in order to gain followers and convince the British to decolonize.

THE ERA SINCE INDEPENDENCE (1960 to the present)

In the first years after independence, Nigeria struggled to make the parliamentary style of government work, and then settled into military dictatorships by 1966, interspersed with attempts to establish a civilian-led democracy. Traditions established during this era include:

- **Parliamentary-style government replaced by a presidential system** – From 1960 to 1979 Nigeria followed the British parliamentary style government. However, the ethnic divisions soon made it difficult to identify a majority party or allow a prime minister to have the necessary authority. In 1979 they switched to a presidential system with a popularly elected president, a separate legislature, and an independent judiciary. However, the latter two branches have not consistently checked the power of the president.

- **Intensification of ethnic conflict** – After independence the Hausa-Fulani of the north dominated the parliamentary government by nature of their larger population. To ensure a majority, they formed a coalition with the Igbo of the southeast, which in turn caused resistance to grow among the Yoruba of the west. Rivalries among the groups caused them to turn to military tactics to gain power, and in 1966 a group of Igbo military officers seized power and established military rule.

- **Military rule** – The first military ruler, Agiyi Ironsi, justified his authority by announcing his intention to end violence and stop political corruption. He was killed in a coup by a second general, but the coup sparked the Igbo to fight for independence for their land – called **Biafra** – from the new country of Nigeria. The Biafran Civil War raged on from 1967 until 1970, creating more violence and ethnic-based conflict. Although the country remained together, it did so only under military rule.

- **Personalized rule/corruption** - During colonial rule, native leaders lost touch with the old communal traditions that encouraged them to govern in the interest of the people. Individualism translated into rule for personal gain, and the military regimes of the modern era generally have been characterized by greed and corruption.

- **Federalism** – In an attempt to mollify ethnic tensions yet still remain one country, Nigerian leaders set up a federalist system, with some powers delegated to state and local governments. Although this system may eventually prove to be beneficial, under military regimes it did not work. Theoretically, power was shared. However, military presidents did not allow the sub-governments to function with any separate sovereignty. Instead, the state remained unitary, with all power centered in the capital city of Abuja.

- **Economic dependence on oil** – In many ways, Nigeria's good fortune has been a liability in its quest for political and economic stability. Its rich oil reserves have proved to be too tempting for most of the military rulers to resist, and corruption has meant that oil money only enriched the elite. Abundant oil also has caused other sectors of the economy to be ignored, so that Nigeria's economic survival is based almost exclusively on oil. When the international oil markets fall, so does Nigeria's economy.

POLITICAL CULTURE

All-important historic traditions have shaped a complex modern political culture characterized by ethnic diversity and conflict, corruption, and a politically active military. However, it also includes a democratic tradition and the desire to reinstate leadership that is responsible to the people. Characteristics of the political culture include:

- **Patron-clientelism (prebendalism)** – Nigeria is the third example that we have seen of a political culture characterized by patron-clientelism. Just as in China and Mexico, **clientelism**, the practice of exchanging political and economic favors among patrons and clients, is almost always accompanied by corruption. The patron (or political leader) builds loyalty among his clients (or lesser elites) by granting them favors that are denied to others. For example, in Nigeria, in exchange for their support, a president may grant to his clients a portion of the oil revenues. This practice invites corruption, and it usually means that the larger society is hurt because only a few people benefit from the favors. In Nigeria, patrons are generally linked to clients by ethnicity and religion.

- **State control/rich civil society** – **Civil society** refers to the sectors of a country that lie outside government control. In Nigerian history, the state has tried to control almost all aspects of life, first under British rule and then under military dictatorship. However, the government has never succeeded in totally dominating civil society. Formal and informal ethnic and religious associations, professional and labor groups, and other NGOs (nongovernmental organizations) have long shaped the society. These groups have related to the government mainly through corporatism and clientelism, but potentially they could form the base of a viable democracy.

- **Tension between modernity and tradition** – Nigeria's colonial past has encouraged it to become a strong, modern nation, but it also has restricted its ability to reach that goal. For many years, Nigeria's status as a colony kept the country in a subservient economic position. Once independence was gained, modernity was difficult to attain because of ethnic-based military conflicts and personalized, corrupt leadership practices. The independence movement itself encouraged Nigerians to reestablish contact with their pre-colonial roots that emphasize communal accountability. Values established in the pre-colonial era conflict with those established in the colonial era, creating the basis for the serious problems that Nigeria faces today.

- **Religious conflict** – Islam began to influence northern Nigeria as early as the eleventh century, at first coexisting with native religions, and finally supplanting them. Christianity arrived much later, but spread rapidly through the efforts of missionaries. These two religions have intensified ethnic conflict, and they also have fed political issues. For example, Muslims generally support *sharia,* or religious law, as a valid part of political authority. Christians, of course, disagree. As a result, an ongoing debate about the role of *sharia* in the Nigerian state has sparked religious conflict.

- **Geographic influences** – Nigeria is located in West Africa, bordered on the south by the Gulf of Guinea in the Atlantic Ocean. Its population of 140 million is greater than all the other fourteen countries of West Africa combined, partly because of its size and the lure of employment in its cities and in the oil industry. Nigeria's ethnic groups may be divided into six geographic zones:

  1. **Northwest** - Dominated by two groups that combined as the **Hausa-Fulani** people, the area is predominately Muslim.

  2. **Northeast** – This area is home to many smaller groups, such as the **Kanuri**, which are also primarily Muslim.

  3. **Middle Belt** – This area also contains many smaller ethnic groups, and it also is characterized by a mix of both Muslims and Christians.

  4. **Southwest** – The large ethnic group called **Yoruba** dominate this area. The Yoruba are about 40% Muslim, 40% Christian, and about 20% devoted to native religions.

  5. **Southeast** – This area is inhabited by the **Igbo,** who are primarily Roman Catholic, but with a growing number of Protestant Christians.

  6. **The Southern Zone** – This area includes the delta of the huge Niger River, and its people belong to various small minority groups.

POLITICAL AND ECONOMIC CHANGE

Political and economic change in Nigeria may be analyzed by dividing its history into three parts: pre-colonial, colonial, and modern eras. Nigeria's political influences in pre-colonial days varied widely according to ethnicity and region, as did its various economic practices. British control during the colonial era brought contradictory political influences – democracy vs. subjugation to colonial rule. Economically Nigeria became highly dependent on British demands, and the colony established a mercantilist role of providing raw materials (like oil) to the industrialized nations. Independence in 1960 meant that one of Nigeria's biggest challenges was just that – How does the new country truly become independent, when it has been dependent for so long? The sources of change have varied with each era, but they have all had important consequences for the modern Nigerian state.

Nigeria's Diversity. Some of the largest ethnicities are identified on the map, but hundreds of ethnically-based groups live within the country's borders. In recent years the capital was moved from Lagos to Abuja in an effort to create a neutral zone in the center of the country.

THE PRE-COLONIAL ERA (800-1860 C.E.)

From the beginning, Nigerian geography has dictated political, social, and economic development. The savanna areas of the north invited easy trade through Saharan Berber traders up to northern Africa, whereas people of the forested areas of the south did not contact the Berbers. Change occurred through **cultural diffusion**, or contact with and spread of customs and beliefs of other people. Most important was the diffusion of Islam, a change that was gradual, with conversion to the religion occurring slowly but steadily over time.

Despite the overall nature of gradual change, an important group – the **Fulani** – came to the north through **jihad**, or Islamic holy war, so this change occurred abruptly. In 1808 the Fulani established the **Sokoto Caliphate**, a Muslim state that encompassed the entire northwest, north, mid section, and part of the northeast. The caliphate traded with Europeans, and eventually succumbed to British colonial rule by 1900. However, it put in place the tradition of an organized, central government based on religious faith.

In contrast, people in the south generally lived communally and in closer contact with the Atlantic Ocean trade. As a result, even before the colonial era, they came into contact with Europeans who converted many of them to Christianity. An important consequence of this contact plagued Nigeria from the 16th through the 19th century in the form of the slave trade. The first contacts were with the Portuguese, but the real displacement of people began in the 17th century, when the Dutch, British, French, and Spanish traders began transporting Africans in large numbers to the New World from the Nigerian coast. The impact on the people is difficult to quantify, but the very nature of the slave trade meant that countless young males were forced to leave their native lands.

THE COLONIAL ERA (1860-1960)

European influence began in the earlier era, but in 1860 the British imposed **indirect rule**, in which they trained natives, primarily from the south, to fill the European-style bureaucracy. The British established the area that would become Nigeria in 1860 as a trading outlet, where they made use of natural resources and cheap human labor. The British influence was strongest in the south, emanating from the ports along the coast.

Because the north was already organized into political hierarchies according to Islamic tradition, the British left that area's government structures primarily intact. These political changes gave more power to the elites, and reinforced their tendencies to seek personal benefit from their positions. It further emphasized differences between north and south, leaving the colony vulnerable to divisions that later caused serious conflict and violence.

Another important influence from the colonial era was the introduction to Nigeria of western-style education. Christian missionaries set up schools subsidized by the British government, primarily for elementary education. In 1934 the first higher education institution was opened, and the first university was founded in 1948. This change had many important consequences, the most obvious being the creation of a relatively literate population. However, it also reinforced some growing cleavages. Elites became more and more separated from the people because they received most of the benefits of education. As a result, they tended to think of themselves as different, and more deserving of economic benefits as well. Another consequence was a deepening of the rift between north and south, since most of the British schools were located in the south, and very few northerners had access to western-style education. In turn, northerners came to be seen as backward by southerners, and northerners came to resent this stereotype.

MODERN NIGERIA (1960-PRESENT)

Nigeria's transition to independence began to take place in the years preceding 1960, with the British trying to "prepare" Nigerians to rule their own country. Indeed, the preparation began early because from the beginning, the British trained natives to join the bureaucracy. Education invariably included the teaching of western political values, including freedom, justice, and equality of opportunity. These lessons were not lost on the native leaders for Nigerian independence, so British education sowed the seeds for decolonization.

An important change in the early post-colonial days came in 1966 when the parliamentary government was replaced by a military dictatorship. This action set in motion the tendency for government to change hands quickly and violently, as the nation began to experience a series of military coup d'etats. In 1979 the military dictator, **Olusegun Obasanjo**, willingly stood down for a democratically elected president, Shehu Shagari, but Shagari was forced out of office in 1983 by a military coup led by General Muhammed Buhari. Two more coups kept Nigeria under military dictatorship until 1999, when a democratic election brought Obasanjo back to power, but this time as a civilian. Each election (1999, 2003, and 2007) has been rife with fraud and violence, with the election of 2007 probably the worst of all. At the same time, the development of nationalism eluded Nigeria, and created the "**national question**," or the possibility that Nigeria would not survive as a country.

The modern era has also seen ethnic identities become the major basis for conflict in Nigeria. Before the colonial era, these ethnicities certainly existed, but the different identities did not lead to constant conflict. Independence brought on a competition among groups, based on heightened awareness of ethnic differences encouraged by the British. Once the British were gone, competition among military generals for control of the country became based on ethnicity, and the heightened tensions have left reconciliation of differences all the more difficult.

LEADERSHIP TRANSITIONS IN NIGERIA SINCE 1960		
RULER	**TYPE OF GOVERNMENT**	**REASON FOR TRANSITION**
1960-1966 Tafawa Balewa (Prime Minister)	Republic	Military coup; Balewa assassinated
1966 Johnson Aguyi-Ironsi	Military dictatorship	Military coup; Ironsi assassinated
1966-1975 Yakubu Gowon	Military dictatorship	Military coup; Gowon replaced
1975-1976 Murtala Muhammed	Military dictatorship	Military coup; Muhammed assassinated
1976-1979 Olusegun Obasanjo	Military dicatorship	Replaced by democratically elected president
1979-1983 Shehu Shagari	Presidential democracy	Military coup; Shagari replaced
1983-1985 Muhammed Buhari	Military dictatorship	Military coup; Buhari replaced
1985-1993 Ibrahim Babangida	Military dictatorship	Military coup; Babangida resigned under pressure
1993-1998 Sani Abacha	Military dictatorship	Death of Abacha; Abdulsami Abubakar rules temporarily
1999-2007 Olusegun Obasanjo	Presidential democracy	Reached end of two-term presidency
2007-Present Umaru Yar'Adua	Presidential democracy	

Leadership transitions. Nigeria's unstable leadership is reflected in the table above as the country first tried parliamentary government that was taken over by military coup, and then changed to a presidential system in 1979, only to have the government seized again by the military in 1983. Since 1999 the country has elected the president in a series of questionable elections (1999, 2003, 2007).

Another change brought about during the modern era has been the institutionalization of corruption among the political elite. This tendency was made much worse by two military presidents: General Ibrahim B. Babangida, president from 1985 to 1993, and General Sani Abacha, from 1993 to 1998. Both generals maintained large foreign bank accounts, with regular deposits being diverted from the Nigerian state. Other funds went to the Nigerian elite through the patron client system. For example, it is estimated that about 2/3 of the windfall Nigeria received in oil sales during the first Persian Gulf War in 1991 ended up in the private hands of Nigerian elites.

Each military leader between 1966 and 1999 promised to transfer power to civilian hands as soon as the country was "stable." In 1993 it seemed as if the time had arrived when civilian Moshood Abiola won the presidential election. However, General Babangida annulled the election, only to lose power to General Sani Abacha in a military coup later that year. When Abacha died suddenly in 1998, a Middle-Belt Muslim General, Abdulsalami Abubakar succeeded him, with the now-familiar promise to eventually hand over the government to a duly elected civilian. He set up a transition team, elections were held in 1999, and the winner, **Olusegun Obasanjo**, became president. Obasanjo was re-elected in 2003, and some hope that these events indicate the long anticipated arrival of a democratic government. However, two facts made it difficult to claim the triumph of democracy: Obasanjo was a former military general, and both elections were characterized by voting fraud. The election of 2007 was even more questionable than the previous two, and so the potential for instability is still a threat to the country.

CITIZENS, SOCIETY, AND THE STATE

The people of Nigeria have some huge challenges in establishing democratic ties with their government. Democratization is always a difficult process because it assumes that citizens have both the time and means to pay attention to political and societal issues. Even in advanced democracies, people often have problems linking their everyday concerns with those of the government. Many societal characteristics of Nigeria make democratization a challenge:

- **Poverty** – About 60% of all Nigerians live below the poverty line, with many people in absolute poverty without the means to actually survive.

- **Large gap between the rich and the poor** – Like Mexico, the distribution of income in Nigeria is very unequal, with a few people being very wealthy and most being very poor. However, Nigeria's economy shows fewer signs of growth, and so the outlook for closing the income gap is bleaker.

- **Health issues** – Like many other African nations, Nigeria has high rates of HIV/AIDS, with some estimating that one of every eleven HIV/AIDS sufferers in the world lives in Nigeria. The toll that the disease has taken on the African continent is incalculable, and the cost to the Nigerian economy, as well as to society in general, is immeasurable. The government has generally made AIDS a secondary priority, leaving much of the challenge to a small group of underfunded **nongovernmental organizations (NGOs)**. The Obasanjo administration provided medications through a small number of clinics, but they reached only a few thousand people in a country where several million people are estimated to be HIV positive.

- **Literacy** – Nigeria's literacy rate for males is 75.7%; for females 60.6%. This is higher than for many other nations in Africa, but is below the world average of 87% for men, and 77% for women.

COMPARATIVE LITERACY RATES

China (2000 census)
Males	95.1%
Females	86.5%

Iran (2002 est.)
Males	83.5%
Females	70.4%

Mexico (2004 est.)
Males	92.4%
Females	89.6%

Nigeria (2003 est.)
Males	75.7%
Females	60.6%

Russia (2002 census)
Males	99.7%
Females	99.2%

United Kingdom (2003 est.)
Males	99%
Females	99%

Source: *CIA Factbook*

The table above shows that Nigeria's literacy rates for both men and women are significantly lower than those for the other five countries. China and Russia's high rates reflect the emphasis that communist leaders put on literacy, as well as equality between the sexes. Nigeria's rates are not only low, but they also show a large gap between male and female literacy rates, as do the rates for Iran. A related statistic for Nigeria is that each woman bears an average of 5.49 children in her lifetime.

CLEAVAGES

Nigeria has one of the most fragmented societies in the world, with important cleavages based on ethnicity, religion, region, urban/rural differences, and social class. Nigeria is similar to Russia in that both have had to contend with ethnic-based civil wars – Russia in the on-going conflict with Chechnya, and Nigeria with the Biafran Civil War between 1967 and 1970. In both countries, ethnic conflicts have undermined the basic legitimacy of the government. The consequences of these cleavages for the Nigerian political system have been grave because they have made any basic agreements about governance almost impossible.

- **Ethnicity** – Nigeria has between 250 and 400 separate ethnic groups with their own array of customs, languages, and religions. The three largest groups – the Hausa-Fulani, Igbo, and Yoruba – have very little in common, and generally cannot speak one another's languages. They live separately in their own enclaves, and virtually no contacts take place among the groups.

- **Religion** – In China and the former Soviet Union, ethnic tensions are (were) managed by imposing communism on the society so that some unifying ideology held the people together. Nigeria has had no such ideology, but instead its political culture is made more complex by competing religions. About half of all Nigerians are Muslim, 40% are Christian, and the remaining 10% affiliate with native religions. Ethnic tensions are exacerbated by religious differences among Muslims, Christians, and those that practice native religions. International tensions between Muslims and Christians are reflected in Nigeria, but their arguments are rooted in the preferential treatment that the British gave to Christians. Disputes regarding the religious law of Islam, the *sharia,* and its role in the nation's policymaking practices reflect the significance of religious cleavages.

- **Region/north vs. south** – Although Nigeria's ethnic divisions are multiple, the country was divided into Three Federated Regions in 1955, five years before independence was official. These regions follow ethnic and religious divisions, and they are the basis for setting election and legislative procedures, as well as political party affiliations. Another way to divide Nigeria by region is north vs. south, with the north being primarily Muslim, and the South mainly Christian.

- **Urban/rural differences** – As in many other countries, significant urban/rural differences divide Nigeria. Political organizations and interest groups exist primarily in cities, as well as newspapers and electronic media sources. Although their activities were suppressed by the annulment of the election of 1993 and the execution of rights activist and environmentalist **Ken Saro-Wiwa** in 1995, most organized protests have taken place in cities.

- **Social class** – The division between elites and ordinary people runs deep in Nigeria. The wealth of the elite stems from their control of the state and the resources of the country. They have maintained their power through appealing to ethnic and religious identities of the people. The elite generally have found it difficult to abandon their access to the government's treasury for personal gain, and yet the educated elite also harbors those who would like to see Nigeria transformed into a modern nation based on democratic principles.

PUBLIC OPINION AND POLITICAL PARTICIPATION

Nigeria is not yet a democracy, and despite a long history of a rich civil society, its citizens have been encouraged to relate to government as subjects, not as active participants. Some activities are now taking place in **civil society**, or the realm outside the government influence, with some professional associations, trade unions, religious groups, and various other interest groups emerging. Even with the presence of military rule, presidents have generally allowed a free press to exist and interest group membership to be maintained.

PATRON-CLIENTELISM (Prebendalism)

Much participation, particularly in rural areas, still takes place through the patron-client system. The special brand of clientelism in Nigerian politics is known as **"prebendalism,"** a term borrowed from

Max Weber's concept of an extremely personalized system of rule in which all public offices are treated as personal fiefdoms. By creating large patronage networks based on personal loyalty, civilian officials have skewed economic and political management to such an extent that they have often discredited themselves. Local government officials gain support from villagers through dispensing favors, and they in turn receive favors for supporting their patron bosses. Of course, most favors are exchanged among the political elite, but the pattern persists on all levels. With patron-clientelism comes corruption and informal influence, but it does represent an established form of political participation in Nigeria.

CIVIL SOCIETY

In Nigeria's postcolonial history, many formal interest groups and informal voluntary associations have actively sought to influence political decisions. Since 1999 many have strengthened, some serving as centripetal forces that encourage Nigerian unity, and others as centrifugal influences that cause Nigeria to fragment along ethnic and religious lines. One group that has managed to do both is the Movement for the Survival of the Ogoni People, or MOSOP, founded by dissident **Ken Saro-Wiwa** in the 1990s. MOSOP has worked to apply national laws to secure financial benefits for the Ogoni in the Niger Delta and to hold foreign-operated oil companies to environmental standards.

Trade unions and professional organizations have been particularly active in trying to protect the rights of their members. For example, the National Union of Petroleum and Gas Workers (NUPENG) has been an influential voice for workers in the all-important petroleum industry. Formal associations for legal, medical, and journalism professions articulate the political interests of Nigeria's growing professional class.

VOTING BEHAVIOR

Nigerian citizens have voted in national elections since 1959, but since many elections have been canceled or postponed by the military and others have been fraudulent, voter behavior patterns are difficult to track. Political parties are numerous and fluid, with most formed around the charisma of their candidates for office, so party loyalty is an imperfect reflection of voter attitudes. Babangida's annulment of the 1993 election also put a damper on political participation during most of the 1990s. However, elections on local, state, and national levels were held in 1999 and 2003, although their results appear to be fraudulent. Nevertheless, Nigerian citizens did vote in large numbers in both the 1999 and 2003 elections. One estimate is that close to 2/3 of eligible voters actually voted in 2003, but the widespread corruption around the election make those figures highly unreliable. The participation rates in the 2007 election are almost impossible to calculate because of voter fraud and inability of legitimate voters to cast their ballots.

ATTITUDES TOWARD GOVERNMENT

Not surprisingly, most Nigerians have a low level of trust in their government. General Abacha was so widely disliked that there was rejoicing and celebration in the street when he died unexpectedly in 1998, with some citizens dubbing the event a "coup from heaven." Nigerians in general are skeptical about the prospects for democracy, and they do not believe that elections are conducted in a fair and honest way. Whether or not Nigerians will remain cynical, however, is yet to be seen. In the early days of independence, attitudes toward the government were generally much more favorable, and many citizens expressed an identity as Nigerians, not just as members of ethnic groups. Perhaps the cynicism results from the notorious rule of Babangida and Abacha in the 1980s and 90s and will soon change. However, without the commitment to democracy from political elites, ordinary citizens are unlikely to see their government in a positive light in the near future.

Nigerian attitudes toward democracy are shared by citizens in many other African countries. According to the Afrobarometer survey published in 2006, 6 in 10 Africans sampled in 18 countries said that democracy was preferable to any other form of government. However, satisfaction with democracy dipped to 45% from 58% in 2001.

Nigerian citizens' negative perceptions of their government are based in some very solid evidence that government officials are quite corrupt. Transparency International, a private organization that compiles statistics about corruption in countries around the world, ranks Nigeria very low in their "Transparency International Corruption Perceptions Index" that they publish every year. In 2006 Nigeria ranked 142nd out of 146 countries in terms of how "clean" its government is.

CORRUPTION PERCEPTION INDEX 2006

COUNTRY	CPI SCORE*	RANK (146 COUNTRIES TOTAL)
China	3.3	70**
Iran	2.7	105
Mexico	3.3	70**
Nigeria	2.2	142
Russia	2.5	121
United Kingdom	8.6	11

*The Corruption Percept Index Score is compiled every year by Transparency International. Countries are ranked from 1 to 10, with a 10 reflecting a corruption-free government.
**Nine countries tied for a rank of 70, including China and Mexico.

Source: *Transparency International*, www.transparency.org

Russia, China, Mexico, and Nigeria all are characterized by patron-clientelism, so it is not surprising that all have relatively low CPI scores. Since Transparency International considers a score of 1 to be "highly corrupt," the chart supports the fact that corruption is a big problem in all of the six countries except for the United Kingdom. In all five cases (China, Mexico, Nigeria, Iran, and Russia) corruption is part of the political culture, and bribes and favoritism are expected to be a part of the ways that governments operate. Nigeria's pre-bendalism permeates the political system to such a degree that political participation cannot yet take place outside its influence.

PROTESTS, PARTICIPATION, AND SOCIAL MOVEMENTS

Since the return of democracy in 1999, a number of ethnic-based and religious movements have mobilized to pressure the federal government to address their grievances. The international oil companies have been major targets, especially in the Niger Delta where the companies and oil fields are centered. A widely publicized protest occurred in July 2002 when a group of unarmed Ijaw women occupied ChevronTexaco's Nigerian operations for 10 days. The siege ended when ChevronTexaco's officials agreed to provide jobs for their sons, and set up a credit plan to help village women start businesses. Although this protest ended peacefully, others ended by being violently suppressed by the Obasanjo government. A major upswing in protests and unrest has occurred since early 2006, with groups organizing to attack the foreign-based oil companies. Armed rebel gangs have blown up pipelines, disabled pumping states, and kidnapped foreign oil workers. These events in Nigeria, the world's eighth largest oil exporter, have affected international energy markets, contributing to higher prices and tighter supplies. As a result, production sites have been shut down, and some companies have left Nigeria, often blaming the government for its inability to stop the problems.

POLITICAL INSTITUTIONS

In its long history, Nigeria has experienced many different regime types. In its pre-colonial days, the regime type varied from one area to another. In the north and west, well-developed large states with hereditary monarchs developed, and in the south, small communal kinship-based rule predominated. The Hausa people in the west were organized into powerful trading city-states. The regime-type changed dramatically with colonization, with the British imposition of indirect rule. Where chiefs did not exist, the British created them, and authoritarian rule under British direction was well developed by the mid-20th century. Authoritarian rule has continued into the independence era, when a military-style regime emerged by 1966.

Today the government structure is formally federalist and democratic, but it has not generally operated as such. The British controlled economic life during the colonial era, and the economy remains under state control today. However, international factors have forced Nigeria to turn to supranational organizations – such as the World Bank and the International Monetary Fund – for help in restructuring the economy.

LINKAGE INSTITUTIONS

Because Nigeria's efforts to democratize are so far incomplete, linkage institutions in general are both newly developed and highly fluid. However, Nigerian citizens have organized themselves in a number of ways with varying degrees of impact on Nigerian politics.

POLITICAL PARTIES

Predictably political parties in Nigeria have almost always been regionally and ethnically based. Unlike Mexico, Nigeria did not develop a one-party system in the 20th century that contributed to political stability. Instead, Nigeria's extreme factionalism led to the development of so many parties that it was almost impossible to create a coherent party system. The resulting multi-party system has reinforced and deepened ethnic and religious cleavages. Parties also form around personalities, and so tend to fade with leadership changes.

Parties have appeared, disappeared, and reorganized frequently. However, in the election of 2007, these parties supported major presidential candidates:

- **The People's Democratic Party (PDP)** – This is one of the better-established parties, having run candidates for office as early as 1998. The PDP is the party of **Olusegun Obasanjo**, and in 2003 he received about 62% of the vote for president. In 2007, amidst widespread fraud, **Umaru Yar'Adua** received almost 70% of the vote. The party also gained the overwhelming majority in the National Assembly, and most of the governors elected were candidates of the PDP. However, because the elections were fraudulent, it is very difficult to know how much real support the PDP actually has. Obasanjo is a Christian and Yoruba from the south, but the party won elections throughout the country. Yar'Adua is Muslim from the north.

- **All Nigeria People's Party (ANPP)** – Former **General Muhammed Buhari**, a Muslim from the north, was the ANPP candidate in 2003 and 2007. In 2003 his running mate was Chuba Okadigbo, an Igbo from the Southeast, who is probably the Igbo's best hope for a run for future presidential elections. Buhari received about 32% of the vote in 2003, and not quite 19% in 2007.

- **Action Congress (AC)** – This political party formed with the merger of the Alliance for Democracy, the Justice Party, the Advance Congress of Democrats, and several other minor political parties in September 2006. The party ran Vice President **Atiku Abubakar** (who defected from the People's Democratic Party) as its presidential candidate in the 2007 presidential election. Abubakar was disqualified from the election by the Independent National Electoral Commission, but the disqualification was later overturned by the Supreme Court. He received more than 7% of the vote.

The fact that several parties merged to form Action Congress may be an indication that the major parties are coalescing. One trend since 1999 is for parties to lose their regional base and to draw support from many parts of the country. The PDP originated in the Muslim north, but deliberately ran Obasanjo, a Christian Yoruba from the south, as its candidate in 1999 and 2003. As a result, it has become the dominant party; however, all three elections were fraudulent, and the violence levels were high enough (more than 200 people were killed in protests surrounding the 2007 elections) that it is difficult for PDP to claim legitimacy.

A flurry of party registrations with the **Independent National Election Commission (INEC)** followed the death of President Abacha in 1998. In order to run candidates for the legislative and presidential elections of 1999, a party had to qualify by earning at least 5 percent of the votes in two-thirds of the states in the December 1998 local elections. This practice effectively cut the number of parties running to three, and also limited the eligible parties to five in the presidential election of 2003. The INEC was widely accused of corruption in the election of 2007, and of complying with President Obasanjo's desire to keep Vice President Abubakar from running for the presidency. The INEC left his name off the list of official candidates, but his disqualification was overturned by the Supreme Court.

ELECTIONS AND ELECTORAL PROCEDURES

Citizens vote for candidates on three levels: local, state, and national. On the national level, they vote for the president, representatives to the House of Representatives, and for senators from their states.

National Elections

- **Presidential elections** – The first presidential election after the annulled election of 1993 took place in 1999, followed by a second election in 2003. If a presidential candidate does not receive an outright majority, a second ballot election may take place. This has not happened yet. An unusual requirement, however, reflects Nigeria's attempt to unite its people. A president also must receive at least 25% of all the votes cast in 2/3 of the states. In other words, a purely regional candidate cannot win the presidency. The requirement also indicates how difficult unification has been for Nigeria since independence in 1960.

- **Legislative elections** - The Senate has 109 senators, three from each of 36 states, and one from the federal capital territory, Abuja. They are elected by direct popular vote. The 539 representatives are elected from single member districts by **plurality vote**. No run-offs take place for these seats. The result in both houses is regional representation, with a wide array of ethnicities that try to form coalitions, even though legislative policymaking power is very weak anyway.

Election Fraud

Many observers believe that Nigeria has made significant progress simply to be able to sustain three regularly scheduled popular elections in a row. During the April 12, 2003 legislative election, about a dozen people died, but many commented that it was not as bad as it could have been. Additionally, several politicians were assassinated, including Marshall Harry, one of the leaders of Mr. Buhari's All Nigeria People's Party. However, the Independent National Electoral Commission (INEC), with outside pressure, made an attempt to cleanse the electoral process when they declared almost six million names to be fraudulent. The names were struck from the voter rolls. On the other hand, international teams that observed the election generally concluded that the election was corrupt, with ballot boxes being vandalized, stolen, and stuffed with fraudulent votes. Some concluded that voting patterns in the south were particularly suspicious.

The elections of 2007 were even worse, with national legislative and presidential races deeply flawed, as well as state and local contests. The year before the election President Obasanjo sponsored a plan to modify the 1999 constitution that would allow him to run for a third term of office, but the National Assembly failed to ratify it. Next, the Independent National Election Committee disqualified Vice President Abubakar from running for president, but the Supreme Court declared that the INEC had no such power. Last-minute ballots were printed and distributed to include him, but the ballots showed only party symbols, not the names of candidates, and lacked serial numbers that help reduce fraud. On election day, international observers, including some from the European Union and some from the United States, witnessed instances of ballot-box theft, long delays in the delivery of ballots and other materials, and a shortage of ballots for the presidential race. Often there was no privacy for voters to mark their ballots in secret. Observers also witnessed unused ballots being marked and stuffed into ballot boxes. Frustrated voters erupted in protest, and the ensuing violence ended in the deaths of about 200 people.

INTEREST GROUPS

Perhaps surprisingly, interest groups have played an important role in Nigerian government and politics. Although the development of an active civil society has been hampered by pre-bendalism and corruption, there is an array of civil society organizations that often cooperate with political parties.

Some of them are based on religion, such as the Christian Association of Nigeria that protested loudly when Babangida decided to change Nigeria's status in the Organization of the Islamic Conference from observer to member. A large number of Muslim civil society organizations in the north work to support the *sharia* court system. They have had to work around military control, but citizens have sought to have an impact on political life through labor unions, student groups, and populist groups.

Labor Unions

Labor unions before the military oppression of the 1980s were independent and politically powerful. Organized labor challenged governments during both the colonial and post-colonial eras, but the Babangida regime devised methods to limit their influence. This was established through **corporatism**, or government approved interest groups that provide feedback to the government. A central labor organization supplanted the older unions, and only candidates approved by Babangida could be elected as labor leaders. However, the labor movement still is alive in Nigeria, and retains an active membership. If democracy indeed is established, labor unions could play a vital role in the policymaking process. For example, in July 2003 labor unions widely and openly protested the government's attempt to raise oil prices for Nigerian consumers.

By 2007 it was clear that labor unions had regained much of their previous power when the **Nigeria Labor Congress** successfully orchestrated a general strike of workers in cities across Nigeria. The strike was organized to protest the government's hike in fuel prices and taxes. The government agreed to rescend their hikes, but strike organizers wanted further reductions. The Nigerian government has subsidized fuel heavily, just as the Iranian government has, and in both cases, the subsidies are quite expensive. Nigeria especially is under international pressure to cut the subsidies so that the immense national debt can be paid.

Business Interests

Business interests have tended to work in collaboration with the military regimes during the last decades, and have shared the spoils of the corruption within the elite classes. However, some business associations have operated outside the realm of government influence in the private sector. Associations for manufacturers, butchers, and car rental firms are only a few groups that have organized. In the 1990s, some of these groups became a leading force in promoting economic reform in Nigeria.

Human Rights Groups

Other interest groups have organized to promote human rights. University students, teachers, civil liberties organizations, and professional groups (doctors, lawyers) protested the abuses of the Babangida and Abacha regimes, and remain active promoters of democratic reform. They staged street demonstrations and protests in 1997-98 as Abacha prepared to orchestrate a campaign to succeed himself. Although the groups are now only loosely connected, their willingness to collaborate and remain active might play an important role in creating a true democracy in Nigeria.

MASS MEDIA

In contrast to most less developed countries, Nigeria has long had a well-developed, independent press. General Abacha moved to muffle its criticisms of his rule when he closed several of the most influential and respected Nigerian newspapers and magazines in 1994. However, the tradition remains intact, although the press reflects, like so many other institutions, the ethnic divisions within the country. Most of the outspoken newspapers are in the south, although a few have been published in the north. Generals from the north have often interpreted criticisms of the press as ethnic slurs reflective of region-based stereotypes. The media actively spread news as the events of the 2007 elections unfolded, and many journalists were highly critical of the government's actions.

Radio is the main source of information for most Nigerians, with newspapers and TV more common in the cities. All 36 states run their own radio stations.

THE INSTITUTIONS OF NATIONAL GOVERNMENT

Nigeria is in theory a **federal political system** with government organizations on local, state, and national levels. Its various constitutions have provided for three branches of government, but in reality its executive branch has dominated policymaking. In the Second, Third, and Fourth Republics (all since 1979), Nigeria has had a **presidential system,** with a strong president theoretically checked by a bicameral legislature and an independent judiciary. Each of the 36 state governments and 774 local governments has an executive and a legislative branch, and a network of local, district, and state courts exists. Currently, neither federalism nor checks and balances operate, and state and local governments are totally dependent on the central government.

THE EXECUTIVE

In 1979, with the establishment of the Second Republic, the parliamentary system modeled after Britain was replaced by a presidential system. Nigeria's many ethnicities fragmented its multi-party system and legislature so seriously that a prime minister could not gain the necessary authority to rule. The belief was that a popularly elected president could symbolize unity and rise above the weak party system. The U.S. presidential model was followed, including a two-term limit for the chief executive. Nigeria followed the model until 1983, when Major-General Muhammadu Buhari (also a candidate for president in the 2003 and 2007 elections) staged a palace coup. He in turn was ousted by General Babangida in 1985, who was replaced by General Abacha in 1993. Civilian rule returned in 1999, and President Obasanjo was reelected in 2003, and in 2007 Nigeria had its first experience of one civilian president handing power to another, no matter how flawed the election.

The Executive under Military Rule

Nigeria's seven military leaders have not all ruled in the same fashion. All have promised a "transition to democracy," but only two have given power over to elected leaders: General Obasanjo in 1979, and General Abubakar in 1999. Generals Buhari (1983-1985), Babangida (1985-1993), and Abacha (1993-1998) are known for their use of repressive tactics during their rule, but virtually all military and civilian administrations have concentrated power in the hands of the executive. The presidents have appointed senior officials without legislative approval, and neither the legislature nor the judiciary has consistently checked executive power.

Patrimonialism

The generals have ruled under a system of **patrimonialism,** in which the president is the head of an intricate patron-client system and dispenses government jobs and resources as rewards to supporters. As a result, cabinet positions, bureaucracy chiefs, and virtually all other government jobs are part of the president's patronage system. The fact that generals repeatedly have been overthrown indicates that the system is unstable, or possibly that the impulse toward democracy is keeping patrimonialism from working.

THE BUREAUCRACY

The British put an elaborate civil service in place in Nigeria during colonial days, allowing Nigerians to fill lower-level jobs in the bureaucracy. After independence, the civil service remained in place, and has grown tremendously over the past decades. Many observers believe that the bureaucracy is bloated, and it is a generally accepted fact that it is corrupt and inefficient. Bribery is common, and jobs are awarded through the patron-client system, or pre-bendalism. Not surprisingly, this system has led to a rapid increase in the number of bureaucratic jobs.

Para-statals

Like Mexican organizations before the 1980s, many Nigerian government agencies are actually **para-statals,** or corporations owned by the state and designated to provide commercial and social welfare services. Theoretically the para-statals are privately owned, but their boards are appointed by government ministers, and their executives are interwoven into the president's patronage system. Para-statals commonly provide public utilities, such as water, electricity, public transportation, and agricultural subsidies. Others control major industries such as steel, defense products, and petroleum.

State Corporatism

As we saw in Mexico in its pre-democracy days, **corporatism** may function in an authoritarian political system where the government allows political input from selected interest groups outside the government structure. Although corporatism in PRI dominated Mexico was far from democratic, political leaders generally did take into consideration the opinions of these selected groups. In Nigeria, as in Iran, para-statals provide this input, and because they are controlled by the government, they create **state corporatism.** Para-statals fulfill important economic and social functions, and they insure that the state controls private interests as well. They serve as contact points between the government and business interests, but the state ultimately controls the interactions. Para-statals generally are inefficiently run and corrupt, and many believe that they must be disbanded if democracy is to survive in Nigeria. One para-statal, founded by President Obasanjo to provide better electrical service, was known as N.E.P.A., but Nigerians joked that the initials stood for "Never Expect Power Again." When the para-statal was renamed the Power Holding Company, the new joke was that it stood for "Please Hold Candle."

THE LEGISLATURE

The Nigerian legislature has taken several different forms since independence, and it has been disbanded a number of times by military rulers. A parliamentary system was in place until 1979, when it was replaced by a presidential system with a bicameral legislature, known collectively as **The National Assembly.** Both representatives and senators serve four-year renewable terms, and elections are held the week preceding the presidential election.

- **The Senate** – Currently the upper house is composed of 109 senators, three from each of 36 states and one from the federal capital territory of Abuja. Senators are elected directly by popular vote. Its equal representation model for states is based on that of the United States Senate, so some senators represent much smaller populations than others do. However, the ethnic and religious diversity of the 36 states means that senators are also a diverse lot.

- **The House of Representatives** – The House of Representatives has 360 members from single-member districts. They are elected by plurality, and like the senators, represent many different ethnicities. After the elections of 2003, only 23 representatives were women, as were only 4 of the 109 senators, but those figures were up slightly from 1999.

Nigerian legislatures under military governments have had almost no power, and even under civilian control, the legislature has only recently become an effective check on the president's power. A notable example is the National Assembly's failure to ratify President Obasanjo's plan to alter the Constitution to allow him to run for a third term in 2007. Even though the president's party (PNP) held a majority in the Assembly, the legislative leaders were highly critical of the fraud and violence associated with the election of 2007. However, like so many other government officials, representatives and senators have often been implicated in corruption scandals. For example, in 1999 the president of the Senate and the speaker of the lower house were removed from their positions for perjury and forgery. In August 2000 the Senate president was removed on suspicion of accepting kickbacks for government contracts.

Nigeria's legislature has a low representation of women, with only 6.4% women in the House of Representatives, and 3.7% women in the Senate. This is probably reflective of traditional society there, although President Obasanjo made it a part of his reelection campaign in 2003 to include more women in his cabinet and top bureaucratic positions. Recent figures indicate that as many as 22% of government bureaucrats are women.

THE JUDICIARY

During the early years of independence the Nigerian judiciary actually had a great deal of autonomy. Courts combined British common law with an assortment of traditional or customary law, including *sharia* in the Northern Region. They were known for rendering objective decisions and for operating independently from the executive. However, the years of military rule ravaged the court system. The judiciary was undermined by military decrees that nullified court decisions, and the generals even set up quasi-judicial tribunals outside the regular system. Judicial review was suspended, and the presidents' cronies were appointed as judges. As a result, many judges today are not well versed in law and render decisions that are manipulated by the government.

Today the judiciary is charged with interpreting the laws in accordance with the Constitution, so judicial review exists in theory. Court structures exist at both federal and state levels, with the highest court in the land being the Supreme Court. The court structure is complicated by the *sharia* courts that exist side by side with courts based on the British model. The 1999 constitution establishes a Supreme Court, a Federal Court of Appeals, and a single unified court system at the national and state levels. Individual states may also authorize traditional subsidiary courts, with the most controversial being the Islamic *sharia* courts, which now function in twelve of the predominantly Muslim northern states.

Two notorious cases from the 1990s indicate to many people how deeply the Nigerian judiciary fell under the sway of military rulers. **Mshood Abiolao**, the winner of the 1993 election annulled by Babangida, was detained and eventually died while in custody. The presiding judges for his detention changed often, and critics of the government believe that justice was not served. In 1995, activist **Ken**

Saro-Wiwa and eight other Ogonis were detained and hanged under orders from a court arranged by the military, consisting primarily of military officers.

THE MILITARY

It goes without saying that the military is a strong force behind policymaking in Nigeria. Yet by becoming so active in political affairs, the military lost its credibility as a temporary, objective organization that keeps order and brings stability. Starting in 1966 when the first coup took place, the military made distinctions between the **"military in government"** and the **"military in barracks."** The latter fulfills traditional duties of the military, and its leaders often have been critical of military control of political power. As a result, the military has been subject to internal discord, and the military presidents often had to keep a close eye on other military leaders. Babangida protected his authority by constantly moving military personnel around and by appointing senior officers through his patronage system.

Although the military is a strongly intimidating force in the Nigerian political system that has often blocked democratic reforms, it is important to understand that it is one of the few institutions in the country that is truly national in character. When the deep ethnic cleavages within Nigerian society have threatened instability, the military has been there to restore order. Nigeria's best, brightest, and most ambitious have often made their way by rising through the military, a fact particularly important for the ethnic Muslims of northern Nigeria who have not had the same opportunities that many in the south have had. Because of these factors, generals had the ability to keep control of the government for many years, and it helps to explain why the democracy has been so fragile so far.

PUBLIC POLICY

Nigeria's years of military rule resulted in a top-down policymaking process. Power is concentrated in the presidency, and much outside input comes to the president and his cabinet ministers through channels established by patron clientelism. Senior government officials are supported by a broader based of loyal junior officials, creating a sort of **"loyalty pyramid**." State control of resources means that those in the pyramid get the spoils, and they alone have access to wealth and influence. These loyal clients have had many nicknames, including the "Kaduna Mafia," "Babangida's Boys," and "Abacha's Boys." Since the military was in control until 1999, the pyramids were backed by guns, so that protesting the corruption could be dangerous.

The system operated under the assumption that the military and political elite operate with only their self-interest in mind. Historically, this pattern of top-down, self-interested rule was put in place during colonial times when the British relied on native chiefs to ensure that Nigerian trade and resources benefited Great Britain. To break this pattern, political elite must get in touch with their older roots – the communalism from pre-colonial days. Democratic rule requires that political leaders are responsible for the welfare of their people, not only to those that they owe favors to.

ECONOMIC ISSUES

One result of the loyalty pyramids has been the squandering of Nigeria's wealth. Currently the country finds itself deeply in debt, and most of its people live in poverty. Tremendous oil revenues have disappeared into the pockets of government officials, and most Nigerians have not profited from them at all. The situation is complicated by ethnic and regional hostilities and by widespread popular distrust of the government. In February 2001 the federal government asked the Supreme Court to allow the federal government to collect oil revenues and pool them into a "federal account." On the surface, this appears to be **revenue sharing**, or allowing the entire country to benefit from offshore oil profits. However, the areas in the south along the Niger Delta protested the practice strongly, partly because they saw the policy as coming from northerners who wanted to take southern profits away. And without trust in the government, almost no one believed that the profits would benefit anyone except corrupt government officials.

Oil: a Source of Strength or Weakness?

The state's main role in the economy is in controlling the nation's revenues, and in spending those earnings, known as **rents,** which came mainly from oil. Individuals, groups, and communities have learned to respond through **rent-seeking** behavior, primarily by competing for the government's largesse. Those that win the competition do so through political connections provided through the patron client system, with the president having control over who gets what. Most Nigerians struggle along without much access, and participate in the **informal economy** of unreported incomes from small-scale trade and subsistence agriculture.

During the 1970s Nigeria's oil wealth gave it a great deal of international leverage. As an active member of OPEC, Nigeria could make political and economic demands because developed countries needed their oil. Through the years Nigeria has gained clout whenever Middle Eastern tensions have cut off oil supplies from that region, forcing developed countries to rely more heavily on Nigerian oil. However, Nigeria's over reliance on oil has meant that the country's economy suffers disproportionately whenever oil prices go down. During eras of low oil prices, Nigeria has amassed great debt, partly because the profits do not remain in the state's coffers long enough to cover the lean years.

One major issue since early 2006 has been the unstable situation in the Niger Delta regarding protests and subterfuge of foreign-based oil companies there. Some groups are idealistic, such as the Movement for the Emancipation of the Niger Delta, which wants more oil money going to the people of the delta states. However, the group has chosen violent methods, such as kidnapping foreign workers, and others have joined in the mayhem, including gangs with no such communal goals. The violence has driven some companies away, such as Willbros, one of the world's largest independent contractors that left Nigeria in the summer of 2006. Other companies have cut production, so that by mid-2007 about a quarter of Nigeria's oil output had been shut down since January 2006. Dealing with this issue is one of the biggest challenges facing the new administration of President **Umaru Yar'Adua**.

Structural Adjustment

After international oil prices plummeted in the early 1980s, Nigeria was forced to turn to international organizations for help in managing its huge national debt. In 1985, the Babangida regime developed an economic **structural adjustment program** with the support of the **World Bank** and the **International Monetary Fund.** The program sought to restructure and diversify the Nigerian economy so that it could decrease its dependence on oil. The government also pledged to reduce government spending and to privatize its para-statals. This "shock treatment" has had mixed results, but generally timelines for debt repayment have been restructured because Nigeria could not keep up with their payments. Para-statals are still under state control, and the private economic sector has not grown significantly. The large national debt remains a major problem for Nigeria today, although the recent rise in oil prices has meant that GDP per capita has improved over the past few years.

"FEDERAL CHARACTER"

Federalism is seen by most Nigerians as a positive, desirable characteristic for their country. Federalism appeals to many countries because it promises that power will be shared, and that all people in all parts of the country will be fairly represented. Federalism also allows citizens more contact points with government, so that true democratic rule can be more easily achieved. In Nigeria, the goal is to seek a **"federal character"** for the nation, a principle that recognizes people of all ethnicities, religions, and regions, and takes their needs into account. The Nigerian Constitution has put many provisions in place that support the goal of "federal character." For example, senators represent diverse states, representatives are elected from diverse districts, and the president must receive 25% of the vote in 2/3 of the regions in order to be elected. However, so far this ethnic balancing has not promoted unity or nationalism, but has only served to divide the country more.

One negative effect of federalism has been to bloat and promote corruption within the bureaucracy. Since all ethnicities must be represented, sometimes jobs have been created just to satisfy the demand. Once established within bureaucratic posts, these appointees see themselves as beholden to ethnic and regional interests. Another negative effect takes place within the legislative chambers. The 36 states vie for control of government resources, and see themselves in competition with other ethnic groups for political and economic benefits.

The "federal character" issue is based squarely on the fact that the "national question" in Nigeria remains unanswered. Do Nigerians have enough in common to remain together as a country?

Many southerners contend that true federalism will exist only when the central government devolves some of its power to the state and local levels. For example, Nigerians of the Niger Delta believe that regions should control their own resources. For them, that means that the federal government should not redistribute their region's oil revenues. Other southerners have suggested that police duties and personnel should be relegated to local and state levels as they are in the United States. Northerners generally don't support the **"true federalism" movement** because their regions historically have not had as many resources or as much revenue to share. Many northern states benefit more than southerners from nationally sponsored redistribution programs.

DEMOCRATIZATION

Some changes have occurred in Nigeria since the last military regime left in 1999. For example, some public enterprises have been privatized, opening the way for limitations on the economic control of the central government. Also, a scheme for alleviating poverty has been set forward. Public wages have increased in recent years, with the hope that well-paid public employees won't be as susceptible to bribery. Some of the money that General Abacha stashed in his foreign bank account has now been returned to the state treasury. Finally, Nigeria's financial reserves have grown, partly because oil prices have been rising over the past few years.

Despite all its problems, Nigeria shows some signs that democracy may be taking root in its presidential system, including these:

- **Some checks and balances between government branches** – The legislature rejected President Obasanjo's attempt to change the Constitution to allow him to run for a third term in 2007, despite a great deal of pressure from the political elite.

- **Some independent decisions in the courts** – President Obasanjo's attempt to keep his vice president, **Atiku Abubakar**, from running for president in 2007 was foiled by the courts after the president's allies used corruption charges to bar his candidacy. The Supreme Court ruled in Abubakar's favor, even though his name was not returned to the ballot until the last minute.

- **Revival of civil society** – Nigeria's many civic and religious groups, driven underground by military rule, have reactivated and freely criticized the government's handling of the 2007 election.

- **Independent media** – During the 2007 election the media sent countless correspondents across 36 states to bring back reports of stuffed ballot boxes, intimidated voters, and phony results. Internet and cell phone connections allowed poll observers, voters, and political parties to freely communicate, making it much more difficult to hide election fraud.

- **A peaceful succession of power** – For the first time in Nigeria's history, power passed between two civilians as President **Olusegun Obasanjo** stepped down in 2007, peacefully allowing **Umaru Yar'Adua** to take over.

- **Improving Freedom House scores** – Freedom House, an organization that studies democracy around the world, ranks countries on a 1 to 7 freedom scale, with countries given a 1 being the most free and those given a 7 being the least free. In 2007 Freedom House gave Nigeria a "4", putting it squarely in the "partly free" category. Nigeria's score has improved over the years, along with those of many other countries in Africa. In 1976, the vast majority, 25 (including Nigeria) were "not free." Today the not-free category has shrunk to 14 states, with most falling into the "partly free" category (including Nigeria).

Are the recent reforms indications that Nigeria may finally be stabilizing as a nation? In many ways, Nigeria's massive economic and political troubles are intertwined in such a fashion that it is difficult to tell where to start in unraveling the issues. Economic problems are rooted in patron-clientelism, which in turn breeds corruption, which makes the economic problems more difficult to solve. Patron-clientelism also has encouraged ethnic discord, and has proved to be a major stumbling block to the development of a democracy.

One of the key characteristics of a true democracy is the existence of regular competitive elections in which citizens have real alternative choices. Recent Nigerian elections may be interpreted to support either an optimistic or pessimistic view for Nigeria's future prospects. On the one hand, it is easy to criticize the Nigerian election process as a farce. After all, the election of 1993 was annulled, and the elections of 1999 and 2003 only put a former military general back in power. The elections of 1999, 2003, and 2007 were also characterized by ballot box theft and stuffing. Several candidates were assassinated, and ordinary people were killed in their efforts to vote. How can this be a democracy? On the other hand, three elections have been held in a row without being suspended or annulled. Some argue that this generation of presidential candidates consists of military men because they are the only ones with the experience necessary to govern. These hopeful ones predict that younger, nonmilitary leaders will emerge as political candidates in the near future. Umaru Yar'Adua, for example, is not a military man. After all, the experience of democracy has deep roots in Nigerian political culture. Perhaps the best question is, "Was this election better than the last one?" If so, perhaps a new, more optimistic pattern is developing in Nigeria.

IMPORTANT TERMS AND CONCEPTS

Abacha, Sani
Abubakar, Atiku
ANPP
Babangida, Ibrahim
Biafra
Buhari, Muhammud
civil society
constitutionalism
corporatism
cultural diffusion
"federal character"
Hausa-Fulani
Ife
Igbo
indirect rule
informal economy
INEC
jihad
Kanuri
kinship-based politics
"loyalty pyramid"
"military in barracks"
"military in government"
National Assembly
"the national question"
nongovernmental organizations
Obasanjo, Olusegun
Oyo
para-statals
patrimonialism
patron-client system (prebendalism)
PDR
plurality vote
rents, rent-seeking
revenue sharing
rule of law
Saro-Wiwa, Ken
sharia
Sokoto Caliphate
state corporatism
structural adjustment program
"true federalism" movement
Yar'Adua, Umaru
Yoruba

MULTIPLE-CHOICE QUESTIONS – NIGERIA

1. Nigeria's "national question" is whether or not it should

   a) have an official state-sponsored religion
   b) remain as one country
   c) keep its presidential system
   d) trade with other countries
   e) disband the military-in-government

2. In comparison to the Iranian Constitution of 1979, the 1999 Nigerian Constitution

   a) is a much less important source of political authority
   b) has been amended less frequently
   c) is based more solidly in sharia
   d) provides for a president as head of government
   e) gives the military much less policymaking power

3. According to novelist Chinua Achebe, Nigeria's troubles are squarely a failure of

   a) political institutions
   b) support from more developed countries
   c) colonialism
   d) leadership
   e) the court system

4. Which of the following influences from the pre-colonial era in Nigerian history was more characteristic of the south than the north?

   a) Islam
   b) trade connections
   c) kinship-based politics
   d) complex political identities
   e) large empires

5. After their arrival, the British intensified ethnic politics in Nigeria by

   a) favoring northerners over southerners
   b) trading with all areas of the country equally
   c) putting British officials directly in charge of the government
   d) reinforcing traditional tribal rule
   e) pitting ethnic groups against one another by selective rewards

6. Informal politics in Nigeria and Mexico in their pre-democracy days were defined primarily by

   a) religion
   b) international politics
   c) their legislatures
   d) open civil society
   e) patron-clientelism

7. Which of the following is a mismatch between ethnic group and region in Nigeria?

   I.   Northwest/Hausa Fulani
   II. Northeast/Kanuri
   III. Southwest/Igbo
   IV. Southeast/ Yoruba

   a) I only
   b) I and II only
   c) III only
   d) III and IV only
   e) IV only

8. The Sokoto Caliphate was founded by the

   a) Hausa
   b) Fulani
   c) Kanuri
   d) Igbo
   e) Yoruba

9. Which of the following is the BEST reason why parliamentary government did not work in Nigeria?

   a) Nigeria's many ethnic groups meant that a majority party could not form.
   b) Nigerians rejected it because they wanted to decrease British influence.
   c) Early constitutions did not provide for direct elections.
   d) The Muslims rejected it as a western style of government.
   e) Nigeria's authoritarian past made it better suited for a presidential system.

10. Which of the following is a major societal problem for both Mexico and Nigeria?

   a) conflict between Christians and Muslims
   b) lack of natural resources
   c) large gap between the rich and the poor
   d) rates of HIV/AIDS higher than most other countries
   e) below average literacy rates

(Questions 11 and 12 are based on the following table):

CORRUPTION PERCEPTION INDEX 2006		
COUNTRY	CPI SCORE*	RANK (146 COUNTRIES TOTAL)
China	3.3	70**
Iran	2.7	105
Mexico	3.3	70**
Nigeria	2.2	142
Russia	2.5	121
United Kingdom	8.6	11

*The Corruption Percept Index Score is compiled every year by Transparency International. Countries are ranked from 1 to 10, with a 10 reflecting a corruption-free government.
**Nine countries tied for a rank of 70, including China and Mexico.

11. According to the chart, which of the following countries have (has) a major problem with corruption?

I. Russia
II. China
III. Mexico
IV. Iran
V. Nigeria

a) I, II, and V only
b) II and III only
c) I, IV, and V only
d) I, II, IV, and V only
e) I, II, III, IV, and V

12. Which of the following is the BEST reason for Britain's CPI score?

a) Britain has a parliamentary system of government.
b) Britain holds direct elections for its political leaders.
c) Britain's political culture has a low level of tolerance for corruption.
d) Britain has a well developed civil society.
e) Britain does not rely on code law.

13. Which of the following countries have the largest number of ethnic minority groups in proportion to their overall population?

    a) Britain and Iran
    b) Mexico and China
    c) China and Iran
    d) Britain and Nigeria
    e) Russia and Nigeria

14. Foreign-based oil companies in Nigeria are based primarily in the

    a) Southwest
    b) Southeast
    c) Northwest
    d) Niger Delta
    e) Northeast

15. Which of the following is the BEST reason why Nigeria does not have as many women in their legislature as Mexico?

    a) Nigeria is a more traditional society.
    b) Nigeria does not have a law that requires parties to run female candidates for office.
    c) Nigeria has not had an active women's rights movement.
    d) Nigerian women are not allowed to vote.
    e) Nigeria's middle class is much smaller in proportion to its total population.

16. Historically Nigerian political parties have been based on

    a) social class
    b) ideology
    c) ethnicity
    d) age differences
    e) gender

17. Which of the following mismatches a party with a country?

    a) Britain/Liberal Democratic Party
    b) Russia/United Russia Party
    c) Mexico/Democratic Revolutionary Party
    d) Iran/National Action Party
    e) Nigeria/People's Democratic Party

18. Which of the following is the BEST indication that Nigeria's political party system may be stabilizing?

   a) Several new parties formed before the election of 2007.
   b) The People's Democratic Party chose to run a Christian presidential candidate from the south in 1999 and 2003.
   c) The Action Congress has run presidential and legislative candidates in all elections since 1999.
   d) The All Nigeria People's Party ran a non-military candidate for president for the first time in 2007.
   e) The Independent National Election Commission disqualified several presidential candidates before the election of 2007.

19. Which of the following countries use a plurality system ONLY for electing representatives to the national legislature??

   I.   Britain
   II. Russia
   III. Mexico
   IV. Iran
   V.   Nigeria

   a) I, II, and IV only
   b) I, IV, and V only
   c) II, III, and IV only
   d) IV and V only
   e) II and V only

20. The most consistent criticism of the Nigerian presidential election of 2007 was that it

   a) had too few candidates
   b) had no international observers
   c) was not well publicized by the media
   d) was fraudulent
   e) was won by an incumbent president who had no right to run

21. Which of the following is the BEST description of labor unions in Nigeria?

   a) All labor unions are controlled by the government.
   b) Labor unions are weak because they were first formed after 1999.
   c) Labor unions have a long, active history in Nigeria.
   d) Labor unions are strong in the north, but not in the south.
   e) Labor unions are numerous but ideologically splintered.

22. Which of the following statements about the Nigerian executive is NOT true?

    a) The executive branch has both a president and a prime minister.
    b) The president is directly elected by the people.
    c) The president must win 25% of all the votes in 2/3 of the states.
    d) The president is limited to serving two terms by the constitution.
    e) The president has generally headed an intricate patron-client system.

23. Which of the following is a para-statal?

    a) the Independent National Electoral Commission
    b) Action Congress
    c) the National Assembly
    d) the Movement for the Survival of the Ogoni People
    e) Power Holding Company

24. The institution in the Nigerian government created to give equal representation to the states is

    a) the Senate
    b) the House of Representatives
    c) para-statals
    d) Supreme Court
    e) vice presidency

25. One indication that the judiciary in Nigeria may be developing some independence is that the Supreme Court

    a) ruled that President Obasanjo could not run for a third term of office
    b) regularly reviews executive actions for their constitutionality
    c) recently freed some political dissidents from jail
    d) ruled that the Independent National Electoral Commission did not have the authority to disqualify candidates for office
    e) ruled that important tax legislation passed by the National Assembly was unconstitutional

26. The institution in Nigeria that is usually seen as the most truly national in character is the

    a) military
    b) House of Representatives
    c) electronic media
    d) Senate
    e) Supreme Court

27. In Nigeria most rent-seeking behavior is directed toward

    a) the government for a share of oil revenue
    b) foreign-based oil companies that control the economy
    c) real estate that is controlled by the government
    d) nongovernmental organizations (NGOs)
    e) other countries in international trade

28. International organizations have developed structural adjustment programs for Nigeria in order to help the country

    a) boost profits from oil
    b) pay down its debt
    c) close the gap between the rich and the poor
    d) compete with Latin American countries in the international market
    e) develop a federal character

29. In 2007 Freedom House gave Nigeria a score of "4." This score indicates that Nigeria is

    a) less free than it used to be
    b) not free and never has been
    c) partly free
    d) free
    e) freer than most other countries in Africa

30. In recent years Nigeria has taken some strides toward democratization in all areas EXCEPT:

    a) checks and balances between government branches
    b) independent judiciary
    c) open civil society
    d) civilian control of the executive
    e) free and fair elections

FREE-RESPONSE QUESTION – NIGERIA

Two major forces shaping world politics today are fragmentation and globalization.

(a) Define fragmentation. Define globalization.

(b) Identify one specific threat that fragmentation has posed to regime stability in modern day Nigeria, and describe one response of the government to this threat.

(c) Identify one specific threat that globalization has posed to regime stability in modern day Nigeria, and describe one response of the government to this threat.

PART III: SAMPLE EXAMINATIONS

SAMPLE EXAMINATION ONE

SECTION ONE: MULTIPLE-CHOICE QUESTIONS

Allow 45 minutes for these 55 questions.

(Questions 1 and 2 are based on the following table):

THE GINI INDEX FOR SELECTED COUNTRIES 2006*	
United Kingdom	.36
Russia	.40
Iran	.43
Nigeria	.44
China	.45
Mexico	.50

1. In comparison to the other countries on the chart, Great Britain's low Gini coefficient indicates that the country has a

   a) higher GDP
   b) healthier, more educated people
   c) more equal income distribution
   d) higher Purchasing Power Parity (PPP)
   e) more democratic government

2. Gini coefficients tend to be higher in

   a) more developed countries
   b) communist and post-communist countries
   c) countries of the Western Hemisphere
   d) less developed countries
   e) developing countries

3. *Sharia* law is used by courts in

   a) China and Mexico
   b) Great Britain and Russia
   c) Mexico and Iran
   d) Iran and Nigeria
   e) Russia and Nigeria

4. One explanation for the failure of French and Dutch voters to ratify the European Constitution is that the European Union suffers from

   a) too many elected officials
   b) enlargement fatigue
   c) the loss of the euro's value compared to the U.S. dollar
   d) the disorganized work of the European Council
   e) fear of terrorist attacks

5. In contrast to proportional-representation systems, plurality electoral systems tend to encourage political party systems characterized by

   a) large, broad-based, and fewer parties
   b) more parties with extreme ideological views
   c) large competitive regional parties
   d) smaller, more ideological, and more parties
   e) parties based on informal patron-client networks

6. Deng Xiaoping Theory differed from Maoism, in that Deng

   a) denounced democratic centralism
   b) allowed capitalism to function within the economy
   c) deemphasized the importance of the military in the policymaking process
   d) took political control from the politburo
   e) dismantled the parallel hierarchies

7. In contrast to the western value of equality of opportunity, Russian citizens tend to value

   a) freedom of speech
   b) wealth
   c) national pride
   d) equality of result
   e) inequality

8. The Pendulum Theory that operated in Mexico during the mid-20th century describes swings between

   a) communism and capitalism
   b) PRI and PAN control
   c) state corporatism and pluralism
   d) control by caciques from the north and caciques from the south
   e) socialist reforms and neoliberalism

9. Which of the following is a function of the prime minister in BOTH Britain and Russia?

   a) issuing decrees
   b) sitting on the cabinet
   c) appointing cabinet members
   d) leading the majority party in the legislature
   e) almost always initiating policy changes

10. Which of the following is the MOST significant source of legitimacy and authority for the Iranian political system?

   a) the Constitution of 1979
   b) *qanun*
   c) *sharia*
   d) popular elections
   e) *velayat-e-faqih*

11. The most important current indication that the Nigerian political system may be unstable is

   a) its inability to shed military rule
   b) a series of fraudulent, violent elections
   c) the failure of the president to abide by the Constitution's term limits
   d) the constant friction between the president and the National Assembly
   e) its inability to participate in international trade

12. Post-modernist values contrast with modernist values in that post-modernist values emphasize

   a) materialism
   b) rationalism
   c) freedom
   d) technology
   e) quality of life

13. Which of the following countries in recent years have experienced significant international pressure to have their debts restructured?

   a) Great Britain and China
   b) China and Russia
   c) Iran and Nigeria
   d) Mexico and Iran
   e) Mexico and Nigeria

14. Which of the following is a feature of the current Mexican political system?

   a) It is a one-party state.
   b) It has a parliamentary system.
   c) Both houses of the legislature have strong representation from three political parties.
   d) The executive is composed of both a president and a prime minister.
   e) It is a unitary state with regional officials appointed by the president.

15. China and the former Soviet Union both have (had)

   a) mass line
   b) Five-Year Plans
   c) equal emphasis on agricultural development and industrial development
   d) multi-party systems
   e) presidential elections

16. Russia probably came the closest to being a totalitarian regime under the leadership of

   a) Alexander II
   b) Vladimir Lenin
   c) Joseph Stalin
   d) Mikhail Gorbachev
   e) Vladimir Putin

17. Which of the following is the BEST description of the current relationship between Britain and the European Union?

   a) Britain has yet to join the EU, but trades with EU countries on a regular basis.
   b) Britain is a member of the EU, but has not yet adopted the euro.
   c) Britain is well integrated into the EU, and generally allows the European Court of Justice to exercise judicial review of decisions made by the British government.
   d) Britain is not a member of the EU, and trades primarily with the United States.
   e) Britain is a member of the EU, and has recently ratified the European Constitution.

18. The legitimacy of the most recent national elections has been seriously challenged in

    I.   Britain
    II. Russia
    III. Mexico
    IV. Iran
    V.   Nigeria

    a) I, II, and III only
    b) II, III, and IV only
    c) III and V only
    d) III, IV, and V only
    e) IV and V only

19. Which of the following ideologies puts the MOST emphasis on individual political and economic freedoms?

    a) liberalism
    b) Islam
    c) socialism
    d) fascism
    e) communism

20. Which of the following institutions in the Iranian political system MOST directly reflects democratic principles?

    a) the cabinet
    b) the Guardian Council
    c) the Expediency Council
    d) the *Majles*
    e) the Revolutionary Guards

21. Prebendalism is the name for Nigeria's version of

    a) interest group pluralism
    b) totalitarianism
    c) patron-clientelism
    d) parliamentary system
    e) conservatism

22. A legal system that is based almost entirely on common law exists in

    a) Russia
    b) China
    c) Iran
    d) Britain
    e) Nigeria

23. A major criticism of a pluralist interest group system is that it

    a) creates confusion and inefficiency in the policymaking process
    b) discourages interest group participation
    c) gives the government too little power in the policymaking process
    d) puts groups in an unequal partnership with government
    e) allows interest groups to be controlled by the political parties

24. The attitude of the youth group called Nashi toward Vladimir Putin is BEST described as

    a) hostile
    b) compliant, but hostile
    c) strongly supportive
    d) confrontational
    e) supportive, but critical

25. Which of the following countries does NOT have a written constitution?

    a) Britain
    b) Russia
    c) China
    d) Iran
    e) Nigeria

26. Britain has a relatively high amount of social capital, which means that the country has

    a) a high GDP per capita
    b) a relatively narrow gap between the rich and the poor
    c) a high Human Development Index (HDI) score, according to the United Nations
    d) a mixed economy with a good bit of capitalism
    e) reciprocity and trust among citizens and between citizens and the state

27. In Mexico, Cuauhtemoc Cardenas and Andres Manuel Lopez Obrador are both

    a) former presidents
    b) former governors
    c) leaders of PRI
    d) leaders of PRD
    e) leaders of PAN

28. "Slavophile vs. westernizer" is a basic issue in Russia's

    a) coinciding cleavages
    b) state corporatism
    c) conflictual political culture
    d) electoral system
    e) separation of powers

29. The British political culture is characterized by insularity, primarily because geographically the country is separated from, yet close to, the European continent. Iran is also insulated from its neighbors, primarily by

    a) the small number of countries that share its borders
    b) high mountain ranges
    c) religion; its population is primarily Shiite
    d) lack of membership in supranational organizations
    e) its multi-nationalism

30. A coup d'etat is LEAST likely to occur in a(n)

    a) less developed country
    b) developing country
    c) authoritarian regime
    d) totalitarian regime
    e) liberal democracy

31. Which of the following countries is generally MOST tolerant of political protests and demonstrations against the government?

    a) Britain
    b) China
    c) Mexico
    d) Russia
    e) Iran

32. The commander in chief of the armed forces in Iran is

    a) the Supreme Leader
    b) the president
    c) the head of the Assembly of Religious Experts
    d) the Chief of Staff
    e) the head of the Guardian Council

33. Asymmetric federalism describes the Russian political system because

    a) the Duma has no real check on the president
    b) the president is much more powerful than the prime minister
    c) some areas are called republics and others are called autonomous regions
    d) some regions are more autonomous than others
    e) governors of states are appointed by the president

34. Despite its authoritarian methods during the time it ruled Mexico, one of PRI's accomplishments was

   a) establishing interest group pluralism
   b) gaining civilian control of the military
   c) developing an independent judiciary
   d) developing checks and balances between the executive and legislative branches
   e) weakening the patron-client system

35. A "mixed economy" is one that

   a) is growing in some areas but shrinking in others
   b) mixes elements of command and market economies
   c) is market based but is regulated by the government
   d) experiences marketization but not privatization
   e) combines both international and domestic trade

36. Britain's gradual inclusion of people in the political process during the 19th century was one reason that few of its citizens were attracted to

   a) a market economy
   b) fascism
   c) religious fundamentalism
   d) Marxism
   e) nationalism

37. All of the following are characteristics of political parties in Nigeria EXCEPT:

   a) fluid and unstable
   b) based on ethnicity
   c) often dominated by personalities
   d) likely to form coalitions
   e) committed to being corruption-free

38. Which of the following conflicts is (was) NOT created by a combination of religious and ethnic cleavages?

   a) Biafran War
   b) conflict in Chechnya
   c) conflict in Northern Ireland
   d) Zapatista rebellion in Mexico
   e) Kurdish conflict in Iran

39. Which of the following one-party states did (does) not allow other political parties to exist?

   I. The former Soviet Union
   II. The People's Republic of China
   III. Mexico under PRI rule

   a) I only
   b) I and II only
   c) I and III only
   d) II and III only
   e) I, II, and III

40. An organized collective activity that aims to bring about or resist fundamental change in society is called

   a) a social movement
   b) political socialization
   c) interest group pluralism
   d) privatization
   e) a coup d'etat

41. When people find common interests with people that live in other corners of the globe through nongovernmental organizations (NGOs), they contribute to the development of a global

   a) nationalism
   b) democratization
   c) "transmission belt"
   d) cosmopolitanism
   e) patron-client system

42. Which of the following leaders is MOST likely to form a coalition cabinet?

   a) Felipe Calderon
   b) Gordon Brown
   c) Mahmoud Ahmadinejad
   d) Vladimir Putin
   e) Hu Jintao

43. Which of the following is the BEST explanation for Britain's high level of risk for homegrown terrorist attacks?

   a) Muslims are just one of many religious minorities.
   b) Most Muslims in Britain are relatively well-off economically.
   c) Most British citizens support the Iraqi War.
   d) Most British Muslims are originally from Turkey and Africa.
   e) The British national culture has not absorbed Muslims into mainstream culture.

44. *Guanxi* in the Chinese political system is a variation of a(n)

   a) political party system
   b) electoral party system
   c) patron client system
   d) military organization
   e) state corporatist system

45. The *maquiladora* district in Mexico developed in response to

   a) joint U.S./Mexico policies to restrict immigration across mutual borders
   b) demands of the Zapatistas for government action
   c) pressures to decentralize the government
   d) the NAFTA agreement
   e) attempts to control drug trafficking

46. A bureaucrat is most likely to have discretionary power in a(n)

   a) authoritarian state
   b) liberal democracy
   c) country with a mixed economy
   d) country that practices state corporatism
   e) developing country

47. In Nigeria the system in which the president is the head of an intricate patron-client system and dispenses favors as rewards to supporters is called

   a) kinship-based politics
   b) patrimonialism
   c) neo-corporatism
   d) *nomenklatura*
   e) *qanun*

48. Which of the following countries all have a bicameral legislature?

   a) Nigeria, China, and Russia
   b) Britain, China, and Iran
   c) Mexico, Russia, and Nigeria
   d) Britain, Iran, and Mexico
   e) Russia, China, and Iran

49. China's elite recruitment takes place primarily through

   a) *danwei*
   b) democratic centralism
   c) the mass line
   d) collectivization
   e) *nomenklatura*

50. Britain, Russia, and Mexico all do NOT have a well-developed

   a) electoral system
   b) civil society
   c) multi-party systems
   d) system for judicial review
   e) system of linkage institutions

51. An important power of the Assembly of Religious Experts in Iran is that it

   a) devises the budget
   b) may dismiss the Supreme Leader
   c) selects vice presidents and cabinet ministers
   d) appoints members of the Guardian Council
   e) may declare war

52. The policymaking powers of quangos in British politics is a reflection of

   a) state corporatism
   b) pluralism
   c) neo-corporatism
   d) democratization
   e) socialism

53. China and Russia both belong to the

   a) United Nations
   b) World Trade Organization
   c) Confederation of Independent States
   d) G-8
   e) NATO

54. The controversy surrounding the Mexican presidential election of 2007 was resolved when

   a) Andres Manuel Lopez Obrador conceded the election
   b) the PRI candidate Roberto Madrazo withdrew from the race
   c) Felipe Calderon threatened Obrador
   d) The United States intervened
   e) the Federal Election Commission declared Calderon the winner

55. In the recent past, "military in government" and "military in barracks" has been an important distinction made in

   a) Russia
   b) China
   c) Iran
   d) Mexico
   e) Nigeria

SAMPLE EXAMINATION ONE
PART II – FREE-RESPONSE

SECTION I (30 MINUTES, 25% OF FREE-RESPONSE GRADE):

Briefly describe or define the concepts below.

1. Define democratic deficit, and explain how the concept applies to the European Union.

2. Describe one defining characteristic of code law. Describe one defining characteristic of common law. Contrast these two characteristics.

3. Describe two differences between the democratization process in Mexico and the democratization process in Nigeria.

4. Define discretionary power as it used by bureaucracies, and explain why discretionary power is more likely to be used in the bureaucracy of a liberal democracy than in the bureaucracy of an authoritarian system.

5. Define GNP per capita. Define Purchasing Power Parity (PPP). Contrast GNP per capita to Purchasing Power Parity (PPP).

SECTION II (30 MINUTES, 25% OF FREE-RESPONSE GRADE):

Conceptual analysis:

Some countries have adopted a semi-presidential system for their governments.

(a) Define one feature of a parliamentary system that may be integrated into a semi-presidential system.

(b) Define one feature of a presidential system that may be integrated into a semi-presidential system.

(c) Explain one disadvantage of a parliamentary system that a semi-presidential system might eliminate.

(d) Explain one disadvantage of a presidential system that a semi-presidential system might eliminate.

SECTION III (40 MINUTES, 20 MINUTES EACH FOR TWO QUESTIONS, 50% OF FREE-RESPONSE GRADE – TWO QUESTIONS AT 25% PER QUESTION)

1. Both Nigeria and Britain have recently had problems with ethnic conflict.

(a) Describe one example of ethnic conflict in each country.

(b) Describe one reason for ethnic conflict that is common to both Nigeria and Britain.

(c) Describe one principal method used by the Nigerian government and one principal method used by the British government to resolve the ethnic conflict.

WOMEN IN NATIONAL PARLIAMENTS

Country	Lower House % Women	Upper House % Women
China	20.3%	___*
Iran	4.1%	___*
Mexico	22.6%	17.2%
Nigeria	6.4%**	7.3%
Russia	9.8%	3.4%
United Kingdom	19.7%	18.9%

* No directly comparable upper house
**2003 figure; data from 2007 election not available

2. The representation of women in national parliaments varies from one country to another.

(a) Describe the level of women's participation in Iran's lower legislative house. Describe the level of women's participation in Mexico's lower legislative house.

(b) Explain one reason for the difference in the level of women's participation in Iran's lower legislative house and the level of women's participation in Mexico's lower legislative house.

(c) Describe one impact that Iran's level of women's participation in the lower legislative house might have on policy.

(d) Describe one impact that Mexico's level of women's participation in the lower legislative house might have on policy.

SAMPLE EXAMINATION TWO

SECTION ONE: MULTIPLE-CHOICE QUESTIONS

1. The political systems of Britain, Russia, and Mexico all have

    a) more than two parties competing in popular elections
    b) two political parties dominating the legislature
    c) one party dominating the executive branch
    d) parties of power that dominate both the executive and legislative branches
    e) coalition parties forming a government

2. The party that has been MOST negatively affected by Mexico's inclusion of proportional representation in the electoral system is

    a) National Action Party (PAN)
    b) Institutional Revolutionary Party (PRI)
    c) Party of the Democratic Revolution (PRD)
    d) Labor Party (PT)
    e) Social Democratic and Farmer Alternative Party (*Alternativa*)

3. Guaranteed employment was part of the political policy of

    a) Vicente Fox in Mexico
    b) Mahmoud Ahmadinejad in Iran
    c) Boris Yeltsin in Russia
    d) Mao Zedong in China
    e) Olusegun Obasanjo in Nigeria

4. All of the following leaders gained their authority based on rational-legal principles EXCEPT:

    a) Vladimir Putin
    b) Tony Blair
    c) Felipe Calderon
    d) Mahmoud Ahmadinejad
    e) Ayatollah Ruhollah Khomeini

5. The greatest social cleavage manifested in modern Nigerian politics is

    a) social class
    b) urban v. rural
    c) immigrant v. native
    d) ethnicity
    e) gender

6. Maoism contradicts Confucianism in that Maoism

   a) emphasizes responsibility of the ruler to the people
   b) does not rely on the teachings of one leader
   c) does not support the idea of a political elite
   d) emphasizes an egalitarian social structure
   e) emphasizes order and harmony

7. Which of the following is no longer a basis for authority and power in Russia?

   a) the Constitution of 1993
   b) the tradition of strong, centralized rule
   c) democratic centralism
   d) rational-legal legitimacy
   e) popular elections

8. The most important motivation for the formation of the Institutional Revolutionary Party (PRI) in Mexico in 1929 was an attempt to gain

   a) a more democratic government
   b) political stability
   c) control by populist leaders
   d) religious freedom
   e) equality in Mexico's relationship with the United States

9. The most common type of political system in advanced democracies is

   a) parliamentary
   b) presidential
   c) semi-presidential
   d) plurality
   e) authoritarian

10. In pre-colonial days, in contrast to groups in northern Nigeria, the Yoruba and Igbo

   a) established larger kingdoms
   b) followed *sharia* law
   c) held their rulers accountable to the people
   d) were quite wealthy
   e) traded vigorously across the Sahara north to the Mediterranean

11. The reforms of Mahmoud Ahmadinejad, the president of Iran, are sometimes collectively called a "white coup" because they are

    a) meant to discourage communists ("reds")
    b) bloodlessly eliminating the reformists
    c) quietly challenging the authority of the Supreme Leader
    d) protecting the authority of *sharia*
    e) helping Iraq resist U.S. control

12. Which of the following countries has been MOST criticized in recent years for holding fraudulent elections?

    a) Russia
    b) China
    c) Mexico
    d) Iran
    e) Nigeria

13. Two revolutions whose major goal was ideological purification were

    a) China's Cultural Revolution and Iran's Cultural Revolution
    b) Russia's Revolution of 1917 and Mexico's Revolution of 1910-1911
    c) China's Cultural Revolution and Russia's Revolution of 1917
    d) Iran's Cultural Revolution and Mexico's Revolution of 1910-1911
    e) China's Revolution of 1911 and China's Cultural Revolution

14. Clerical authority is most associated with a political system called a(n)

    a) monarchy
    b) military dictatorship
    c) illiberal democracy
    d) theocracy
    e) oligarchy

15. Mexico's inclusion of proportional representation in their electoral system directly resulted in

    a) a more powerful legislative branch
    b) a clear majority in both legislative houses for PAN
    c) three well-represented parties in both legislative houses
    d) a rubber-stamp legislature
    e) growing representation for minority parties in the lower house only

16. When grouped by religious affiliation, the largest single group of Russian citizens

    a) do not practice a religion
    b) are Russian Orthodox
    c) are Muslim
    d) are Roman Catholics
    e) are Protestant Christian

17. Which of the following courts has used the power of judicial review most effectively?

    a) the British law lords
    b) the Russian Constitutional Court
    c) the Supreme Court in Mexico
    d) the European Court of Justice
    e) the People's Courts in China

18. In Iran, religious persecution is MOST likely to be directed at

    a) Christians
    b) Azeris
    c) members of the Baha'i faith
    d) Zoroastrians
    e) Persians

19. In contrast to Mexico and Iran, in recent years the Nigerian political system has been controlled by

    a) a president
    b) clerics
    c) an ethnic minority
    d) its legislative branch
    e) the military

20. In Mexico, both the Revolution and 1810 and the Revolution of 1910-1911 were attempts to

    a) overthrow colonial rule
    b) bring stability to the country
    c) quiet populist demands
    d) overthrow authoritarian rule
    e) restore military rule

21. A corporatist interest group system is usually characterized by

    a) high levels of control by populist groups in policymaking
    b) a relatively small number of interest groups having input into the policymaking process
    c) a great deal of competition among interest groups for the government's attention
    d) a lack of access of business elites to the government
    e) almost no interest group activity in civil society

22. Which of the following is most obviously a party of power?

    a) Mexico's PAN
    b) Nigeria's Action Congress
    c) Russia's United Russia
    d) Britain's Labour Party
    e) Iran's Executives of Construction Party

23. Which of the following is MOST likely to be a member of the Chinese Communist Party's Politburo?

    a) a wealthy entrepreneur
    b) a peasant that rose through *nomenklatura*
    c) a well educated member of a traditional Chinese aristocratic family
    d) a technocrat that rose through *nomenklatura*
    e) an influential professor at one of China's prestigious universities

24. Magna Carta, the Bill of Rights, and common law are basic to British

    a) rational-legal authority
    b) plurality electoral system
    c) conflictual political culture
    d) mixed economy
    e) charismatic authority

25. As an economic measure of comparison, Purchasing Power Parity (PPP) is different from Gross Domestic Product (GDP) per capita in that it takes into consideration

    a) the Gini Index
    b) adult literacy
    c) life expenctancy
    d) educational enrollment
    e) what people can buy in the local economy

26. Which of the following is an accurate comparison of privatization and marketization in China and Russia since 1980?

    a) Russia infused capitalism slowly; China made a rapid transition from a command to a market economy.
    b) China and Russia have both infused capitalism slowly.
    c) Russia and China have both made rapid transitions from a command to a market economy.
    d) Leaders of both countries vigorously opposed privatization and marketization.
    e) China infused capitalism slowly; Russia made a rapid transition from a command to a market economy.

(Questions 27 and 28 are based on the following table):

COMPARATIVE LITERACY RATES

China (2000 census)
Males	95.1%
Females	86.5%

Iran (2002 est.)
Males	83.5%
Females	70.4%

Mexico (2004 est.)
Males	92.4%
Females	89.6%

Nigeria (2003 est.)
Males	75.7%
Females	60.6%

Russia (2002 census)
Males	99.7%
Females	99.2%

United Kingdom (2003 est.)
Males	99%
Females	99%

27. The gap in literacy rates between men and women is highest in

   a) China and Iran
   b) China and Russia
   c) Iran and Nigeria
   d) Nigeria and Mexico
   e) Mexico and Russia

28. Which of the following is probably the BEST explanation for why the gap between male and female literacy is high in the two countries you identified in #12?

    a) The countries don't have as much disposable income as the others do.
    b) The countries have weak central governments.
    c) The countries have low PPP per capita.
    d) The political cultures of the two countries don't place as much emphasis on education for women.
    e) The Gini coefficiencies of the two countries are higher than those of the other countries.

29. Party systems in Britain and Mexico are both characterized by

    a) two dominant parties
    b) a one-party dominated legislature
    c) a one-party dominated executive
    d) no viable regional parties
    e) parties on the left, center, and right

30. Modern day China's regime type is BEST described as

    a) parliamentary democracy
    b) illiberal democracy
    c) authoritarianism
    d) monarchy
    e) presidential democracy

31. Which of the following interest groups in Britain has been the MOST likely to use guerilla warfare tactics?

    a) Trades Union Council
    b) Irish Republican Army
    c) Whigs
    d) Confederation of Business Interests
    e) Euroskeptics

32. An arrangement in which state-selected interest groups have the right to speak for the public is called

    a) co-optation
    b) state corporatism
    c) neo-corporatism
    d) patron-clientelism
    e) pluralism

33. The political systems of China, Mexico, and Russia all have

    a) code law systems
    b) legitimacy primarily based on a written constitution
    c) prime ministers
    d) active military participation in the policymaking process
    e) separation of power among government branches

34. A unitary system of government is one that

    a) rules in an authoritarian manner
    b) has a weak central government
    c) cooperates with other countries under the umbrella of a supranational country
    d) has managed to tame strong centrifugal forces
    e) concentrates policymaking powers in one central geographic place

35. A logical reaction by a government of a country with strong centrifugal forces is to institute a policy of

    a) globalization
    b) devolution
    c) pluralism
    d) checks and balances
    e) conservatism

36. Separatist movements by minority groups are most likely to occur

    a) when the economy is good
    b) when the government does not give them what they want
    c) around a country's periphery
    d) among people that are uneducated
    e) when other countries interfere

37. According to the Constitution of 1917, the Mexican political system is

    a) presidential
    b) parliamentary
    c) semi-presidential
    d) a theocracy
    e) unitary

(questions 38 and 39 are based on the following chart):

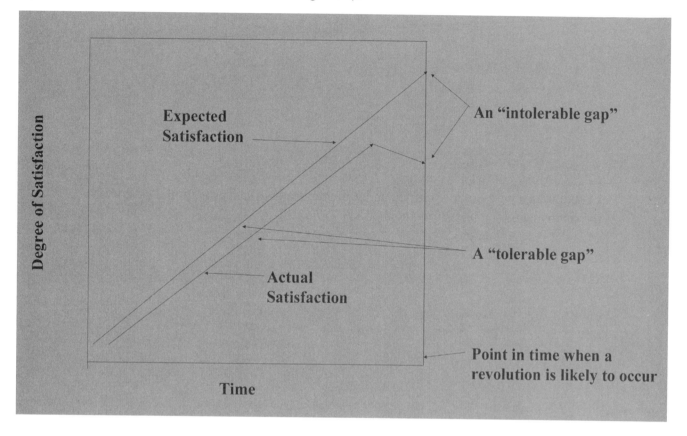

38. According to the chart, under what circumstance is a revolution most likely to occur?

   a) when expected satisfactions go up
   b) when actual satisfactions go up
   c) when the difference between expected and actual satisfactions is not great
   d) when a big gap appears between expected and actual satisfactions
   e) when expected and actual satisfaction go down

39. Applying the circumstance that you identified in #36, in which of the following situations would a revolution most likely be spawned?

   a) Russia in 1945
   b) Iran in 1979
   c) Mexico in 2007
   d) Nigeria in 1998
   e) China in 1982

40. Which of the following groups of countries is MOST affected when the price of oil goes up or down?

    a) Britain, Russia, and China
    b) Mexico, Iran, and Nigeria
    c) China, Mexico, and Nigeria
    d) Russia, China, and Iran
    e) Britain, Mexico, and Nigeria

41. A cabinet coalition is most likely to form in a(n)

    a) authoritarian state
    b) country with a two-party system
    c) illiberal democracy
    d) country with a multi-party system
    e) presidential system

42. Which of the following groups of countries have a mixed electoral system for national elections?

    a) Britain and Iran
    b) Britain and Nigeria
    c) Mexico and Russia
    d) China and Russia
    e) Nigeria and Iran

43. The All-China Federation of Trade Unions is an example of an organization that formed under the practices of

    a) neo-corporatism
    b) interest group pluralism
    c) socialist market economy
    d) cosmopolitanism
    e) state corporatism

44. In contrast to a referendum, an initiative

    a) is started by the people
    b) is a plebiscite
    c) is binding on the government
    d) requires citizens to vote for particular candidates
    e) requires citizens to vote on a issue, not for candidates

45. An example of a "transmission belt" interest group is the

   a) Trades Union Council in Britain
   b) Power Holding Company in Nigeria
   c) Movement for the Survival of the Ogoni People in Nigeria
   d) *Majles* in Iran
   e) Youth League in China

46. Russian elections may be criticized as undemocratic because

   a) they have become progressively less competitive
   b) very few people voted in the last presidential election
   c) no elections are held on the local level
   d) people can only vote for the president, and not for any legislators
   e) the Constitution does not provide for a referendum

47. Which of the following events have occurred recently in both Mexico and Iran?

   a) A violent, flagrantly fraudulent election threatened legitimacy.
   b) A president has refused to step down from power at the end of his term.
   c) A peaceful succession of the presidency has occurred in which power passed between two civilians.
   d) A presidential candidate has been assassinated.
   e) The military has had to seize political power in order to restore stability.

48. Which of the following is the BEST description of the political system of Iran?

   a) It is a unitary state, but has taken significant steps toward devolution.
   b) It is a unitary state, with few signs of real authority granted to local officials.
   c) It is a federalist state in name, but in reality is a unitary state.
   d) It is a federalist state in name and in reality.
   e) It is a confederal state, with little power granted to the central government.

49. Which British political party usually captures the most votes in urban and industrial areas?

   a) Conservatives
   b) Labour
   c) Liberal Democrats
   d) National Unionists
   e) Scottish Nationalists

50. Which of the following is designed to measure the social welfare of a country's people?

   a) PPP
   b) PPP per capita
   c) GDP
   d) GNP per capita
   e) HDI

51. The Mexican and Nigerian political systems both currently have

    a) para-statals
    b) military rule
    c) electoral rules that include proportional representation
    d) two-party systems
    e) small bureaucracies

52. "Political power grows out of the barrel of a gun."

    The statement above is attributed to

    a) Vladimir Putin
    b) Mao Zedong
    c) Deng Xiaoping
    d) Ayatollah Ruhollah Khomeini
    e) General Sani Abacha

53. Which of the following countries has a "1" on the Freedom House freedom scale?

    a) Britain
    b) Russia
    c) China
    d) Mexico
    e) Nigeria

54. Which of the following is an example of a way that the British political system holds the prime minister and cabinet accountable?

    a) The House of Commons may override an executive veto of a bill.
    b) The law lords may declare executive policies to be unconstitutional.
    c) The prime minister and cabinet face Question Time almost every week.
    d) The House of Lords may delay policies indefinitely.
    e) The speaker of the house may choose to ignore the cabinet's request to bring bills to the House of Commons.

55. The presidents of both Mexico and Russia have the power to

    a) appoint the prime minister
    b) dissolve the lower house of the legislature
    c) issue decrees
    d) appoint cabinet members
    e) write a new constitution

SAMPLE EXAMINATION TWO

PART II: FREE-RESPONSE QUESTIONS

SECTION 1 (30 MINUTES, 25% OF FREE-RESPONSE GRADE):

1. Contrast a coinciding cleavage to a cross-cutting cleavage.

2. Define head of state and identify the official who is head of state in Russia. Define head of government and identify the official who is head of government in Russia.

3. Identify one advantage and one disadvantage of a federalist system for a democracy. Identify one of the six countries in the AP Comparative Government and Politics course that has a federalist system.

5. Describe one defining characteristic of a coup d'etat. Describe one defining characteristic of a revolution. Contrast these two characteristics.

6. Describe a patron-client system, and identify one of the six countries in the AP Comparative Government and Politics course that has had a patron-client system in the last ten years.

SECTION II (30 MINUTES, 25% OF FREE-RESPONSE GRADE):

Conceptual analysis:

Interest groups may function in a democracy in either or both a pluralist or a neo-corporatist system.

(a) Define interest group pluralism. Define neo-corporatism.

(b) Describe one implication of interest group pluralism for the policymaking process.

(c) Describe one implication of neo-corporatism for the policymaking process.

SECTION III (40 MINUTES, 20 MINUTES EACH FOR TWO QUESTIONS, 50% OF FREE-RESPONSE GRADE – TWO QUESTIONS AT 25% PER QUESTION)

EU 15

New Countries 2004-07

1. The European Union is a good example of the forces of supranationalism at work in the modern world.

    (a) Define supranationalism.

    (b) Identify two advantages of supranationalism, and explain how each has benefited member states of the EU illustrated above.

    (c) Identify one disadvantage of supranationalism, and explain how the admission of new countries to the EU illustrates the disadvantage.

2. China and Russia both have political parties and party systems.

    (a) Describe the party system that currently exists in China. Describe the party system that currently exists in Russia.

    (b) Discuss one factor that has contributed to the structure of the party system in China. Discuss one factor that has contributed to the structure of the party system in Russia.

    (c) Describe one impact that the party system in China has on the policymaking process. Describe one impact that the party system in Russia has on the policymaking process.

Order Information

Four ways to order:

1) **Fill out and send this form to:**
   WoodYard Publications
   P.O. Box 3856
   Reading, PA 19606

Full payment must accompany the order. Make checks payable to WoodYard Publications.

2) **Purchase Orders (for schools only) - Send purchase order to the above address or Fax to 610-372-8401.**

3) **Order from Amazon. Go to www.amazon.com for order information.**

4) **Pay for one student book through Pay Pal. Go to the website (http://apcomparative.home.comcast.net), click on "Order Form," and order.**

Phone: 610-207-1366

E-Mail: apcomparative@comcast.net

Please use order form on the reverse side.

Order Form

Please send _____copies of AP Comparative Government and Politics: A Study Guide (3rd Edition) to:

Name_____

Mailing Address_____

City, State, Zip_____

Phone_____

E-mail Address_____

School_____

School Address_____

City, State, Zip_____

Please check one: Please send book(s) to _____Home Address

                                        or

                                  _____School Address

Prices:

      1 book - \$17.95 + \$4.60 Priority Mail shipping = \$22.55

      2-9 books - \$14.95 + 8% shipping

      10 books or more - \$12.95 + 8% shipping

Mail this form with check payable to WoodYard Publications, P.O. Box 3856, Reading, Pennsylvania 19606. School purchase orders also accepted.

ANSWER KEY
FOR
AP COMPARATIVE GOVERNMENT AND
POLITICS: A STUDY GUIDE
3RD EDITION

Ethel Wood

 WoodYard Publications, Reading, Pennsylvania